A GUIDE TO
ETHNIC FOOD
IN LOS ANGELES

ALSO BY LINDA BURUM

Asian Pasta: A Cook's Guide to Noodles, Wrappers, and Pasta Brownies

The Cook's Market Place: Los Angeles (with Sherry Virbila)

A GUIDE TO

ETHNIC FOOD
— I N —
LOS ANGELES

Restaurants, Markets, Bakeries,

Specialty Shops for the Foods of

Cambodia, China, Ethiopia, Greece,

Guatemala, India, Japan, Mexico,

Morocco, Thailand, Vietnam, and Others

LINDA BURUM

Photographs by Andrea Elovson

HarperPerennial
A Division of HarperCollins*Publishers*

HarperCollins Books may be purchased for educational, business, or sales promotional use. For information, please write: Special Markets Department, HarperCollins Publishers, Inc., 10 East 53rd Street, New York, NY 10022.

FIRST EDITION

Designed by Jessica Shatan
Maps by Paul Pugliese

Library of Congress Cataloging-in-Publication Data
Burum, Linda.
   A guide to ethnic food in Los Angeles / Linda Burum : photographs by Andrea Elovson.—1st ed.
      p.   cm.
   Subtitle: Restaurants, markets, bakeries, specialty shops for the foods of Cambodia, China, Ethiopia, Greece, Guatemala, India, Japan, Mexico, Morocco, Thailand, Vietnam, and others.
   Includes indexes.
   ISBN 0-06-273038-X
   1. Restaurants, lunch rooms, etc.—California—Los Angeles—Guidebooks.
2. Grocery trade—California—Los Angeles—Guidebooks. 3. Los Angeles (Calif.)—Description—1981-   —Guidebooks.
I. Title. II. Title: Ethnic food in Los Angeles.
TX907.3.C22L673   1992
381'.45641'02579494—dc20   91-44320

---

   93   94   95   96   CG/RRD   10   9   8   7   6   5   4   3   2

This book is dedicated to Stephen Burum,

my patient, good-natured husband,

who endured countless experimental meals—

whether the restaurants that served them

made the "A" list or the circular file.

And to my mother, Adele Vesco,

for being a good sport.

Contents

Acknowledgments ✦ ix

Introduction ✦ xi

CHINA ✦ 1

JAPAN ✦ 37

KOREA ✦ 67

THAILAND ✦ 83

VIETNAM ✦ 99

SOUTHEAST ASIAN CULINARY CROSSOVERS
*Cambodia, Indonesia, Malaysia,
and the Philippines* ✦ 115

INDIA ✦ 131

MEXICO ✦ 147

CENTRAL AMERICA, SOUTH AMERICA,
AND THE CARIBBEAN ✦ 173

EUROPE ✦ 191

GREECE, THE MIDDLE EAST,
AND AFRICA ✦ 211

City Index ✦ 243

Geographical Index ✦ 245

General Index ✦ 259

Acknowledgments

Without a wealth of good advice no one could accurately survey Los Angeles' thousands of ethnic food stores and thousands more ethnic restaurants. Only with the help of many friends and local "experts" was I able to cull out the best places that illustrate our city's extraordinary supply of excellent ethnic food resources.

For their special contributions I would like to thank: Ruth Reichl and Charles Perry at the *Los Angeles Times*, without whose encouragement I would probably never be writing about food; my agent Martha Casselman, who unselfishly spent many hours helping me polish the Chinese chapter; Linda Zimmerman, Carolyn Miller, and Joyce Glasser, for their editorial guidance.

Also thanks to the following food lovers for their generous gifts of time and information: my colleagues at the *Times*—Laurie Ochoa and Jonathan Gold, for their hot tips on Mexican restaurants, and Max Jacobson, for answering all my questions about Asian food and restaurants; Tom Wan and Kathy Siu, for patiently escorting me around the San Gabriel Valley to track down the best Chinese food in the area, and Donjean Gardner for introducing them to me as well as supplying menus and tips from her neighborhood; Nona Demetre, for introducing me to Tony and Michelle of Taiwan, whose wonderful list of regional Chinese restaurants was invaluable; Robert Tolone and Janice Hisu, for more good tips on Chinese restaurants; Baldwin Marchack, for weeding out the dead wood on my Chinese restaurant list, and Chris Woo, for her information on Chinese food terms.

For their help on Korean food, Mrs. Grace Kim, David Kim, Daniel Oh, Heisun Chung, and Ginsook Chang and Young Song; Regina Cordorva, for her knowledge of Mexican shops; Peter Konenakeaw, for helping me explore the Thai community; Neelam Batra and Mira Advani, for their help with Indian food information; Haimanot Habutu, for her insight into the Ethiopian community; Albert and Terry Bezjian and Shant Kuyumjian, for answering my endless questions about Middle Eastern shops and restaurants; Yasuko Hamada, Maggie Hale, and Mrs. Natsue Wakana, for their insight into Japanese specialty restaurants and shops; Helen Tran, for her tips on Vietnamese restaurants and markets; and Kit Snedaker, for the use of her cookbook library.

Also thanks to these fearless diners and contributors of good restaurant information: Tom Martin, Chrys Chrys, Nina Segovia, Naomi Williams, Laurie and Elliot Swartz, Daisy Gerber, Larry Alexander, Louis Hubbell, Rex McGee, Kendall Gyler, Larry and Barbara Caretto, Sue Young, Peg Rahn, Margaret Dennis, Willie and Lorna Veliz, Don and Sue Levy, Anne Sprecher, and Debbie Slutsky.

And finally to Sheila Merrill, for hours of typing the data base and other assistance.

Introduction

I began gathering information for this guidebook in the mid-eighties quite by happy accident. When it was suggested that I collaborate with Sherry Virbila on an L.A. version of *The Cook's Market Place* (a series of food shopping guides), I jumped at the chance. My job would be to search out the best cheese, the finest greengrocers, and the highest quality meats. What could be more fun, I thought, than seeking out good food?

Like most Angelenos, I was accustomed to getting on the freeway and driving past every neighborhood but my own. But now, while doing my research traveling on the surface streets, I explored worlds I'd never imagined existed. I discovered that Los Angeles was filled with Old World food artisans, most of whom were barely known outside their own ethnic communities. In East Hollywood, for example, a Lebanese baker hand-stretched his filo dough to make the lightest, flakiest baklava I'd ever eaten. Next to a body shop in a Mar Vista no-man's-land at the modest Aloha Grocery, a Japanese-American handcrafted batches of exquisitely fresh nigari tofu—the sort rarely found except in small (and disappearing) shops in Japan. Even more remarkable was the Spanish housewife turned professional sausage maker. Her regional recipes, including those for chorizo de bilbao, Catalan butifarra, and Basque chistorra, were culled from her visits with sausage makers throughout Spain.

Most astonishing, though, was the number of big-business food concerns I encountered in the larger ethnic communities. Competing with the stereotypical mom-and-pop enterprises are huge supermarket chains that dispense a vast range of imported foods. Their shelves are filled with locally grown specialty produce and goods from Los Angeles factories that manufacture everything from Korean kimchee and microwavable Indian dinners to Vietnamese meatballs. And in some cases California's high-quality production standards made these ethnic products even better here than in their homeland.

After eight months of driving around Los Angeles, I found myself deeply immersed in the city's ethnicity. I discovered that while some nationalities have obvious centers (such as Koreatown or Little Tokyo), many others blend with everyone else in L.A. County's 4,070 square miles of semisuburban sprawl. Ethnic markets, I soon realized, were the keenest indicator of who lived where, and inevitably there were restaurants nearby that catered to that market's patrons. Many of these bore no resemblance to any I'd ever eaten in or read about, and frequently they specialized in a particular food. Depending on the area, countless signs announced such things as Mexican mariscos, Japanese ramen, or Vietnam's national soup, pho.

Exploring these specialties was often the key to understanding an ethnic group's food culture. The Japanese don't simply go to a restaurant, they seek a sushi-ya for the best sushi and a ramen-ya for noodles. Mexicans get the best tacos in a taqueria and best birria in a birriaria. Such subjects became the basis for the articles I began to write for the *Los Angeles Times*. Tempting story ideas materialized everywhere I looked: Korean pubs, Indian snack shops, and Taiwanese delis. Eventually these authentic establishments became the focus of this book.

The Chapters and Their Selections

With nearly three dozen ethnic cuisines to choose from, Angelenos can eat from a different culture every day for more than a month without duplication—even longer if they explore such regional differences as southern Indian or northeastern Thai. But it's not just diversity that has inspired such L.A. appellations as "Ellis Island West" and the "New Melting Pot." Many Los Angeles ethnic groups are the largest outside their country of origin. About 50,000 Cambodians, at least 300,000 Vietnamese, and 250,000 Iranians live here, along with almost half a million Koreans; Latino residents constitute nearly one third of Southern California's total population.

These enormous ethnic communities have created a ready market for restaurants that serve their own nationality. As a result, Los Angeles has an undiluted view of many ethnic food cultures, yielding incredible rewards for those wishing to explore new tastes. In the right restaurants, adventurous diners can savor the clean spiciness of Thai cooking as Thais eat it, Cantonese seafood with the same fresh pure flavors of dishes cooked in Hong Kong, and tamales that taste as if they were made in a Mexican home.

I've also tried to make each chapter or section in the book function as a primer for exploring a cuisine. Where possible, I've selected a broad range of establishments that, when viewed together, illustrate the eating customs and culture of an ethnic group. I could, for example, fill a chapter with excellent all-purpose Korean restaurants. But Koreans also seek out their particular style of sushi in seafood houses, and they enjoy pubs that serve rice wine and anju (snacks) to accompany it. You'd miss some of the best Korean dining if you didn't know about these restaurants. The same thinking applies to Chinese food. If you simply ate in the best all-around Chinese restaurants, you might never guess how much the Chinese love noodles and dumplings and how many dozens of restaurants are devoted to these delicious habit-forming specialties.

Many of the people who patiently answered my relentless questions on how their food was made—and how it was eaten—often slipped in a little cultural lore. Their advice enabled me to take this book beyond a standard where-to-eat-and-shop guide, turning it into a culinary handbook as well. I'm hoping this book will make Indian chat, Persian khoresh and Salvadoran pupusas as familiar as pizza or sushi.

How to Use This Book

Because the area covered by this guide is so huge, I've divided it into seven geographical areas: Central; South; West; S.F. Valley (San Fernando Valley); San Gabriel Valley; East of L.A.; and also OCounty (Orange County).

With Los Angeles' ethnic communities so spread out I've tried to include almost every kind of restaurant and a large variety of markets within each geographical area.

- Each listing includes an address and area locator (such as SOUTH) indicating the section of the county in which a shop or restaurant lies.
- A map on pages xviii–xix illustrates the geographical divisions. If you're reading about a place whose address is 11650 Santa Monica Boulevard, Hollywood, CENTRAL, you can quickly locate it on the portion of the map labeled CENTRAL.
- The lists that follow tell you which cities and towns are in which geographical area.

CENTRAL

Boyle Heights	Koreatown
Chinatown	Little Tokyo
Eagle Rock	Los Angeles (parts)
Highland Park	Silverlake
Hollywood	

EAST OF L.A.

Bell	Huntington Park
Covina	Montebello
East Los Angeles	Pico Rivera

Pomona
Rowland Heights

West Covina

OCOUNTY (Orange County)

Anaheim
Buena Park
Costa Mesa

Garden Grove
Santa Ana
Westminster

S.F. VALLEY (San Fernando Valley)

Burbank
Canoga Park
Chatsworth
Encino
Glendale
North Hollywood
Northridge
Pacoima
Panorama City

Reseda
Sepulveda
Sherman Oaks
Studio City
Tarzana
Toluca Lake
Van Nuys
Westlake Village
Woodland Hills

SAN GABRIEL VALLEY

Alhambra
Duarte
El Monte
Monterey Park
Rosemead

Pasadena
San Gabriel
San Marino
Temple City

SOUTH

Artesia
Bellflower
Carson
Cerritos
Gardena
Harbor City
Hawthorne
Hermosa Beach
Inglewood
Lakewood

Lawndale
Lomita
Long Beach
Lynwood
Norwalk
Rancho Palos Verdes
San Pedro
Torrance
Wilmington

WEST

Brentwood	Santa Monica
Beverly Hills	Venice
Culver City	West Hollywood
Los Angeles (parts)	West Los Angeles
Marina Del Rey	Westwood
Pacific Palisades	

- In addition, the City Index at the back of the book lists cities alphabetically and gives their geographical areas. If you are looking for a shop or restaurant in Long Beach, for example, either the map, the above list, or the City Index will tell you that Long Beach is in the SOUTH area.
- The Geographical Index at the back of the book lists the establishments within each area according to cuisine. If you want a Thai restaurant in the SOUTH area, look under SOUTH and then under Thai in the Geographical Index.

Please remember the golden rule of using any guidebook: Call ahead. Change is inevitable. Restaurants close or move or they suddenly decide not to serve lunch on Saturday, though they've been doing so for years. I've done my best to make all the information here as accurate as possible, but inevitably a book will lag behind current circumstances.

A Word About Spelling

Bulgogi, pulkoki, bulkoki—the menu spelling of this Korean barbecued beef depends on who is doing the transliterating from the Hangul alphabet. Formal systems for translating alphabets such as Thai or Arabic into English are used by scholars and journalists, but few menu writers seem to pay them any mind. Words commonly crop up with different unofficial spellings. Chinese is particularly tricky. Current proctocol suggests we use Mandarin transliterated by the pinyin system. But many dishes such as Peking duck and chow mein have been familiarized in their Cantonese spelling. Who ever heard of Beijing duck (officially spelled Bei jing tian ya) or chao mian? So, generally I've used the most popular menu spellings rather than insisting on "official" but unfamiliar spellings.

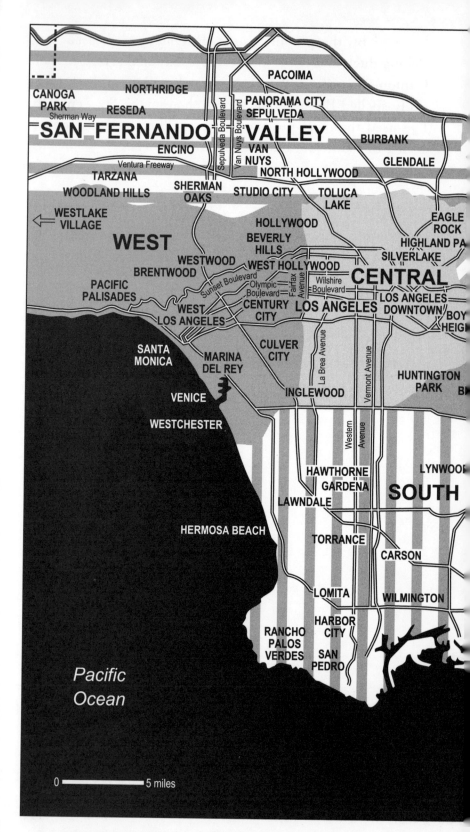

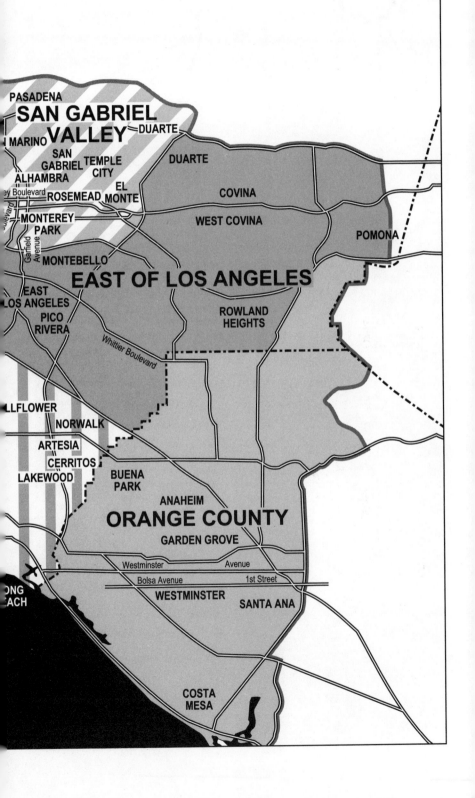

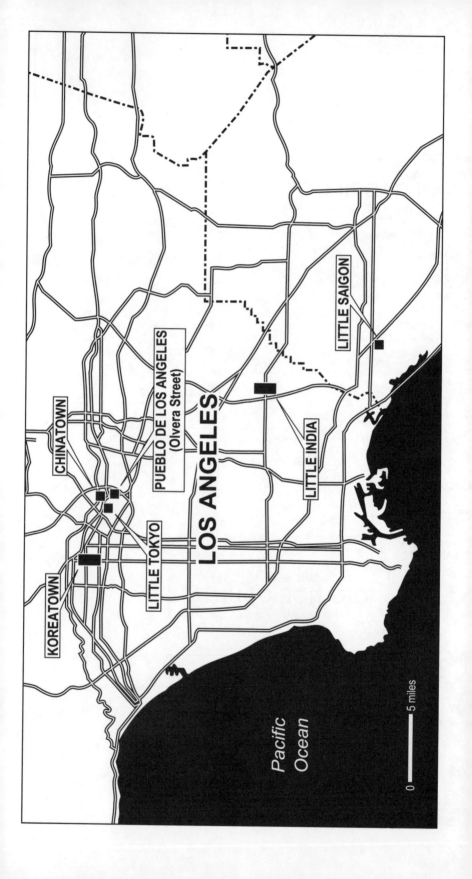

A GUIDE TO
ETHNIC FOOD
IN LOS ANGELES

CHINA

A man cannot be too serious about his eating.

—CONFUCIUS

Even more than the French, the Chinese discuss food before they eat, while they are eating, and after they have
eaten. In Monterey Park, L.A.'s most affluent Chinese suburb, crowds line up at the best dim sum parlors an hour
before opening time, noodle shops stay jammed past 2:00
A.M., and no respectable Cantonese restaurant has fewer
than three tanks filled with live fish and shellfish.

While the Chinese obsession with food has been cultur-
ally ingrained for centuries, Angelenos have witnessed it
only during the past two decades. In that time, California's
Chinese population has more than doubled, primarily due
to a change in immigration laws. Arriving from Singapore,
Taiwan, and Hong Kong, these well-educated, cosmopolitan, and often wealthy immigrants demanded the same
quality of food they knew at home. And, unwilling to leave
their meals to chance, they imported master chefs and in-
vested heavily in restaurants.

Adventurous diners who traveled out to Monterey Park

found that real Cantonese food was exquisitely fresh and simple—nothing like the dreary Column A, Column B school of American-Chinese family dinners many of us grew up with. That originated before the turn of the century in Chinatown.

The Chinatown of the nineteenth century, as depicted in silent films and stories, was a mysterious enclave with narrow, unpaved alleys and mah-jongg parlors behind secret doors. The image isn't entirely fabricated. Turn-of-the-century Chinese lived in a ghetto east of Olvera Street; most were men who immigrated as indentured servants, leaving their families behind in Canton. Cooking for themselves, they tried to re-create their native food with Southern California's ingredients.

A few enterprising souls opened coffee shops that dished up "chop suey" to Chinatown's workers and the occasional daring Anglo looking for a taste of adventure.

By 1934, only a block of old Chinatown remained, the rest having been razed to make way for the huge new Union Station. But on that surviving block, along with the Asiatic Costume Company and a curious herb shop, sat the Dragon's Den Restaurant, a basement opulently decorated with Hollywood-style orientalia. It became a hangout serving exotic almond duck and wonton soup to bohemians and entertainment-world figures, including Walt Disney and Sydney Greenstreet.

"New" Chinatown, centered on Broadway between Sunset and Bernard Street, started in 1938 with 18 stores and a tofu factory. Restaurateurs with an eye to tourism embellished their buildings with Asian tile roofs, foo dogs, and colorful chinoiserie. More often than not, though, their cooks would be guys who used to drive tofu delivery trucks.

After World War II, an influx of Chinese women brought with them authentic Chinese techniques and dishes. Most of these dishes, however, were served only at home or eaten by the help in restaurant kitchens. The food that went into the dining rooms omitted any unusual ingredients; dishes were tailored to American tastes (cooks added pineapple chunks to sweet and sour pork drenched in a garish orange sauce); and the fortune cookie came into being.

The latest wave of Chinese immigration began in 1965, and many newcomers settled eight miles east of Chinatown in Monterey Park and its neighboring suburbs of Alhambra, San Gabriel, and Rosemead. Today the area, with a population more than 60 percent Asian, is thick with exceptional food sources, from glitzy supermarkets and high-end restaurants to casual places serving wonderful "popular" food: dumplings, deli snacks, and regional noodle dishes.

And although "New" Chinatown still has its colorful chinoiserie, and you can occasionally find chop suey on the menu, new investments have meant luxurious restaurants offering shark's fin soup and live crab for sophisticated diners. This is food Confucius would take seriously.

— CHINESE GLOSSARY —

Pinyin spellings, which may sometimes be encountered on menus, follow the most common spelling, where applicable.

See also Taiwanese Breakfast and Snacks Glossary (page 9) and Dim Sum Glossary (pages 23–24).

Bao: Steamed wheat buns with various fillings. For the various types, see the Dim Sum Glossary, pages 23–24.

Bon bon chicken: A Sichuan-style cold chicken and cucumber salad with a hot, garlicky sesame paste dressing.

Chiao-tzu (jiao-zi): When pan-fried, these dumplings, filled with various chopped meats or vegetables, are known as pot stickers. They are also served boiled or steamed.

Chow fun (chao fen): Flat fresh rice noodles stir-fried with other ingredients.

Chow mein (Cantonese) or chao mian (Mandarin): Thin wheat noodles stir-fried with other ingredients.

Congee or jook (zhou): A porridge made by simmering cooked rice in water or stock until it has the thick, almost smooth texture of oatmeal. Congee is garnished with your choice of various meats or other pungent additions such as preserved pickled cabbage.

Dim sum: The Cantonese-style morning meal of tea with assorted small dishes. For a glossary of dim sum dishes see pages 23–24.

E-fu noodles: A Cantonese-style wheat noodle that has been deep-fried and dried. Usually used in soup, it has an unusual chewy texture and needs little cooking.

Fujianese-style food (or Fukienese): From the southeastern province of Fujian, bordering the South China Sea, this is related both to Cantonese and eastern-style cooking and is the provincial cuisine that most influences Taiwanese cooking.

Fun (Cantonese) or fen (Mandarin): Fresh, flat rice noodles.

Ja jang mein (jia chang mian): Thick Beijing-style wheat noodles in a spicy sauce.

Kung pao (gongbao): A western-central stir-fry dish originally made with chicken and great quantities of garlic, ginger, whole dried chilies, and fried peanuts (formerly corn kernels were used). Kung pao dishes are now often made with shrimp or vegetables.

Lion's head meatballs: Shanghainese-style pork meatballs wrapped in cabbage that resembles the lion's mane, served in a rich brown sauce.

Lo mein (Cantonese) or lao mian (Mandarin): Thin wheat noodles with a stir-fried or sauce topping.

Ma po bean curd (also called mapo doufu): A Sichuan-style tofu dish with a sauce of sautéed ground pork, tree ear mushrooms, garlic, hot chilies, and Sichuan pepper.

Mein (Cantonese) or mian (Mandarin): Thin, wheat noodles.

Mu-shu (muxu): A thin wheat pancake brushed with sweet bean paste and filled with a meat, scrambled egg, and vegetable mixture. Pork was the original mu-shu dish, but beef, chicken, shrimp, or vegetables now often replace the pork.

Shao bing: Northern-style flaky hollow sesame seed-topped buns.

Shark's fin: The Chinese prize this expensive and nearly tasteless fin for its gelatinous texture. It's considered an appetite stimulant. Any flavor in a shark's fin dish comes from the other ingredients with which it is cooked.

Tan tan mein (or dan dan mian): Cold thin wheat noodles in a spicy, garlicky Sichuanese peanut sauce.

Tilapia: An aquaculture-raised freshwater fish with a texture and flavor resembling striped bass served in most Cantonese seafood restaurants.

Yue bing: Moon cakes. These consist of short pastry enclosing various sweet fillings made of bean pastes, nuts, or fruits surrounding a piece of salted duck egg yolk. Yue bing always have a decorative design imprinted on them.

Wonton (hun tun): A bite-sized meat- or seafood-filled dumpling served in soup or deep-fried.

REGIONAL CHINESE RESTAURANTS

Like most other cities in the world with a diverse Chinese population, authentic Chinese restaurants in Los Angeles often represent a city rather than a region: We have Taipei-style, Shanghai-style, and

Hong Kong–style restaurants. These kitchens mix the cuisine of their own region with a variety of influences brought to those cities by immigrants from all over China, so to put them into precise regional categories is often impossible. That's why I've grouped some establishments by city of origin and others by region.

But here in Los Angeles, even places that emphasize the food of a specific province, say Hunan, may also list the most popular dishes from other areas of China. To get their best cooking, stick to the regional specialties. A Cantonese kitchen may serve Sichuan wontons but it's best to order the Cantonese dishes instead.

SHANGHAINESE RESTAURANTS

Shanghai's eclectic cuisine didn't really develop until after the 1840s, when the once provincial village opened to the West. A strategically situated port, Shanghai rapidly grew into China's most cosmopolitan city. International merchants, bankers, and political refugees from the West and Chinese from every region poured in, bringing their own culinary traditions. The Shanghai kitchen was quick to adopt a variety of provincial and even Western influences. For instance, the elaborate cold appetizer platter, found in most Los Angeles Shanghai-style restaurants in a less elaborate form, was inspired by the Russian zakuska, a lavish cold premeal buffet.

Such food fashions were an overlay on the already complex style of the Shanghai area. The region's year-long growing season, copious rivers, and long shorelines offer an amazing array of ingredients that Shanghai cooks combine in dishes of extreme intricacy. Shanghai's chefs blend six or eight vegetables in a dish, often cutting them into different small shapes, where most other regional cooks use one or two. Shanghai-style

sauces are dark and full-bodied, based on a complicated brown stock with wine, soy sauce, and rich Chinkiang vinegar, which, like balsamic, is aged for decades.

From nearby Shantung, a wheat-producing area, come flour products. *Chiao-tzu* dumplings, the pride of Shanghai, are done with style in several Los Angeles restaurants.

Lake Spring Cuisine, 219 E. Garvey Avenue, Monterey Park, SAN GABRIEL VALLEY, 818-280-3571. Lunch and dinner daily. It's the very personal style of Lake Spring's chef, Bin Kun Cheang, who once added his extraordinary talent to the kitchen at Ja Shang Low in Taiwan, that makes this small restaurant's food such a standout. The traditionally robust Shanghai tastes are all there—this is not nouvelle Shanghai-style cooking, you understand—but Cheang's discipline at the stove and artistry at honing in on flavors gives his Shanghai food a finesse found nowhere else. Cold appetizers include Shanghai-style wine chicken, pressed duck, and aromatic smoked fish served with a fermented black bean and fresh green chile condiment.

Shanghai Palace, 932 Huntington Drive, San Marino, SAN GABRIEL VALLEY, 818-282-8815. Lunch through dinner daily. With crowds constantly overflowing Lake Spring's small dining room, its owners expanded the business by converting a tired neighborhood Chinese place in San Marino into the light and airy flower-filled Shanghai Palace. Its Shanghainese-Cantonese menu is almost identical to Lake Spring's. And the same talent runs the kitchen.

Dragon Villages, 301 W. Valley Boulevard, No. 112, San Gabriel, SAN GABRIEL VALLEY, 818-284-4769. Lunch through dinner daily. One of the city's most popular Shanghai-style restaurants, Dragon Villages has forgone the baroque golden dragon and red lantern motif popularized by the old-time Shanghai restaurateurs. Instead, the simple modern room is a backdrop for several contemporary Chinese paintings.

When baskets of steamed buns and dumplings arrive at the tables, diners carefully lift their covers as if opening gifts. Along with the buns, listed on the menu under Shanghai pastries, are onion puffs, sweet bean pancakes, and crab meat dumplings.

While the menu lists every item in English, the names do little to describe the complexities of this Shanghai food. When it came time to order, we simply looked around the room and pointed out a few dishes that appealed to us, a stratagem that proved successful. Our first dish, called "eight delicacy ingredients" (with a list of ingredients long enough to supply a small banquet), was typical of the style: smoky ham, perfectly cooked plump shrimp, anise-infused pressed tofu, pork, water chestnuts, and mushrooms were each cut into a different shape, tossed in a rich, intricately flavored pepper-laced sauce, and scattered generously with roasted peanuts. The sliced beef in garlic sauce sounds simple enough, but it too had nearly as many differently cut ingredients.

Tennis-ball-sized lion's head meatballs went to almost every table. Apparently it's the restaurant's signature dish, though Dragon Villages' English menu calls it "braised meatball in brown sauce."

To do justice to this excellent menu, you must return often. If you've never tried Shanghai-style food, Dragon Villages is a fine introduction.

The illustrious **3 6 9** restaurant in Shanghai has spawned imitators in Shanghainese colonies all over the world. Two 3 6 9 restaurants in the San Gabriel Valley are not related to the famous one nor to each other, but the carefully made pastries and Shanghai-style dumplings from both kitchens live up to the famous name.

3 6 9, 120 E. Valley Boulevard, No. K, San Gabriel, SAN GABRIEL VALLEY, 818-571-5369. Lunch through dinner daily. While 3 6 9 in Alhambra is a snack-style place, this newer San Gabriel 3 6 9 is a full restaurant. A refrigerated buffet case displays beautifully arranged little cold dishes that Shanghainese love, such as crabs imported from Asia, cured in salt, and served uncooked like Latin American seviche. These come cracked open and garnished with their luscious coral roe. Plates of thinly sliced cured beef and smoked pomfret fish look as though an artist had arranged them. An assorted cold plate holding an incredible selection of smoked fish, meat, and chicken includes a paper-thin tofu sheet wrapped around smoky vegetables and called "vegetarian goose."

A long tradition of Buddhism has given Shanghai an elaborate vegetarian cuisine that exemplifies the region's finely cut and richly flavored foods. A brilliant example, "braised assorted vegetable with bean curd," has slivered vegetables wrapped in thin tofu sheets formed into bird shapes and braised together with meaty black Chinese mushrooms in a luscious brown sauce.

Pan-fried meat-filled bao, crusty-bottomed in the Shanghai tradition, are another wonderful specialty. In fact, it's hard to go wrong with anything on this menu. 3 6 9's affable co-owner, Debbie Yeh, will offer excellent suggestions.

3 6 9 Shanghai, 1277 E. Valley Boulevard, Alhambra, SAN GABRIEL VALLEY, 818-281-9261. Lunch through dinner daily. At the older and more cafélike 3 6 9 in Alhambra, the famous dumplings are succulent juicy bites. Marvelous onion cakes, fried sesame buns, dainty crab meat bao, and tea-smoked fish with noodles have kept this tiny place on top of the competition.

It's not all snacks at 3 6 9: Salt-and-pepper pork chop, a Shanghai classic, has a crunchy, spicy exterior that encases moist meat. A saucer of spiced salt comes alongside for dipping. Refreshing cucumbers in chili sauce from the upright glass refrigerator go best with this. And in typically eclectic Shanghai style, 3 6 9 has entrée-sized kung pao chicken and chicken in "Szechwan" sauce on the same menu.

Mandarin Shanghai, 970 N. Broadway (Mandarin Plaza No. 114, behind Fu Ling), Chinatown, CENTRAL, 213-625-1195. Lunch and dinner daily. Behind the touristy Fu Ling in the Mandarin Plaza, Mandarin Shanghai is a hidden Chinatown treasure. Not incidentally, it's one of the few L.A. restaurants with Shanghai in its name that actually turns out excellent Shanghai-style cooking. Even so, the waitresses seem trained to steer "tourists" toward the sweet and sour pork, shrimp with snow peas, and other non-Shanghai-style dishes. But without too much effort, you can usually persuade them to describe their Shanghai specialties: the deeply flavored cold wine-braised chicken—white as snow with a buttery smooth texture; the "shang-yee" shrimp with black mushrooms in a typically rich Shanghai sauce; and whole yellow fish with a deep brown sauce. The lion's head meatballs here have a marvelously light, silky texture.

Mandarin Shanghai has free underground parking, just a few steps from the restaurant's door.

CHIU CHOW RESTAURANTS

Chiu Chow cooking at its most refined comes from the kitchens of **Chiu Chow Garden** (111 N.

CHIU CHOW

Though the Chiu Chow's heritage is eastern, these ethnic Chinese settled close to Canton and then migrated to Southeast Asia, where their food absorbed local culinary influences. Chiu Chow cooking, considered by many the most distinctive blend of Chinese styles, is a true hybrid: Light, quickly cooked Cantonese dishes merged with the intricate spicing of eastern food and Southeast Asian flourishes. Chiu Chow cooking emphasizes clean, fresh tastes, fine textures, and a minimum of oil.

Atlantic Boulevard [No. 351 Landmark Center], Monterey Park, SAN GABRIEL VALLEY, 818-282-7666; lunch and dinner daily), across from Harbor Village Restaurant. The pale green marble and cool colorings of the airy dining room suggest this food's patrician qualities.

Fried chicken with chinjew sauce displays Chiu Chow's dual eastern and Cantonese heritage: Thin slices of chicken thigh, barely cooked in the Cantonese way, come glazed with an intricately spiced filmy brown sauce typical of eastern-style cooking. The dish arrives on a luxurious bed of deep-fried julienned chile leaves that curl into crispy wisps.

The kitchen's remarkable talent with frying shows up in the juicy little appetizer nuggets of shrimp balls and crab balls—so lightly breaded and quickly fried they seem oil-free. An accompanying trio of dipping sauces from which you mix and choose is characteristic of Chiu Chow service.

As is often the case, the menu translations aren't particularly illuminating, but the management's descriptions are exceptionally reliable. A few of the more exotic dishes can be pricey, though many run from $6 to $9. Two can eat well for about $30.

Driving down Garvey Boulevard at night, you can't miss **A A A Seafood** (220 W. Garvey Avenue, Monterey Park, SAN GABRIEL VALLEY, 818-571-8898; lunch through dinner daily), glowing like a power station. Light pours from its massive second-story dining room through a huge bay window facing the street. Under the shimmering lights, large crowds are cracking crabs, plucking lobster meat from the shell, and relishing whole crispy salted fish just netted from one of the tanks installed in the apricot-colored marble of the back wall.

The food here is even lighter than what you'll be served at nearby Cantonese restaurants. Still, many dishes are boldly flavored; baked crab with garlic sauce will banish vampires. Oysters on the half shell are lightly cooked under just enough pungent black bean sauce to let the briny oyster flavor prevail.

When it's available, fresh abalone from the tanks, thinly sliced and flash-cooked with black mushrooms, is out of this world.

Among some of A A A's eastern-influenced dishes are duck soup with sour plums and Chiu Chow–style roast goose.

See also **Kim Chuy** for Chiu Chow noodles in the Specialty Section, page 25.

Taiwanese-Style Restaurants and Delis

A million Chinese fleeing the mainland during the post–World War II revolution brought the flavors of Hunan, Shanghai, Beijing, and Sichuan to Taiwan, reshaping the island's food by adding new flavors to the local cooking—particularly in restaurants. Scarcely any restaurants serve the kind of regionally pure cuisine that native Taiwanese cook at home.

Typically, most places serving Taiwanese cooking, both in Los Angeles and on Taiwan, are delis that offer small snacks, cold plates, soups, and noodle dishes. Most also serve a sprinkling of multiregional items and even a few Japanese dishes, a carryover from 50 years of Japanese occupation.

Because the Chinese snack throughout the day, these light meals play an important part in everyday eating, and the delis often are open early until way past midnight. One, Good Shine Kitchen, in Monterey Park, is open 24 hours.

The delis are also popular spots for "northern"-style dim sum breakfasts—an entirely different meal from the Cantonese dim sum morning repasts. These Taiwanese-style breakfasts usually include a big bowl of soy milk soup, dumplings, and long crispy unsweetened Chinese crullers called yu t'iao.

TAIWANESE BREAKFAST
AND SNACKS GLOSSARY

Dou fu jiang: Either sweet or savory soybean milk served warm in a bowl. You add chili oil to taste to the savory version.

Gua-bao (Taiwanese): A steamed bread disk folded around marinated Chinese bacon and minced pickled vegetable.

Guo tie jiao: Pan-fried meat dumplings.

Jing-jiao: Steamed, meat-filled dumplings, usually served in their own steaming basket.

Shao-bing: Flat, hollow sesame-topped buns made of flaky pastry, eaten with soy milk. Shao-bing are also served along with barbecued meats, which diners sandwich inside the buns.

Shui jiao: Boiled dumplings filled with either pork, shrimp, or vegetables.

Siao lung bao (xiao long bao): Small dumplings filled with broth and meat.

Tienstin-style bun (tian jing man tou): A yeasted dough filled with minced pork and vegetables.

Yu t'iao (you-tiao): Two long strips of wheat dough fried together. The result is an unsweetened crullerlike pastry, usually eaten with soy milk. The crullers also come stuffed with shredded meat and crushed dried shrimp enclosed in sticky rice.

Other non-Cantonese dishes you'll find on Taiwanese deli menus are: *scallion cakes* (pancakelike, rather chewy, semiflaky pastry flecked with Chinese chives—which are larger and with a stronger taste than Western chives); *turnip cakes* (small baked buns filled with grated turnips); *sweet bean cakes* (buns filled with sweetened bean paste); *northern-style thick wheat noodles* in soups of various flavors; *oyster omelets; and chewy rice cakes,* sliced and stir-fried with bits of meat, Chinese pickled vegetable, and hot pepper.

TAIWANESE DELIS

Yung Ho (533 W. Valley Boulevard, San Gabriel, SAN GABRIEL VALLEY, 818-570-0860; open 7:00 A.M. through 10:00 P.M. daily), a busy, noisy café, is so popular on weekend mornings that you may have to wait for a table, but fortunately the tables turn fast. In spite of the crowds, our waitress didn't mind explaining unfamiliar dishes. But hubei-dubei (on their dim sum list) was beyond her explanatory powers. Out of curiosity, I ordered it and got a three-layer extravaganza of sticky rice topped with a savory, crispy bean pancake over a layer of garlic- and onion-laden minced pork. Another marvel of manifold textures from the dim sum list was "salty rice roll"— sticky rice again, but this time molded around yu t'iao stuffed with intensely flavorful shredded dried meat. Along with a bowl of sweet or savory soy milk, these items make an ample meal for under $3.

But people come here in groups and order lots of things. The tables are virtually covered with platters of seafood dumplings, pork-and-vegetable-stuffed buns, leek-filled pancakes, white turnip with fried eggs, and sink-sized bowls of meatball soup.

Deli World Cafe (127 N. Garfield Avenue [inside Hong Kong Market], Monterey Park, SAN GABRIEL VALLEY, 818-288-7482 or 288-3052; open 9:00 A.M. to 9:30 P.M.) is a trip to Taipei without an airplane ticket. To get there you go up a flight of stairs inside the huge Hong Kong Supermarket; the deli overlooks the store. Through large plate-glass windows you can watch a throng of shoppers stocking up on 1000-year-old eggs and mushroom soy sauce to the beat of rock music.

The long dining room is divided into stations, each preparing a different specialty. These are reflected by headings on the menu: "Cold Appetizers," "Taiwanese Deli," "Soups," "Noodles," and a section called "Lucky Mouth," which lists small entrées. Almost anything you try in this curious snacky way of eating will be marvelously authentic, amazingly delicious, and incredibly inexpensive.

The most popular section with non-Asians, "Dumpling King," offers, in addition to dumplings, a stuffed leek pancake enclosing an inch-thick mixture of Chinese chives, transparent noodles, and plenty of chopped garlic, and the popular pork gua-bao that you eat like a sandwich.

To woo nostalgic Taiwanese, **Sun Shine** (819 W. Las Tunas Drive, San Gabriel, SAN GABRIEL VALLEY, 818-284-0255; lunch through midnight and Friday and Sturday until 3:00 A.M.; closed Monday) has a picture on its business card of a mobile vendor serving his customer from a cart. Although the long knotty-pine-paneled dining room is almost as small as those carts, Sunshine is definitely stationary, with a good deal more seating. Up by the cash register is a glass display case from which you can point out steamed rice cake with pork: Sticky rice and meat are formed into a cupcake shape and served with a sprinkling of ground peanuts. Another sticky rice dish is molded around shrimp, pork, and mushroom, and wrapped in a bamboo leaf like a tamale. Sticky rice cakes are popular in many Taiwanese delis, but rarely are they this good.

The case also holds thick ribbons of spiced braised seaweed folded and speared with a wooden pick, and rich Taiwanese sausages. An extensive menu lists more familiar items. Try the delicate little oysters with scrambled eggs, or the cold noodles in a spicy sesame sauce with shredded chicken. Prices for these dishes are as low as you might pay at a street cart.

At **Good Shine Kitchen** (235 S. Garfield Avenue, Monterey Park, SAN GABRIEL VALLEY, 818-572-9666; open 24 hours daily), a 24-hour-snack-and-light meal dispensary of the sort found in the night markets and many other places in Taipei, a number of dishes reflect the Japanese influence on Taiwanese food. There's Chinese celery tempura, check-a-mein: tempura over Japanese-style noodles in soup. Good Shine's owner, Mr. Hsu, likes to recommend three-flavored chicken, a dish he knows everyone loves. The chicken is first fried, then stewed in a rich bean paste–sake sauce loaded with ginger and whole garlic cloves until it glazes the crisp skin. Chicken smoked over tea leaves and hot rock sugar in a covered wok is equally sensational. Other more strictly Taiwanese dishes are the salt-fried oysters, the several varieties of rice cakes with meat, and the anise-flavored roasted pressed tofu.

The large glass cases that dominate **MaMa's Kitchen** (543 W. Valley Boulevard, San Gabriel, SAN GABRIEL VALLEY, 818-308-1414; open daily), a strictly take-out Taiwanese deli, hold rows of small Styrofoam trays. Under their shrink-wrap covering you might find meaty cured duck legs that taste like rich ham, tiny clams cooked with whole garlic cloves and chiles, or Taiwanese rice cake wrapped in lotus leaves. In the Taiwanese manner, customers buy several small portions of food for one meal. Pickled radish with pork and chile, or the aforementioned clams, will spice up your rice or congee.

MaMa's makes on the premises many ingredients that most places buy from commercial manufacturers, including smoked fish and various styles of pressed tofu. In one version, tofu is cut into long fine strands resembling noodles. MaMa's tosses them with wisps of vegetable and a tart-sweet vinegar dressing for a salad. Besides what you see in the deli cases, MaMa's offers a small list of hot rice plates, noodles, and amusingly translated hot snacks (how about "sodium glutinous rice"?).

BEYOND SNACKS: TAIWANESE RESTAURANTS

Meitze, 321 W. Garvey Avenue, Monterey Park, SAN GABRIEL VALLEY, 818-288-0898 or 288-0899. Lunch through dinner daily. "Meitze is where nostalgic Taiwanese come when they want home cooking," said my Chinese friend. He was right. Just as we finished our dinner, a busload of Taiwanese tourists filed in past our table, cameras strapped over their Universal Studios T-shirts.

Meitze's little dishes, many of which are illustrated with color photographs, are more substantial than what you get in the delis: shelled clams with scallions and black beans, or fried baby eel in chili sauce garnished with fresh chile slices. And Meitze is known for a regional-style congee with boiled yams. This rice porridge, a staple during times of famine, is, like oatmeal, pure comfort food.

As in the delis, the fun of eating here is in trying a little of this and that. We sampled the steamed pork with preserved egg—a sort of minimeatloaf flecked with bits of pickled vegetable with the cooked egg yolk on top—then a plate of cold sliced beef in a delicious jelly, and a thick, warming cabbage soup with salty shreds of dried fish.

Formosan Restaurant, 18846 Norwalk Boulevard, Artesia, SOUTH, 310-924-0366. Lunch through dinner daily. Offerings at the Formosan Restaurant, in the small but growing Chinese enclave of Artesia, are similar to Meitze's. The Formosan doubles as a deli, too, with a substantial list of terrific appetizers and Taiwanese-style dim sum, including sticky rice rolls like the ones at Sun Shine.

Color photographs illustrate many dishes (this seems to be the current fad in Taiwanese restaurants), both unusual and familiar, from spare ribs with bitter melon and pig's-blood-cake soup, to kung pao chicken and fish steamed with black bean sauce. Some dishes that sound weird on the menu—"bamboo shoot w/pig's leg," for example—turn out to be rather familiar food: This is simply lean pork and bamboo shoots in a rich eastern-style brown sauce. Just about everything listed under "chicken" is a winner. Try "drunk chicken," smoked chicken, or the chicken assortment plate with five versions of the bird.

Live Fish, 230 N. Garfield Avenue, No. 12, Monterey Park, SAN GABRIEL VALLEY, 818-572-4629. Lunch through dinner daily. In the heart of Monterey Park—the Cantonese live-seafood capital of America—Live Fish, unlike its Cantonese neighbors, serves up Taiwanese-style seafood. The sauces are richer, more pungent, and spicier than the Cantonese variety. The dining rooms, decorated with marine paraphernalia, weathered boards, and paper banners announcing the daily specials in Chinese characters, give the impression of an old Maine seafood house hastily occupied by a makeshift Chinese restaurant.

The restaurant's Chinese name, Stone Door Dam, is meant to remind nostalgic Taiwanese of a famous dam and lake area near Taipei. The lakeside restaurants there are renowned for carving up a large lake fish and presenting it in 13 different dishes. The fish comes to the table as a savory fish head soup, and a fish tail braised in luscious brown gravy, then as a parade of fish fillets in various guises: steamed, deep-fried, and in various hot, sweet, and tart sauces. Live Fish usually prepares smaller fish in fewer versions, but the effect is the same.

From the concrete tanks at Live Fish, you can select Santa Barbara spot prawns, sheepshead, or bluefish. You choose seafood either stir-fried with garlic, deep-fried and served with pepper salt, or braised in a chafing dish.

If you go the chafing dish route you can select other ingredients for the pot from the menu. These add-ons range from oysters and cabbage to pig's-blood squares. You have a choice of braising sauces too.

Start your meal with a selection of appetizers that the waitress brings over on a tray: cold smoked duck, sweet marinated bamboo shoots, diced pressed bean curd with preserved egg, or spiced boiled peanuts.

WESTERN CUISINE: SICHUAN AND HUNAN RESTAURANTS

The heat for which Sichuanese cooking is so famous is only the first flavor, say Chinese gastronomes. After the blast of hotness subsides, other tastes emerge in waves: the sweet flavor of cooked garlic; the fresh snap of ginger; and the mellow richness of bean paste. Sichuan's "multiple flavors" captivated Chinese—and everyone else—outside the region in a relatively few years.

Prior to World War II, Sichuanese food was almost unknown outside its province. But when the Nationalist government had to hide from the Japanese by moving their operations to a remote section of Sichuan, officials ate nothing but the local food for eight years. When they reestablished headquarters in Shanghai and Nanking, their cooks came with them. After the war, many chefs moved to Taipei, where they opened restaurants of their own.

Few Sichuanese chefs have traveled to Los Angeles; what we usually get are blander adaptations of this hearty peasant food. But **Fu Shing** (512 W. Valley Boulevard, San Gabriel, SAN GABRIEL VALLEY, 818-570-0725; lunch through dinner daily), a Taipei-style Sichuan restaurant, serves, hands down, the best Sichuan cooking in the city.

Attempts have been made to upgrade the coffee-shop ambience of its decidedly out-of-character A-frame building, which once belonged to the House of Pies chain. The setting may not be glamorous, but nothing could diminish the glory of this kitchen. The dishes Fu Shing turns out have lots of style and clean, sharp flavors you can taste individually. Cold diced chicken with spicy sauce, for example, is bright with the individual notes of hot fresh chile and cilantro in the filmy sauce. Laced with crunchy Sichuan peppercorns and topped with crushed fried peanuts, the chicken is arranged on a ruffle of red lettuce with a tomato wedge cut like a bird. An ample cushion of shredded scallions was the base for Hunan beef, chunky with whole black beans and masses of garlic and chile.

Waiters at Fu Shing will always ask you how spicy you want your food, and many plainer dishes act as a counterpoint to all the spice. Try a plate of sautéed spinach garnished with a generous heap of beautiful coral crab roe. The roe's crunch and saltiness perfectly accent the plain vegetable.

Green Jade, 750 N. Hill Street (or 747 N. Broadway) (in Chunsan Plaza), Chinatown, CENTRAL, 213-680-1528. Lunch and dinner daily. Often the most superlative western Chinese food comes from Hunan, an area with much more to offer agriculturally than the mountainous Sichuan province. Fish and shellfish also are more abundant. Although Sichuan and Hunan cuisines are often lumped into the same pot, they do use different cooking styles, as a meal at Green Jade, the best Hunan restaurant in Los Angeles, can easily demonstrate.

Oftentimes, Hunanese food is thought to be even hotter than Sichuanese, a notion many chefs refute. Let me say that if you order

Green Jade's popular Chicken à la Viceroy, sauced with knee-buckling quantities of very fresh hand-chopped garlic, ginger, and ample chiles, you'll want to sample milder but no less remarkable dishes with it. Tea-smoked duck here is one of the few versions I've had with a thin, really crackly skin. Scallops with broccoli, a dull-sounding dish I almost passed up, was incredible: pillow-soft scallops seared in bacon or fresh lard heated to exactly the right temperature gave the scallops a subtle, aromatic flavor. An addictive Hunan honey ham, steamed to rid it of saltiness, came sliced and served with steamed buns.

Green Jade's understated dining room sits quietly beneath the huge, hyperactive Ocean Seafood in Chinatown. The restaurant employs two Hunanese chefs who cooked at Green Jade in Taiwan, a kitchen with a reputation for the best Hunan chefs in Taipei. Many of the restaurant's specialties, we were told, are not on the menu, as they need 24 hours to prepare. But with a reservation you can order a meal of dishes from the "diplomatic dinner" for upward of $12 per person.

Wei Fun, 708 E. Las Tunas Drive, No. 4, San Gabriel, SAN GABRIEL VALLEY, 818-286-6152. Lunch through dinner daily. My Taiwanese friends Tony and Michelle, always a great source of good restaurant tips, recommended this rather plain Hunanese restaurant on the growing restaurant-row area of Las Tunas Drive. "It's famous for the hundred-layer pancake," they told me. As usual, they were right on the money. On almost every table was a large, flaky pastry disk with airy tullelike layers resembling a mother-of-the-bride hat. Everyone just tears off pieces to munch with whatever else they're eating.

Once we convinced our waitress we were brave enough to try anything, she happily advised us, recommending "two plate," an economical way of ordering any two cold dishes from the appetizer list. We tried anise-spiced cold duck and something called "buddle flavored chicken." The "chicken" turned out to be braised dried tofu sheets tightly rolled into a loaf and sliced like a coldcut. Hunan-style lamb, the best dish to accompany the pancake, was a plate of tender lamb slices with lots of garlicky brown sauce, chopped black beans, and still-crunchy stir-fried leeks.

The unappealingly named "sauté glue rice cake" was a real winner. Typical of the western region, it came blazing with chile that was sufficiently tamed by the bland, chewy, noodlelike slices of rice cakes, and shredded chicken.

NORTHERN-STYLE RESTAURANTS

While Sichuan, Cantonese, and even Chiu Chow cooking are acclaimed beyond their provincial borders, one sees few northern-style restaurants outside that region. This is probably because many northern specialties—Peking duck, noodles, dumplings, buns, and Mongolian hotpot—are now eaten all over China, so a northern restaurant might seem redundant.

Once in a while, though, you find a restaurant like Royal House that serves the north's delicious lamb dishes and other specialties not often available elsewhere. Mongolian barbecue and hotpot dishes, now eaten in all the regions, are classics of northern cooking, so I've included here restaurants focusing on them. And I've included Muslim cooking, also a northern specialty.

Wheat, not rice, is the staple grain in the region; the north was the first area in China to develop all sorts of noodles, dumplings, and breads. Restaurants featuring these dishes are listed under "Chinese Specialties," page 22.

Royal House, 628 W. Valley Boulevard, Alhambra, SAN GABRIEL VALLEY, 818-289-4328. Open 9:00 A.M. to 10:00 P.M. daily. Royal House has been around for 20 years, first on Eighth Street near Chinatown and currently in Alhambra. The wood-panel decor of its present location hasn't changed much since the days when the restaurant housed a family-run Italian restaurant and pizzeria.

Royal House came recommended for its northern-style breakfast, but the excellent northern regional entrées and soups are what make it a great find. Express your interest in these house specialties and the friendly staff will happily discuss the details of any dish. (Avoid the familiar mu-shu shrimp and chicken with cashew nuts, or you'll miss the point of this kitchen.)

Lamb with green onions was more exotic than its name: The tender lamb strips are stir-fried with masses of garlic and shredded scallions. Alongside come dainty wheat pancakes that you smear with plum sauce and wrap around the meat. Another gem of a dish, lamb soup with pickled cabbage, is filled with clear noodles that soak up a marvelous, faintly tart broth. And don't pass up one of the better starters: cold Shantung chicken served on a bed of cucumbers.

Breakfast gets rolling around 11:30 A.M. on weekends. Order Tientsin-style buns stuffed with meat and pickled cabbage; hollow flaky sesame bread; fat steamed dumplings; steamed turnip cake; and sweet or savory bowls of soy milk.

China Islamic, 7727 E. Garvey Avenue, Rosemead, SAN GABRIEL VALLEY, 818-288-4246. Lunch and dinner; closed Wednesday. Chinese Muslim cooking originated in the northwest, and its heritage is

Central Asian Islamic. Wherever they go, Muslims have their own butcher shops and restaurants, since pork or anything cooked in the same kitchen with it is forbidden. Religious considerations aside, the hearty, richly seasoned, and often spicy dishes at China Islamic are so good that the restaurant attracts Chinese gastronomes of every persuasion. Indian and Middle Eastern Muslims also frequent it for Chinese food that suits their dietary requirements.

The most popular items—thin-skinned juicy lamb dumplings, rich mutton-shank soup, giant pan-fried sesame bread, and hearty stews in sand-pot casseroles—are distinctly northern. Buckwheat noodles with lamb and pickled cabbage, a northern dish rarely seen elsewhere, has a nutlike flavor. At China Islamic, cooks use garlic and hot chiles with enthusiasm, and many dishes have real punch. But guests with all tastes are catered to, even those with a fondness for chicken chop suey or sweet and sour shrimp.

China Muslim, 18331 E. Colima Road, Rowland Heights, EAST OF L.A., 818-810-2499. Open lunch through dinner; closed Tuesday. China Islamic's sister restaurant, China Muslim, in the newer Asian enclave of Rowland Heights, offers many of the same Islamic-style dishes.

Cocary, 112 N. Garfield Avenue, Monterey Park, SAN GABRIEL VALLEY, 818-573-0691. Open 11:00 A.M. to 1:00 A.M. daily. The Mongolian hotpot, with its charcoal-fueled chimney in the center, and the dome-topped Mongolian grill are familiar symbols of Mongolian cooking. Nowhere is the legacy of both the grill and the hotpot more deliciously apparent than at Cocary, a northern restaurant in the Taipei style.

Each table in the large open dining room holds a grill divided into six curved segments. Attached to its center is a cooking pot, which your waiter fills with soup stock as soon as he lights the grill. The food you select may either be simmered in the pot or grilled. Cocary has three huge high-tech refrigerated cases along one wall. The first is stocked with various meats, including deliciously marinated beef and sliced sausage. Another holds such seafood items as tiny clams and fish dumplings wrapped in ultrathin omelets. Still another case is filled with all sorts of vegetables, noodles, condiments, and appetizers. Three-tiered wire baskets are stacked next to the cases for carrying your selections.

The pace is hectic. Whole families get into the act of cooking while waiters rush around to the beat of Chinese rock music. At meal's end the waiter totes up the stack of dishes on the table and presents the bill.

Coriya, 1200 E. Valley Boulevard, Alhambra, SAN GABRIEL VALLEY, 818-576-1857. Open 11:00 A.M. to 2:00 A.M. daily. If you prefer more leisurely table service, Coriya (that's the Chinese name for Korea) has sit-down service. You select items from colored pictures on the menu, then cook them, as you do at Cocary, in a combination hotpot and grill.

Big Wok, 24012 Vista Montana (corner of Anza and Pacific Coast Highway), Torrance, SOUTH, 310-375-1513. Lunch and dinner Monday through Friday; dinner only weekends. Except for the small statue of a camel by the buffet area and the huge steel Mongolian grill, nothing in the dining room at Big Wok suggests the rugged Mongolian steppes where the idea for this barbecue originated. The very civilized space is large and elegant: Dainty black banquettes stand out against peach-toned grasscloth-covered walls and etched-glass room dividers.

For Big Wok's do-it-yourself

meals, you select your meat (raw wafer-thin slices of lamb, beef, chicken, pork, or turkey) and assorted vegetables from a buffet. It's up to you to flavor your dish from the pots of various sauces on the buffet. To guide you, the place mat offers several recipes. You then hand your ingredients to one of the chefs manning the grill. As soon as the food hits the blistering hot steel, puffs of sizzling steam erupt. Seconds later you're handed the cooked food on a china dinner plate. Some Mongolian barbecue aficionados like to stuff the grilled food into the flaky, hollow shao bing that come with the meal, to eat their barbecue like a sandwich. A second Big Wok (1200 Pacific Coast Highway, Hermosa Beach, SOUTH, 310-798-1155) is open the same hours and features the same menu.

CANTONESE RESTAURANTS

The fresh simple food coming out of our newest wave of Cantonese restaurants bears little relation to the syrupy-sauced sweet and sour shrimp we once thought of as Cantonese food. In the Hong Kong tradition, these places always have a collection of tanks holding lively sea creatures; a squadron of servers rushes them from tank to kitchen to table.

Many of the new restaurants have immense, opulent dining rooms that teem with intense business meetings by day and overflow with lavish wedding banquets by night. On weekends, when throngs line up for dim sum, crews of waitresses circle dining rooms pushing carts piled high with baskets of steaming dumplings and fragrant pastries. Diners spend hours leisurely putting away order after order of seductive little dishes, ignoring the anxious tapping feet of those waiting at the door.

Smaller places have their individual charms and, usually, a more casual ambience. The food may be

wonderful or it may be just all right, but the best part of dining in any of these restaurants is the feeling you've been transported to Asia without leaving L.A.

◆ **THE BEST CANTONESE-STYLE RESTAURANTS IN THE SAN GABRIEL VALLEY**
Peony, 7232 N. Rosemead Boulevard, San Gabriel, SAN GABRIEL VALLEY, 818-286-3374. Lunch through dinner daily. It is, perhaps, a tad peculiar to find a former assistant chef from Hong Kong's deluxe Regent Hotel cooking in a converted International House of Pancakes in a relatively obscure part of San Gabriel, where Peony is situated. But a meal from Chef Vincent Cheng's kitchen explains why this place so quickly developed a loyal following. The pointy-roofed exterior may kindle visions of pancake breakfasts, but inside, Peony has a kind of Paris bistro elegance, albeit with gurgling tanks by the kitchen door. Simply but comfortably appointed, the restaurant focuses, in true Parisian style, on flawless food and a well-selected list of boutique wines.

Cheng's dishes explain the Chinese enthusiasm for Cantonese quick-cooking techniques. They coax flavors from the very freshest ingredients, heightening them with a few well-chosen seasonings. In Cheng's lobster vermicelli casserole, juicy fresh cracked lobster rests on a bed of translucent noodles that absorb the lobster's juices and its rich cooking broth; the combination gives the dish a sort of double-whammy lobster flavor. Crab is done the same way, unfettered by sauces that might obscure its sweetness. For the best meal at Peony, always consider recommendations from the knowledgeable maître d'.

Harbor Seafood, 545 W. Valley Boulevard, San Gabriel, SAN GABRIEL VALLEY, 818-282-3032. Open 11:30 A.M. to 3:00 A.M. daily.

Harbor Seafood has a casual feel to it. There's the buzz of an animated clientele, open fish tanks with humming pumps at the back of the room, and waiters in snappy white cotton tuxedo jackets with red lapels patrolling the sea of white-linen-covered tables.

Harbor may be casual, but the menu still offers such things as braised shark's fin with partridge. Most tables, however, seem to order the huge (almost minilobster-sized) prawns steamed or boiled in the shell. These come with a tart dipping sauce, all you need to enhance their flavor. Look for them in the tanks; they aren't listed on the menu. More items for serious seafood-lovers: geoduck clam, either Japanese style (sashimi) or parboiled (quickly whisked through boiling water) and served with dipping sauce; oysters steamed in their shells in black bean sauce and ordered by the piece; and deep-fried bean curd stuffed with minced shrimp. Harbor caters to diners whose sole purpose is eating fresh fish and seafood, and who don't mind bringing their own wine or beer.

Seafood City, 7540 E. Garvey Avenue, Rosemead, SAN GABRIEL VALLEY, 818-571-6066 or 571-5454. Lunch through dinner daily; dim sum 9:00 A.M. to 3:00 P.M. A Taiwanese friend claims Seafood City became one of the most popular seafood destinations less for its splendid seafood than for its Cantonese-speaking Latino busboys who trade jokes with the clientele. In its former location across the street, Seafood City had a rather drab dining room crowded with mobs of Chinese eating at huge round tables with lazy susans in the center. But its new location—in keeping with the onslaught of competition among fancy restaurants like Harbor Village and N B C Seafood (see below)—is a huge, high-ceilinged

space embellished with rose marble, rosewood trim, and brass pillars. All those rosy colors, along with the starched pink tablecloths and the pink menus, make the room fairly vibrate with pinkness. And barely a swish or gurgle can be heard from the fish tanks, encased in more rose marble on the back wall.

I tasted my first shark's fin soup here when a friend held a minibanquet at one of the huge tables. This version of the gelatinous fin came floating in a broth with luscious smoky Virginia ham. Shark's fin has cachet, but the huge prawns, sliced open, steamed, and sprinkled with finely diced sautéed garlic, were what everyone talked about on the way home.

Seafood City's vast menu of well over 200 items (not all of them seafood) offers more preparations of shrimp than I've seen anywhere, with ingredients that range from potent chiles and black beans to fresh asparagus or chewy taro root. And Seafood City serves good traditional dim sum from carts every day until 3:00 P.M. Reservations are advised for this busy place, especially on weekends.

Harbor Village, 111 N. Atlantic Boulevard, Monterey Park, SAN GABRIEL VALLEY, 818-300-8833. Lunch and dinner daily; dim sum from 10:00 A.M. weekends, 11:00 weekdays. Harbor Village, a branch of the Hong Kong chain, is a palatial 450-seat room, ablaze with crystal chandeliers. The main room is rimmed with ornate private dining rooms furnished with Chinese antiques. Silver chopstick rests on heavy damask tablecloths complement the imperial-style Cantonese cuisine. This is the fanciest and most original food in all L.A.

But the prearranged banquet dinners, not the regular menu, are what show off the kitchen's skill. As the waiters will tell you—sometimes with a hint of disdain—the

English menu is a simplified version of the chef's repertoire.

The real master of this restaurant, however, is the dim sum chef. His wares, a quantum leap past what we've been eating, have been called the most inventive selection of dim sum this side of Hong Kong. From ten in the morning until 3:00 P.M., carts glide around the vast dining room bearing shrimp-and-chive dumplings in a translucent wrapping, dumplings filled with soup that squirts when you bite into them, chile-flecked octopus salad, silky rice noodle rolls with pork filling, and glutinous rice cakes filled with peanut paste. Harbor Village is a little piece of imported Hong Kong at its most exuberant. One caveat: There are no reservations for dim sum, so arrive early or you'll find the wait long.

N B C Seafood, 404-A S. Atlantic Boulevard, Monterey Park, SAN GABRIEL VALLEY, 818-282-2323. Open 8:00 A.M. to 10:00 P.M. daily. The monolithic N B C Restaurant (with the same ownership as A B C in Chinatown and the much more casual Ocean Star) should be experienced at least once in every Cantonese seafood diner's lifetime. Sitting in the ultrabright 700-seat dining room beneath the high-voltage glare of enormous crystal chandeliers is like floating in some surreal Hong Kong fantasy. Even with all those seats, I've actually had to wait for a table on weekends; N B C is Monterey Park's most popular venue for parties and banquets.

From the tanks that line the room, you can order a simple meal of exquisite, satiny steamed tilapia with a little ginger and light soy sauce to enhance its flesh. Or have the more exotic pan-fried "dual" squid: The chewy texture and intensified flavor of the reconstituted squid enhance the briny subtleties of fresh squid. You could just as well dine magnificently without any seafood at all from N B C's colossal list of decidedly unfishy choices.

Ocean Seafood, 25 W. Valley Boulevard, Alhambra, SAN GABRIEL VALLEY, 818-282-1828. Lunch and dinner daily until 3:00 A.M. The building that houses Ocean Seafood was clearly once a forties-style drive-in diner. Its tall art deco spire, rimmed in neon, juts up like a peacock's comb from the building's round coffee-can shape. And though the designers have stylized the exterior with smart pin-striping and bowed awnings, I have a hard time erasing my early memories of roller-skating carhops bringing burgers on a clip-on metal tray.

Inside, etched-glass mirrors and restrained color give the dining room a postdeco supper club feel. The predecessor of the huge Ocean Seafood in Chinatown, this branch still draws a good crowd of San Gabriel Valley regulars.

It's a good idea to come with at least three other people. Many dishes run in the $10, $15, and up price range, but portions are generous. You probably won't want to pass up the "double pleasure" sole, in which perfectly cooked strips of fish are arranged over the deep-fried crispy carcass, lightly coated in a slightly salty breading reminiscent of potato chips. The combination is amazing. And there are scallops from the tanks, the females bearing creamy orange-colored roe, and live lobster cooked in garlic sauce with meat so sweet you'll wonder why you ever ate the frozen kind.

Dragon Regency, 120 S. Atlantic Boulevard, Monterey Park, SAN GABRIEL VALLEY, 818-282-1089. Open 9:30 A.M. to 10:00 P.M. daily. One of the first Cantonese seafood restaurants to gain recognition beyond Monterey Park, Dragon Regency still has egg rolls on the menu—some say to make

Western customers happy. But there's also bird's nest with crab soup and shredded duck with jellyfish that will appeal to the adventurous. Exotic as it once was, Dragon Regency's menu now seems standard for Monterey Park. But while it offers few surprises, the kitchen still holds its own in the intense seafood-restaurant competition.

If you can gather ten friends together, Dragon Regency offers some extraordinary bargains on set dinners ranging from $99 to $148 for the whole meal. Each starts with a combination platter of barbecued meats and includes a whole steamed fresh fish. If you order the $128 menu, you'll be served deep-fried plump oysters, pan-fried scallops with vegetables, pan-fried crab with ginger, steamed chicken with Chinese broccoli, and several other dishes. Dragon Regency's dim sum is acceptable, but there's better to be had close by.

Ocean Star Seafood, 112 N. Chandler Avenue, Monterey Park, SAN GABRIEL VALLEY, 818-300-8446. Open daily, 5:00 P.M. to 3:00 A.M.; until 4 weekends. When he opened Ocean Star, a small seafood house on a side street just off Garvey Avenue in Monterey Park, the owner already had the gargantuan N B C and A B C Seafood to his credit. An astute businessman, he saw an unfilled niche in the culinary market for a less ostentatious place with the same high-quality seafood.

Ocean Star has the offhand feel of an after-hours café, and actually does stay open until 3:00 A.M. during the week and 4:00 A.M. on weekends. Unlike the owner's other, more formal restaurants, where waiters wear tuxedos, this is a place where I'm not embarrassed to slurp oysters out of their shells. At mealtimes, a young, hip, primarily Chinese crowd comes in for unfussy Cantonese dishes like

lobster simply baked with butter, or cooked with a little ginger and green onion to complement its sweetness. To accompany a steamed sheepshead (the fish we'd selected from a tank), we ordered a rich hotpot of roast pork and oysters that came in a meaty-tasting gravy. Steamed chicken with ham and vegetables arrived in a surprising arrangement of layers alternating the meats with greens like a lasagna.

◆ **THE BEST CANTONESE-STYLE RESTAURANTS IN CHINATOWN**
Empress Pavilion, 988 N. Hill Street, Chinatown, CENTRAL, 213-617-9898. Lunch through dinner daily; dim sum 9:00 A.M. to 5:00 P.M. Just a few years ago, the venerable Yee Sing Chong Chinese market and its asphalt parking lot turned into the elegant Bamboo Plaza. The five-level structure, filled with a supermarket and shops, holds the Empress Pavilion restaurant. Both are evidence of important changes under way in Chinatown.

To get to the restaurant you take glass elevators from the top parking area and glide down to the second floor of the plaza, which overlooks a shady central courtyard. In typical Hong Kong style, the 600-seat space subdivides into banquet rooms when a series of decorative screens is unfolded. There's also a comfortable lounge and bar.

At the moment, Empress Pavilion is the undisputed leader for refined Cantonese meals in Chinatown. There's live seafood and an extensive menu with all the expected Cantonese classics and Sichuan dishes. A "gourmet specialties" section emulates the latest currents in Hong Kong–Cantonese cooking, with oysters on the half shell under a peanut-curry cream sauce, or scallops stuffed with shrimp mousse.

The restaurant is busy throughout the day with a bustling dim sum lunch, dim sum teatime from 2:30 to 5:00, and pretheater dinner. And Empress Pavilion's dim sum vies with Ocean Seafood's as the best in Chinatown. Har gow, siu mai, and other standards are expertly crafted; often a cart holds more exotic choices, such as steamed lotus seed buns, or pale green disks of Chinese squash stuffed with minced shrimp, pork, and mushrooms. Be sure to ask about the five varieties of exotic teas to go with the dim sum or you'll get the prosaic jasmine variety.

For a change, the service, which in many Chinese restaurants resembles what you expect from surly countermen in New York delis, is delightfully pleasant.

Ocean Seafood, 750 N. Broadway, Chinatown, CENTRAL, 213-687-3088. Lunch through dinner daily; dim sum 8:30 A.M. to 3:00 P.M. Almost overnight the venerable Miriwa, which had been so famous for dim sum, was transformed, as if by a genie waving a magic joss stick, into Ocean Seafood. The dim sum menu was revitalized, the dining room sprouted tanks, and there was an overall upgrade of the regular food as well. Live seafood and other entrées almost duplicate what you'll find at A B C and V B C (see below). Now Ocean is the best-known dim sum parlor in the neighborhood (although I don't think it's as good as Empress Pavilion). Besides the full morning dim sum service, you can get a limited selection of dim sum at all hours, or purchase it from Ocean's deli next to the restaurant.

The rest of the food is competently done. But Ocean caters huge Chinese wedding banquets, and when the kitchen is overtaxed, some dishes suffer the usual problems encountered while attempting to serve 400 people at once.

Fortune, 750 N. Hill Street, No. F, Chinatown, CENTRAL, 213-680-0640 or 680-2615. Lunch and dinner until 1:00 A.M. daily. At dinnertime, if I don't feel like getting fancy, I prefer Fortune restaurant just below Ocean in the same Chunsan Plaza. This little jewel is a simple room with heavy white tablecloths and a marvelous chef who knows how to make flavors sing. Shrimps from the tanks come bursting with juice. Pan-fried oysters with ginger and green onions are full of briny flavor and aromatic accents. Many dishes go beyond the tried and true: spinach and lettuce stir-fried with Chinese sausage and bacon, or scallops sauteed with pine nuts on a bed of crunchy deep-fried preserved cabbage.

Hop Li Seafood, 526 Alpine Street, Chinatown, CENTRAL, 213-680-3939 or 680-3417. Lunch through dinner daily. Unlike the cookie-cutter sameness of the menus at larger restaurants, Hop Li's has an inset menu of monthly specialties, and each selection has little quirks of individuality. One night the restaurant recommended beautiful live scallops quickly cooked and served with their coral; on another, a huge plate of small tender mussels steamed with ginger and scallions. The clean oceany flavor of oysters on the half shell blended with a light touch of spicy Sichuan sauce was the sort of combination that inspires legends. And the pork chop in a fresh orange glaze is another unusual example of this delightful kitchen's handiwork. With all the competition, Hop Li, a smallish, off-the-beaten-path restaurant on Alpine, sometimes gets overlooked. It shouldn't be.

Full House Seafood, 963

N. Hill Street, Chinatown, CEN-TRAL, 213-617-8382. Open 11:30 A.M. to 3:00 A.M. daily. Full House is a good place for late suppers after a show downtown. The menu isn't as nouveau as some of the glitzier places. No shrimp with macadamia nuts—just dependable favorites from the well-stocked tanks and the lengthy menu that includes succulent salt-baked shrimp; roast pork and oysters cooked in a sand pot with a rich brown sauce; delicate tofu triangles stuffed with minced shrimp; and lettuce-and-shrimp-meat-stuffed crab claws, all modestly priced. The small selection of beer and wine is best ignored.

Mon Kee, 679 N. Spring Street, Chinatown, CENTRAL, 213-628-6717 or 628-1090. Lunch through dinner daily. Until Mon Kee caught on in the early eighties, most Angelenos hadn't tasted anything resembling true Cantonese food. Mon Kee must be credited for introducing the taste of lobster and catfish drawn from the tank just moments before it appears on the table; for a well-turned-out plate of fresh clams with pungent black bean sauce; and for stir-fried vegetables that hadn't seen more than a few seconds in the wok.

Mon Kee may not be at the zenith of the great Cantonese food that has more recently swept Monterey Park, but the restaurant still draws crowds, even with all the new competition.

There are two more Cantonese–style restaurants worth noting. **V B C Seafood,** 711 N. Broadway, Chinatown, CENTRAL, 213-680-0888. Lunch and dinner daily. Live seafood in a posh setting with a dreamy view of Downtown L.A. **A B C Seafood,** 205 Ord Street, Chinatown, CENTRAL, 213-680-2887. Lunch and dinner daily; dim sum from 8:30 A.M. to 3:00 P.M. The same ownership and menu as N B C in Monterey

Park. This jammed, noisy dining room is popular for dim sum and live seafood.

♦ **THE BEST NEIGHBORHOOD CANTONESE-STYLE RESTAURANTS**
Oriental Seafood Inn, 4016 Lincoln Boulevard, Marina Del Rey, WEST, 310-306-9088. Lunch and dinner daily. West Side residents no longer need to brave the freeways to Chinatown or Monterey Park for live seafood. The Oriental Seafood Inn opened quietly several years ago in a former hacienda-style Mexican restaurant. Most of the tables are filled with large groups of former Hong Kong residents living on the West Side. Busboys fish crabs and lobsters from tanks, and the food is beautifully garnished. There's a second branch of the Oriental Seafood Inn at 16161 Ventura Boulevard, Encino, S.F. VALLEY, 818-907-0427.

The Sea Food House, No. 3 18329 S. Pioneer Boulevard, Artesia, SOUTH, 310-860-7794. Lunch and dinner daily; dim sum from 10:00 A.M. to noon. Another branch of the well-respected Seafood Paradise II restaurant in Westminster has wisely located in Cerritos/Artesia, a rapidly growing Asian enclave. Dim sum served

---

OTHER GOOD PLACES TO EAT IN CHINATOWN

- Green Jade, Hunan (page 13)
- Luk Yue, Cantonese noodles (page 25)
- May Flower, village chicken and won tons (page 26)
- Mandarin Deli, dumplings and noodles, (page 24)
- Kim Chuy, Chiu Chow noodles, (page 25)
- Family Pastry, dim sum, pastries (page 31)
- Mandarin Shanghai, Shanghai style (page 7)

---

from carts has the same excellent quality as at the Orange County branch. And the seafood selection, including live seafood, is vast: The selection of shrimp dishes rivals what you find at Seafood City and includes such rarely found items as heads-on giant prawns in their shells with Thai-style mint dipping sauce. The offerings aren't strictly Cantonese. You'll see lots of stars indicating hot, spicy dishes sprinkled around the menu: Sichuan kung pao frogs' legs and the chile-garlic-laced ma po bean curd, for example. Clams also come in a spicy Southeast Asian mint sauce or are pan-fried with hot bean paste.

CHINESE SPECIALTIES

◆ NOODLES AND DUMPLINGS

You can't walk more than a few feet in Asia without bumping into a seller of noodles or dumplings. Like sandwiches in the West, noodles are China's all-purpose food: Delivery boys bicycle noodles to offices; late-night stands and coffee shops offer them as midnight snacks. Asians even eat noodles for breakfast.

Invented in the wheat-growing north, noodle doughs quickly caught on everywhere, and each region perfected its own noodle and dumpling style. In the south, for instance, doughs made from rice, the region's staple, are turned into many noodle shapes and stuffed for dumplings.

Noodles

As L.A.'s noodle-shop competition mounts, owners have started to specialize. We are now heirs to all sorts of handcrafted noodles and various regional dumpling styles. Sichuan dan dan mein, Cantonese chow fun, or Shanghai-style Yang Chow fried noodles may one day rival sandwiches.

With noodles so much a part of daily eating, it's easy to see why the Chinese appreciate their subtle variations: A simple change in the noodle's shape makes a big difference in the dish. Chinese chefs are masters of manipulating dough in an amazing variety of ways. Each of the following restaurants makes its noodles using a different technique. The most astonishing method to watch is northern-style noodle pulling.

As far as I know, **Dumpling House** (5612 Rosemead Boulevard, Temple City, SAN GABRIEL VALLEY, 818-309-9918) is the only San Gabriel Valley restaurant where the art of noodle pulling is carried out. To watch the noodle chef, who works by a window facing the parking lot, you have to stand outside. He takes a blob of dough and slaps, stretches, and twists until it magically separates into firm, silky noodles with a character no machine can duplicate.

Dumpling House offers ten dishes with hand-pulled noodles, ranging from a rich brown meat sauce to a light seafood broth and soups from fiery to mild. I love the beef stew soup noodles, a clear peppery broth loaded with beef slices; the wheaty noodles temper the broth's intense dry chile taste. And, of course, Dumpling House makes dumplings, wonderful satiny-skinned pork dumplings with a shrimp embedded in the center of each.

At **Dow Shaw Noodle House** (432 E. Valley Boulevard, San Gabriel, SAN GABRIEL VALLEY, 818-572-0617), the chef, who makes the dow shaw northern-style noodles at this plain café, works behind a pizzeria-style window visible from the street. He kneads a massive ball of dough into a fat cylinder the size of a football and, holding it with one arm, uses a cleaver to shave off thin dough slices into boiling water at lightning speed. The noodles emerge slightly thick and chewy, with an angular edge where the cleaver has sliced them from the dough. Their extraordinary texture is firmer than the

Dim Sum

im sum, the southern Chinese morning tradition of taking tea with sweet and savory pastries and other nibbles, evolved from China's teahouses. The term literally means "dot the heart," but "hit the spot" captures the true sense. A few of the top dim sum restaurants are Empress Pavilion (page 19), Harbor Village (page 17), Joss (page 29), Ocean Seafood (page 20), A B C Seafood (page 21), Seafood City (page 17), The Sea Food House (page 21) and **Sun T. Lok** (400 S. Arroyo Parkway, Pasadena, SAN GABRIEL VALLEY, 818-584-6719).

Two gourmands select dim sum from a cart at Empress Pavilion in Chinatown.

DIM SUM GLOSSARY

Pinyin spellings, which may sometimes be encountered on menus, follow the most common spelling, where applicable.

Bao: These slightly sweet yeast-risen wheat buns hold various fillings that include Chinese sausage *(lop cheong bao);* chicken with vegetables and salted duck egg *(gai bao);* date and sweet bean paste *(tou sha bao);* and barbecued pork *(char siu bao).*

Chang fun (chang fen): Steamed rice flour sheets rolled around fillings of beef, shrimp, or barbecued pork.

Dan ta: Short pastry tarts filled with a sweet, dense egg custard.

Har gow (xia jiao): Steamed shrimp-filled dumplings with a slightly chewy, wheat starch and tapioca flour covering.

Jar woo kwok or gok: Deep-fried taro flour turnovers.

Jeen duey (jian dui): Deep fried rice flour balls stuffed with sweet bean paste.

Jing joon or dong: Glutinous rice mixed with dried shrimp and chunks of sausage (or other meats), wrapped in lotus leaves and then steamed.

Lin yun bao: Steamed lotus buns with sweet bean paste filling.

Lo bok goh (lo bo gao): Rice flour and shredded turnip cakes with chopped sausage, steamed and pan-fried to a golden brown.

Ma lye goh: Steamed sponge cake.

Ngau yuk siu mai (niu rou shao mai): Steamed beef meatballs flavored with fresh coriander served on steamed greens.

Pai gwat (pai gu): Bite-sized pieces of steamed spare ribs in black bean sauce.

Sieaw gai (shao ji): Soy sauce-braised chicken.

Siu mai (shao mai): Steamed open-faced dumplings shaped with a "waist" near the top, filled with minced pork, or shrimp and pork.

Yu jao (yu jiao): Stuffed balls or ovals of deep-fried, mashed steamed taro filled with pork, shrimp, and mushrooms.

---

rolled and cut flat noodles at Dumpling Master and Mandarin Deli, and they're heftier than the hand-pulled noodles at Dumpling House.

Dow Shaw's many toppings and soups are as fine as its noodle-making display. Try hot and sour soup, a mild and tart, slightly thick broth with pork and smoky mushrooms; shreds of brilliant red fresh pepper add a tingle of heat. Or try the noodles in a rich brown beef shank stew perfumed with star anise. (Dow Shaw is closed on Wednesday.)

"House special noodles are best," the kindly man at the cash register desk told me in confidential tones. This man knows his noodles. The cook at **Dumpling Master** (423 N. Atlantic Boulevard, No. 106, Monterey Park, SAN GABRIEL VALLEY, 818-458-8689) rolls out noodle dough by hand and cuts it into thick ribbons. The hefty noodles soak up a light but rich-tasting broth. And the toppings are cooked by someone with an impeccable sense of timing: In the "house special noodles," the shrimps are juicy and the pea pods still snap. The kitchen turns out several other versions, but be sure to insist on the special noodles or you'll get the factory-made kind.

Topping Dumpling Master's menu are the portly pork dumplings and the scallion pie that built the café's reputation. But at the small mirrored room's Formica tables, diners are also putting away juicy-looking pork chops, glistening wok-fried vegetables flecked with chile, and velvety rich corn soup in bowls the size of a laundry sink.

Since its inception, the fish and scallion dumplings with their light, flaky filling and the meat dumplings, which look like flower buds, have drawn crowds to the **Mandarin Deli** (727 N. Broadway, No. 109, Chinatown, CENTRAL, 213-623-6054). But a growing number

---

of regulars have also found the Deli's homemade noodles addictive. Some of the best noodles the Deli makes are the oddly named "ground noodles in soup." They are similar to the hand-rolled noodles at Dumpling Master, but cut into large squares, not strips, dropped into boiling broth, and garnished with bits of meat and vegetables. Mandarin Deli makes more kinds and styles of noodles than any other Chinese noodle outlet. Cold sesame noodles, as well as noodles bathed in a serious chili sauce, have devotees across the city.

Now a chain, the Deli has four branches citywide. A rather opulent Little Tokyo branch features colored photographs of most items. The original Monterey Park location, called **Mandarin Noodle House,** is said to have the best food, though you may have to endure rude service. Other branches: 701 W. Garvey Avenue, Monterey Park, SAN GABRIEL VALLEY, 818-570-9795; 9305 Reseda Boulevard, Northridge, S.F. VALLEY, 818-993-0122, and 356 E. 2nd Street, Little Tokyo, CENTRAL, 213-617-0231.

Regional Noodles

Just next door to the China Mandarin Deli, **Kim Chuy** (727 N. Broadway, No. 103, Chinatown, CENTRAL, 213-687-7215) serves Chiu Chow–style noodles. The Chiu Chow Chinese fled to various parts of Southeast Asia years ago. In the case of Kim Chuy's owners it was Vietnam. This explains the Vietnamese writing on the signs and the Southeast Asian influence in the food.

Kim Chuy uses three types of fresh noodles: wide flat rice noodles; thin square-edged rice noodles; and thin Cantonese-style egg noodles. Each is prepared with a long list of toppings, sauces, and soups. "Beef variety rice noodle," for example, is a huge bowl of silky flat rice noodles topped with sliced steak, chunks of braised beef, and chewy beef balls. The "spice beef rice noodle bowl" is a version with thin fresh rice noodles and a mildly spicy red sauce. Noodles with soup come garnished Vietnamese-style with fresh herbs and a sliver of lime. The flat rice noodles are also delicious in stir-fries; Kim Chuy's chef scrambles in an egg along with the other ingredients.

After your noodles, have a glass of Vietnamese-style iced coffee with condensed milk; it tastes like liquid coffee ice cream.

Luk Yue (853 N. Broadway, Chinatown, CENTRAL, 213-687-0330), a Cantonese noodle parlor with a spirit altar above the cash register, has a loyal following for its congee—22 kinds, to be exact. Though it's an acquired taste for many, for any Chinese congee is as comforting as Jewish penicillin.

Luk Yue's noodles, on the other hand, have instant appeal. They come in four classic Cantonese varieties: skinny Cantonese-style egg noodles called mein; wide rice noodles called fun; rice vermicelli; and precooked dried e-fu noodles.

Luk Yue's kitchen turns out all the traditional Cantonese noodle preparations; thus you can get any of the four noodles in lo mein or in "soup noodles" (that is, noodles *flavored* with soup as opposed to noodle soup). Stir-fried dishes include chow fun and chow mein. Rice vermicelli comes either stir-fried or in broth.

Ginger-chicken lo mein, full of sharp clean flavors, is the dish I'm hooked on. And lo mein topped with Chinese greens and crispy roast duck, which Luk Yue prepares in its own barbecue kitchen, is a close second.

The Chinatown Luk Yue closes at 10:00 P.M. But its two branches in Monterey Park are always jumping way into the wee hours of the morning. Also at: 123 N. Garfield

Avenue, Monterey Park, SAN GA-
BRIEL VALLEY, 818-280-2888, and
735 W. Garvey Avenue, Monterey Park, SAN GABRIEL VALLEY, 818-
284-6638.

Silver Wing (1265 E. Valley
Boulevard, Alhambra, SAN GABRIEL
VALLEY, 818-308-1890) serves
wonderful Yang Chow (Shanghai-
style) coldcuts and dim sum, so I
couldn't figure out why my Hong
Kong friends referred to it as a
"northern" restaurant. (Most
Cantonese, I later found out, tend
to dismiss any place north of
Guangdong Province, including Sichuan in the west and Shanghai and
Taipei in the east, as northern.) Silver Wing *does*, however, specialize
in something truly northern: the
fat, slightly chewy northern noodles served in more than a dozen
variations. One version comes in a
powerfully spicy red broth with
shreds of long-simmered brisket—
the menu calls it "braised beef
stringy in soup." The chile in this
dish really clears the sinuses and in-
fuses the bland noodles with plenty
of flavor. A milder dish comes
loaded with shredded pork perked
up with tangy preserved vegetables.

As for defining Silver Wing, you
could call it a northern noodle
house with Shanghai dishes, or a
Shanghai restaurant with northern
noodles (unless, of course, you're
Cantonese).

Dumplings and Wontons

Sir Charles Dumpling House
(11746 Artesia Boulevard, Artesia, SOUTH, 310-865-7694 or 865-
2315)—where did they get that
name?—a small café in Artesia,
makes 11 dumpling varieties of impressive quality. Dumpling devotees come in and tote off bags of
them (they are sold frozen, 50 to
the bag). Or they plop down at the
counter and spend a few euphoric
moments savoring each juicy bite
of dumplings as good as the ones
they remember from Taipei or

Hong Kong. The house specialty,
with a combination shrimp, scallop, pork, and vegetable filling, is a
dumpling to risk rush-hour traffic
for. There's a lightness to the generous filling, and the dough coverings are rolled precisely to the
right thickness. Sir Charles's other
dumpling varieties include fish with
leeks, pork with Chinese mushrooms, beef with napa cabbage,
and vegetarian.

The world's best shrimp dumplings come from **Pearl's Oriental
Restaurant and Dumpling
House** (644 W. Garvey Avenue,
Monterey Park, SAN GABRIEL VAL-
LEY, 818-284-2761). When we ordered the house speciality, "shrimp
and leeks boiled dumpling," we got
nods of approval from the café's
all-Chinese clientele. The thin-
skinned little pockets surround a
chopped shrimp filling that barely
holds together. Pearl's also prepares ja jang mein in a hearty
brown meat sauce (noodles in a
mildly tingly "spicy beef noodle
soup") and Taipei-style cold appetizers. But these dishes don't hold
a candle to Pearl's dumplings. Pearl
herself works the cash register,
and though her English is minimal
she beams when you order more
dumplings to go.

Wonton devotees will want to put
wonton soup and village chicken
from **May Flower** (800 Yale
Street, Chinatown, CENTRAL, 213-
626-7113) on their list of Best
Dishes. The plain-wrap Formica
café, obscurely located away from
the touristy part of Chinatown
near the French Hospital, makes
meaty, meltingly tender fillings
swathed in translucent dough.
These come crowded into a vat-
sized bowl of luscious broth. Of
the many toppings for the soup,
"village chicken" is the most outrageous. May Flower devotees
rhapsodize about the chicken's
crisp, slightly dry meat suffused

with a sweet ginger-garlic soy. Go early for lunch; this item always runs out early.

Even before most West Side Chinese-food lovers were driving to Monterey Park for a meal of dumplings, small portions of smoked chicken, and little plates of pickled cabbage, Philip Chiang had brought this kind of food to his West Hollywood restaurant, **Mandarette Chinese Cafe** (8386 Beverly Boulevard, West Hollywood, WEST, 213-655-6115). Chiang, whose mother then owned the well-known Mandarin in Beverly Hills, wanted to introduce his customers to the eating style he grew up with and the sorts of foods he often ate at home.

So in an artfully plain café—a sort of postmodern take on the functional nonstyle of Chinese dumpling houses and tearooms—Chiang began serving little plates of noodles with minced Sichuan pork, cold tofu with 1000-year-old egg, and steamed pork buns—in short, food that had yet to grace a table west of the Harbor Freeway.

Mandarette's kitchen prepared these dishes to suit Chiang's contemporary taste: Unlike the hole-in-the-wall versions, they were incredibly low in fat. That's what inspires fans of Mandarette to pay $6.75 instead of $2.95 for bon bon chicken, $10.50 instead of $6.75 for clams in black bean sauce, and $8.25 for cold noodles with shredded chicken instead of $3 to $4 a bowl.

Since Chiang has taken over **The Mandarin** (page 29), it too offers a wide selection of small plates.

Another outpost for dumplings of an entirely different sort is **Hong Kong Restaurant** (9635 Reseda Boulevard, Northridge, S.F. VALLEY, 818-886-6928). On the 25-item dim sum menu (with additional items on weekends), look for Sichuan wontons in red chili sauce, mushroom and chicken bao, and shrimp har gow. And there's dan dan mein: cold noodles, tangy picked vegetables, and cooling shredded cucumber tossed in a palate-warming sesame sauce. Hong Kong also specializes in soup noodles with fresh rice noodles.

MORE CHINESE SPECIALTIES

One of the first restaurants to bring Chinese **vegetarian** food to our attention, the **Fragrant Vegetable** (108–110 N. Garfield Avenue, Monterey Park, SAN GABRIEL VALLEY, 818-280-4215) offers Buddhist-style dishes in an elegant dining room graced with statues and Taoist paintings. The fare is a far cry from a monk's starvation rations. An assortment of meatlike appetizers arrives at the table around a bowl of smoking dry ice with a carved carrot phoenix rising from the center. Gluten, the base of many meatless entrées, isn't the dreadful canned stuff you find in Asian markets; it's made here fresh every day. Gluten doesn't quite duplicate meat, but when it absorbs the Fragrant Vegetable's delicious sauces the result is marvelous.

This imperial vegetarian cuisine is based on China's rich repertoire of mushrooms, creamy coconut milk curries, and elaborately conceived eggplant dishes, including taro-stuffed eggplant in a pungent black bean sauce. (Also at 11859 Wilshire Boulevard, West Los Angeles, WEST, 310-312-1442).

A bookcase full of Buddhist literature set back from the entryway acts a foyer at **Merit Grove,** (206 S. Garfield Avenue, Monterey Park, SAN GABRIEL VALLEY, 818-280-7430). The utilitarian dining room isn't nearly as posh as the Fragrant Vegetable's, but this kitchen's painstakingly prepared vegetarian dishes have the same appeal. "Buddha's feast," an assortment of nuts, gluten, tofu, and mushrooms in a rich brown sauce, arrives encircled with bright green broccoli florets. Many items are fairly simple vegetable dishes: spicy kung pao cabbage with peanuts; braised fresh mushrooms; pressed meaty tofu sautéed with bean sprouts.

At **Shau May** (15 E. Valley Boulevard, Alhambra, SAN GABRIEL VALLEY, 818-282-4560), watching the server fashion the house specialty, **Taiwanese slush,** is worth the price of admission. A large block of ice is clamped into the stout, hand-cranked ice shaving machine, and, with a turn of the handle, fresh ice shavings fall into a bowl. First a bit of sweet syrup is poured over the ice. Then you select your toppings from the row of containers in the deli case. You get three toppings for $1.50: pearl tapioca, sweet red beans, or lichee nut. Four items cost $1.75; you could add grass jelly cubes or, for richness, a dollop of sweetened condensed milk. Shau May also sells hot snacks and rice plates. A recently opened second branch is at 127 S. San Gabriel Boulevard, San Gabriel, SAN GABRIEL VALLEY, 818-451-0077.

Among the customers at **Plaza Deli** (729 E. Valley Boulevard, San Gabriel, SAN GABRIEL VALLEY, 818-307-5664), stern-looking Chinese businessmen can be seen at the ice cream parlor tables reading their Chinese newspapers and sipping **ice shakes** similar to those at Shau May (above). Plaza Deli also makes extremely refreshing shakes of blended ice and fruit.

The sibling of a well-known Taipei café, **Lu's Garden Taiwanese Congee Shop** (534 E. Valley Boulevard, No. 12, San Gabriel, SAN GABRIEL VALLEY, 818-280-5883) specializes in the regional **rice congee** with boiled yams, and a buffet full of congee toppings to chose from.

Move your tray along the cafeteria-style counter and point to the selections that interest you: whole broiled pike; steamed baby clams in soy sauce; tofu stewed in sweet pungent sauce; salted mustard greens; tiny sardines with chiles; or white-cut chicken wings. At lunch, three selections are $3.50 with congee. Lunch and dinner are served until 1:00 A.M. daily.

With McDonald's and Kentucky Fried Chicken all the rage in Asia, younger generations prefer the frenetic energy of fashionable **Chinese-style Western coffee shops** to the staid fading teahouses of their elders. In Bangkok it's the Highlight or the Uptown, in Hong Kong, Mickey D's. Now the East's version of Western eateries has descended on the San Gabriel Valley.

Litz (201 E. Garvey Avenue, Monterey Park, SAN GABRIEL VALLEY, 818-288-8882) draws high school and college students on dates who sip ice cream floats, and eat Asian versions steak in wine sauce and macaroni. For the less acculturated there are rich plates, chow fun, and Asian-style–curries. Litz is open from 11:00 A.M. to 1:00 A.M. on weekdays, and until 3:00 A.M. on weekends.

Helena Restaurant (156–158 S. San Gabriel Boulevard, San Gabriel, SAN GABRIEL VALLEY, 818-285-2108, with branches in Alhambra and Monterey Park) offers its Western dishes with *karaoke* (customers singing to background music). The young waitresses flip on the music and large-screen projection video the minute a customer is seated. Caddies on the tables hold song request cards. The closest thing to Asian food on Helena's otherwise "continental" menu is curry over rice. The vegetable borscht is recommended, filet mignon wrapped in bacon is the house speciality, and baked pork chop with spaghetti sells briskly.

You can get a B.L.T. and French toast, too. Ice cream soda flavors run to red bean, mango, and longan. The San Gabriel Helena, open from noon to 1:30 A.M., is the only branch with karaoke. The other branches stay open until 2:00 A.M.

♦ **NEIGHBORHOOD SPOTS WORTH A DRIVE**
Plum West, 1057 Tiverton Avenue (enter parking lot at 1100 Glendon Avenue), Westwood, WEST, 310-208-3977. Lunch and dinner daily; brunch 11:00 A.M. to 3:00 P.M. Saturday and Sunday. Just a few feet from the staid Bullock's Westwood, Plum West serves northern-style breakfasts on weekends. People are hungrily gobbling up steamed pork buns, pot stickers, scallion cake, and stir-fried "gluey rice cake" as though they were going out of existence. In the evening, live lobster and oysters on the half shell are plucked from the kitchen's tanks, and there's an excellent pan-regional menu.

The Mandarin, 430 N. Camden Drive, Beverly Hills, WEST, 310-272-0267. Dinner nightly; lunch Monday to Saturday. In 1975, when Cecilia Chiang opened the Mandarin, her Sichuan and Peking-style dishes were considered revolutionary. Today her son Philip, who recently took over the restaurant's management, continues in his mother's pioneering footsteps by introducing an eating style still unfamiliar to most non-Asians. Philip's new menu follows the Chinese tradition of "small tastes."

The younger Chiang brought Chinatown uptown, putting a barbecue and dim sum kitchen right in the middle of the dining room. His chefs, who make dumplings, steam breads, and pull the best Peking duck in town from the oven, work in full view of the diners. And while Chiang kept kung pao shrimp and even sweet and sour pork on the menu, he also introduced small tastes of spicy boiled wontons with vegetable preserves, slightly sweet glazed walnuts served on a crinkly bed of deep-fried spinach leaves, and cold tofu topped with chopped 1000-year-old eggs. These may be authentically Chinese, but they're not quite the little dishes you find in Monterey Park's Formica-table snack shops. Chiang has culled his offerings from a broad repertoire, refined them to suit Beverly Hills tastes, and priced them accordingly.

Joss, 9255 Sunset Boulevard, Beverly Hills, WEST, 310-276-1886. Dinner nightly; lunch Monday to Friday. Only the chopsticks in this spartan dining room hint that Joss is a Chinese restaurant. A quick glance at the menu—scallops stuffed with pear mousse, and breast of chicken in a light Chinese mustard sauce—could give the impression that French influences are at work here. "Not so," says owner Cecile Tang, who frequently travels to Hong Kong on exploratory eating trips. "Most dishes compare with what you find in Hong Kong's most au courant kitchens."

Tang has also kept many familiar dishes like tangerine beef and kung pao chicken on the menu too. "When it comes to introducing new food, you can't move people along too fast," Tang says.

These aren't my favorite dishes here. The dim sum, which is worth every dime of its high tariff, is my pick. Nowhere in Los Angeles will you find honey-apricot glazed spareribs, toasted rice-pastry shrimp dumplings, Yunnan siu mai, or pot stickers stuffed with lamb and leeks that are turned out with such finesse.

Twin Dragon, 8597 W. Pico Boulevard, West Los Angeles, WEST, 310-657-7355 or 855-1550. Lunch and dinner daily. Right down to its mint-flavored toothpicks, its

Long Island tea, its mai tais with little umbrellas, and its English-only menu, Twin Dragon is the consummate Chinese-American restaurant. This kitchen turns out American-style Chinese food but it's not the humdrum soggy egg roll variety. A house speciality, Twin Dragon beef steak, is a pair of well-aged filet mignons seared, painted with oyster sauce, and served with baby corn, mushrooms, and broccoli florets. The lengthy menu includes excellently prepared Sichuan and Shanghai-style dishes. And for the nostalgic, there's egg fu young.

Fortune West, 12733 Ventura Boulevard, Studio City, S.F. VALLEY, 818-760-3867. Dinner nightly; lunch Monday through Saturday. Obscurely located at the far end of a large rambling shopping center, Fortune West isn't a restaurant you stumble across accidentally. But the kitchen outshines the neighboring competition. Its chef seasons his food with authority; his sauces are silky and light. And dishes arrive in stylish presentations. Su-tzah beef, shredded, deep-fried, then cooked in a powerful chile-garlic sauce, assaults your senses with its intriguing mix of crispy textures and multifaceted flavors. A northern and western emphasis shows up in most dishes. There's a long, better-than-average dim sum list to assuage your dumpling cravings, though most of these items are not an absolute rave.

Hunan Garden, 2439 Pacific Coast Highway, Lomita, SOUTH, 310-530-1180. Lunch through dinner daily. Chef Roger Lee, partly responsible for the excellent reputation of the food at the old Mandarin, is a man whose fans have followed him from restaurant to restaurant over the years. Now he has installed his woks in his own place in Lomita.

Lee's varied repertoire covers every region and does so with exceptional skill. Even the dumplings (which are usually disastrous except in dumpling-specialty places) are sublimely filled, with properly thin, toothsome skins. His green onion pancakes are equally fine. Years ago, Lee put tangerine beef on the Los Angeles culinary map. At Hunan Garden, you see this dish—in voluptuous proportions—going to almost every table. Even common-sounding dishes have the stamp of Lee's culinary artistry.

Golden Lotus, 31176 Hawthorne Boulevard, Rancho Palos Verdes, SOUTH, 310-377-5892. Lunch and dinner daily. At the very end of Hawthorne Boulevard, where it winds down to the Palos Verdes Peninsula bluffs overlooking the ocean, Golden Lotus caters to the Asian millionaires whose homes and estates dot the peninsula's bucolic landscape. It's a fitting room, large and gracious with dignified, upholstered banquettes and an opulent bar near the entryway. Although chop suey is available, listed under "American Chinese Dishes," there's tea-smoked duck perfumed with a lingering smoky flavor; wispy strips of marinated tripe in a zingy chili sauce, and a lengthy list of whole fish dishes. The whole fish in Hunan sauce with masses of garlic and a slightly sweet soy and vinegar sauce truly deserves your attention.

Jasmine Tree, 11057 Santa Monica Boulevard, West Los Angeles, WEST, 310-444-7171. Lunch and dinner daily. One of the more spirited Chinese kitchens on the West Side, Jasmine Tree resides in the former second-story home of Captain Pepper's Shrimp Boat, a sunny space with windows overlooking Santa Monica Boulevard.

Jasmine Tree does all the obligatory Sichuan and Mandarin favorites, but the kitchen also serves a few Shanghai cold plates: smoked fish, grilled pressed bean curd, and jellyfish seasoned with sesame oil—not your everyday pu pu platter. Complex Shanghai-style brown sauces show up on the hot-braised whole fish and the clams with brown sauce.

Szechuan Garden, 17719 Van-owen Street, Reseda, S.F. VALLEY, 818-343-2665. Lunch and dinner daily. This is really a Shanghai-style eastern restaurant masquerading as an everyday neighborhood place. The back pages of the lengthy menu (and the untranslated Chinese menu) list dozens of Shanghai items under "Old Fashioned Chinese Dishes," "Chef's Specialties," and "Cold Dishes." Smoked fish and vegetarian goose head the cold listings; shredded pork may be had eastern-style with dense pressed bean curd and zingy pickled vegetables. Eel comes in an unctuous brown sauce sprinkled with yellow leeks. And tea-smoked duck isn't a dish you find often—if at all—in the Valley. I always get the feeling I'm missing something wonderfully authentic from the Chinese menu, but I'm not complaining.

Hunan Taste, 6031 W. San Vicente Boulevard, Los Angeles, CENTRAL, 213-936-5612 or 936-6133. Lunch through dinner daily. This popular restaurant was one of the first to do really good spicy western Chinese dishes (it's yet another fine Chinese kitchen in a converted House of Pies). But the once hokey interior has been turned into spacious dining rooms with subdued coloring and comfortable seating. Hunan Taste's chile-and-orange-tinged General Tsao's chicken seemed almost revolutionary in the restaurant's early days, and it's still one of the best versions in the city. Popular favorites here include cold Hunan noodles; plump, spicy Hunan wontons; and hot, garlicky Hunan lamb. Ma po bean curd (on the menu as "hot, spicy bean curd with pork") comes explosively spiced with

quantities of garlic, ginger, and chile—a dish that redefines tofu.

CHINESE SPECIALTY SHOPS AND MARKETS

♦ BAKERIES

Yi Mei Bakery (736 S. Atlantic Boulevard, Monterey Park, SAN GABRIEL VALLEY, 818-284-9306) is known among Monterey Park Chinese residents as a very good traditional bakery whose bakers come from Taipei. Everything in this small shop is handmade. The traditional yue bing, or moon cakes, made with a wheat pastry stuffed with such fillings as sweet date, pineapple, or winter melon, are lined up in straight rows in the pastry case. I like the small turnovers stuffed with pork curry and green onions, as well as the pork and vegetable bao—the covering is thin and not too sweet.

The bakery is also known for northern-style breakfasts centering on large bowls of soy milk that may be ordered slightly sweetened or seasoned with a dash of sesame oil and salt and eaten with yu t'iao. Everybody enthusiastically soaks up the milk with the yu t'iao, then noisily (it is impossible to do this quietly) consumes it. Try the sumptuous scallion cakes—the bakery is famous for these—or the baked Mandarin bread made from a lightly yeasted sweet dough flavored with green onions.

By 8:00 A.M., big trays of lightly sweetened baked Mandarin-style buns line the back wall of **Family Pastry** (715 N. Spring Street, Chinatown, CENTRAL, 213-622-5255). There are a few nondescript tables, the tea is free, and those buns—just from the oven—are a wonder! They come stuffed with ham or barbecued pork. Steamed buns such as chicken, egg, and sausage bao or scallion buns showered with green onion and twirled into a delightful figure eight also make a delicious breakfast. Other savories include curry pork turnovers, pork or beef stuffed siu mai, and steamed half-moon dumplings. Chewy taro turnovers are filled with meat and deep-fried.

As for sweets, Family Pastry makes lovely dan ta, tarts with tender, crumbly crusts, *jeen duey* stuffed with dates, and steamed egg cakes sweetened with honey. Family Pastry is open from 7:00 A.M. to 5:00 P.M. daily.

With its marble and granite façade in subdued oriental colorings, **Kuo's Bakery** (1430 W. Valley Boulevard, Alhambra, SAN GABRIEL VALLEY, 818-458-0688) is the city's glitziest and most modernized Chinese bakery. Taiwanese know the Kuo Yuan Ye shop in Taipei. It began in 1867 as the Yuan Ye Cake store in the Taiwanese village of Shee-Lin. In the beginning, all its pastries were made by hand and loaded into bamboo baskets and sold along Shee-Lin street. But the fifth generation, now running the shops, has turned to the latest in Western and Japanese baking technology to create the precisely ornamented traditional Mandarin-style pastries Kuo's Bakery is known for.

The shop's reputation was built on "four seasons pastries": cookielike pastries molded into flowers and geometric shapes, stamped with an intricate design, and filled with sesame paste, peanut, sweet bean, or black bean filling. Classic yeast buns come filled with lightly sweetened pastry cream, pork, or sweet red bean paste. The filled flaky pastries are quite light as such pastries go. These may be traditional, but they are the most refined versions you'll ever encounter.

♦ **CHINESE MARKETS**
99 Ranch Market, 988 N. Hill Street, Chinatown, CENTRAL, 213-625-3399. (Also 1340 W. Artesia Boulevard, Gardena, SOUTH, 310-323-3399, and 140 W. Valley Boulevard, San Gabriel, SAN GABRIEL

VALLEY, 818-307-8899. And also in Montebello, EAST OF L.A., Rowland Heights, EAST OF L.A., Anaheim, OCOUNTY, and Westminster [see page 113]). Tawa, Inc., whose eight 99 Ranch or 99 Price supermarkets are scattered throughout the city, has moved to the top of the Asian supermarket heap in just a few years. The company, like its non-Asian counterparts, advertises heavily in the local media. At Tawa's product-promotion tasting fairs, consumers sample Chinese convenience foods: frozen scallion buns ready for the oven, frozen dumplings, and myriad premixed sauces. Its produce, which includes Chinese celery, water grass, winter melon, and giant white radish, is procured from California growers.

Tawa's Chinatown 99 Ranch Market, underneath the Empress Pavilion restaurant in the high-tech Bamboo Plaza, sets the tone for the chain with its vast and spectacular meat and seafood department. Along one wall, in sparkling, fastidiously clean tanks, are live catfish and briskly swimming tilapia of various sizes. Humming pumps gush freshly oxygenated water into the tanks, which house lobsters, and Dungeness, blue, and rock crabs. Other containers hold live oysters and clams. On banks of ice are multihued fish in the round: soles, dabs, rockfish, and the silvery, almost paper-thin moon fish. A team of butchers is on hand to custom-carve meats from the enormous selection of primal cuts on display. Like many Asian markets these days, the 99 Ranch stores stock a basic selection of pan-Asian goods that run the gamut from Thai curry pastes to Japanese ice cream.

Older Chinese markets cater to a Cantonese clientele, but Tawa's shelves hold many ingredients specific to eastern (i.e., Taiwanese) cooking: Fresh gluten products are

Selecting dinner from the live seafood tanks at 99 Ranch Market.

found in bins of water across from the produce department, and various forms of pressed and grilled tofu are stocked in the cooler case.

Man Wah Supermarket, 758–762 New High Street, Chinatown, CENTRAL, 213-628-7490. Also in Chinatown, Man Wah Market continues to be excellent, with a large and varied packaged goods department (nearly an entire gondola is devoted to Chinese and Southeast Asian hot sauces). This supermarket goes all the way through from Spring Street to New High Street. On the New High Street side, you will find Cantonese noodles and dumpling skins in the cooler cases, and chrysanthemum tea and big bags of dried mushrooms packaged by the store. Look for Asian baking and dessert supplies on the shelf with the cake mixes: almond powder in jars, agar-agar, boxes of taro flour, and rice flour for sticky cakes.

Take the ramp up to the Spring Street side of the store, where the produce is kept and where the seafood department offers live turtles with their eyelids at half mast.

Hong Kong Supermarket, 127 N. Garfield Avenue, Monterey Park, SAN GABRIEL VALLEY, 818- 280-8888. (Also 137 S. San Gabriel Boulevard, San Gabriel, SAN GABRIEL VALLEY, 818-309-1111, and in Chinatown.) The Chinatown Hong Kong Market is small and caters primarily to a Vietnamese clientele. But the two huge San Gabriel Valley branches offer all the Western supermarket amenities—including coupons and spiffy neon signs indicating the various sections: meats, fish, produce, and so on—coupled with several typically Asian touches. Along the north side of the Monterey Park store, a series of independent shops, modern versions of Asian market stalls, sell their wares.

Lao Dah Fung bakery stocks leaf-wrapped Taiwanese rice rolls, curry beef pies, and airy steamed Chinese-style sponge cakes. Of note are the various deli items: smoked chicken, Taiwanese-style sausage made with rice and peanuts, and Chinese-style hot or sweet meat jerky. Other shops sell Vietnamese submarine sandwiches called banh mi and freshly squeezed juices, including sugar cane and longan. **World Book Company** is the source for Chinese-language magazines; there's a minibranch of **Sun Long Tea** and a sundries store that stocks over-the-counter medical remedies from Taiwan and Hong Kong.

The huge market's dry noodle, canned goods, and Chinese convenience foods sections stretch into the mists with a variety that boggles the mind.

After shopping, walk up the stairs to **Deli World Cafe** (page 10) for Taiwanese-style dumplings and tea, or next door to **Luk Yue** (page 25) for noodles and barbecue.

The San Gabriel Boulevard Hong Kong Supermarket, also with the same tea and bakery outlets, has a Cantonese-style noodle and barbecue restaurant for after-shopping refreshment.

Ai Hoa Supermarket, 421 N. Atlantic Boulevard, Monterey Park, SAN GABRIEL VALLEY, 818-308-3998. (Also at 7235 Reseda Boulevard, Reseda, S.F. VALLEY, 818-996-8383. And in Alhambra and Chinatown.) With its elaborate upswept oriental tile roof, the Vietnamese-owned Ai Hoa on Atlantic Boulevard is equally large and excellently stocked. Sliced and diced wok-ready meats are well priced here, and the produce section offers Chinese and Southeast Asian herbs and vegetables. The chain is of interest to San Fernando Valley residents for its branch on Reseda Boulevard. And there's another branch in the City of Industry.

DiHo, 720 S. Atlantic Boulevard, Monterey Park, SAN GABRIEL VALLEY, 818-282-9182, and 11700 E. 183rd Street, Artesia, SOUTH, 213-422-0512. DiHo market seems a very modest-sized store these days, but not so long ago it was king of supermarkets in the Monterey Park area. Catering to the demands of its neighborhood (Monterey Park has been called the Chinese Beverly Hills), DiHo was the store that introduced what you might call Chinese convenience food: diced skinless chicken breast, julienne strips of pork, and beautifully cut noisettes of pork tenderloin, all ready for the wok. Apart from excellent quality meats and well-manicured produce, considerate service has helped DiHo keep its reputation.

Monterey Fish Market, 724 S. Atlantic Boulevard, Monterey Park, SAN GABRIEL VALLEY, 818-282-3486. The fish department at DiHo is fairly modest, but just next door at Monterey Fish Market, bubbling tanks hold madly paddling Santa Barbara spot prawns, live abalone, and Dungeness crab. Catfish and red snapper swim in tanks against the wall. Monterey Fish Market skins eels for its customers and imports small Taiwanese crabs used for stuffing or for pickled crab. You can also buy chunks of Indonesian beltfish and ready-to-cook large sea cucumber (the large ones are the most tender).

Sun Long Tea, 748 S. Atlantic Boulevard, Monterey Park, SAN GABRIEL VALLEY, 818-576-1289. In the same shopping plaza is a branch of Sun Long Tea, importers of rare and fine teas from Taiwan. King's tea, at this writing $118 a pound, is picked from bushes grown on a certain mountain where the weather is perfect for fine Oolongs. Teas made from the tender whole young leaves command the highest prices. Solid brass containers that line the walls of the dignified room hold green, fermented, and semifermented teas of different grades, and 50 types of ginseng of varying qualities. They also sell lovely unglazed earthenware tea sets: tiny pots and miniature cups for enhancing tea's fragrance. (Also in Chinatown, CENTRAL, at 811 N. Broadway, 213-626-3888.)

Vinh Hao Super Market is an excellent Chinese and pan-Asian supermarket in the Long Beach area (see page 118).

♦ POULTRY SPECIALTIES

Everyone knows the Chinese like their fish just minutes from the water. They also prefer to buy chickens while they're still clucking. Chinatown has several live poultry shops that hard-core cooks should know about. At **Canton Poultry** (717 N. Broadway, Chinatown, CENTRAL, 213-680-2588; open daily), cages of cackling chickens and quacking ducks are stacked outside the entryway. You go inside to strike a deal on your bird. Pick up some of their marvelous fresh eggs, which are best for poaching. In addition to everyday cluckers, Canton carries chukars, partridge, and quail. You can also order out-of-the-ordinary poultry such as guinea hen.

On Spring Street, **Shang Lee Poultry** (711 N. Spring Street, Chinatown, CENTRAL, 213-617-2635; open daily), justifiably proud of its fine silkies (black Chinese chickens) and fat squab, also takes special orders. **Superior Poultry** (750 N. Broadway, Chinatown, CENTRAL, 213-628-7645; open daily), one of the first of these live bird emporia in Chinatown, looks like a forlorn pet shop with its drab, dusty gray exterior. Cages stacked just inside the door make for a rather overwhelming aroma, but cooks have been coming here for decades for fat Christmas geese, mallard ducks, and pheasant in season.

United Foods Company, 736 N. Broadway, Chinatown, CENTRAL, 213-624-3788. Open daily. Whole sides of pork and glistening ducks hang in the window, big pans of stewed exotic meats—pigs' intestines in soy sauce, stewed duck, or chicken feet in broth—fill the deli case. It's all very old-time Chinatown. But United has a few hidden virtues the casual visitor might miss. In a separate building at the rear of the shop, it sells speciality ingredients to many of the city's major restaurants. You can request an air-dried uncooked duck. Cooks say these roast up crispier; more fat renders from the skin. United also carries mallard ducks, rare poultry, and duck livers for pâtés. One fan says it's the only place she trusts for fish to be served raw. United's second location at 419 Alpine Street, 213-620-0368, a fish store, is a fine source for good-quality low-priced shrimp. Tanks with live turtles, and fish including perch and skulpin, are constantly replenished.

JAPAN

When the New Otani Hotel opened its Weller Court shopping area in Little Tokyo about ten years ago, it ushered in a new era of Japanese restaurants. In the food court were the sort of specialty places you find in Japanese cities, where they are crammed together like tiny boxes in every alleyway, and located around subway terminals and on the top floors of department stores. At Weller Court there were yakitori and noodle shops, along with Unashin, a restaurant devoted entirely to eel dishes.

None of these restaurants served the predictable teriyaki combination plates, nor the sort of home-style dishes that Japanese Americans have cooked for generations. Instead, they "catered to Japanese businessmen," a description that was fast becoming the best thing you could say about a Japanese restaurant.

But catering to Japanese businessmen doesn't have to mean a place where the expense-account set makes deals in secluded tatami rooms over $200-a-person dinners. Most of the restaurants opening now are the sort of places you'd find in travel guides titled *Japan on a Shoestring.* And the food served in them is exactly what you'd get in Tokyo or Osaka.

In fact, more than a few establishments have branches in Japan. Several, including Chin Chin Tei, Furiabo, and Yoro no Taki, are Japanese chains. Their kitchens, says Showa Marine, a wholesale purveyor of Japanese foodstuffs, use staples and even fresh ingredients from home. "We bring in approximately a thousand different items from Japan, including daily shipments of fish flown in from Tsukiji, the huge wholesale fish market in Tokyo." Other food companies import everything from soy sauce to Japanese mayonnaise.

Everyone is familiar with sushi bars and Benihana-style teppan-yaki grills. But Japan has more than 16 other restaurant categories—and assorted subcategories—and most of them are represented in Los Angeles. So in the Japanese tradition, I've emphasized specialty restaurants. But I've also included my favorite restaurants with good, all-around variety.

⸺ *JAPANESE GLOSSARY* ⸺

Aji no tataki: *Horse (or Spanish) mackerel chopped into pieces and served with a vinegar-soy sauce.*

Ankimo: *Cooked monkfish liver served in slices. Ankimo resembles foie gras.*

Anpan: *A yeast roll with a sweet red bean filling.*

Bento: *Japan's traditional lunch box, which includes an assortment of varied small food portions surrounding a large serving of rice.*

Bincho: *A special hard charcoal named after a renowned charcoal dealer and produced in Wakayama prefecture, bincho is primarily used for yakitori and kushiyaki grills.*

Bonbochi or bonchiri: *The "pope's nose" or chicken's tail.*

Chakin: *A form of sushi: thin sheets of omelet filled with a seasoned rice mixture and shaped into rolls or balls.*

Chashu: *Japanese-style Chinese barbecued pork.*

Chazuke: *This began as tea poured over rice to help wash it down. Today chefs use broth and add other ingredients.*

Chirashi sushi: *Sushi ingredients artistically arranged on top of seasoned rice in a bowl.*

Dobin mushi: A clear soup, often flavored with fresh pine needles and cooked and served in a small teapot.

Domburi: A meal in a bowl consisting of rice with a wide range of topping choices.

Edamamé: Boiled fresh soy beans served in their pods.

Enoki or enokitake: Tiny white mushrooms with a strawlike stem.

Ganmodoki: Mashed tofu, nori, and vegetables pressed into a cake and deep-fried.

Gobo: Known as burdock in English, this long slender orange root with a hairy brown skin could be called the Japanese carrot. It is eaten as a cooked vegetable or made into pickles.

Gyoza: Japanese-style Chinese meat-filled grilled dumplings.

Ika soba: Squid cut into strips as fine as noodles and served chilled.

Ikura: Cured salmon roe similar to red caviar.

Ippin-ryori: A meal of small à la carte dishes.

Izaka-ya: A Japanese pub.

Kaiseki: This highly refined multicourse meal, based on the best seasonal foods, evolved out of tea ceremony cooking. Its courses include foods from each cooking style in the Japanese repertoire.

Kamameshi: Rice cooked ''country style'' with assorted ingredients in a special iron pot.

Kappo-ryori: The most refined cooking style in the ippin-ryori category.

Karaoke: The latest entertainment fad in Japan. Restaurant or club patrons sing popular songs to taped background music in front of other customers.

Kasu zuke: A marinade for fish using sake lees, a by-product of sake making.

Kazunoko konbu (or kombu): Thick seaweed with a layer of unseasoned cod roe over it.

Kissaten: Similar to the idea of a French café, these coffee- and tea-drinking lounges serve snacks and offer a place to relax, socialize, and listen to music.

Koryori-ya: Restaurants serving meals composed of a series of small à la carte dishes prepared to order using only traditional Japanese cooking styles and ingredients.

Kushi-age: Morsels of food coated with Japanese-style bread crumbs (panko), skewered and deep-fried.

Kushi-yaki: Assorted skewered and grilled foods prepared the same way as yakitori.

Mabo ramen: Ramen noodles in a spicy Chinese-style ground pork sauce.

Maguro: The leanest cut of raw, red-meat tuna.

Maki-zushi: Sushi served in a roll form wrapped up in crisp roasted seaweed.

Matsutake: A huge fragrant seasonal mushroom that grows wild in Japanese forests (and now in the northwestern United States).

Miso: A paste made from fermented soy beans and grains, miso is used as a flavoring for everything from soup to dips and salad dressings. Like cheese, miso's many varieties depend on its aging process and ingredients. Misos range from pale creamy ''white'' miso to deep red aka miso.

Mochi: A chewy confection made from sweet rice pounded to a powder, mochi are often stuffed with sweet red bean or soybean paste.

Mushi: Implies steamed foods.

Nabeyaki udon: Udon noodles in

a fish-based broth with assorted ingredients and usually topped with shrimp tempura.

Nigari: A extract of sea water (bittern) used to make nigari tofu—a special variety.

Niku: Implies a dish using beef. Yaki-niku is soy-marinated grilled beef.

Nomi-ya: A neighborhood pub with informal cooking.

Nori: Dried marine algae pressed into thin sheets, this is often mistakenly thought of as seaweed. Nori is the familiar crisp wrapping enclosing sushi and is also used as a garnish.

Okonomiyaki: Grill-your-own savory pancakes with various toppings.

Omakase: The custom of having the chef select the dishes for your meal.

Onigiri: Rice formed into a ball or triangle around a small morsel of strong-tasting food such as a pickled plum or salted cod roe. Yaki-onigiri are grilled rice balls.

Oshibori: The small wet cloth offered to diners before a meal to freshen up.

Otsumami: Tidbits and small plates of food usually eaten while drinking sake or other alcoholic drinks.

Ponzu sauce: A lime juice, soy sauce, and rice vinegar mixture used for many sushi preparations.

Ramen: These thin wheat noodles are a Japanese version of Chinese mein. The word ramen has been borrowed into the Japanese language from the Chinese lo mein.

Robata: A hearthside grill restaurant.

Ryori: Cooking or cuisine.

Sarashina: A highly refined buckwheat flour used for a particular kind of high-quality soba.

Sashimi: Fish or seafood served raw.

Shabu-shabu: Japanese-style beef fondue in which thin sliced beef and vegetables are cooked in broth at the table.

Shiitake: A type of Japanese mushroom with a dense meaty texture.

Shio-yaki: A cooking term (salt-broiled) meaning food is dry-marinated in salt and grilled.

Siu mai: Shrimp and pork-filled open-faced dumplings.

Soba: Slender noodles made primarily from buckwheat flour.

Somen: Slender white wheat noodles; the angel hair pasta of Japan.

Sunomono: This means "vinegared things," and comprises a wide range of cold foods dressed in a sweet, slightly tart rice vinegar dressing.

Sushi-ya: A restaurant or shop specializing in sushi.

Tamago or tamago yaki: A Japanese-style omelet cooked in a thin sheet and rolled to form a loaf. Tamago is served in sushi bars.

Tanmen: Ramen in a clear pork broth with vegetables.

Tare: Sauce, usually the barbecue sauce for yakitori.

Tatami room: A private dining room that has its floor covered in straw tatami mats.

Tatsuta-age: Chicken chunks that have been marinated and then deep-fried.

Teishoku: A prearranged multicourse meal.

Tempura: Foods dipped in a light batter and deep-fried.

Teppan-yaki: A style of cooking done on a large grill in front of diners.

Tonkatsu: Deep-fried breaded pork cutlets.

Tori meshi: Rice cooked together with chicken and seasonings.

Tori no karaage: Deep-fried chicken.

Toro: Tuna belly; the fatty cut of raw prime tuna used for sushi and sashimi.

Tsuke-jiru: A soy sauce-based dipping sauce for cold noodles.

Udon: A thick white wheat noodle usually served in soup but also served cold.

Umeboshi: A small, very sour pickled plum.

Unagi: Freshwater eel.

Wafu: Japanese-style.

Warabi: Similar to fiddlehead fern.

Wasabi: A pungent root unrelated to horseradish, as is commonly thought. The light green paste, reconstituted from dried wasabe root, is the ever-present sushi condiment.

Yaki soba: Stir-fried dish that uses a thick ramen noodle known as chuka soba (Chinese soba). In spite of its name, yaki soba is never made with soba.

Yakitori: Chicken parts grilled on skewers and glazed with a sweet-savory barbecue sauce.

Yamaimo: Taro root. Literally the name of this tuber means "mountain yam." It is eaten grated and has a slimy texture that the Japanese love.

Zaru: A mat made from thin bamboo sticks used for cold noodles.

Zōsui (or O-zōsui): Rice boiled in a soup seasoned with soy sauce and sometimes other ingredients.

Zuke: Pickled foods.

KORYORI-YA

Ita-Cho, 6775 Santa Monica Boulevard, Hollywood, CENTRAL, 213-871-0236. Dinner nightly. Ita-Cho, a koryori-ya, looks like a neighborhood minimall café with a sushi bar. But where you usually find maguro or toro behind the bar's glass front are instead artfully arranged stacks of mushrooms, vegetables, and whole fish, which the chef cooks to order. Sometimes the fish will be flounder and other times plaice. The mushrooms could be fresh shiitakes or fan-shaped oyster mushrooms.

You can leave the preparation of your meal in the chef's hands or follow the suggestions on the printed menu. There might be snow-white chunks of chicken breast rolled in lettuce, steamed, and served in an unctuous broth, or shrimp with yamaimo (that's taro root) tucked into nori and quickly deep-fried. Texture is played against texture, and flavors complement but rarely merge. This cooking is the best introduction to ippin-ryori I know. Dishes average around $3.50 to $4.50; you'll probably want to order about five per person.

Hirozen, 8385 Beverly Boulevard, West Hollywood, WEST, 213-653-0470. Lunch and dinner; closed Tuesday. Ignore the familiar teriyaki-tempura dinners on Hirozen's standard menu. Instead, sit at the counter in front of the spotless kitchen and browse over the daily offerings. The best food here is Hiro Obayashi's home-style ippin-ryori. Hiro's wife, Yasuyo Obayashi, will enthusiastically guide you through the many possibilities. We had a fresh, grilled tuna burger and swordfish kushi-yaki. After that, a cold soba noodle salad was the perfect starchy counterpoint. If the season is right, you could try the warabi—similar to fiddlehead fern—in a vinegary sauce, and the clear pungent matsutake mushroom soup. The dozens of wonderful choices, from salmon mousse to grilled matsutake, will encourage your return. And when you do, there will always be something new on the menu.

Issenjoki, 333 S. Alameda, No. 301 (Yaohan Shopping Center), Little Tokyo, CENTRAL, 213-680-1703. Lunch and dinner daily. Aged wood beams and lovely old Japanese antiques give Issenjoki the feel of a Japanese country inn. Several shelves above a bar area hold whiskey bottles filled to various levels; these belong to the restaurant's regular customers, who buy their whiskey by the bottle, not the glass.

It's easy to order ippin-ryori here, for not only is the menu well translated, but color photographs illustrate many dishes. As tradition dictates, the foods are listed under categories according to their preparation: sashimi, kushi-yaki, and so on. Many grilled items—the fish cake steak, for example—arrive on little sizzling metal plates balanced on a wooden paddle, and simmered dishes come in tiny iron kettles. Salads are abundant and artfully piled on platters. Issenjoki's food makes you forget you're in a shopping mall: It tastes as good as it looks. At lunchtime the restaurant serves udon and soba noodles in beautifully crafted Japanese ceramic bowls.

JAPANESE PUBS:
BEER, SAKE, AND LITTLE DISHES

Japanese pubs are called nomi-ya or izaka-ya, and the line between them is fine: Izaka-ya are usually larger public bars, while nomi-ya are small neighborhood "home cooking" style places. Both are eating and drinking establishments to which much of the Japanese male population adjourns after a long day. Each is often a boisterous place where everyone sits in large groups, and each has its own carefully cultivated personality. Although the food is designed to go with drinks, much care goes into its making. Modern izaka-ya, especially in Los Angeles, are visited equally by men and women who love the casual, satisfying food.

Fukuhime, 17905 S. Western Avenue, Gardena, SOUTH, 310-324-7077. Lunch and dinner until midnight; closed Sunday. Fukuhime, with its decor of fishnets, dangling blowfish, marine paraphernalia, and rustic tables, evokes a Japanese seaside tavern. The whole place is plastered with Kirin and Suntory posters, and Fukuhime's regulars order from the calligraphed strips of paper pasted all over the walls. If you don't read Japanese, Mr. Kono, Fukuhime's owner, has provided a well-translated menu in English, and daily specials are written on a board. Be sure to insist on the *appetizer* menu or you'll get the tourist combination list.

As the ambience suggests, Fukuhime's food is straightforward. One night, the simplest dish of lightly sautéed asparagus tips with thick lean, smoky Japanese bacon was just the sort of thing good sake requires. And that night's fish special, steamed baby bass, came lightly brushed with a teriyakilike glaze. It was meltingly buttery, fresh, and perfectly cooked.

On the printed menu are all the familiar izaka-ya staples: The broiled category offers *tsukune-yaki* (skewered chicken meatballs) and grilled smelts. And you can get standard-issue sushi and sashimi from Fukuhime's tiny sushi bar.

Daruma, 15915 S. Western Avenue, Gardena, SOUTH, 310-323-0133. Open 5:30 P.M. to midnight; closed Sunday. At Daruma, Japanese *sararimen* (salaried men) on a Los Angeles assignment begin to filter in around six, and by eight all the drinking rooms are filled

Restaurants Serving Ippin-Ryori Style (Japanese Pubs, Koryori-ya, Kappo, and Robata Restaurants)

A good many of the new authentic restaurants cater to an eating style called "ippin-ryori." Literally, ippin-ryori means "single-plate cooking," but in a restaurant it translates to a series of small dishes that you order at random, like sushi or Spanish tapas.

Several different types of restaurants serve *ippin-ryori*-style. These include koryori-ya, restaurants that offer à la carte dishes based on seasonal fresh fish and vegetables. Koryori-ya are popular places to drink sake and beer, as are the other kinds of restaurants serving ippin-ryori style. More informal ippin-ryori cooking may be had at Japanese pubs.

Finally, in its most elegant form, ippin-ryori cooking is called kappo-ryori. Kappo chefs are the most highly trained, and their dishes are what the Japanese term "Cordon Bleu caliber." Business VIPs do their entertaining in kappo restaurants, and there's always plenty of sake flowing.

Quite a few sushi bars now serve ippin-ryori and I've grouped some good ones under "Raw Fish and Assorted Dishes," (page 56).

IPPIN-RYORI TERMS

Ippin-ryori menus usually list dishes under headings denoting their cooking styles: *namamono* (raw); *yakimono* (grilled); *nimono* (simmered); *agemono* (deep-fried); and *mushimono* (steamed). You choose one or more dishes from each category, customarily beginning with sashimi and ending with the heaviest and most strongly flavored foods. These meals usually end with o-zōsui, a thick rice soup, or with grilled rice balls called yaki-onigiri.

with groups knocking back sakes and calling the waitresses for more pickled squid. There's a nice long counter for couples or lone diners and a menu that's completely bilingual. The counter is a good place to sit if you care to have Mr. Hanoka, Daruma's owner, explain any of the dishes while you munch on edamamé: soybeans that you squeeze from their fuzzy, caterpillar-green shells. Many dishes are self-explanatory, though. Tiny delicious enoki mushrooms come in a sesame dressing. Conservative choices are Nagasaki-style braised beef and stewed pork and potatoes.

Terried Sake House, 11617 Santa Monica Boulevard, West Los Angeles, WEST, 310-477-9423. Open 6:00 P.M. to 1:00 A.M.; closed Monday. In spite of its corny, touristy-sounding name, this typical nomi-ya has wonderful and inexpensive food. A board lists a changing array of sakes and daily specials. And there's quite a long printed menu supplemented with a separate table list of yakitori offerings. Examples include grilled, skewered chicken breast chunks with green mustard; a stew of pork and potato in a pungent broth; asparagus sautéed with butter; and a huge bowl of clams braised in sake.

Yuu, 11043 Santa Monica Boulevard, West Los Angeles, WEST, 310-478-7931. Dinner; closed Monday. Obscurity is the first bit of authenticity about Yuu, an izaka-ya with a cosmopolitan edge and an international clientele. It's almost invisible in a corner of a strip mall. Yuu's food is slightly more polished, the sake list more sophisticated (and longer) than in your average izaka-ya. But the dishes on its long traditional menu are so familiar most Japanese would know them by heart—for example, ankimo, the velvety-textured pâté of the sea. There's a long list of vegetable dishes: broiled, grilled, simmered, and steamed. The list of seafood preparations is impressive: try *shiromi isobe,* whitefish wrapped in nori and deep-fried; it's both crunchy and moist.

Mitsuki, 201 N. Western Avenue, Los Angeles, CENTRAL, 213-871-0703. Open 5:00 P.M. to 2:00 A.M.; closed Monday. Waitresses in traditional cotton kimonos enhance the warm country-style theme at this Koreatown-area pub that has a large non-Japanese clientele. People gather at the communal table or in private booths, and there's also a sushi bar. Mitsuki has translated all of its dishes into English, giving English speakers a good idea of what they can expect to be eating. And the fine pub food and long sake list keep them returning.

Yoro No Taki, 432 E. 2nd Street, Little Tokyo, CENTRAL, 213-626-6055; 192 S. Vermont Avenue, Los Angeles, CENTRAL, 213-388-3179; 15462 S. Western Avenue, Gardena, SOUTH, 310-323-3742; also, West Los Angeles WEST, 310-444-9676. Dinner nightly. Yoro No Taki, an everyman's pub, has more than 3,000 branches in Japan and several more here. The food, as you might expect from a chain, is predictable, commercial, and not too refined. Still, it's fun to sit in the rough-hewn room with its thick rope-tied beams and soak up the atmosphere of everyday Japanese urban life. There's always a roar of conversation, sake flows like a river after a heavy rain, and the waitstaff rushes around attentively. Order from the Technicolor-bright plastic menu with photographs of many items. There's something for every taste, from fried chicken wings to the yakitori combo. If you want to get fancy, try the $5.00 Harushinka or Otokoyama sakes instead of the $2.50 house sake.

KAPPO AND ROBATA RESTAURANTS: LITTLE DISHES WITH MORE STYLE

Kappo Kyara, 333 S. Alameda Street, No. 313, Little Tokyo, CENTRAL, 213-626-5760. Lunch and dinner; closed Sunday. At Kappo Kyara, the ippin-ryori, elevated to the kappo level, is a more sophisticated version of the food in Japanese pubs. Kappo chefs know the spawning cycles of all manner of flora and fauna and the ideal season to acquire each ingredient at its peak, so most kappo food is highly seasonal. Kappo Kyara has a menu, but longtime patrons often prefer to order omakase-style ("at the hands of the chef"). For $50 or more, owner Kozo Terajima prepares an array of intriguing seasonal specialty plates. These are delivered to your table one after the other, appropriately paced to aid in the enjoyment of the excellent sake. Terajima prefers advance notice for such a meal.

Even if you order from the printed menu, Kappo Kyara's dishes are pretty exotic. There might be snapping turtle bisque, or a crab and whitefish mousse wrapped in a tissue-thin sheet of tofu called *yuba chakin. Soboro manju,* a pale yellow ball of mountain yam stuffed with minced chicken, sits in a delicate pool of bronze-colored sauce.

Kappo Kyara's bento box lunch is one of the city's most extraordinary. Served in a treasure-laden stack of graduated lacquered boxes, it too changes monthly according to the season.

Matsuhisa, 129 N. La Cienega Boulevard, Beverly Hills, WEST, 310-659-9639. Lunch Monday through Friday; dinner daily. Already renowned for such flamboyant presentations as garlic-laced raw salmon stuffed with cucumber and wrapped in seaweed, chef Matsuhisa has developed a stellar reputation for innovative sushi. But his kappo-style dishes are even more imaginative and, I think, even better. The Japanese-style Peruvian seviche and the use of hot peppers and garlic in his food must have been inspired by Matsuhisa's seven years as a sushi bar owner in Peru. He imbues kappo with daring little quirks of individuality: asparagus in a cloudlike hollandaise is sprinkled with salmon eggs; a zingy pepper sauce enlivens halibut cheek; a miniature basket comes filled with elegantly fine somen noodles in three flavors (plain, plum, and green tea) with a clear mushroom dipping sauce. Every dish is a gustatory adventure.

Robata Beverly Hills, 250 N. Robertson Boulevard, Beverly Hills, WEST, 310-274-5533. Lunch and dinner Monday to Friday; dinner Saturday. Robata restaurants in Japan evoke the warmth and camaraderie of people gathered around the fireside, cooking on the hearth. These places ooze rustic charm, with chefs in country-style kimonos standing behind stacks of beautifully arranged raw ingredients. Diners point to what they want, and the robata chef cooks it before them. He uses a long-handled paddle to scoop the food from the fire and present it to his customer. This leaves us wondering why the Robata Beverly Hills—an elegant, modern room of sleek granite surfaces, shimmering glass, and no stacks of food—is called a robata. A few dishes do hint at the simple, earthy qualities of down-home robata cooking: dobin mushi, a soup in an earthenware pot, fragrant with a smoky perfume of the forest, manages to suggest the hearthside cooking of times past. And if you sit at the marble dining counter, you can watch chefs cook before you in a modified open kitchen.

But there are also Western-style tables and chairs, and most of what

Robata serves is inventively executed kappo: a tiny seaweed salad in a chilled glass is topped with a buttery rich foie gras. Fresh wasabi is grated for sashimi dishes—something you'll rarely see here *or* in Japan—and imported *yuzu,* a Japanese lime, seasons salads and seafoods.

You might want to order à la carte but the best way to experience Robata is with one of its multicourse kaiseki meals. Some dishes are exquisitely designed mouthfuls, others dazzle with richly married flavors. Expensive? Yes. But the price is less than if you ate such a meal in Japan. At this writing kaiseki dinners are priced at $50, $70, and $100. I still wonder, though, why they didn't name the restaurant Kaiseki.

Kayo, 816 S. Atlantic Boulevard (at Cadiz), Monterey Park, SAN GABRIEL VALLEY, 818-282-7525. Lunch and dinner, closed Monday. Kayo is more like a true robata, and while its decor only hints at rusticity, the restaurant *does* have Chef Kitamura standing behind a horizontal display case of exotic and not-so-exotic delicacies, ready to prepare them as you order. (He does not serve them with a paddle, however.) One night he grilled small Japanese river trout and large scallops from the icy waters around Hokaido. Cod kasu zuke, marinated in sake mash, was beautifully moist with crispy edges, and ika soba—tender squid cut to look like noodles—was served, as noodles often are in the heat of the Japanese summer, over ice.

There's a sushi bar, a nice list of set-course dinners, and many standard à la carte items.

JAPANESE SPECIALTY RESTAURANTS

Specialty restaurants, the Japanese feel, provide the finest examples of a particular type of cooking: You get the most perfectly executed tempura in a tempura bar and the best sushi in a sushi-ya (*ya* means "restaurant" or "shop"). Like their counterparts in Japan, L.A.'s specialty restaurants raise the cooking of even ordinary foods like noodles and grilled yakitori chicken to an art. Here is a sampling of places whose specialties run the gamut from Japanese fried chicken to eel.

♦ YAKITORI: BARBECUE BY THE SKEWERFUL

Every big train station in Tokyo is surrounded by yakitori-ya. These grilleries, like Japanese pubs, cater to the after-work crowd looking for a few beers and a light meal before catching the train home. They billow with charcoal smoke and roar with conversation. And the food is often as cheap as that in a fast-food franchise.

True yakitori-ya are restaurants serving nothing but various forms of grilled skewered chicken (*yaki* means "grilled" and *tori* means "chicken"). Kushi-yaki places, on the other hand, serve all sorts of skewer-grilled foods.

But at Torimatsu and Koekokko, what you get is chicken, chicken, and more chicken: chicken parts (wings, thigh meat, chicken hearts, gizzards, or livers), chicken ground into seasoned meatballs, and chunks of white meat with mushrooms or zucchini are threaded onto small bamboo skewers and grilled over charcoal on a long narrow stove.

Though he's often cooking about 20 orders at a time, a good yakitori chef deftly rotates the skewers, plucking them off the grill at precisely the right moment to leave the morsels still running with juices. He cooks the food until it's almost done before dipping it into the tare (glazing sauce). Then he cooks it a few seconds more. Inevitably, some of the grilled chicken's drippings flow into the sauce, adding flavor and depth. It is said that good yakitori chefs keep their sauces going for years, adding more of the sauce base at the end of each day.

Torimatsu (1425 W. Artesia Boulevard, No. 28 (near Normandy), Gardena, SOUTH, 310-538-5764; open 5:30 P.M. to 11:00 P.M.), like the very best yakitori-ya, serves not just chicken but also quail and duck. My favorite item is the large mushrooms stuffed with seasoned ground chicken. One à la carte selection I've not seen elsewhere is bonbochi, the chicken's tail. First-time guests might try the Shinjuku course, which comes with soup, rice, pickles, and seven varieties of skewered chicken.

Kokekokko (360 E. 2nd Street [or 203 S. Central Avenue], Little Tokyo, CENTRAL, 213-687-0690; open for dinner until midnight Monday through Saturday)—the name is "cock-a-doodle-doo" in Japanese—is a brightly lit, joyously noisy place with a team of young waiters in jeans, polo shirts, and matching aprons. For variety you always can rely on the "half-course set" of five different skewers or the full course of ten skewers. If you don't like organ meats, get the five skewers, or look around and point to what appeals to you.

♦ **KUSHI-YAKI**
Kushi-yaki, like yakitori, is grilled skewered food, but instead of just chicken, the food can be almost anything: meats, vegetables, fish, tofu, and so on.

Sakura House, 13362 Washington Boulevard, Marina Del Rey, WEST, 310-306-7010. Lunch and dinner Tuesday to Sunday. At Sakura House, a polished black and red lacquered space, the aura is smart and cosmopolitan. A few specialties not listed on the menu are seen on the plates of the knowing (one night it was grilled oysters on the half shell). The à la carte kushi-yaki is perfect and traditional: skewered fresh asparagus wrapped in tissue-thin beef; tender little eggplants with a sheer, sweet glaze. At the end of the meal the Japanese order *cha soba,* soba noodles flavored with green tea. Set-course meals arrive in well-paced succession, so each skewer is still sizzling when it reaches your plate. Included in the four dinner sets is an all-chicken meal. The most luxurious set, with seafood and vegetables, features a grilled small half lobster along with the skewered items.

Nanban-Tei of Tokyo, 123 S. Weller Street (Weller Court), Little Tokyo, CENTRAL, 213-620-8744. Lunch and dinner; closed Sunday. With one branch in Tokyo's Roppongi—the city's nightlife area—and another in the Ginza area, Nanban-Tei in Weller Court is familiar to visiting Tokyoites. Its name, which translates as "the Restaurant of the Southern Barbarians," refers to Dutch traders living in Nagasaki during the Edo period in the mid-seventeenth century; they introduced skewer grilling to the Japanese. It's not likely, however, that the Dutch flavored their beef in a staggeringly good ginger-soy marinade, or slathered it with bean paste, as Nanban-Tei's chefs do. Kushi-yaki, like many Japanese adaptations, has acquired a definite Japaneseness. Nanban-Tei's long kushi-yaki list includes jumbo clam, stuffed mushrooms, and crisp grilled chicken wings.

Nanbankan (11330 Santa Monica Boulevard, West Los Angeles, WEST, 310-478-1591; dinner nightly), in the Little Tokyo West area, uses the famous extrahard bincho Japanese charcoal to provide even, long-lasting heat for its succulent skewered morsels. À la carte items include vegetables, grilled quail eggs, chicken wings, beef tongue, and prawns.

Tori-zen (16410 S. Western Avenue, Gardena, SOUTH, 310-323-8600; lunch and dinner Monday to Friday; Saturday, dinner only), fairly opulent for a grilling restaurant, was one of the first Gardena-area Japanese places to specialize in yakitori and kushi-yaki. Although most of the restaurant's regulars order à la carte, the deluxe combination dinners are a fine way for beginners to get the hang of eating kushi-yaki and yakitori-ya-style. These include either siu mai or tatsuta-age, and your choice from the various traditional rice preparations that always go with yakitori and kushi-yaki: tori-meshi rice is flecked with chicken and shiitake mushrooms; zōsui and cha-zuke are both savory, warming rice porridges.

♦ **NOODLES: A JAPANESE INSTITUTION**
L.A.'s ramen consciousness was raised with Juzo Itami's 1987 film *Tampopo,* the metaphorical tale of a struggling noodle-shop proprietress who timed her ramen cooking with a stopwatch. Needless to say, the Japanese are fussy about their noodles. So fussy, in fact, that ramen, the Japanese version of Chinese lo mein noodles, isn't served in the same restaurants that sell true Japanese noodles such as soba and udon. The strong tastes and aromas of ramen dishes interfere with the more delicate Japanese udon and soba flavors, it is believed.

Connoisseurs of soba (thin, tan buckwheat noodles) and udon (fat, chewy wheat noodles) seek out gourmet shops staffed by noodle masters with years of training. Some soba shops go so far as to grind their own specially farmed buckwheat and to roll out the soba dough in small batches. The two **Sarashina** shops here in L.A. do this. (1747 W. Redondo Beach Boulevard [in Tozai Plaza], Gardena, SOUTH, 310-323-3820; lunch and dinner daily; and at 345 E. 2nd Street [in Japanese Village Plaza], Little Tokyo, CENTRAL, 213-680-0344.) At the Gardena shop, soba master Satoshi Aoki, who plied his craft for 20 years at Yokohama's well-known Sarashina-Ikkyu, uses the most refined buckwheat flour (sarashina) and a small quantity of pulverized seaweed to give his noodles a silky resiliency that plainer noodles lack. Mr. Aoki prepares both soba and udon in the shop each day.

Try cold zaru soba or sansai soba with mountain vegetables. Both come as a tangle of chilled noodles served on a bamboo lattice called a zaru. Pick up a few noodles with your chopsticks and barely flick them into the accompanying tsukejiru (dipping sauce). It's considered gauche to saturate the noodles with tsuke-jiru—you must taste the noodles themselves.

Houtou nabe is udon in a steamy miso broth with slivers of meat, oysters, and vegetables. Other versions come with chicken and egg, beef, or a long list of additions that may be selected to go with hot or cold soba or udon.

Sanuki no Sato, 18206 S. Western Avenue, Gardena, SOUTH, 310-324-9184 or 324-9185. Lunch and dinner daily. Sanuki no Sato, which has noodles made to its specifications with flour imported from Japan, is a little more opulent than your average workaday noodle shop. There are small tatami rooms and, along one wall, a row of tables under hooded fans where customers who've ordered udon suki cook their meal in steaming hotpots. First the diners cook crab, shrimp, chicken, and vegetables, which enrich the broth that will later cook the udon.

On the noodle menu (written on one side in English and the other in Japanese), white dots indicate cold dishes and black indicate hot. One of my favorite cold soba preparations, the ikura oroshi, comes garnished with salmon eggs and grated daikon radish—a bright contrast of salty and fresh tastes with the slightly musky soba. *Kanitama udon,* noodles in hot soup with a scrambled egg and crab topping, is one of the best versions I've tried. In the evening the restaurant offers a full menu of ippin-ryori (see page 43).

At **Mishima** (11301 Olympic Boulevard, No. 210, West Los Angeles, WEST, 310-473-5297; open daily), the sound of the thick udon appreciatively slurped in chorus drowns out the Muzak. The shop serves soba or udon topped with a wonderful mixture of grilled beef and egg called niku toji udon (or soba) and a fine version of the traditional shrimp tempura-topped soba or udon. The chirashi sushi and noodles combination, a bowl of sushi rice with assorted sashimi on top, is accompanied with your choice of any noodle style.

♦ **RAMEN SHOPS**

For the last few years, ramen shops have been popping up like shiitakes after a fall rain. L.A. has dozens; the selection here includes the best to be found in almost every part of L.A. County.

Yokohama Ramen, 11660 Gateway Boulevard, West Los Angeles, WEST, 310-479-2321. Open for lunch and dinner; closed Tuesday. It's not surprising that Yokohama Ramen, serving regional ramen variations—even going so far as to fly its fresh noodles in from Japan—should open in West Los Angeles near Sawtelle Boulevard. The area, now called "Little Tokyo West," was settled by Japanese farmers in the 1920s and has been an enclave ever since.

Yokohama Ramen's namesake, the bustling Japanese trade center south of Tokyo, is where Chinese immigrants first introduced their noodles to Japan. But the dish, which spread everywhere, soon

acquired regional variations. And Yokahama offers several of them. *Chanpon* ramen, a Kyushu regional specialty, is a bowl of long-simmered chicken broth garnished with barely cooked vegetables, whole baby clams, and other seafoods. The *ja ja men,* ramen with a zingy and peppery miso-laced sauce, is probably the spiciest dish in any Japanese restaurant.

On Sawtelle, **Asahi Ramen** (2027 Sawtelle Boulevard, West Los Angeles, WEST, 310-479-2231; lunch and dinner; closed Thursday) boasts some of the city's best and juiciest gyoza. The wonton ramen, a vast portion of noodles in soup bobbing with plump wontons, appears at your table in a fragrant mist of steam, and the mabo ramen, topped with lean ground pork, floats in a gently sinus-clearing spicy broth.

Two ramen aficionados display proper noodle slurping etiquette at Yokohama Ramen.

At the corner of Fountain and Vine, cheek by jowl with a Cuban nightclub and a French pastry shop, **Atch-Kotch** (1253 N. Vine Street, No. 5, Hollywood, CENTRAL, 213-467-5537; lunch through dinner; closed Sunday) organizes its menu in a mix-and-match format. It lists three traditional broths—the soy-based *shoyu* broth, the clear tanmen pork broth, and a miso-based broth—and then lists the toppings;

you select one or more toppings as if you were ordering pizza. Try the sautéed vegetables with shrimp, the *chashu* (Chinese roast pork), or one of the delightful ramen salads.

The San Fernando Valley now has two good ramen shops. At **Ramen Nippon** (6900 Reseda Boulevard, No. D, Reseda, S.F. VALLEY, 818-345-5946; lunch through dinner daily), there's a definite emphasis on the spicier ramen dishes like mabo ramen with its peppery ground pork sauce, and the fried dumplings with ramen in a spiced-up shoyu broth. At **Kyu-shu Ramen** (15355 Sherman Way, Van Nuys, S.F. VALLEY, 818-786-6005; lunch through dinner daily), try the cold ramen with white-meat chicken and omelet shreds, the Japanese-style Chinese salad, or the yaki soba, a Japanese version of chow mein.

I had written off **Tampopo** (2015 Redondo Beach Boulevard, Gardena, SOUTH, 213-323-7882; lunch and dinner daily) as an attempt to capitalize on the movie *Tampopo*'s fame until a ramen connoisseur vouched for the quality of their noodles and delicious broth. Everything is served in beautiful, heavy, rough-textured earthenware. And besides the standard ramen dishes, Tampopo offers ''set'' ramen meals of several courses and a nonramen daily special.

Mikoshi (8162 Sunset Boulevard, Los Angeles, WEST, 213-654-5024; lunch through dinner daily) may soon be the Pizza Hut of ramen sellers. The aggressively expanding chain is reaching for a general audience with its all-English, full-color-photographed menu in lieu of the traditional plastic models of food. What I've tasted so far has been reasonably good and well priced. Try the chicken yaki soba, which is a nice meaty hunk of grilled chicken on a bed of stir-fried noodles with a small mixed green salad on the side. (Also in Los Angeles [near USC], 213-746-7874, and Koreatown, CENTRAL, 213-387-2079.)

The Redondo Beach Boulevard branch of **Umemura** (1724 Redondo Beach Boulevard, Gardena, SOUTH, 310-217-0970; lunch through dinner daily), a Japan-based ramen chain, stays open until 3:00 A.M., making it handy for late-night gamblers from Gardena's casinos. The trencherman-sized servings in enormous white porcelain bowls and on platters could easily serve two, which makes Umemura one of the biggest ramen bargains around. There have been reports though, of gluey, overcooked ramen in the cold dishes. Also in Little Tokyo, CENTRAL, and West Los Angeles, WEST.

BEYOND NOODLES: JAPANESE SPECIALTIES FROM TEMPURA TO EEL

Tonkatsu, the breaded pork cutlet introduced by the Portuguese, caught on wildly in Japan after the government ban on meat was lifted during the Mejii restoration in the late 1860s. Closely related to tonkatsu and prepared the same way is **kushi-age:** bite-sized pieces of various breaded, deep-fried foods on skewers. Both kushi-age and tonkatsu show up on many menus but everyone knows the best—with a light flaky pastrylike coating—are served at tonkatsu-ya, like the ones following.

Apple (333 S. Alameda Street, No. 312 Yaohan Plaza, Little Tokyo, CENTRAL, 213-626-5858; lunch through dinner daily) offers tonkatsu in three traditional styles: the more expensive tenderloin cutlet, the standard cutlet, or bite-sized loin chunks individually fried. These always come with rice, ultrathin shredded cabbage, and Japanese-style ''Worcestershire sosu'' for dipping. Apple's magnificently crisp chicken cutlet and the cutlets served with an egg over rice extend tonkatsu-lovers' options and Apple's kitchen also turns out plump oysters, whitefish, shrimp, and scallops prepared tonkatsu style.

To find **Rokumeikan Cutlet Parlor** (15607 S. Normandie Avenue, Gardena, SOUTH, 310-324-4477; dinner nightly; lunch Monday to Friday) you have to go to the second story of a Travelodge Motel, but Rokumeikan's tonkatsu is worth the search. The substantial kushi-age combination dinner gives you little tastes of everything, from chicken to salmon.

On a grander scale, **Kushinobo** (123 S. Weller Street [3rd Floor, Weller Court], Little Tokyo, CENTRAL, 213-621-0210; lunch and dinner daily) is, I believe, L.A.'s only kushi-age bar. Skewered morsels emerge still sizzling from the oil, and the way Kushinobo breads and fries them, their breading seems almost weightless. From over 30 meat, seafood, and vegetable selections, several combination set-course meals are offered. Or you may want to try the omakase (chef's choice). The chef will keep all manner of skewers coming until you've signaled you've had enough. Kushinobo is also known for its delicious shabu-shabu— loosely translated as beef fondue. Shabu-shabu actually means "swish-swish"; you cook thin slices of beef and vegetables at your table in a hotpot, swishing them through the simmering broth.

Fried chicken may be as American as apple pie, but the Japanese have *tori no karaage,* their own version of this down-home staple. The best Japanese fried chicken to be had is at **Furaibo** (1741 W. Redondo Beach Boulevard, Gardena, SOUTH, 310-329-9441; lunch and dinner; closed Monday), a chain with about 62 franchises in Japan and one in Gardena, whose signature dish is *"teba sake* chicken wings."

Furaibo's chicken is first marinated, then fried in oil so hot it sears the chicken, leaving a grease-less crackly surface and a moist interior. The chicken comes in a range of flavors from sweet to extra spicy, and you can be picky about which chicken parts you eat: Order the Tarzan and you get half a chicken, the Jane is a chicken breast, Chita is the leg and thigh, and teba a whole order of wings. Furaibo also serves a long list of ippin-ryori plates.

Okonomiyaki has been called Japanese pizza. But the griddled pancake (literally, it means "as you like it") is more like a scrambled egg-topped crêpe; it's deliciously filling and fun to eat. At **Tomo** (2106 W. Artesia Boulevard, Torrance, SOUTH, 310-324-5190; lunch and dinner; closed Monday) and **Okonomiyaki Koma** (123 S. Weller Street [No. 304 Weller Court], Little Tokyo, CENTRAL, 213-620-9345; lunch and dinner daily), you cook your own okonomiyaki on a griddle at the table and, depending on the additions you have ordered, add meat, fish, or vegetables to the batter. The Japanese love to smother the pancake with a thick sweet sauce, which I think obliterates the good taste. Fortunately the sauce comes on the side.

Focus Salon de Café (319 E. 2nd Street [No. 202, Little Tokyo Mall], CENTRAL, 213-680-3015) is L.A.'s first **kissaten,** or coffee-drinking lounge. The hundreds of such lounges that dot Tokyo—a surrealistically hectic city of tiny cramped apartments and crushing crowds—offer respite, breathing room, and a place to relax, listen to music, and be alone or with friends.

Focus has the feel of a large living room, with low couches, a baby grand piano, and a greenhouse window that lets in a patch of downtown sky. Mellow jazz plays over a superb sound system, and behind the coffee bar an attendant brews your coffee in a gizmo that looks a little like Frankenstein's chemistry set: Tiny glass flasks are mounted with a brass ring over a Bunsen burner—it's called a siphon. The five coffee varieties include Brazil and Blue Mountain, or you may order a blend of any. The beans are ground in front of you just before your coffee is brewed.

Japanese-style French pastries and light meals are offered: sandwiches cut in canapelike triangles, spaghetti dishes, afternoon teas. Japanese-style Western breakfasts include omelets, huge thick slices of toast, and sunny-side-up eggs served with salad.

An attendant mans the siphon coffee maker at Focus Salon de Café.

Japanese specialty chefs turn **unagi** (eel) into velvety-textured fillets somewhere between chicken and whitefish, with a slightly sweet smoky flavor similar to yakitori. The eel is first steamed to render it of fat, then marinated, grilled, sauced, and regrilled. The Japanese love unagi so much that Tokyo alone has more than 3,000 unagi restaurants (unagi-ya).

Masukawa (page 60), is a fine, all-around Japanese restaurant and one of its house specialties is live eel flown in from Japan. The kayabayaki, or grilled eel dinner, may be had, like Maine lobster, in three sizes: the single, the 1½, or the double eel portions. Eel sukiyaki is also available in three sizes along with several other eel options. Another of Masukawa's specialties, kamameshi, is discussed below.

In Japan's **kamameshi** restaurants, rice cooked with a variety of ingredients comes served in its own individual iron cooking pot with a two-legged wooden lid. Some have likened this traditional country-

style dish to paella, especially when it's made with seafood. The better kamameshi-ya offer a staggering number of ingredients and combinations, with each portion prepared to order. Masukawa serves kamameshi seven ways, including shrimp, crab, chicken, grilled eel, and vegetable variations.

In Little Tokyo, at **Takaya** (305 E. 1st Street, CENTRAL, 213-689-4837; lunch and dinner Monday to Friday; continuously from noon Saturday and Sunday), the best-selling kamameshi is the oyster version, and there's also salmon, chicken and beef.

Bento, portable boxed meals, have been a part of Japanese life for centuries. They began as refreshments for traveling royalty, whose food was transported in elegant lacquered boxes. Today you find bento at every train station and at the theater, where they're called maku-no-uchi ("between the curtains") bento. Bento can be elegant or humble; they're even sold at baseball games.

Moc-Moc (1431 W. Redondo Beach Boulevard, Gardena, SOUTH, 310-515-9911; lunch and dinner daily; closed Sunday), a fast-food operation familiar in Japan, sells a maku-no-uchi bento that's great for the sheer fun of sampling a wide assortment of tastes. Its five-compartment tray holds an egg roll, fried siu mai, and gyoza. The grand assembly includes sundry vegetables, tempura, chicken chunks, and tamago, plus a compartment of soy- and wine-simmered beef slices. Moc-Moc is liberal with the pickles and sesame-topped rice, too. Typical of many other simpler bentos is the grilled-salmon-and-tempura box with salad.

A good many restaurants feature more luxurious bentos than the take-out variety. At **Kappo Kyara** (page 45) the lunchtime bentos that change seasonally are exquisitely arranged and generously served. And **Tatsuki** (416 Boyd Street, Little Tokyo, CENTRAL, 213-613-0141; lunch and dinner daily; closed Sunday) is the only restaurant I've found that offers chakin bento. The centerpiece of this elaborate meal is a paper-thin sheet of omelet wrapped around a seasoned-rice-and-vegetable mixture, then tied up with an edible bow of nori.

You'll find classic bentos that include every form of cooking—sashimi, simmered foods, grilled foods, and something fried—all arranged like museum displays at **Kanpachi Sushi** (see next column), **Ranzan** (page 54) and **Katsu** (page 54).

When you crave the lightest, featheriest **tempura,** the best place to find it is at a tempura bar, where the chef waits until you have finished one portion before he cooks you another. You can find tempura bars at the following restaurants: **Inagiku** at the Bonaventure Hotel, 404 S. Figueroa Street (6th level), 4th & Flower Street, Los Angeles, CENTRAL, 213-614-0820; **Edo Sushi** (page 60); and **Senbazuru (A Thousand Cranes)** (page 61).

SUSHI

Sushi may have taken a place next to the Brie and tortellini in the supermarket deli case, but a meal at the hands of a gifted sushi chef still reminds us that sushi can be the world's most luxurious food. Fortunately, Los Angeles has a number of masterly sushi chefs capable of reminding us.

Seafood Club, 1757 W. Carson Street, No. 5, Torrance, SOUTH, 310-782-0530. Lunch and dinner daily. It's the marvelous theater of Seafood Club, as much as its elegant food, that makes this restaurant worth the price of admission. Instead of the usual refrigerated glass cases, the bar surrounds tanks of live fish and shellfish. Once selected, these creatures are readied quickly in the kitchen for the sushi chef, who will work his magic turning them into kappo dishes, or sushi and sashimi.

Not everything is still swimming when you order it. Seafood Club has a small case of conventional items at fairly moderate sushi prices (from $3 to $4.50 for a two-piece order). There's a nice long list of ippin-ryori, $45 and $55 prix fixe dinners, and other meals for about $25.

Kanpachi Sushi, 1425 W. Artesia Boulevard, No. 27, Gardena, SOUTH, 310-515-1391. Lunch and dinner; closed Monday. Not as showy as Seafood Club, but certainly as good, is Kanpachi Sushi. The chef and owner, Mr. Kido, keeps the restaurant's small tank stocked with live abalone, shrimp, and sometimes lobster. One evening live flounder was on hand. There are often lush slabs of kazunoko konbu—a cushion of cod roe on kelp—and house-cured salmon. Each evening Kido-san prepares several ippin-ryori specialties, and at lunch there's a fine, moderately priced bento.

Kanpachi is an intimate one-man-band sort of place, with a coterie of regulars who often entertain clients in the restaurant's small tatami room. Many parties order Mr. Kido's delightful sushi kaiseki (beginning at $50 without drinks, with a two-day notice requested).

Tsukiji, 1745 W. Redondo Beach Boulevard, Gardena, SOUTH, 310-323-4077. Monday to Saturday 5:30 P.M. to midnight. At Tsukiji, even before we'd unfurled our warm cloth oshibori, a square ceramic plate with otsumami—the little tastes offered before you get down to serious ordering—was set before us. The assortment had a visual wit rarely present in Americanized Japanese food. A daikon slice split to open like a little taco was filled with ikura. Ankimo came on a canape of cucumber beside a slice of matsutake mushroom. The meal was all uphill from there. Aji no tataki, the Spanish mackerel that usually comes as a simple bowl of chopped fish in lime juice and soy ponzu sauce, was filleted before us and prepared three ways: in julienne strips, in tiny cubes, and minced with onion—each technique presenting a different nuance in flavor. The three preparations came arranged around wispy mounds of seaweed and the gracefully curving mackerel skeleton, its head still on. We tried several kinds of unfamiliar clams, and a steamed crab from the tank was sweet and vaguely briny.

Tsukiji has a clubby feel to it: Businessmen joke and pour each other drinks of Scotch. International tycoon types drift in solo; they seem to know the staff well. There's a list of kappo dishes in Japanese; the staff helps with translations. But sometimes it's more fun to say *"Onaji mono o kudasai"* ("please bring me the same").

Ginza Sushi-Ko, 3959 Wilshire Boulevard, No. A-11, Los Angeles, CENTRAL, 213-487-2251. Lunch and dinner Monday to Friday, dinner Saturday. You can't simply walk into this shrine of incomparable sushi, which charges $200 for a meal, and which those in the know say is worth it. You must be introduced by a regular patron—as Madonna, Warren Beatty, and a host of Japanese business executives presumably have been when I was there. The sushi, selected by the chef, "will help you commune with the Japanese experience," says one knowledgeable food writer.

Katsu, 1972 Hillhurst Avenue, Silverlake, CENTRAL, 213-665-1891. Lunch and dinner Monday to Friday, dinner Saturday. When a restaurant prides itself on a "no California roll" policy and has no sign on the door, you wonder if you're going to run into a lot of irksome pretensions. But Katsu's melodramatic, monochromatic, high-tech room, hand-fashioned ceramic plates, and sushi cut with a sculptor's flair will seduce even the most jaded. Katsu also features sumptuous bentos at lunch, and nightly specials.

Shibucho, 333 S. Alameda Street, Little Tokyo, CENTRAL, 213-626-1184. Also at 3144 Beverly Boulevard, Silverlake, CENTRAL, 213-387-8498. Lunch and dinner; closed Sunday. There are two Shibucho sushi bars. The one in Little Tokyo's Yaohan Plaza is owned by Mr. Shibuya, who also founded the original Shibucho on Beverly Boulevard, now owned by his former assistant. Both are filled with Japanese who prefer to eat sushi in a setting where it won't have to vie with the stronger aromas of tempura or other cooked foods, and where they won't find such offending ingredients as mayonnaise, avocado, or imitation crab in their sushi rolls.

Ranzan, 2621 Pacific Coast Highway, Torrance, SOUTH, 310-534-5445. Lunch and dinner; closed Monday. With a door identical to all the other powder-blue doors in the huge Rolling Hills shopping complex, Ranzan appears to be just another restaurant. But there are wonderful surprises here: fresh scallops still in the shell with their coral, glistening little pompano, and the tiniest baby octopus imaginable. A sushi kaiseki meal may be arranged on one day's notice for lunch and two days' notice for dinner (approximately $12 and $50, respectively). Ranzan's interesting à la carte selections include steak *no ta taki* (grilled on the outside and raw within), grilled duck breast, and crab sunomono.

U-Zen (formerly **Ike-Ichi**), 11951 Santa Monica Boulevard, West Los Angeles, WEST, 310-477-1390. Dinner nightly; lunch Monday to Friday. A comfortable, casual neighborhood spot with better-than-neighborhood sushi made with exotic ingredients like blood clams and the hard-to-find pompano. Regulars receive bottles of sake at Christmas, and once a month there's a karaoke night when customers croon to an audience to taped background music—none of which detracts from the great sushi at reasonable prices.

Iroha, 12955 Ventura Boulevard, Studio City, S.F. VALLEY, 818-990-9559. Lunch and dinner; closed Sunday. One friend described this place as Matsuhisa (see page 45) with low prices. Well, not quite. But Iroha does serve many adventurous sushi rolls, and while tradition-bound purists might look askance at the spicy tuna roll or special hand roll No. 4 filled with rice and tempura, many adore them. Sushi-making is, after all, an art, and art by its very nature evolves.

Shihoya, 15489 Ventura Boulevard, Sherman Oaks, S.F. VALLEY, 818-986-4461. Lunch and dinner; closed Tuesday. To get the splendid sushi here you must endure lessons in traditional sushi-tasting protocol. Orders must go from light to heavy (eat the mild, less oily fish before you indulge in eel or ikura). Souls of an aggressively rebellious disposition will have difficulty with this restaurant's authoritarian nature. But those who can conform will be treated to some of the best sushi in the Valley. Kaiseki, or tea-ceremony-style gourmet dinners, are available ordered in advance.

Sushi Nozawa, 11288 Ventura Boulevard, No. C, Studio City, S.F. VALLEY, 818-508-7017. Lunch and dinner Monday to Friday, Saturday dinner only. The sign behind the bar that reads "Today's special: Trust me" is the only glimmer of humor at this otherwise ultraserious, ultratraditional sushi bar. Some days you may not find your favorite toro or yellowtail, because Nozawa-san buys only what's freshest and best. You won't miss them, for Mr. Nozawa has an unerring eye at the fish market.

♦ **SUSHI BARGAINS**

If you crave a satisfying hit of vinegary, sweet, fish-topped rice without the ritual of the bar, here are the top places to find the best-quality sushi for a modest sum.

Megu's Japanese Food Mart, 22330 Sherman Way, No. 12-C, Canoga Park, S.F. VALLEY, 818-704-1459. Open daily. This tiny six-stool sushi bar squeezed into a minuscule Japanese market reminds me of take-home sushi-ya in suburban Japan. Customers call in their orders, then come and pick them up. When the stools are filled you can always explore the snappily packaged Japanese groceries or flip through the glossy Japanese magazines while you're waiting. Megu's also caters beautifully arranged sushi trays.

Cho Cho San, 19010 Ventura Boulevard, Tarzana, S.F. VALLEY, 818-881-8518. Lunch and dinner daily. And **Tokyo Sushi,** 1831 W. Redondo Beach Boulevard, Gardena, SOUTH, 310-516-0499. Lunch through dinner; closed Sunday. At these sushi emporia, there is no refrigerated case before you, but a moving belt on which orders of sushi glide by. You pick your favorites, and when you're finished the waitress adds up the bill by counting the stack of plates you've amassed. Don't see what you like? The chef will whip it up to order and, like the brass ring, you catch it as it goes by.

At **Sushi Boy,** (11698 San Vicente Boulevard, West Los Angeles, WEST, 310-207-1003, and 3948 Sepulveda Boulevard, Torrance, SOUTH, 310-378-4565; lunch and dinner daily), a fast-food sushi shop import from Japan, sushi is prepared to order (the nori is still crisp and the rice not gummy). But picking up your order can be time-consuming when a busload of Japanese tourists disgorges its cargo in front of the place for lunch—a not infrequent occurrence.

♦ **RAW FISH AND ASSORTED DISHES**

These sushi bars tempt with eclectic nonsushi specialties.

Ueru-Ka-Mu, 19596 Ventura Boulevard, Tarzana, S.F. VALLEY, 818-609-0993. Lunch and dinner; closed Sunday. The sushi is good at Ueru-Ka-Mu, but it's not the whole attraction. This restaurant's selection of ippin-ryori is the best and most complete in the Valley. Ueru-Ka-Mu's talented cook has such a knack for honing in on flavor, that you're tempted to order the same dish again and again instead of experimenting with new items. Beef sashimi, with its thin border of seared meat around raw meat, is a perfect balance of tart and lightly salty; niku *jaga* (stewed lean pork chunks with potato) is braised in a light but deeply flavored broth. And *chiri* mushi, whitefish steamed with tofu and vegetables, is delicate without being bland.

Kushiyu, 18713 Ventura Boulevard, Tarzana, S.F. VALLEY, 818-609-9050. Lunch and dinner; closed Monday. Kushiyu is the best of two worlds: a sushi bar and a kushi-yaki bar under the same roof. At first, the restaurant drew mainly Japanese clientele, but the combination has caught on mightily with everyone. Sushi aficionados will know the familiar list by heart, although daily specials from the board often go beyond the usual clichés: we had pompano *nanban-zuke*—the little fish was marinated, deep-fried, and crunchy. The dinner combinations may be all sushi, all kushi-yaki, or a mix.

Asuka, 1266 Westwood Boulevard, West Los Angeles, WEST, 310-474-7412. Lunch Monday to Friday; dinner nightly. Asuka, a well-loved West Los Angeles sushi bar, has always done things in a timely way. In the late seventies it installed a second sushi bar when the sushi it had long been serving suddenly became trendy. Now, in another timely move, Asuka has converted one of its bars into what it calls Robata-Que. The à la carte menu offers large grilled juicy scallops and bacon, whole tiny mackerel, chicken meatballs, and beef short ribs—not your everyday kushi-yaki.

Kazu Sushi, 11440 Ventura Boulevard, Studio City, S.F. VALLEY, 818-763-4836. Lunch Monday to Friday; dinner nightly. It's the salads I really love at Kazu, though the restaurant serves ippin-ryori and excellent sushi too. A salad of baby lettuces comes topped with sliced albacore, seared on the outside and raw within; it's a dish of bright, uncomplicated flavors. "Mountain salad," filled with typical Japanese vegetables, has slivers of orangy gobo, potatolike ya-maimo, and warabe (marinated fiddle head ferns). Kazu's chicken salad, according to my Japanese friend Yasuko, is the best version she's ever had.

Mako Sushi, 13905 Ventura Boulevard, Sherman Oaks, S.F. VALLEY, 818-789-1385. Lunch and dinner Tuesday to Friday; Saturday, dinner only. Mako Sushi's menu says it specializes in "healthy Japanese cuisine." This translates into good traditional home-style Japanese cooking and ippin-ryori plates like sautéed gobo and carrots or *sansai* soba, a dish of vegetables with buckwheat noodles. In the brown-rice vegetarian sushi, fat rolls of nutty mellow brown rice come layered with such things as vegetable tempura or a kaleidoscopic array of vegetables and avocado in the crispiest toasted nori. There is also "regular" sushi.

Hakone Sushi, 1555 W. Sepulveda Boulevard, No. G, Torrance, SOUTH, 310-539-9602. Open 11:30 A.M. to 10:00 P.M. Monday to Saturday; Sunday, dinner only. Another ippin-ryori-sushi find in the South Bay is Hakone Sushi. Owner Shun Adachi keeps his case filled with an ever changing array of roes, assorted clams, and fish that may include white salmon. Don't let the waitress give you the "Combination Dinners" menu. Ask instead for the side orders list, where you'll find the cockles simmered in sake, ultraplump gyoza dumplings, and the smelly *nato*: the fermented bean paste that most Japanese adore. There's continual service through the day.

BORROWED FOODS

◆ A SHOKUDO: JAPANESE-STYLE WESTERN AND CHINESE FOOD

Chin-Chin Tei, 1320 W. Redondo Beach Boulevard, Gardena, SOUTH, 310-327-8500. Lunch through dinner; closed Monday. In Japan the *shokudo* or "mixed" restaurant offers foreign foods tailored to Japanese tastes: Western rice dishes, curries, and a few Chinese dishes. Chin-Chin Tei, with its

JAPAN'S BORROWED FOODS

Where else but in Japan would you find green tea cheesecake, *umeboshi*-flavored chewing gum, and spaghetti sprinkled with nori? Like cowboy boots and jazz, certain Western foods have captivated the Japanese. These have been expertly translated to satisfy Japanese palates.

While Japanese-French fare is familiar enough to have its own category in a number of restaurant guidebooks, the Western-style Japanese coffee shops, spaghetti joints, and curry rice shops, so much a part of eating in Japan, are just beginning to attract non-Japanese. Their presence is indicative of just how much modern Japanese culture we've imported.

air-brushed neo–Pacific Rim art on the walls, is a hip version. It caters to a jeunesse moderne who saunter in wearing floor-length vinyl trench coats over ripped jeans. Japanese-style Chinese stir-fries include mabo *nasu*: sautéed eggplant with ground pork in a peppery miso sauce. There's wafu steak, marinated and charbroiled; hamburger curry; and coffee ice cream float for dessert.

◆ KARI-RAISU

If you had to guess Japan's most popular borrowed food it probably wouldn't be curry. But *kari-raisu,* as the Japanese call the dish they adopted from British-style Indian restaurants, is found everywhere: in luncheonettes, coffee shops, and packaged in cans or "instant" mixes in every market. Every L.A. Japanese enclave has its curry shop: Curry Hut, Curry Land, Curry Emporium; I like the following three.

Curry Club (6623 Melrose Avenue, Hollywood, CENTRAL, 213-939-4627; lunch through dinner Monday to Friday; Saturday from 2:00 to 10:00 P.M.), undoubtedly the only curry bar in an art gallery, makes a delicious scallop curry with sweet crunchy Japanese pickles replacing chutney. Noncurry offerings like sautéed chicken breast with a light cream sauce have prices that make you forget you're eating near the trendy part of Melrose. **Curry House** (21215 Hawthorne Boulevard, Torrance, SOUTH, 310-540-8980; lunch and dinner daily) is part of a Japanese chain that has spread its curry empire to Southern California. The curry, more like a stew with plenty of gravy, can be had with assorted meats, and Curry House offers a small menu of Japanized spaghetti dishes. On the West Side, **Hurry Curry of Tokyo** (2131 Sawtelle Boulevard, West Los Angeles, WEST, 310-473-1640; lunch and dinner daily) offers the usual array of curry flavors plus chicken cutlet and beef cutlet curry and a small menu of side dishes: fried calamari, fried chicken chunks, and chicken pasta salad.

♦ **BAKED GOODS AND COFFEE SHOP**
Pasco, 1600 Redondo Beach Boulevard, Gardena, SOUTH, 310-515-5828; 8:00 A.M. to 7:00 P.M. daily. You could call Pasco the Entenmann's of Japan. The giant Japanese baked goods manufacturer, which now has a plant in Torrance, supplies various supermarkets and its own stores with such cross-cultural delights as anpan, a light sweet roll filled with sweet bean paste; fluffy Japanese-style raisin bread; and Japanese-style mocha layer cake.

Pasco has recently opened a coffee shop where, in addition to siphon coffee (see page 52) and a vast sparkling case of Pasco's baked goods, you'll find Japanese luncheon and breakfast favorites: tonkatsu sandwiches, onion soup

gratinée, and, for breakfast, eggs Benedict or the Pasco Morning Set with toast, an egg, and salad.

♦ **JAPANESE-STYLE SPAGHETTI**
The Japanese love spaghetti as much as they love ramen or udon. At L.A.'s oldest Japanese spaghetti emporium, **Spoon House** (1601 W. Redondo Beach Boulevard, Gardena, SOUTH, 310-538-0376; breakfast through dinner; closed Tuesday), the spaghetti is far, far from the Via Veneto. Pastas with flying-fish caviar or sea urchin sauce sprinkled with crispy nori are grouped separately from the "Italian" spaghettis on the menu. But even the Italian offerings are interesting examples of what can happen when the Japanese fondness for clean-tasting, greaseless food merges with the Italian soul. A plate of Spoon House's white-sauced spaghetti is delicate even with the optional topping of sausage, meatballs, or bacon and egg.

Japanese pasta and other marvelous examples of Japanized Western dishes are served forth at **Pasta House** (4454 Van Nuys Boulevard, Sherman Oaks, S.F. VALLEY, 818-986-7076; lunch through dinner; closed Monday). Try spaghetti with clams and soy butter; fettuccine with shrimp in a creamed tomato sauce, sliced steak in garlic cream with red peppercorns; and a heavenly Grand Marnier crêpe.

♦ **JAPANESE-STYLE**
KOREAN BARBECUE
The Japanese learned to love Korean barbecue at the many hole-in-the-wall Korean immigrant-run *bulgogi* joints in Tokyo. Inevitably, Japanese restaurateurs began serving a slightly more Japanized version: The kimchee is less incendiary, and the marinade, though garlicky, not quite so pungent.

Seiko-En and **Totoraku**—two very similar establishments in opposite parts of town—specialize in "Tokyo-style" Korean barbecue.

For grilling at your table you can select the prime rib with bone, the top loin, or variety meats. Totoraku also offers scallops and shrimps to barbecue. **Genghiskhan Bar-B-Q Buffet House** has an all-you-can-eat arrangement. You get your meats, vegetables, rice, pickles, and salad at the buffet, but grill your own meat at your table.

- **Seiko-En,** 1730 W. Sepulveda Boulevard, Torrance, SOUTH, 310-534-5578. Lunch Tuesday to Friday; dinner Tuesday to Sunday.
- **Totoraku,** 2125 Sawtelle Boulevard, West Los Angeles, WEST, 310-473-7747. Dinner Tuesday to Sunday.
- **Genghiskhan Bar-B-Q Buffet House,** 1151 W. Pacific Coast Highway, Harbor City, SOUTH, 310-534-5766. Lunch and dinner daily. Also in Alhambra, SAN GABRIEL VALLEY, 818-282-5636.

♦ **PATISSERIE**

One little-known but exceptionally toothsome translation of Western food is Japanese-style patisserie. Those pastries, usually made by chefs who've studied in France, are lighter and less sweet, and sometimes incorporate Asian ingredients. In Japan, these shops are everywhere and now they're starting to spread throughout Los Angeles. The following ones, each with its own character, are my favorites.

Former surfer and restaurant manager Makoto Takahashi fell in love with California's relaxed way of life. "But," he says, "I missed the kind of French pastries we have at home." He opened **Mousse Fantasy** (2130 Sawtelle Boulevard, West Los Angeles, WEST, 310-479-6665; lunch through dinner; closed Monday). The shop's Japanese-trained baker makes Japanese pumpkin and green tea mousse cakes as well as the more customary vanilla or lemon. And Mousse Fantasy has a small dining area in which you can enjoy Danish with cappuccino, or lunch on East/West entrées.

After you have the noodles at Sanuki no Sato, amble a few doors down to **Bonjour French Pastry** (18222 S. Western Avenue, Gardena, SOUTH, 310-323-1468; also in Pacific Supermarket [page 65]) in the same mall. Their fruit mousse cakes—mandarin orange, strawberry, or pear—are light but satisfyingly flavored. Apple pastry cream comes in a feathery millefeuilles crust, and the strawberry tart has a rich layer of pastry cream. **Frances** (404 E. 2nd Street, Little Tokyo, CENTRAL, 213-680-4899) comes closest to being truly French. In the afternoon, you're likely to see proper Japanese women at the dainty tables in front of the baroque French armoire, sipping excellent coffee and nibbling pick-me-ups of pear mousse ringed with ladyfingers and topped with almost translucent pear slices. The opera cake is rich with a dark chocolate top, and there are beautiful fruit tarts.

At **Ginza Ya Bakery** (333 S. Alameda Street, Yaohan Plaza, No. 106–107, Little Tokyo, CENTRAL, 213-626-1904, and 11301 W. Olympic Boulevard, West Los Angeles, WEST, 310-575-1131), the goods look as though plucked from a Parisian boulangerie. Don't be deceived—these are Japanese-style baguettes, almond Danish, raisin bread, petits pains, and beautiful butter cookies in shimmery cellophane packets tied up with bows.

GENERAL RESTAURANTS

Sai Sai, 501 S. Olive Street (Biltmore Hotel), Los Angeles, CENTRAL, 213-624-1100. Breakfast, lunch, and dinner daily. More than at any other Japanese restaurant I know, the cuisine at Sai Sai, in the Biltmore Hotel's lower level, illustrates the Japanese culture's intimate link to nature and seasonal change. Changing tableware depicts the mood of each season: porcelain expresses the refreshing feeling of spring; cool glass is used in summer; in autumn, the dishes are earthenware; and in winter, wooden plates add a warm touch. The tableware may even be changed to suit the mood of the day or hour. The dishes listed on the multicourse kaiseki menu aren't described, because they change every two weeks.

"This food is true Japanese ryori," a Japanese gourmand assured me. Of course the real seasonal Japanese ryori can be cooked at home or in a tiny koryori-ya, but at Sai Sai it is of kaiseki caliber. It's expensive to order from the à la carte menu, but if you choose the lowest-priced $35 multicourse menu for dinner or the $28 lunch, you will be served six elaborate courses and the inevitable pickles, rice, and soup. Sai Sai also offers a multicourse traditional breakfast.

Masukawa, 1328 W. Rosecrans Avenue, Gardena, SOUTH, 310-323-1922. Lunch and dinner Monday to Friday; dinner Saturday. Acclaimed for its live eel imported from Japan and its sophisticated daily appetizer specials (zensai moriawase), Masukawa is, deep in its soul, a Japanese country-style restaurant. Most of the dishes are Japanese home cooking, which emphasizes flavor over flair. Nothing could be simpler than the salted, broiled shio-yaki-style seafood and meats, the country-style kamameshi, or the cook-at-the-table nabe mono dinners that include the old-fashioned Japanese-style bouillabaisse, kaizoku nabe mono. There's also an excellent sushi bar, and wonderful tempura including a standout lobster version.

Tsukuba, 2210-2 W. Artesia Boulevard, Torrance, SOUTH, 310-538-4828. Lunch and dinner daily. My Japanese friends go to Tsukuba

for its enticing lineup of specialties: snapping turtle nabe (a souplike stew), shrimp-stuffed fried shiitake mushrooms, and seiro meshi (a lacquered box filled with a square of rice topped with such "delicacies" as salmon roe or cured salmon). Some Americans complain that seiro meshi is "too small" (but you don't eat large portions of caviar or foie gras, either). For these folks, Tsukuba's English-language menu is filled with familiar dishes and combination dinners. But for anyone seeking a more adventurous taste of Japan, it's best to consult Tsukuba's owner, Mr. Yajima. He translates expertly, and he'll describe the kani no yoshinori or arani nimono and the restaurant's impressive $55 to $85 multicourse kaiseki menus.

Oishii, 4744 Pacific Coast Highway, Long Beach, SOUTH, 310-498-2314. Lunch Monday to Friday; dinner nightly. Oishii, meaning "delicious," which started out life as a beautifully appointed kushi-yaki bar and restaurant with an enticing appetizer list and inexpensive dinners, had something for almost everyone—but not quite. "Customers would come in asking for sushi; they didn't know what kushi-yaki and yakitori were, so they left," says co-owner Barbara Kuo. Oishii has now added sushi, and customers who try the kushi-yaki love it. Now Oishii has something for everyone.

Edo Sushi, 22737 Ventura Boulevard, Woodland Hills, S.F. VALLEY, 818-887-3200. Lunch and dinner daily. Edo Sushi took the opposite approach: This popular Valley sushi bar installed a separate tempura and kushi-yaki bar just last year. The tempura, ordered one piece at a time, emerges cloudlike from the fryer to the counter in front of you; the yakitori is juicy and sizzling. And the appetizer list is long. If à la carte eating isn't your style, there are familiar combination dinners and "Samurai" dinners in which several courses are arranged in a bamboo boat.

Teru Sushi, 11940 Ventura Boulevard, Studio City, S.F. VALLEY, 818-763-6201. Lunch Monday to Friday; dinner nightly. Teru gained notoriety as a flamboyant show-biz sort of place with costumed sushi chefs banging gongs. But sushi acolytes agree that the bar is as high in quality as in entertainment. Because so many people equate the restaurant with sushi, the other excellent food often gets overlooked. Over a dozen appetizer plates include beef sashimi with a ginger-garlic-infused soy sauce, and niku maki, shrimp and avocado wrapped up in beef and sautéed. Entrées include innovative grilled dishes such as chicken in a crushed sesame seed sauce. If you aren't enthralled with the hyperactivity of the bar, there's a quiet heated garden patio with a pond and a waterfall.

Tokyo Kaikan, 225 S. San Pedro Street, Little Tokyo, CENTRAL, 213-489-1333. Lunch and dinner Monday to Friday, dinner Saturday. Tokyo Kaikan, the granddaddy of authentic Japanese restaurants in Los Angeles, is still a favorite with downtown Japanese businessmen. Many of the city's top sushi chefs once plied their craft at its always reliable sushi bar. In the recesses of the rustic dining room, there's a shabu-shabu bar that offers both beef and seafood, which you swish through the steaming broth and eat piping hot from the kettle. A large selection of appetizers and the entrées are fine but fairly standard.

For the more adventurous, Tokyo Kaikan's parent company, the Ewa Group, also owns the spectacular **Kitayama** in Newport Beach (714-725-0777), one of the *L.A. Times* top-40 Southern California restaurants.

Senbazuru (A Thousand

Cranes), 120 S. Los Angeles Street (New Otani Hotel & Garden), Little Tokyo, CENTRAL, 213-629-1200. Breakfast, lunch, and dinner daily. My favorite meal at this dining room, which overlooks a trompe l'oeil garden atop the New Otani Hotel, is the traditional Japanese breakfast. While many Japanese have become toast and egg converts, in the past, morning meals included bowls of rice, miso soup, and salted salmon or other fish, all washed down with green tea. Senbazuru offers this morning ritual presented to you by a kimono-clad waitress. The breakfast also includes dainty squares of Japanese-style omelet, simmered vegetables, and myriad side dishes.

The restaurant has separate sushi and tempura bars; the tempura alone is worth a trip. For many years Senbazuru's other food, though good, was unimaginative. Now, however, a revamped menu includes a series of marvelous kaiseki multicourse meals comparable to the stylish, contemporary Tokyo-style cuisine served at the New Otani's hotels in Japan.

Horikawa, 111 S. San Pedro Street, Little Tokyo, CENTRAL, 213-680-9355. Lunch and dinner. Also Santa Ana, OCOUNTY, 714-557-2531. In a world of green tea cheesecake and Japanese-Italian spaghetti, Horikawa is a restaurant that holds steadfastly to tradition. The restaurant's tatami rooms shelter Pacific Rim industrialists making deals over kaiseki meals. The sushi bar is excellent, and the teppan-yaki grill room serves without the Benihana fanfare (and with far less salty sauces).

Suehiro, 337 E. 1st Street, Little Tokyo, CENTRAL, 213-626-9132. Open 11:00 A.M. to 3:00 A.M. Monday through Saturday; Sunday 11:00 A.M. to 1:00 A.M. A funky coffee shop atmosphere with turquoise tuck-and-roll booths is an all-purpose restaurant where you can get everything but sushi at rock-bottom prices until 3:00 A.M.

FOOD SHOPPING IN L.A., JAPANESE STYLE

L.A. has plenty of supermarkets battling it out for the Asian shopper's dollar. But some stores offer more than sheer size and variety. One small unassuming market on a quiet West Los Angeles street, **Aloha Grocery** (4515 Centinela Avenue, West Los Angeles, WEST, 310-822-2288. Monday through Saturday 9:00 A.M. to 7:00 P.M.) makes its own specialty tofu products—the best in town. In a glassed-in minifactory behind the produce department (you can watch if you get to the store early), tofu master Hiroshi Uyehara still forms his big blocks of silken and regular tofu the old-fashioned way: by hand.

Hiroshi Uyehara demonstrates tofu-making at his Aloha Grocery tofu boutique: stirring the coagulated soy milk;

With automated factories spewing out thousands of pounds of tofu a day for the Los Angeles market, he resolved to keep making the kind of flavorful tofus that must be produced in small batches. To hone his technique, Uyehara traveled all over Japan studying with tofu masters. Old-fashioned nigari tofu, fast disappearing even in Japan, is made without calcium sulfate as a coagulant. It's tricky to make, but many swear by nigari's sweet, beany flavor.

Aloha also makes cooked tofu products. Ganmodoki—mock goose—is wonderful for vegetarian dishes, as are the fried tofu squares and pouches.

The market also flies in and prepares an interesting variety of Hawaiian items: Portuguese sweet bread, poi, and lomi lomi (Hawaiian-style cured salmon seviche).

Yaohan Market, Little Tokyo Square (Yaohan Plaza), 333 S. Alameda Street, 3rd floor, Little Tokyo, CENTRAL, 213-687-6699. Open 7 days. Also 21515 Western Avenue, Torrance, SOUTH, 310-516-6699, and Costa Mesa, OCOUNTY. At Yaohan Market you can find everything from Japanese designer socks to matsutake mushrooms. All the Southern California branches of this worldwide Japanese chain rival any American food-market-drug-department-store complex both in size and in variety of ingredients. Yaohan owns 114 or so retail outlets, not just in Japan, but in Singapore, Malaysia, and Costa Rica, and in cities across the United States including Edgewater, New Jersey, and Fresno.

Wandering the aisles, you almost feel as if you've been flown to Japan. And you will probably get a better idea of the range of Japanese consumer goods here than most tourists will on a Tokyo stopover. You'll find curry raisu mix—the modern Japanese housewife's equivalent of Hamburger Helper—and fresh noodles with packets of sauce. Lush-looking produce is often packaged, in the

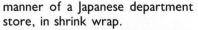

transferring the stirred coagulated soy milk to a muslin-lined pressing form; cutting the formed tofu into blocks;

taking the finished product off the line, ready for labeling.

manner of a Japanese department store, in shrink wrap.

There are prepared foods to go: precut sashimi trays, ready-made sushi, and pristine slabs of fish to make your own. Along with a mind-boggling assortment of packaged goods, you'll discover at least 15 kinds of soy sauce.

Within Yaohan is a branch of **Fugetsu-Do,** a traditional Japanese confectionery shop that has been in Los Angeles since 1903. Fugetsu-Do's original store is still nearby at 315 E. 1st Street, Little Tokyo, CENTRAL, 213-625-8595. The shop makes delicate white-and-green red bean-filled rice cakes called mochi that are one of Japan's favorite confections. Some mochi have chunky whole-bean filling, others are smooth oblongs of mochi dusted with roasted crushed soybeans. A small selection of more Westernized pastries include a delicate cake roll spread with the thinnest imaginable layer of jam.

On the ground floor just outside

Yaohan is **Mikawaya,** another long-standing but more commercial confectionery shop with branches in Pacific Square in Gardena and in Japanese Village Plaza (page 65). Mikawaya is famous for its baked sweet cakes filled with bean paste, known as manju. And here you can get red bean or green tea ice cream cones.

Japanese confectionery lovers should also know about two Gardena shops. **Sakura-Ya** (16134 S. Western Avenue, Gardena, SOUTH, 310-323-7117), a family-run business for nearly 30 years, is the most personal. Their completely handmade mochi are remarkably tender, and the smooth rice exterior is never overwhelmed with an (sweet red bean filling). The otamochi, with an on the outside, are excellent here. And Sakura-Ya is famous for kuri manju—steamed wheat flour cakes shaped like chestnuts and filled with snowy white sweet bean filling.

Chikara Mochi (16108 S.

A Saturday afternoon food demonstration of Japanese-style Chinese bao at Yaohan Market in Little Tokyo.

Ready-to-eat foods at Yaohan Market.

A visible Japanese menu: Plastic food replicas in a window at Little Tokyo Square (Yaohan Plaza) shopping center.

Western Avenue, Gardena, SOUTH, 310-324-5256, open 10:00 A.M. to 6:00 P.M. daily) makes traditional mochi of all sorts. For Girl's Day, an-filled *sakura* mochi uses a special variety of rice, and each little cake comes wrapped in a plum leaf. Boy's Day brings leaf-wrapped un-stuffed mochi with a sweeter taste, and for other holidays, mochi is formed into incredibly realistic-looking plums, peaches, flowers, and fish.

Tea lovers shouldn't leave Yaohan Plaza without making a visit to **Ryoku Shu En** (Yaohan Plaza, Little Tokyo, CENTRAL, 213-613-0066, on the third floor). The shop offers about 60 kinds of Japanese tea. The several varieties of green tea include *gyokuro,* or "jewel dew." It's made from selected young buds of the tea plant and has a fragrant aromatic flavor unlike restaurant green tea. There's also *kagabocha,* an uncaffeinated brew; *genmai-cha,* mixed with roasted popped rice grains; and *gen-mai matcha* of tea ceremony fame.

Leaving Yaohan Plaza and walking toward San Pedro Street along Second Street will take you to **Japanese Village Plaza**—look for the blue-tiled roofs—and **Enbun Market** (213-680-3280), a pre-Yaohan supermarket with a large and loyal following of locals. The meat counter cuts the best beef to order for shabu-shabu and sukiyaki. Then walk across the plaza to **Ikeda Bakery** (213-624-2773), possibly the oldest Japanese-Western bakery in Los Angeles. Ikeda distributes its tall, thickly sliced white bread—the kind you always get with your "morning set"—to most Japanese markets. Ikeda's version of this bread tastes a little better than many brands. You may also want to try their curry-filled doughnuts, cream-filled buns called *anpan,* beautifully manicured cakes, cream puffs, and the delicious brown rice bread. Ikeda Bakery is also at 1824 W. 182nd Street, Torrance, SOUTH, 310-323-0482.

Still farther west is **Modern Food Market** (332 E. Second Street, Little Tokyo, CENTRAL, 213-680-9595. Its clientele is drawn from the long-established Japanese American community, and it is slightly more economical than the pricey Yaohan. I like the fish counter here for its marinated *tara* kasuzuke (cod marinated in sake mash that broils up flavorful and juicy) and for its several kinds of cured salmon.

In Gardena, **Pacific Supermarket** (1620 W. Redondo Beach Boulevard, Gardena, SOUTH, 310-321-4734; also at 3030 W. Sepulveda Boulevard, Torrance, SOUTH, 310-539-8899), formerly called New Meiji Market, was L.A.'s first Japanese supermarket. A decade ago, non-Asians were amazed by the mind-boggling selection of rice crackers and the dazzling assortment of colorful zuke: pickles from sweet crunchy radish to the sourest umeboshi plums (sometimes called Japanese mouthwash). Here, too, are wonderfully fresh fish in the round, all sorts of clams, and dozens of fish cakes.

Pacific's produce department has heaps of Japanese pumpkins with an intense flavor, gobo, Asian pears and eggplants, and even rolls of vegetable sushi. **Bonjour French Pastry** (page 59) has a concession here.

Tofu lovers in this part of town will want to know about **Meiji Tofu** (16440 S. Western Avenue, Gardena, SOUTH, 310-538-0403), a minifactory and retail store owned by Hiroko Nakayama, where freshly made silken and regular-style tofu is prepared daily. Meiji also makes soy milk and deep-fried tofu pouches.

Shoppers for Japanese groceries in West Los Angeles go to **Safe and Save** (2030 Sawtelle Boulevard, West Los Angeles, WEST, 310-479-3810), a fixture in this Japanese neighborhood since the thirties. The store has a real butcher and fish cutter and a display of ready-to-cook meats—diced chicken breast, julienne pork, and shabu-shabu beef, cut with the precision of a jewel cutter. Safe and Save isn't large, but it stocks a full array of sauces, mixes, seaweeds, and fresh and dry noodles, and offers a good selection of Asian vegetables.

Finally, bargain hunters in the market for Japanese packaged foods and tableware will love **Daiyu Discount Warehouse** (7968 Garvey Avenue, Rosemead, SAN GABRIEL VALLEY, 818-572-4152).

KOREA

Koreatown, with its blocks of banks and commercial buildings flanking Wilshire Boulevard, its huge Korean supermarkets, Korean movie theaters, dozens of car dealerships, and Korean churches, is Central L.A.'s most visible ethnic enclave. The area from Beverly Boulevard to Pico between Western and Vermont is the most concentrated Korean neighborhood in the United States. But Koreans have also moved to the San Fernando Valley, Gardena, and Orange County. Los Angeles is home to the largest Korean population in America and to the newspaper *Korea Central Daily* (which has a worldwide circulation of 2 million). All this explains our stupendous number of Korean restaurants: about 500 at last count.

To woo Western customers, some Korean restaurateurs have tried user-friendly menu descriptions—calling pindaettuk "griddled pancakes," for example. But a griddle cake made from mung beans still seems pretty odd. It's not until customers taste pindaettuk, with its crispy edges and soft savory interior, that they warm to the idea of eating something as strange-sounding as a mung bean pancake.

It's not hard to understand why most Korean food, beyond barbecue, is still a mystery to most Angelenos. All over Koreatown, many small restaurants with delicious aromas wafting from their kitchens have no printed menu at all. I've had some of my best meals in these places with Korean friends whose method of ordering was to discuss the nightly offerings (in Korean, of course) with the cook. One was at Ham Kyung Do Abaii Soon Dae, a place that sells only two dishes—grilled Korean sausage (soon dae) and Korean sausage in soup.

But things are looking up. My favorite mandu place on Third Street uses a brochure of colored photographs to describe the many ways their specialty, dumplings, are served. And the latest rage on the Korean restaurant scene is all-you-can-eat buffet restaurants. These provide a great opportunity to see and taste all kinds of foods you might miss by choosing a meal from the cryptic translations on many menus.

Several years ago, Korean restaurateurs started getting out of the saturated barbecue restaurant market to open specialty restaurants, the same kinds you find in Korea. Now, not only do you see good seafood restaurants and various kinds of noodle shops, but foods as esoteric as pigs' knuckles and goat. You also find, scattered around Koreatown and other Korean enclaves makkolli houses—pubs that serve rice wine to drink along with small plates of food called anju—and tearooms called tabangs, where gossip, rather than the drinks and snacks, seems to be the main attraction.

— KOREAN GLOSSARY —

Anju: Small servings of food, similar in style to tapas, usually consumed with alcoholic drinks.
Bibim bap: A meal in a bowl consisting of assorted vegetables and meats over rice with a spicy sauce on the side to mix in.
Bulgogi (or pulgogi) and

barbecue: Bulgogi is only one of the many meat preparations that Koreans love to cook and eat at the table. It is thinly sliced beef, marinated in a garlic-laden soy and sesame mixture. But kalbi—beef short ribs cut either across the bone or entirely off the bone—is equally popular. Other meats include twaeji-gogi, sliced pork (in a different marinade); tak gogi, marinated chicken meat; and ch'onyop, tripe. Several other organ meats and even eel or fish may also be offered.

Chap che: A stir-fry of clear noodles, beef, and assorted vegetables—the Korean version of chow mein.

Chige (or tchige): A variety of thick soupy stew.

Chowmamein: Wheat noodles, often the hand-tossed variety, in a broth seasoned with red chile. When prepared with seafood, chowmamein often goes by the name "three sea delicacies."

Doenjang chige (or tchigae): A tofu, meat, and bean paste stew (see chige).

Gu jeol pan: A special-occasion dish of thin crêpes surrounded by an arrangement of cut vegetables and meats, which are rolled in one of the crêpes to eat.

Haejangkook: A beef soup made with abundant bones, marrow, and blood pudding that is thought to cure hangovers; some call it Korean menudo.

Haemul pajeon: See pajeon.

Hamhung noodles: Northern-style potato starch noodles eaten cold in a spicy sauce with various toppings.

Hware: A brazier—either gas-fueled or charcoal fueled—used to grill foods at the table.

Hwedobap: Sliced raw fish served over rice topped with shredded lettuce and cucumbers accompanied with a slightly sweet red pepper sauce to mix in.

Jajaingmein: Wheat noodles, often the hand-tossed variety, in a rich brown meat and bean paste sauce.

Jeon: A style of cooking that involves dipping foods in an egg batter and then grilling them. Some versions (see pajeon) resemble pancakes.

Kalbi: Beef short ribs.

Kejang: Raw crab cured in salt and served cold in an extremely hot red pepper sauce.

Kimchees: These salted, fermented, and often heavily seasoned foods served as side dishes at almost every meal (even breakfast), are the cornerstone of Korean eating. Although the chile-hot cabbage version is most prevalent, kimchees can range from bland turnips in salted water to whole pickled jalapeño peppers with baby oysters. Many families make their own kimchees, but every Korean supermarket has dozens of varieties.

Komtang: A beef soup.

Kulbossam: An anju composed of separate dishes of oysters, sliced salt pork, and a variety of kimchees, eaten rolled in salted cabbage leaves that accompany them.

Maeun t'ang: An assortment of seafood in a light pepper-laced broth.

Makkolli: A cloudy rice beverage made from fermented rice. Pubs serving makkolli may be called makkollijip or suljip.

Mandu: These meat- or vegetable-filled dumplings, similar to Chinese dumplings, are served either in soup, boiled, steamed, or pan-fried.

Minari: A leafy green that resembles flat-leafed parsley.

Naeng myun: Long thin chewy buckwheat and potato starch noodles, usually served in a bowl of cold or hot broth, and topped with sliced beef, egg, and turnip kimchee.

Pajeon: Savory pancakes with small oysters in the batter, eaten with a soy-sauce-based dip. Haemul pajeon is often made with assorted seafood.

Panchan: Side dishes other than kimchee.

Perilla: Also called beefsteak plant, perilla, a member of the mint family, will be familiar to sushi devotees as shiso, the wide multipointed pungent leaf. A red variety, sold in bunches in Korean markets, is used in many casseroles and soups.

Pindaettuk: A grilled pancake made from deliciously seasoned ground mung beans and eaten as anju.

Sae u jeon: Prawns dipped in egg and sautéed.

Saeng son jeon: Batter-dipped grilled fish (see jeon).

Sin sul ro: A meal of assorted meats, seafood, and vegetables which diners warm in broth in a Mongolian hotpot at the table.

Soon dae: Korean-style blood sausage.

Soon tofu: Soft unpressed tofu, usually served in a spicy broth garnished with bits of meat or seafood.

Suljip: A drinking and eating pub specializing in makkolli and tongdongju. Less formal pubs are called makkollijip.

Tang: The Korean word for soups with a light broth base. Kalbitang is a beef rib version.

Tongdongju (or dongdongju): Another rice brew, more refined than makkolli, that is similar to sake.

Yuk-hwe: Minced raw beef served with condiments and lettuce to use as an edible wrapper.

KOREAN BARBECUE SPECIALISTS

You can expect to find barbecue in almost every Korean restaurant except noodle parlors and tofu soup shops. But to get the ultimate—the best meat and marinade and the hottest grills for searing ribs and bulgogi—only a specialty barbecue restaurant will do.

Soot Bull Jeep, 3136 W. 8th Street, Koreatown, CENTRAL, 213-387-3865. Dinner nightly. Koreatown's most popular barbecue gets so crowded at mealtimes that the owners have wisely installed one of those take-a-number dispensers by the door. Soot bull jeep, a special hardwood charcoal that Koreans favor for cooking, is what the restaurant uses for its barbecue rather than the gas-jet grills you find at most other places. One of the dining rooms has a pit housing the glowing coals. After you order, the waitress carries over a tray full of coals and sinks it into a deep well in the center of your table. Next comes the usual array of soup, rice, kimchees, a few panchan, and a huge plate of bronze-leaf lettuce. The lettuce is used to wrap the barbecued meat with the accompanying condiments or with sesame-oil-dressed scallion shreds, and is eaten like a burrito. Or you can simply eat the meat, still sizzling, straight off the barbecue, with rice.

Soot Bull Jeep's menu lists a dozen different kinds of meat. You can get rib eye, spencer steak, tongue, and the ever popular beef ribs, or kalbi, on or off the bone. The menu also lists chicken and eel. Some cuts are marinated; the pork has a peppery marinade rather than the sweet, garlicky sauce that flavors the beef. But many beef cuts are offered plain, brushed only with a little sesame oil to facilitate barbecuing. Along with the meat, Soot Bull Jeep offers a list of cold noodle dishes, which seems to be de rigueur in barbecue restaurants.

Pete Wood B-B-Q, 910 E. Garvey Avenue, Monterey Park, SAN GABRIEL VALLEY, 818-571-6950. Lunch and dinner Monday to Saturday; 4:30 P.M. to 10:30 P.M. Sunday. Similar to Soot Bull Jeep, Pete Wood B-B-Q in Monterey Park is smaller and less frenetic. But they use the same hardwood charcoal for barbecuing. The barbecued chicken on the bone is popular with non-Koreans. Meals come with a lightly peppered refreshing lettuce salad as well as the lettuce for wrapping and several mouth-torching kimchees.

The Corner Place, 2819 W. 9th Street, Koreatown, CENTRAL, 213-487-0968, and 19100 S. Gridley Road, Cerritos, SOUTH, 310-402-8578. Lunch through dinner daily. At mealtimes all 25 hooded table fans hum, waitresses rush from the kitchen with platters of meats, and busboys whisk used grills from their sockets to replace them in seconds; efficiency is the Corner Place's middle name. Most barbecue restaurants require a minimum of 2 diners before they'll dirty up a grill, but the Corner Place accommodates single diners. Barbecue, noodles, and soup constitute the entire menu; the choice of meats is incredibly varied.

The 9 styles of kimchees served with every meal are another draw. More than at any restaurant I know, the selection here—ranging from impossibly hot pickled cucumbers with sliced fresh hot peppers to the cooling and sweet giant radish slices that come in a bowl of ice and brine—gives a glimpse of kimchee's range of flavors. The white cabbage kimchee is garlicky but not hot, and the zucchini slices, though marinated in a bright red sauce, are only slightly spicy.

Ham Hung, 809 S. Ardmore Avenue (at 8th), Koreatown, CENTRAL, 213-381-1520 or 381-1865. Lunch through dinner daily. I used to go to Ham Hung just for the special northern-style cold noodles but Daniel Oh, Ham Hung's jovial proprietor, a man who always seems to be on the cutting edge of the Korean restaurant scene, has now installed efficient oak-burning hware (grills) imported from Korea. These are a little daintier than the smoke-puffing stoves at Soot Bull Jeep, but they still impart that wonderful woody aroma to the grilled meats.

Hamhung noodles, a regional dish of the Hamhung area of northern Korea, are similar to naeng myun, the chewy buckwheat noodles that Koreans love to eat cold. The restaurant employs a noodle chef to prepare the Hamhung-style noodles. He uses a huge noodle press imported from Korea and makes each serving to order from potato starch and other starches. In the northern style, the cold clear chewy noodles are served in a mildly spicy sauce.

Also notable here are the hot-

Cooking over live coals in the hware at Ham Hung restaurant in Koreatown.

In the last few years, several Korean buffets have sprung up around Koreatown. With literally everything from soup to nuts displayed in plain view, these offer an inexpensive way to taste-test a wide range of dishes. Each buffet has its own personality and a different selection.

pot noodle dinners kept warm on a little stove at your table. The beef hotpot dinner (No. 14) with clear noodles is loaded with fresh vegetables and meaty mushrooms, while the spicy seafood version swims with clams, crab, shrimp, squid, and egg noodles.

BUFFET RESTAURANTS

For many years **V.I.P. Buffet Palace** (3014 W. Olympic Boulevard, Koreatown, CENTRAL, 213-480-8949; lunch through dinner daily), a posh mecca for Korean business wheelers and dealers, had been growing a little frayed around the edges. The vast space has been transformed into a rather elegant cafeteria. Barbecue isn't the main attraction here. V.I.P.'s food is more what you'll find Koreans cooking at home: Soups might be creamy Asian pumpkin or Chinese vegetables with tofu in a broth. Instead of serving only white rice, V.I.P. also offers a homey mixture of grains cooked with rice and red beans. There is meat, but the profusion of vegetable dishes and salads (one included wild mountain grass with sesame dressing) are a draw for Koreans who are tired of clichéd Koreatown menus. Entrées change daily and many aren't spicy at all.

At **Lotte Buffet** (401 S. Vermont Avenue, No. 11, Koreatown, CENTRAL, 213-487-6960; lunch and dinner daily; closed Sunday), the grilling goes on behind the cafeteria-style serving counter. You are handed steaming dumplings or sizzling meat straight from the grill. A long line of panchan and kimchees includes baby octopi in chili sauce, sweet black beans, and zucchini slices dipped in egg and fried. You might want to sample the naeng myun noodles that you eat in cold broth and garnish with hot mustard and cool marinated turnips.

ALL-PURPOSE RESTAURANTS

Until a few years ago you had to make a trip to Koreatown for the best Korean food. But many Korean restaurants have been opening in the suburbs. The following all offer wide-ranging menus, tabletop barbecue, and combination dinners that are an excellent introduction to Korean food.

At **Shilla** (16944 S. Western Avenue, Gardena, SOUTH, 310-770-3858 or 538-8848; lunch and dinner; closed Monday), intimate booths, hand-carved dragons and a *koi* (carp) pool at the entryway offer the ambience of a luxurious Seoul dining house. The restaurant has two elegant bars (sushi and cocktail). Owner Sam Chung prides himself on the hot-rock stoves on which guests can barbecue meat without any oil. Shilla's combination dinners called *"jangban jung sik"* (meaning an abbreviated chongsik meal), are noteworthy. Select a grilled meat or casserole entrée, and with it comes a plate of fat juicy mandu (dumplings); chap che; along with velvety sautéed egg-dipped fish and a tableful of side dishes.

Green Oaks, 7126 Van Nuys Boulevard, Van Nuys, S.F. VALLEY, 818-989-7791. Lunch through dinner daily. Once you've been introduced to Korean food, you might want to expand your horizons at Green Oaks. The art-filled restaurant, done in lovely natural woods and owned by former actress Sae Mi Hong, has the San Fernando

The Korean Meal

Korean meals, unlike Western ones, don't have a series of courses but rather many dishes served simultaneously. There is one or more "main" dishes and always an array of accompanying dishes known as panchan. Panchan can be likened to Italian antipasti in that you nibble on an assortment of items and sometimes, along with rice, soup, and kimchee, they comprise the whole meal. Panchan change with the season and the whim of the cook, and can range from the simplest foods—perhaps a few sweet black soy beans—to more substantial dishes such as tiny oysters in chili sauce or piece of stewed meat. Several kinds of kimchees, or fermented vegetables—the Korean equivalent of pickles—round out the meal.

Barbecue and panchan: some of the best eating in Koreatown.

Everyday meals include only a few panchan, but on special occasions when Koreans serve a *chongsik* dinner it may have up to 100 of these small plates of food.

Nam Kang, 3055 W. 7th Street, Koreatown, CENTRAL, 213-380-6606. Lunch through dinner daily. The success of a Korean meal depends in part on the number and quality of panchan. While most Los Angeles restaurants serve only a few simple items such as boiled spinach with sesame oil, boiled soybean sprouts, and a few kimchees, Nam Kang offers one of the most lavish selections of panchan in Koreatown. Even the regular $8.95 Korean barbecue is an opulent affair. Before the waitress lights the grill, she brings a huge oval tray covered with little dishes and sets them on your table: raw oysters in chili sauce, squares of pancake flecked with vegetables, hard-cooked quail eggs, and 13 other items that barely leave table space for the barbecue, soup, and tea that follow.

Nam Kang also serves chongsik dinners (these must be ordered a day in advance), which make the above mentioned generous spread pale by comparison. Diners at these feasts should merely nibble on the first assortment of dishes that comes to the table, as many more (about 20, plus an assortment of kimchees) will follow in rapid succession. The small dishes include large meaty clams, baked and served sauced in their shells, and tender slices of whitefish fried in an eggy batter. Among the larger dishes are a peppery Korean-style seafood gumbo called maeun t'ang and a rich beef short rib stew. Everything is left on the table until the end of the meal, so by the time the last item arrives the tiny banquet room is a sea of plates and bowls.

Valley's most skilled Korean kitchen. Green Oaks' imaginatively crafted ten-course meal—plus various kimchees—offers miniversions of classical dishes that ordinarily require a large group to sample. But here the famous Mongolian hotpot meal, sin sul ro, comes individually tailored for one serving. The minipot even has a little center well with live coals to heat it. Though small, the hotpot includes all the elements of its larger counterpart: deep-fried tiny meatballs, several kinds of meats, seafood, and chrysanthemum leaves stacked in layers and deep-fried tempura style, all in a bubbling broth. Still more unusual is gu jeol pan, which usually is a stack of thin pancakes surrounded by precisely cut meat and vegetables that diners roll in a pancake to eat. In the Green Oaks version, the pancake is replaced by an almost sheer slice of giant white radish softened in a sweet and sour marinade.

The meal includes grilled dishes, soups, and stews, each more refined than the next. And Green Oaks also serves the traditional barbecue and casserole dinners.

Yet Gol, 1835 W. Redondo Beach Boulevard, Gardena, SOUTH, 310-329-7343. Lunch and dinner; closed Monday. After a quiet opening several years ago, Yet Gol has developed a devoted following for its carefully turned out traditional dishes. Barbecue is secondary here, since the restaurant has only a few tabletop grills. The kitchen emphasizes freshness over elaborate preparations, and dinner might include a novel kimchee of tiny young radishes with the tops still on or a preserved-chestnut kimchee. Yet Gol's bibim bap—the meat-and-vegetable-garnished rice you mix with condiments—comes in a scalding hot stoneware casserole. Koreans favor this traditional serving dish, called a tukkpeggi, for its ability to keep foods hot during even the coldest Korean winter. On top of the rice and meat is a carefully arranged mountain of vegetables that includes swirls of fern buds.

There are also wonderful fat mandu, perfectly cooked pajeon, crisp saeng son jeon, and rich, meaty grilled eel—the best I've had in a Korean restaurant. Korean artifacts lend a subtle touch of grace to the open room, and the waitstaff in modern-day Korean-style uniforms adds to the charm of the place.

Korean Gardens, 950 S. Vermont Avenue, Koreatown, CENTRAL, 213-388-3042. Lunch and dinner daily. When Korean Gardens opened in 1975, it was the first Los Angeles restaurant to have tabletop hware. Back then it was called Woo Lae Oak, and the hware were such a novelty the local *Two on the Town* television magazine show filmed the restaurant. Korean Gardens continues to serve some of the best Korean fare. Their cooks never make the barbecue marinade too sweet, nor do they overmarinate the meat to mask the taste of the beef.

The restaurant's *han jung sik*—a miniversion of the 100-course dinner—is an extraordinary value that includes barbecue plus a tableful of such items as oyster pancakes, tiny beef-stuffed peppers, yuk-hweh, and doenjang chige (a tofu-and-meat stew in a robust bean paste sauce). These aren't panchan, but full-sized servings accompanied with a host of kimchees.

Siyeon, 721 S. Western Avenue, Koreatown, CENTRAL, 213-382-2277 or 382-2278. Lunch through dinner daily. This former bowling alley is one of the most popular restaurants in Koreatown. Brass, wood, and etched-glass dividers make Siyeon's huge space elegant and comfortable, but you can't help noticing the high, echoing ceiling. Waitresses trundle through the huge dining area with carts to dish out kimchees and panchan. Besides the items for grilling and many spicy casseroles, a long list of appetizers includes the popular Korean steak tartare, which you roll up in lettuce with kimchee and condiments; deep-fried oysters, and sae u jeon. Unfortunately, Siyeon's kitchen is uneven. Sometimes you get wonderful food—sometimes not.

Woo Lae Oak of Seoul, 623 S. Western Avenue, Koreatown, CENTRAL, 213-384-2244. Lunch through dinner daily. This is the L.A. branch of an international restaurant chain with restaurants in Seoul, New York, and Washington, D.C. Woo Lae Oak has a reputation as a place Koreans entertain their Western business friends. And many say the cooking is tailored to American tastes. Like Siyeon, Woo Lae Oak offers a broad selection of standard Korean dishes and gas grills for barbecuing in the middle of its tables.

Pine Tree Korean BBQ, 8967 Tampa Avenue, Northridge, S.F. VALLEY, 818-886-1512. Lunch and dinner daily. Pine Tree, a commodious restaurant across from the Northridge Fashion Center, serves inexpensive and generous lunch specials. The menu is nicely translated, although occasionally you find a translation like "wrapped with lettuce and beef." This turns out to be marinated meat grilled in the kitchen and served with a pile of red lettuce leaves, minari, sliced raw garlic, and hot and mild kimchees. You wrap the meat with your choice of these condiments, burrito style, to eat. Pine Tree's waitresses watch over you to be sure you don't burn your bulgogi barbecue, and they do their best to explain what goes into such items as the short rib stew and kimchee casserole. And the menu teaches you to say *kam sa ham ni da:* "thank you" in Korean.

SPECIALTY RESTAURANTS

In Seoul, Myong Dong is a lively area known for good shopping and tiny one-specialty places serving foods not always offered at larger establishments, perhaps hand-cut noodles, beef shank soup, or tofu stew. Collectively, Koreatown's minimalls have become a microcosm of the Myong Dong district.

♦ **KOREAN SEAFOOD SPECIALISTS**
Song Do Sea Food (377 N. Western Avenue, Koreatown, CENTRAL, 213-464-9010; open for lunch and dinner until 2:00 A.M.; closed Tuesday), a simple whitewashed room with a tiny sushi bar at the back, is my favorite place for hwedobap, an enormous bowl of rice strewn with shredded lettuce and cucumbers, and topped with three kinds of sashimi. Pour on a spicy, slightly sweet red sauce and mix the whole thing up like a salad. You can easily regulate spiciness and add soy sauce too. The effect of cool cucumber, starchy rice, salty-sweet fish, and that

Except for the Chinese border of North Korea, the entire country is surrounded by ocean, and its most valuable harvests come from the sea. As in Japan, fresh fish is eaten raw but Korean sashimi has an earthier style.

At Korean seafood restaurants, sashimi always comes on a huge plate blanketed with shredded white radish and at least half a dozen varieties of fish. Guests wrap the sashimi morsels in lettuce with a few crunchy radish shreds, and fresh hot pepper slices or raw garlic cloves. For dipping, try the accompanying lusty red hot-sweet sauce, the rich brown bean paste, or the familiar Japanese soy-sauce-with-wasabi combination. Some diners skip the wrapping ceremony altogether and dip the fish directly into one of the sauces.

After the sashimi comes a tang (a clear broth seafood soup with a penetrating chile heat), a *chige* (similar to a tang but more like a stew), or a crispy, salt-broiled whole fish. Each restaurant serves a different variety of cooked specialties.

open 10:00 A.M. to 4:00 A.M. daily) serves the usual large sashimi platters that everyone sits around the table and shares. But it also offers many sautéed seafood dishes you don't see elsewhere; we ordered pan-fried green onion and oysters. And we couldn't resist getting one of the tangs listed on the menu as "fish egg stew." It turned out to be a wonderful spicy broth filled with vegetable chunks and slices of uncured fish roe resembling sliced sausage. Kejang (raw crab marinated in a scalding spice mixture that cures it like seviche) is fresh and meaty here. But not every item is exotically spiced: Steamed whole crab or a plate of unshelled steamed shrimp comes plain and simple. These go perfectly with the many spicy side dishes that arrive at your table.

♦ **KOREAN PUBS:**
MAKKOLLI AND ANJU

Suljip—casual pubs frequented by students and working-class Koreans—are virtual institutions of Korean life; every neighborhood has at least one. And Koreatown has quite a few.

Koreans pour into these pubs at day's end for a bit of after-work socializing and makkolli, the national rice brew. But no one in Korea ever drinks makkolli without eating plenty of anju: hearty pub snacks that are Korea's most appealing foods.

In Korea, suljip range from tiny nondescript holes-in-the-wall to more elegant gathering places. **Yeejoh** (2500 W. 8th Street, No. 108, Koreatown, CENTRAL, 213-380-3346; lunch to midnight; closed Sunday), with its intimate wooden booths lined in multicolored silk pillows and its elegant private rooms, ranks with the classier ones. The house specialty, tong-dongju, a mellow golden sakelike brew with a centuries-old history, is a refined version of makkolli. It

sauce together is like a complex musical arrangement. In addition to a generous sashimi plate—$20 buys enough for two or three people—Song Do's offerings include a light, spicy crab soup made with half a female crab and its roe, and a rich-tasting broiled marinated eel.

In Cheon Restaurant (3177 W. Olympic Boulevard, Koreatown, CENTRAL, 213-738-8717;

is brought to the table in a large bowl and ladled out with a dried, hollowed gourd into chinaware cups. Tongdongju is to spicy Korean food what vodka is to caviar, and people instantly love its mild flavor.

Though Koreans don't consider anju "dinner," they often linger long enough at Yeejoh to make a meal of them. Anju have much the same appeal as Spanish tapas or Japanese kappo—you can eat a little and then decide what you feel like next.

One of my favorite foods with rice wine is kulbossam, which is rather like an oyster taco. Its components come on several plates, and you assemble them by piling a few baby oysters onto a piece of salted cabbage, topping them with a bit of finely shredded radish kimchee, and sprinkling that with fresh pine nuts and rolling it all up.

Kobawoo House (4271 Beverly Boulevard, Koreatown, CENTRAL, 213-660-6271; open nightly), named after Kobawoo, a popular Korean cartoon strip character, has a more workaday style than Yeejoh. It serves anju plus soups and stews in tightly packed surroundings. At mealtimes you might find yourself waiting for a table out on the sidewalk. The English menu, a somewhat shortened version of the Korean one, suggests "Korean pancakes": crisp-edged pindaettuk and the similar seafood-filled pancake haemul pajeon. In the meat category, listed under appetizers above the pig's foot, is "brisket meat." The brisket has been braised and pressed into a compact loaf, and a little plate of thin, meltingly tender overlapping slices comes with a tart, soy-based dipping sauce and several kimchees. The plain but savory beef is perfect foil for these fiery condiments.

Toad, 4503 W. Beverly Boulevard, Koreatown, CENTRAL, 213-

460-7037. Dinner; closed Sunday. From the tiny dining area decorated like a vineyard, you can watch the cook behind a glass-enclosed grill flipping various kinds of pancakes including delicious crisp-edged potato pancakes. These, and many egg-battered items, are Toad's specialty. Jeon at the end of a menu item indicates batter-dipped grilled foods, such as *gogi kouju-jeon:* thumb-sized peppers, scooped out and filled with beef, then lightly dipped in egg and grilled. Saeng son jeon, pieces of fish cooked the same way, have a miraculously velvety texture. Ask the waitress and she'll describe the meat and vegetable versions. Another specialty, soon dae, a well-seasoned blood sausage that's a favorite snack with makkolli, comes either grilled or in a peppery soup. These homey dishes are always appealing, even to the novice Korean diner. But if you're after something exotic, Toad serves bibim bap, a rice casserole made with—you guessed it—toad.

♦ **NOODLE RESTAURANTS**
Myung Dong Noodle House, 910 N. Western Avenue, Koreatown, CENTRAL, 213-462-9135. Lunch through dinner; closed Tuesday. One of Koreatown's oldest noodle shops, this is the only place I know that still rolls out and cuts its "knife noodles"—called *khal kooksoo*—by hand. An enormous mound of the khal kooksoo comes in huge steaming bowls of richly flavored broth, either chicken or anchovy. And on every one of the tiny shop's half dozen or so tables are pots of the house-made, glow-in-the-dark red chili sauce to add to your taste. After 17 years in business, Myung Dong's menu still isn't translated into English. But the owner's English-speaking sons now run the shop. Moreover, mastering the menu is no problem, because the only things Myong Dong

serves are its noodles and juicy, delicious homemade mandu.

Hand-Pulled Chinese Noodles, Korean Style

Most of the places I've found that make Chinese-style hand-pulled noodles are Korean-owned Chinese restaurants. It's worth seeking them out for their gloriously chewy, silky noodles with a slightly irregular texture that can't be attained any way but by hand.

Koreatown is loaded with Chinese restaurants where you get kimchee with your meal. Their chefs, ethnic Chinese who've lived most of their lives in Korea, cater to the Korean palate. A few still make hand-pulled noodles (though many have started to use pasta machines). I can't always recommend the other Chinese dishes in these places, and you should know that not every noodle dish features handmade noodles; it's a good idea to check which ones do. Virtually all restaurants serving the noodles will offer them in traditional brown-bean-and-meat-sauced dishes called jajaingmein and also in a chile-laced soup called chowmamein. Prepared with seafood, chowmamein becomes "three sea delicacies," another standard dish.

- **Peking Yuen,** 3185 W. Olympic Boulevard, Koreatown, CENTRAL, 213-382-3815.
- **Mandarin Garden,** 1001 S. Vermont Boulevard, No. 106, Koreatown, CENTRAL, 213-380-0075.
- **Mandarin House,** 3074 W. 8th Street, Koreatown, CENTRAL, 213-386-8976.

SEOUL FOOD FOR THE ADVENTUROUS: TOFU, DUMPLINGS, AND SOUP

In a charming setting with tables made from slices of tree trunks, **Beverly Soon Tofu Restaurant** (4653½ W. Beverly Boulevard, Koreatown, CENTRAL, 213-856-0368; lunch through dinner daily) devotes its entire menu to dishes

The noodle master hand-pulls noodles at

featuring soft (soon) tofu (pronounced "soon doo-bu"). The tofu, made without any added coagulant, comes plain or in a spicy soup that ranges from mild to splendidly sinus-clearing. You choose from a list of additions: meat, various seafoods, or sheets of toasted seaweed that you crumble over the top. The tofu is so fresh it's like creamy clouds, and absorbs the flavors of the soup.

After pouring a special iced tea made from roasted corn into drinking bowls and setting out three varied kimchees, the waitress brings the tofu in individual cast-iron pots so hot the sauce is still boiling violently as she sets them on the table. If you like, she will ceremoniously break a raw egg into the center of each and spoon the boiling sauce over it. A three-minute egg results if you let it sit. (A second branch is at 2717 W. Olympic Boulevard, No. 108, Koreatown, CENTRAL, 213-380-1113.)

Though Beverly was the first soft tofu shop in Los Angeles, competitors have surfaced. Of

Peking Yuen Korean-style Chinese restaurant in Koreatown.

particular note is **Jangtoh Soon-tofu** (4451 Beverly Boulevard, Koreatown, CENTRAL, 213-665-8664; lunch through dinner daily), specializing in both soft tofu and *kongbiji,* a thick, hearty meat-and-vegetable soup made with ground soybeans. The restaurant serves makkolli and has a small menu of anju, including oyster pancakes and *pindaettuk.*

Ddo Wa Dumpling (3542 West 3rd Street, Koreatown, CENTRAL, 213-387-1288; lunch through dinner; closed Sunday) is a six-table restaurant that makes mandu, mandu, and mandu. Lately a few uptown touches have been added: A portfolio of glossy colored photos illustrates each dish. But the tender dumpling coverings are still made by hand, and the filling seems even lighter and better than before. Ddo Wa's chef prepares mandu three ways. The fillings are the same, yet each rendition has its own character: The crisply fried mandu seems like pastry; the steamed mandu has the texture of

a firm meatball; and the mandu in a luscious soup garnished with fluffy scrambled egg and garlic chives is meltingly tender. Ddo wa means "come back again"—and you will want to.

Another excellent dumpling shop, **Panda Dumpling** (928 S. Western Avenue, Koreatown, CENTRAL), is located in the Koreatown Plaza Market's food court (see page 81).

At the soup shop **Nakwon Jip** (1001 S. Vermont Avenue, Koreatown, CENTRAL, 213-388-8889; open 24 hours), a Korean talk-radio show plays in the background, muffling the soft slurps of customers bent over giant bowls of soup. A worker fills hundreds of tiny takeout cups with a coarse salt mixture and readies plastic bags for an onslaught of called-in orders. This busy soup shop in Koreatown has many competitors, but it's one of the few such places with an English menu (if somewhat abbreviated).

Soups play an enormous role in

Korean eating. One of my Korean advisers tells me there are 120 kinds of traditional beef soup alone, each made from a different part of the animal, including the skin, the fat inside the skin, the front foot, the back foot, the tail, various organs, and so on.

The most popular beef soup, haejangkook—known for its chicken soup–like restorative qualities—is a favorite of men who've been out drinking too much rice wine. Haejangkook's rich broth is a product of long simmered beef bones, and it's garnished with vegetables and cooked blood cubes. You season the unsalted soup with coarse salt and the sliced scallions in huge covered bowls set on every table.

Another hearty nourishing "morning after" soup, komtang, gets its creamy white color from shin-marrow bones that have been simmered for hours to make its broth. If shin isn't your thing, don't give up on Korean soup shops—you have 119 other types of beef soup to choose from. The spring chicken soup, another white broth, boasts a whole little game hen stuffed with sweet glutinous rice, garlic, and a Chinese date. A slice of ginseng and a whole chestnut rest at the bottom of the soup.

Goat specialty restaurants in Korea cater to Koreans who believe black goat has strength-giving qualities. It is often eaten by people recovering from a serious illness. **Kong-Joo** (3029 W. Pico Boulevard, Koreatown, CENTRAL, 213-737-9487; lunch through dinner; closed Sunday), a black-goat specialty restaurant, has been open for several years now. When I saw the crowd relishing their stews and barbecues, I suspected health had little to do with why they were eating goat. The mild meat of the barbecued goat is infused with pepper and has a crisp finish. A seri-

ously hot-spicy goat soup comes garnished with pungent perilla leaves and strips of red pepper. The black-goat dishes are printed boldface in the Korean script on an otherwise English menu; non-Korean speakers will have to use the handy index finger method of ordering—just point. Kong-Joo's menu also offers a selection of familiar dishes, but almost everyone eats the goat.

KOREAN MARKETS

The mom-and-pop Korean markets of 15 and 20 years ago are swiftly disappearing. A few mid-sized stores still serve the Valley and smaller Korean enclaves in Glendale and Hacienda Heights, but in Koreatown the supermarket wars are on and the competition is fierce.

These stores resemble standard supermarkets with their banks of upright freezer cases, bar code scanners, and computerized cash registers, but they also have an undeniable—if thoroughly modern—Asian quality.

Hannam Chain Super Market, 2740 W. Olympic Boulevard, Koreatown, CENTRAL, 213-382-2922. Open daily. The Hannam Chain Market, one of my favorites, boasts a huge area devoted to deli-style prepared foods. Set out in a salad-bar-style arrangement are panchan heaped up in stainless-steel containers. The spinach in sesame dressing or the braised short ribs are familiar enough, but there's lots here to get the conversation rolling at your next buffet: perhaps a seaweed salad, whole heads of pickled garlic, or the cooked mountain ferns.

In the deli-kitchen behind a counter, workers constantly package up freshly cooked dishes that include pindaettuk and grilled Korean sausage packaged under shrink wrap with a little container of dipping sauce and a few hot red chiles. Trays with beautifully arranged as-

The kimchee selection at Hannam Chain Super Market in Koreatown.

파티용 캐더링과
도시락 주문을 받

Anju to go: A Korean appetizer display at Hannam Chain Super Market in Koreatown.

sorted anju come ready to set on the cocktail table.

Hannam's produce department has bins of bulk items: roasted barley for tea, sweet rice, roasted sesame seeds, red beans, and more. Of course there are mounds of snowy cabbage, piles of white radish, sesame, and chrysanthemum leaves for hotpot dishes and soups. Explore the cookware aisle, too. You'll find enormous brass teapots, covered rice bowls, rice cookers, and wonderful large stoneware crocks—about the size of a five-gallon water bottle—for preserving kimchee.

Koreatown Plaza Market and International Food Court, 928 S. Western Avenue, Koreatown, CENTRAL, 213-385-1100. Open daily. In a posh green and mauve marble bilevel shopping mall, the splashy Koreatown Plaza Market keeps company with a group of chic Euro-mode boutiques. There's validated parking and a drive-up grocery-loading area in the plaza's covered lot. The sparkling, brightly lit store has adopted many packaging and merchandising techniques from the Japanese.

The merchandise, however, is undeniably Korean. Frozen mandu filled with meat or vegetables are good to have on hand when a dumpling craving hits. You simply boil or steam the mandu and serve them with a soy-vinegar dipping sauce or in soup. In the state-of-the-art meat and seafood department, which seems about a city block long, you'll find precut sashimi, assorted clams, and fish in the round. Imaginative cooks will find many uses for the presliced beef and pork, and short ribs are butchered for bulgogi, kalbi, stewed dishes, and soups. The aisles burst with dozens of varieties of seaweed and dry and fresh noodles, either plain or with convenient sauce or soup packets.

In the produce department look for minari, *kongnamul* (soy-bean sprouts larger than the usual mung bean variety), and *hangkuk kochu* (almond-sized fresh red and green semihot peppers).

Part of the fun of shopping at Koreatown Plaza Market is a visit to the **International Food Court** just outside its doors. It's a microcosm of Koreatown's specialty restaurants. **Korean Express** (213-480-0387) has a hot table where you can look over the braised casseroles, assorted kimchees, stir-fries, and rice cakes in neon red sauce, and point to what appeals. **Boh Tong Zip** (213-480-0679) offers meal-in-a-bowl soups and buckwheat noodles called naeng myun. These grayish brown chewy noodles are an acquired taste—especially the bland *mool* naeng myun in a pool of chilled beef broth—but Koreans love them. The best item, I think, is kalbi tang a beef rib soup with rice, or the very spicy *yukgejang,* a peppery broth loaded with flank steak. If you love mandu don't pass up **Panda Dumpling** (213-385-1881). The server there insisted I would like the steamed or fried dumplings best. These come with fluorescent yellow turnip pickles, kimchee, and a soy dipping sauce. Panda also serves up water dumplings (boiled) and monumental-sized servings of mandu in soup with wisps of egg garnishing the soup's surface.

THAILAND

The flamboyant cooking in the first bare-bones Los Angeles Thai restaurants was a flavor revelation. It used chiles in completely new ways, combining them with creamy coconut milk, lively herbs, and a sweetness that seduced us.

Chiles weren't the only thing that made this food hot. A good Thai meal cost little more than a burger and fries. And it wasn't long before it was just as handy: The L.A. Thai Chamber of Commerce estimates Los Angeles now has at least 350 Thai restaurants—that's more than any other city in the world outside of Thailand.

The intense competition spurred restaurateurs to lure customers with high-tech rainbow neon, rock music, and midnight delivery. They lowered their chile quotient and cut down on the smelly fish sauces. But most restaurants served the same handful of popular dishes that all Thai food lovers know by heart: sates, mee krob, and tom kha kai. It was as though a standard menu for every Thai restaurant had been ordained by Buddha.

A trip I took through different regions of Thailand introduced me to all sorts of dishes I'd never tasted before. And when I returned to L.A., Thai friends took me to restaurants that served these regional foods. There was more to L.A.'s Thai food, I discovered, than the Buddha-ordained menus; there were noodle shops, dessert stores, dinner cabarets featuring popular entertainers from Thailand, and even a Thai breakfast joint.

Now a few restaurateurs recognize that some of us, having mastered the finer points of pad thai and tom yam kung, are ready for something new, and regional dishes are beginning to work their way onto mainstream menus. These dishes would not have been as authentic ten years ago, but Thai chefs can get better ingredients now. Imports have escalated and local farmers grow and supply the marketplace with typical Thai produce: kaffir lime, morning glory leaves, and those pale green golf-ball-sized eggplants.

⸺ THAI GLOSSARY ⸺

Gwaytio: Fresh rice noodles; gwaytio sen lek are thin fresh rice noodles.

Gwaytio lod: A rolled uncut sheet of fresh rice noodle with meat or seafood and vegetable stuffing.

Gwaytio rangsit: This spicy beef and rice noodle soup, often made with organ meats, is named for a Bangkok suburb where vendors once sold it from portable boat kitchens along the klong (a canallike waterway).

Hormok: This custardlike mixture of minced fish, coconut milk, lime leaves, and seasonings is steamed either in clay cups or wrapped in banana leaves. Hormok is also made with chicken.

Isaan cooking: The spicy cooking style of Thailand's northeastern provinces.

Joke: A relative of the Chinese congee (or jook), joke is rice cooked to a smooth purée in broth. It is served topped with assorted condiments.

Kaeng (or gaeng): The word means liquid, and it also refers to soups and soupy curries. Kaeng leung, for example, is a yellow southern-style soupy fish curry with fermented bamboo shoots; kaeng hung lae, is a red, northern-style pork and garlic curry; kaeng kae is a yellow northern-style chicken and vegetable curry; kaeng tai pla is a yellow southern-style curry flavored with pickled fish stomach.

Kaeng (or gaeng) rong pla bang: An Issan-style hot and sour soup made with freshwater fish.

Kaffir lime: Only the leaves and

---

rind of this tropical lime are used in curries, soups, and salads. The leaves, called bai makrut, are available dried and occasionally fresh, while the rind, pew makrut, usually comes dried (and often ground).

Kai yang: Barbecued chicken originally from northeastern Thailand.

Kanom: The word means "little cakes" and refers to sweetmeats made from wheat, rice, or tapioca flours, mixed with coconut milk. Kanom may also be fashioned from agar or other gelatinous substances. Desserts that are more puddinglike are not called kanom.

Kapi: A fermented fish or shrimp paste used as a seasoning.

Keap moo: Northern-style light and crispy deep-fried pork rinds often eaten with nam prik oong.

Kha: Known as galangal in English, this is a relative of ginger but has a taste all its own. Kha is sold sliced and dried in packages, and can occasionally be found fresh.

Khao soi: A northern noodle dish in a creamy, soupy yellow curry, served with many condiments on the side.

Khao tom: A rice soup, with chunks of chicken, meat, or seafood.

Kra-thong-tong (also gah-thong thong): Tiny pastry shells filled with ground meat and vegetables served as an appetizer.

Kra-tip: A northeastern-style three-legged basket used to serve sticky rice.

Larb: A northeastern-style warm salad of grilled minced meat or fish dressed with lime juice, dry chile, and roasted rice powder. Larb is usually made with beef or chicken, but larbs made with duck (larb pet) and freshwater fish (larb paduk) are also popular.

Mee: The name for thin noodles. Mee includes ba mee (egg noodles), and sen mee (rice vermicelli). The later is the major ingredient in mee krob, a dish of deep-fried rice noodles with a sweet dressing.

Mussaman curry: A yellow curry—the word is a corruption of the word Muslim—borrowed from India, which includes non-Thai spices such as cinnamon and nutmeg.

Naem sod: A warm salad of sautéed ground pork with herbs and ginger in a lime-chile dressing.

Nam pla: A clear liquid sauce made from fermented fish. Known as the soy sauce of Thailand, it is the cuisine's major seasoning.

Nam prik num: A thick green vegetable curry from northern Thailand usually eaten with sticky rice.

Nam prik oong: A northern-style thick red chili sauce made with ground pork, usually accompanied with sticky rice.

Nem: A raw-cured sausage fermented with large quantities of garlic, chiles, and rice.

Neua dad deal: Thai-style beef jerky.

Neua nam tok: A salad of sliced beef and lettuce in a lime-chile dressing.

Panaeng: A dry red curry paste, usually used with beef and always cooked with coconut milk.

Phed: The term for chile heat in Thai.

Pla kung (or goong): A shrimp salad dressed with a chile and lime-juice dressing. The best versions are made with charcoal-grilled shrimp.

Sai krog: Northern-style pork sausage usually served grilled.

Sataw: A highly odoriferous beanlike tree fruit favored by southern Thais. Pad sataw is a stir-fry containing sataw.

Sate: Small pieces of marinated meat, skewered, charbroiled, and served with a dipping sauce (peanut sauce is the most common).

Seua rong hai: Literally means "it makes a tiger cry," referring to the spicy heat of a tamarind-chile dipping sauce served with grilled, sliced steak.

Som tam: A salad of shredded unripe papaya topped with dry shrimp and roasted peanuts and an exceptionally hot lime-chile dressing.

Sup nor mai: An extremely spicy northeastern-style salad of sour shredded bamboo shoots.

Tom kha kai: Chicken and coconut milk soup flavored with kha, chile, and lemon grass.

Tom yam kung (or goong): Also called hot and sour shrimp soup, this clear shrimp broth is flavored with lime juice, lemon grass, and chile. The chicken version is tom yam kai.

NEW CALIFORNIA THAI

A few Thai restaurants that clearly cater to an American clientele are becoming more adventurous with their offerings and more stylish with their presentation—as though a Franco-Japanese chef were looking over the shoulder of a Thai grandmother, adding his refinements.

Talesai, 9043 Sunset Boulevard, West Hollywood, WEST, 310-275-9724. Lunch and dinner; closed Sunday. At Talesai, a lovely art-filled restaurant, Prakas Yen-bamroong was one of the first Thai restaurateurs (serving a non-Thai clientele) to put larb, the searingly hot meat salad from northeastern Thailand, on his menu. He also offered the seldom seen hormok: a savory, creamy coconut custard studded with chunks of seafood and spiked with galangal and Thai basil.

Over the years Talesai's food has acquired certain delightful nouvelle leanings: Grilled salmon, presented in one piece as it would be in the West, is napped with a chile-coconut sauce of clearly Thai origins. "Super-wild" grilled shrimp in a chile-lime juice sauce is a deluxe update (larger shrimp and less fish sauce) of the traditional Thai "naked shrimp."

The much newer Valley **Talesai** (11744 Ventura Boulevard, Studio City, S.F. VALLEY, 818-753-1001) has introduced the sate bar to L.A. Sizzling skewers of marinated meats, chicken and even shrimp plus a handful of Bangkok-style street foods are lightened up by this stylish restaurant's chefs. You can nibble your way through a whole range of mostly unfamiliar but delicious little tastes. The bar is the perfect spot for single diners too.

Suvanee Siam, 713 E. Garvey Avenue, Monterey Park, SAN GABRIEL VALLEY, 818-280-8655. Lunch and dinner daily. Food-lovers usually equate Monterey Park with either posh Hong Kong–style live-seafood restaurants or hole-in-the-wall noodle joints with fabulous food. A meal at Monterey Park's Suvanee Siam might get them thinking in a new direction. As to ambience, it's a stylish little boite—powder-gray walls are splashed artily with fruit sherbet colors matched by the tablecloths and the Mexican stoneware dishes. The menu features colored photographs of some of the beautifully garnished presentations. But what impresses even more is the kitchen's meticulous attention to detail. Crispy fried catfish sits in a pool of intense red sauce and is scattered with whole fresh Thai basil leaves. A salad of meaty duck strips over crisp spinach leaves comes garnished with little flowers carved from red peppers. These sensations are some of the best examples of what made us love Thai food in the first place.

Tusk Thai Cuisine, 10925 W. Pico Boulevard, West Los Angeles, WEST, 310-470-7570. Lunch and dinner daily. A sleek marble floor paves the entryway leading into to Thai Tusk's well-appointed East-West dining room, where you can recline on Thai triangular floor pillows to dine traditionally, or choose a Western-style table. Thai Tusk's food reflects the same multicultural mix. A sumptuous duck salad with Thai ginger dressing mimics a popular California-French salad: lean shreds of duck meat and sliced mushrooms are laid over a bed of fresh spinach leaves and topped with strips of crispy duck skin. There's also a palate-detonating green curry, a dish that's seldom found in Cal-Thai restaurants. And Thai Tusk keeps a well-bred selection of California wines.

Talking Thai, 119–121 Broadway, Santa Monica, WEST, 310-451-2483. Lunch and dinner; closed Monday. On their large, curving, boldly colored platters, Talking Thai's lunch combinations appear like little set pieces with vegetable art as a backdrop. This high-ceilinged, airy trattorialike space across from I. Cugini, an Italian restaurant in Santa Monica, attracts shoppers from Santa Monica Place and an early evening business crowd. But it deserves to have a much wider audience. On the menu, most selections may seem like the same familiar dishes, but pla goong, the spicy shrimp salad, rings with the sharp intensity of shredded kaffir lime leaf—an ingredient most places leave out. Other dishes are indicative of Talking Thai's adventurous bent. Several northeastern Isaan selections come presented with a style far from their rustic roots, and the spicy beef curry salad with noodles alone is worth a journey.

L.A.'S REGIONAL THAI RESTAURANTS

◆ NORTHERN THAI RESTAURANTS

A good place to get the feel of a northern regional meal is **Alisa** (2812 W. 9th Street, Los Angeles [one block east of Vermont], CENTRAL, 213-384-7049 or 487-1927; open 10:30 A.M. to 10:00 P.M. daily)—Chao Nue in Thai—a quintessential "hole in the wall." The modest dining room sports handwoven tablecloths and souvenir fans from the city of Chiang Mai.

You'll usually be offered the menu bearing the restaurant's English name. It lists a humdrum collection of central Thailand-style dishes. But check your table and you'll probably find a menu of northern dishes, handwritten in Thai; an English version is available for the asking.

Order the two staples of northern cooking: nam prik oong, a red ground-meat chili, and nam prik num, a green vegetable chile. Another good dish to try with these is *jin bing,* Alisa's garlicky grilled marinated pork. Then sit back and wait for the parade of dishes.

Sticky rice comes in a little straw basket; as you lift the lid, a waft of fragrant steam floats out. A platter of vegetables is served to munch on or dip into the nam prik dishes. You might also want to order keap moo to dip into your nam prik oong. These light-as-air crisps of deep-fried pork skin are sold in the open markets everywhere in the north; Thai tourists buy bags of them to take back home.

Alisa also serves kaeng, or soupy "wet curries." If you are lucky, kaeng hung lae will be one of that day's special curries. It's a fabulous long-simmered mixture of pork, spices, slivers of ginger, and whole garlic cloves cooked until they turn soft and sweet. There's also a mild red beef curry, kaeng *hom,* and kaeng kae, a strong yellow curry with a mixture of vegetables, pea-sized bitter eggplant, long beans, chicken, and much more. (Note: Alisa's parking lot is several buildings west of the restaurant.)

V.P. Cafe, 4814 Melrose

NORTHERN THAI FOOD

The central Thailand-style food that most Thai restaurants serve has aristocratic roots. Its major influence, the royal palace kitchens, is evident in such fancy dishes as deep-fried stuffed chicken wings and carved vegetables. And because Chinese own a good portion of Thailand's urban eating places, it often includes lots of Chinese-inspired food. But in northern Thailand, in the area around Chiang Mai, the food changes dramatically. People eat sticky rice, which they roll into little balls to pick up morsels of food. To accommodate this eating style, most foods are cut into small pieces or chopped and sharply seasoned with lots of garlic, lemon grass, and "dry" curry mixtures. Chiang Mai, often called "hog butcher to the nation," has a reputation for good pork dishes and charcuterie, especially the pungent nem. This dry-cured sausage isn't cooked, but rather pickled in massive amounts of garlic and chile.

Avenue, Hollywood, CENTRAL, 213-663-7079. Open 10:00 A.M. to 9:00 P.M. daily. The V.P. Cafe on Melrose serves nam prik oong and nam prik num with a nice subtle glow without the hot-pepper buildup evident in most authentic Thai food. Their kaeng hung lae is also an exceptionally mellow version.

Khao soi, a Thai/Burmese-style noodle dish sold around every corner in northern Thai cities, is a bowlful of fine flat egg noodles in a creamy curry sauce topped with crispy fried noodles. As with many Thai dishes, you can add your own garnishes, which include minced shallots, chili sauce, and pickled Chinese greens.

You'll find the V.P.'s northern dishes written in Thai at the back of its standard menu. The café also has a translated northern menu for the asking.

♦ ISAAN RESTAURANTS

Renu Nakorn, 13041 E. Rosecrans Avenue, Norwalk, SOUTH, 310-921-2124. Lunch and dinner; closed Monday. A few Isaan dishes, such as larb, and Isaan barbecue chicken (kai yang), have long been seen on mainstream Thai menus in L.A. But at Renu Nakorn in Norwalk, situated between a barbershop and a fishing tackle store, the selection goes well beyond a few popular items. And with them comes the requisite sticky rice and an authentic array of side condiments and vegetables—the only proper way to eat Isaan foods.

Norwalk may seem an unlikely place to discover Thailand's most exotic dishes. But when you are brought seua rong hai, sup nor mai, and No. 29, a dish of minced lightly cooked beef lavished with fresh mint and fresh cilantro, you'll know why this place is worth the drive.

One of my favorite items at Renu Nakorn is the deep-fried

Isaan Food:
Dishes from Thailand's
Northeastern Provinces

I n the northeast, or Isaan, region of Thailand, the cooking is rustic, uncomplicated, and extremely spicy. Isaan cooks transform a limited range of ingredients into glorious fusions of taste and texture: Meats are simply charcoal-grilled, or served raw, and accompanied with fiery dipping sauces. Or they are sliced and tossed with chile and lime into fresh herb-filled salads. The Isaan eat the northern-style sticky rice, as well as food that shows more Cambodian influences than central Thailand food.

Isaan regional cooking has recently become wildly popular among foodies in Bangkok. But the people who first brought this region's food to the city were northeastern rice farmers, who come to work there between the planting and harvest seasons. Some set up shop as food vendors, catering to other workers from the region. Gradually, certain side streets in Bangkok became known for the enticing smell of grilling kai yang wafting from outdoor stalls. The stalls attracted college students, cabbies, and others seeking a supremely tasty meal for small change. Now many of these students are Thai yuppies who live here.

dried beef called neua dad deal. Drying intensifies the beef's flavor; it is succulent and chewy, yet much softer than jerky. With its peppery dipping sauce and accompanying greenery, neua dad deal typifies the finger-food style of the Thai northeast. Isaan dishes are listed under the "Renu Nakorn Special" category. Others, which your waiter can translate, are written in Thai on a small card attached to the menu; these are the best dishes to order.

Thai Villa, 5921 South Street, Lakewood, SOUTH, 310-920-3785 or 867-9118. Lunch and dinner; closed Monday. Neither Thai Villa's sign ("Thai and Chinese Food") nor its menu, with such very familiar offerings as mee krob, shrimp tempura, and cashew chicken, inspire much curiosity. But keep reading and you'll find lots of Isaan dishes and sticky rice (called "sweet rice") served in a kra-tip. In Thailand, these woven baskets on small legs transport a typical meal of rice, salted fish, and a spicy sauce to the fields.

The best dishes one evening were the warm bamboo shoot salad with a traditional chile-lime roasted-rice dressing hot enough to smelt copper. The red pepper–spiced chicken larb and the spicy Thai stewed beef soup (No. 10) were polished off down to the last green-bean garnish. But nearly all the dried fish fried with Chinese greens was taken home for someone's cat. There is entertainment—usually a popular Thai singer—on weekend evenings.

Thai Nakorn Restaurant, 8674 Stanton Avenue, Buena Park, OCOUNTY, 714-952-4954. Lunch and dinner; closed Monday. In many northeastern provinces near the Laos border, the people are of Lao extraction. And at Thai Nakorn, located just at the edge of Knotts Berry Farm in Buena Park, this influence is particularly apparent in a dish like gaeng rong pla bang, a hot and sour soup with whole catfish slices, sweet Asian pumpkin, and oyster mushrooms. The dish, from the unskinned fish to the pungent tamarind leaves and large pieces of lemon grass stalk, might be a tad too native for some palates—my group ate only half of it.

On the other hand, there was nothing left of the catfish larb (*larb paduk*), the *lin nam tok* (slightly chewy but succulent barbecued beef tongue slices on a bed of salad), and the Isaan-style grilled sausage. The sausage comes accompanied with slivered ginger, roasted peanuts, shallots, and whole chiles, along with cabbage leaves for wrapping the various tidbits. You eat your choice of these condiments with each sausage slice and with the sticky rice that arrives in a classic Isaan-style kra-tip basket. Many more Isaan items are written in Thai on a little chalkboard above the kitchen door, and the owner will happily help you organize an Isaan meal.

Pi Yai Restaurant (Yai), 5757 Hollywood Boulevard, Hollyood, CENTRAL, 213-462-0292. Open 11:00 A.M. to 10:00 P.M.; closed Tuesday. When Thais in central L.A. have a craving for Isaan food you're likely to find them at Yai in Hollywood, a beige-and-linoleum-decorated café next to a Seven-11 market. Yai isn't, strictly speaking, an Isaan restaurant, but its Isaan dishes taste authentic and, almost as important, the menu is translated into English. A chat with the owner garnered a checklist of Yai's Isaan dishes (Nos. 5 through 8 and 13 through 16 on the front page of the menu). Som tam and sup nor mai are incredible foils for Yai's pork sate and barbecued chicken, which, though well flavored, are deliciously bland by contrast.

◆ **A SOUTHERN THAI RESTAURANT** Several restaurants in Los Angeles serve a southern dish or two, but the best place for *ahan pak thai* (southern Thai food) is **Satang Thai** (8247 Woodman Avenue [at Roscoe], Panorama City, S.F. VALLEY, 818-989-5637; lunch through dinner; closed Tuesday). There's no mention of southern dishes on Satang's printed menu, but at least four are available daily. The most popular of the four is kaeng leung, an ultrahot sour curry of catfish and broad slabs of bamboo shoot with fermented overtones. Like most southern Thai kaengs, the heat is not modified with coconut milk. And its taste is one that even the staunchest champion of unique Thai flavors must adapt to. The same can be said for kaeng tai pla, an explosively seasoned soupy curry made with cashew nuts, vegetables, and pickled fish stomach. These and most other southern Thai meals are accompanied with a plate of varied raw vegetables. You munch these in between bites to refresh your palate.

More appealing, perhaps, to Western tastes is *pla kabog tod:* a

In the far southern provinces of Thailand, where Muslim mosques with gilded domes take the place of Buddhist temples, the curries are renowned for their assertive pungency. Isaan food may be hot, but southern cooking is what *Bangkok Post* restaurant writer Ung Aang Talay once dubbed "the limit of phedness": as hot as food can possibly get.

delicious, crispy, deep-fried, dried fish garnished with fresh chile slices, red onion, and lime. Satang's final southern offering, pad sataw, is a stir-fry of pork, chicken, and shrimp with a highly aromatic beanlike vegetable. The advice someone once gave me regarding limburger cheese definitely applies to sataw: "If you don't breathe while you eat it, you'll love it."

Many of Satang's nonsouthern specialties are also excellent. Try the delicious mussels steamed with chile and lemon grass, or the gingery naem sod sprinkled with peanuts.

CLASSIC L.A. THAI

Jitlada Restaurant, 5233½ Sunset Boulevard, Hollywood, CENTRAL, 213-667-9809. Lunch and dinner; closed Monday. "Jitlada," Thais always say when I ask them for the name of a great Thai restaurant. Never mind that it's in a dusty, nondescript storefront. When you step inside you find two rooms tastefully decorated with traditional Thai artifacts and tables draped in linen. Jitlada also has two menus: one printed only in Thai, from which all the Thais seem to be ordering, and the "tourist" menu, from which you can still get a wonderful meal. We saw a platter of giant prawns go by (minilobsters actually) and told our

waiter, "Bring us those." A bowl of creamy green curry with stuffed fish balls on the next table looked wonderful; it was. Jitlada is still introducing L.A. to some of the best central Thailand-style food anywhere.

Jitlada West, 11622 Ventura Boulevard, Studio City, S.F. VALLEY, 818-506-9355 or 769-4831. Lunch and dinner Monday through Friday; dinner only Saturday and Sunday. Jitlada West, no longer associated with the more authentic Hollywood Jitlada, manages to be among the best California-style Thai restaurants in the Valley. And given the overwhelming abundance of Thai places there, that's saying a great deal. The setting, food, and prices are upscale Thai. My fried catfish was seasoned just right—hot but mellowed out with coconut cream—nothing that would make you dive for your beer. Sautéed asparagus, perfectly crunchy, was marred by the addition of synthetic bacon bits, but the Thai sausage salad, though made with Chinese sausage, had a pleasantly refreshing lime juice dressing and good greens. One thing is missing—the really hot green curry most authentic and adventurous restaurants serve.

Tommy Tang's, 7473 Melrose Avenue, Los Angeles, CENTRAL, 310-651-1810. Lunch and dinner daily; closed Sunday. Can Tommy Tang's, on seriously trendy Melrose, be a serious Thai restaurant? When Tang was the chef at Chan Dara he helped the restaurant build a reputation for excellent food. At his own restaurant he's stayed on top of the trends, installing a sushi bar and adding Cal-Thai dishes to the menu. Tang also demystified Thai cooking with his how-to-cook-Thai-food video, and he expanded to a New York outpost. Tommy's food, while California-esque, doesn't stint on the chiles; it's fresh and bright and not too sweet and, in short, worth considering if you want to catch the trendy scene in Tommy's neighborhood.

Chan Dara, 1511 N. Cahuenga Boulevard, Hollywood, CENTRAL, 213-464-8585; 310 N. Larchmont Boulevard, Los Angeles, CENTRAL, 213-467-1052; 11940 W. Pico Boulevard, West Los Angeles, WEST, 310-479-4461. Chan Dara is nearly as trendy as Tommy Tang's, serving well-made versions of all our old Thai favorites. But I can't recommend the yuppified Pico Boulevard branch unless you don't mind eating overpriced, only slightly better than average Thai while forgoing any dinner conversation and risking a splitting headache from the din.

Thai 'n I, 17544 Ventura Boulevard, Encino, S.F. VALLEY, 818-783-8424. Lunch and dinner; closed Monday. Thai 'n I on Ventura Boulevard, a citified version of Thailand's kai yang stalls, has its barbecue facing the street enclosed in glass. You can smell the smoke, and the sight of those sizzling chickens and Thai-style ribs is a real lure. And so is the taste. It's irresistibly garlicky, heightened by a sweet-hot dipping sauce. There's also a basic menu of Thai soups, salads, and entrées. Stir-fried chicken and green beans in a sauce of roasted chiles is one that will really call your taste buds to attention.

Anajak Thai, 14704 Ventura Boulevard, Sherman Oaks, S.F. VALLEY, 818-501-4201. Lunch and dinner; dinner only Saturday and Sunday; closed Monday. Anajak Thai, another Valley favorite, was where we discovered years ago that mee krob didn't have to taste like Cracker Jacks. And chef owner Ricky Pichetrungsl keeps us on our toes with his ever evolving special dishes. Lately it's been *kai ho kao phoed* (marinated chicken

chunks wrapped in corn husks, then broiled and served with sate sauce) and New Zealand mussels steamed with lemon grass, with a chile-lime sauce on the side. And even his everyday offerings—beef sate and coconut-chicken soup—are pleasantly fresh.

Siamese Restaurant, 1628 E. 7th Street, Long Beach, SOUTH, 310-436-3123. Lunch through dinner daily. Siamese Restaurant started 13 years ago with a small dining room and a cook who grilled chicken over charcoal on a hibachi. That chicken made Siamese famous, and the restaurant has evolved over the years to keep an increasingly sophisticated clientele satisfied. The new two-room dining area has an imported marble floor from Thailand and comfortable booths.

The chow mein and chop suey that have been on the menu for years are still there. But the sautéed chicken with almonds and whole chiles, the crunchy shrimp rolls, and the *tom kha kai* are what keep Long Beach Thai-food-loving customers coming back.

Sompun, 4156 Santa Monica Boulevard, Los Angeles, CENTRAL, 213-669-9906 or 661-5350. Lunch through dinner; closed Tuesday. During the era of clone Thai menus, Sompun went its own way. It served many dishes not usually found on the Buddha-ordained menus, and the food tasted as if it was cooked for Thais. The restaurant served more and better noodle dishes than anyone. Even today you'll find dishes that seem quite original: zucchini scrambled with egg, mushrooms, and garlic; eggplant stir-fried with mint, green chile, and a little black bean sauce. With its peaked entry and charming garden, the restaurant is a little bit of Thai heaven hidden away where Santa Monica obscurely meets Sunset.

Because they cater primarily to a Thai clientele, these restaurants offer specialties and sometimes use ingredients not found in the majority of everyday Thai neighborhood restaurants.

♦ **NOODLES**

Sanamluang Cafe, 5176 Hollywood Boulevard, Hollywood, CENTRAL, 213-660-8006; open 10:00 A.M. to 5:00 A.M. daily. 12980 Sherman Way, North Hollywood, S.F. VALLEY, 818-764-1180; open 10:00 A.M. to midnight. Also in Pomona, OCOUNTY. The three Sanamluang Cafes serve more kinds of noodles than you'll ever see on other restaurant menus. The Hollywood branch is jammed to the rafters around 2:00 A.M., and, if it is a warm night, the crowd spills outside.

In a dish called "General's Noodle," mee, fine egg noodles, are topped with barbecued pork, roast duck, and a few shrimp, then sprinkled with crushed roasted peanuts and scallions. "Emperor's Noodles" are made with gwaytio sen lek, the flat fresh rice noodles; these came lightly fried, with chicken, seafood, and egg scrambled into them. Indian curry noodle, another good choice, is flat rice noodles in a rich coconut milk sauce with peanuts, hard-cooked egg, and slices of beef.

Sanamluang has much more than noodles. Their salad of roast duck slices, dressed with a sweet-tart-hot lime dressing and lots of crunchy red onions and herbs, is always a nice counterpoint to the pasta dishes. And the restaurants are a good source for joke and khao tom, but only after 10:00 P.M.

Sunshine Thai Restaurant, 861 N. Western Avenue, Koreatown, CENTRAL, 213-462-0234. Open 11:00 A.M. to 11:00 P.M.; closed Sunday. Many people I know love this tiny café for its great noodle dishes, but Thais often go for the desserts. On a table near the door, a row of cooking pots is filled with foods that can only be described as warm puddings. Such exotica as cassava cubes in a slightly sweet syrup are spooned out into a bowl and smothered in rich, creamy coconut milk. Other "puddings" include cooking bananas, large tapioca balls, or sweet black beans. For many years Sunshine was the only place that made mango and sticky rice, the Thais' favorite sweet.

The dessert table, which has a large following of take-out customers, is only one of the reasons Sunshine has survived at least a dozen years. It's the kitchen's authenticity and attention to freshness that has made its home-style foods stand out.

♦ **CURRIES AND KANOM**

• **Indra,** 517 S. Verdugo Road (at Maple), Glendale, S.F. VALLEY, 818-247-3176. Lunch through dinner; closed Monday.

• **Khun Kao,** 13550 Roscoe Boulevard, Panorama City, S.F. VALLEY, 818-786-6969. Lunch and dinner; closed Monday.

Like their counterparts in Thailand, these two family-run curry kitchens offer a changing daily selection of specials plus an extensive menu at rock-bottom prices. At both places, where children may be doing their homework or coloring at a corner table, you get the feeling you're in an extended family. Indra, Formica-plain on a shady tree-lined street, is a hangout for Glendale Thais who drop by at any time of day. A monk dressed in saffron robes was eating there one time I visited.

Both restaurants make homemade Thai desserts known as kanom. An array of sweets and colorful jellies is displayed in a glass case. One of my favorites, banana and sweet sticky rice, is steamed in fragrant banana leaf packets. An almost chewy cassava pudding is topped with snowy whipped coconut cream and a single rose petal for decoration. The changing assortment might include squares of Asian pumpkin custard to be eaten in slices, and bite-sized taro balls stuffed with sweet-salty ground pork.

At Khun Kao, business is particularly brisk on weekends when Thais congregate at Wat Thai, the Buddhist Temple nearby. On weekends there's a "chef's specialties" menu written in Thai, which the owner translated for me. From it I ordered a marvelous plate of deep-fried mussels stir-fried with egg and vegetables—a Thai Hangtown fry of sorts. The mild dish came with a flaming red dipping sauce on the side.

Renoo's Kitchen, 3960 Beverly Boulevard, Hollywood, CENTRAL, 213-480-8786. Open 9:00 A.M. to 10:30 P.M. daily. Renoo's Kitchen, a small and rather drab dining room across from the Cathay Market on Beverly Boulevard, is reminiscent of neighborhood curry kitchens you still see in Thai towns and urban neighborhoods. Renoo's has an impressive hot table spread with intense earthy-colored curries and other ready-to-go dishes. The offerings rotate throughout the day, so you are never sure exactly what will be available. But for $3.25 you can get a huge mound of rice and two substantial selections.

Renoo's daily specials are posted on the wall in Thai. But the servers behind the counter can show you what they are. On Friday there's *mi gati,* thin rice noodles in a coconut milk sauce that are a favorite with children. Wednesdays Renoo's serves the famous noodle soup gwaytio rangsit. The rich, spicy-beef-and-meatball broth is garnished with pieces of lightly cooked liver (they'll omit the liver on request) and topped with deep-fried garlic slices, fresh herbs, and puffs of pork rind.

From 7:30 A.M., Renoo's offers comforting Thai breakfasts of khao tom or joke. Both are topped with your choice of chicken or meat and egg, and garnished with ginger and herbs. Renoo's has a good translated menu of cooked-to-order dishes too.

♦ **SUPPER CLUBS**

Palm Restaurant, 5273 Hollywood Boulevard, Hollywood, CENTRAL, 213-462-5073. Open 11:00 A.M. to 1:00 A.M. daily. I discovered the Palm (and the whole Thai cabaret scene) by accident. A friend had recommended it for Isaan food, and I expected a quiet storefront restaurant. But when we walked in one Saturday evening, we could barely hear the hostess over the din of a Thai rock combo. When the music stopped, a stand-up comedienne took the small stage and soon had the group in a state of side-splitting laughter. She was followed by a young woman singing slow ballads in Thai.

As for the Isaan food, the Palm has a small but good selection. Thais prefer these spicy dishes with alcoholic drinks. They're not really considered dinner, rather something to nibble between sips. The Palm also serves reasonably good familiar Thai fare.

Tepparod Thai Restaurant, 5151 Hollywood Boulevard, Hollywood, CENTRAL, 213-667-9800. Lunch and dinner until 3:00 A.M.; closed Monday. In the early days of Los Angeles Thai restaurants, Tepparod Thai was part of a small family-owned chain. These days, with only two restaurants in the family, Tepparod Thai owner Chow Burana concentrates on bringing popular recording stars from Thailand to sing at his cabaret. But with three performers

Entertainment imported from Thailand at Tepparod Thai Restaurant in Hollywood.

each night and no cover charge, expect to find talent drawn from the local pool of Thai entertainers too.

Whenever a big-name singer appears at Tepparod, Burana advertises in several local Thai newspapers. On those occasions, unless you arrive before 9:00 P.M. you may not find a seat in the tiny cabaret.

The best things to eat are Tepparod's grilled sates, and their seafood salads with a distinctively smoky flavor. Try pla goong: butterflied char-grilled shrimp on lettuce with a lemon-grass-infused chile-lime dressing. Tepparod's thick, rich curry dishes are a good contrast to the salad's sharp flavors.

♦ JOKE

Torung, 5657 Hollywood Boulevard, Hollywood, CENTRAL, 213-464-9074. Open 5:00 P.M. to 4:00 A.M. nightly. When the discos close and all the partying is over, Thais head for specialty shops or the night market stalls that sell warm soothing bowls of khao tom (rice soup) or joke (rice porridge). Either dish will remedy the ills of too much drink or, like a glass of milk, lull you to sleep. As bland as these may sound, they become a feast of contrasts in the hands of Thai cooks. Chicken, pork, or seafood go into the basic soups, along with an optional raw egg that cooks in the scalding broth. Sprinkled over all of this are plenty of fresh ginger slivers and a few leaves of fresh coriander. Chinese sausage, pickled Chinese greens, and other sharp-tasting accompaniments are often ordered on the side.

Torung serves my favorite version of joke. The menu is translated into English, but you may still want to consult your waiter if you don't know what such additions as "ancient egg" or "preserved vegetable salad" might be. Torung's other Thai food is right up there with the best.

Torung's other dishes, such as the raw shrimp salad bathed in garlic-laden chile-lime dressing and called "dancing shrimp," are deservedly popular with Thais.

GOOD NEIGHBORHOOD SPOTS

Gulf of Siam, 22984 Ventura Boulevard, Woodland Hills, S.F. VALLEY, 818-702-8721. Lunch and dinner; Sunday, dinner only. The suitably named Gulf of Siam has the longest list of seafood items— more than 25 shrimp dishes, for example—I've found in a Thai restaurant, and their quality is consistently high. Prices for certain dishes are just a tad higher than the norm. But seafood lovers will appreciate the lack of iodine-tasting clams and flabby shrimp that often find their way into seafood dishes at many Thai restaurants. The cooking is also exemplary, and nonseafood dishes are priced competitively. I can especially recommend the deep-fried Siamese scallops topped with an only-slightly-fiery chili sauce.

Pataya Cafe, 1525 E. Colorado Boulevard, Pasadena, SAN GABRIEL VALLEY, 818-356-0404. Lunch through dinner Monday to Saturday; Sunday lunch and dinner. Pataya Cafe, across from Pasadena City College, advertises low prices, but this charming place has much more. There's an enclosed patio garden with a gurgling fountain, and a separate menu of vegetarian dishes filled with wonderful-sounding curries. A small selection of Isaan dishes includes the authentic sticky rice. Pataya's spicy salads don't stint on the chiles, nor does the beef in green curry.

Natalee Thai Cuisine, 10036 Venice Boulevard, Culver City, WEST, 310-202-7003. Lunch through dinner daily. Just a block from M-G-M Studios, Natalee gets a sprinkling of Hollywood power-lunch types. Like most authentic Thai restaurants, Natalee puts those caddies holding jars of tiny fresh and dry chiles on the tables in case you find your tom kha gai or disco shrimp (pla koong) too mild. The kra-thong-tong—those little pastry cups filled with ground chicken and vegetables—are Natalee's most popular appetizer.

Thai Tiffany, 2211 Pacific Coast Highway, Lomita, SOUTH, 310-539-8878 or 539-8923. Lunch and dinner Monday to Friday; dinner Saturday and Sunday. With its flower-filled room appointed with Thai statues and artifacts, Thai Tiffany is my choice for the best Thai food in the South Bay. The larb is plenty spicy, the mee krob not too sweet, and a dish called ''noodles supreme'' (a spicy rice noodle stir-fry with mint and chiles) is aptly named.

Thai Dynasty, 208 E. Valley Boulevard, Alhambra, SAN GABRIEL VALLEY, 818-289-6378. Lunch and dinner daily. Plenty of Isaan dishes, sticky rice, and exotic finds like *nam ya* curry (fresh rice noodles topped with minced fish) in coconut milk and fish, and hormok *thalay* offer something for the adventurous. There is also a full range of popular standards in this dazzlingly neoned dining room.

D. J. Thai, 15207 Sunset Boulevard, Pacific Palisades, WEST, 310-459-9927. Lunch through dinner daily. D.J. started out as a plain little take-out joint, then moved into larger quarters in a former Pacific Palisades sushi bar. But size and decor are almost beside the point; D.J.'s appetizers are the main attraction. You can munch sai krog—pieces of the northern-style sausage—and finger foods that include the remarkable combination of peanuts fried with green onions and chiles. Gwaytio lod is a sheet of sheer rice noodle rolled around shrimps and bean sprouts and served with a sweet dipping sauce, and the deep-fried sweet potatoes in a coconut-milk batter come flecked with sesame seeds. There is also a complete lunch and dinner menu.

THAI MARKETS

Bangkok Market, 4757 Melrose Avenue, Los Angeles, CENTRAL, 213-662-9705. Open daily. Bangkok Market was once a rather unkempt little store on the opposite side of Melrose from its present location, now called Bangkok Market, Inc. The supermarketlike new store is much more inviting, especially the well-lit and neatly kept meat department. Frozen foods are now in orderly upright freezer cases instead of the old deep-freeze where you used to find frozen frogs under a pile of packaged young coconut. Bangkok is the retail outlet of a large Thai food importing and produce distribution company that serves many smaller stores around L.A. and Orange County. And it has branches of its wholesale business in San Jose and Texas.

Since the store is so popular with non-Thai cooks, the managers are used to fielding questions about ingredients. This is the place you're likely to get the most assistance finding frozen kha or kapi. The produce section is one of the best in town, and you can usually find several varieties of Thai basil and such unusual vegetables as morning glory leaves and the smelly durian fruit in season. Likewise, the packaged and dry goods include more ingredients than any English-language Thai cookbook would ever call for. There are fresh rice noodles, dozens of chili sauces, and unusual snacks by the check-out counter.

Bangluck Market Inc., 5170 Hollywood Boulevard, Hollywood, CENTRAL, 213-660-8000. Also 12980 Sherman Way, North Hollywood, S.F. VALLEY, 818-765-1088. Also in Pomona, OCOUNTY. The minichain of Bangluck markets—each with a Sanamluang noodle shop and a B.B.Q. Heaven in the same "Bangluck Plaza" has evolved nicely over the past few years. The formerly slightly tacky Valley branch has now moved next door into larger and spiffier quarters, and they've expanded their inventory substantially; the produce department is also excellent.

The hard goods section at the Valley branch has the most astonishing selection of prepared Thai curry pastes I've seen in one spot. In addition to the familiar cans of green, yellow mussaman, and red curry pastes, I came across sour curry paste with tamarind, *Panaeng* curry paste, southern-style gaeng (kaeng) *som* and gaeng (kaeng) tai pla curry pastes among the lot. These are packaged in sizes ranging from a half cup to plastic quart-sized buckets. And I found large packets of chile paste in oil to blend with freshly crushed lemon grass, shallots, and garlic for homemade curries. I have the feeling a good many small restaurants do their shopping here. Despite its other changes, Bangluck still has a wonderfully ornate Thai spirit house, with burning incense and offerings of food on little plates, in the corner of each plaza.

Cathay Supermarket, 3969 Beverly Boulevard, Hollywood, CENTRAL, 213-660-7211. Cathay is a big barnlike store that's a little less spiffy than Bangkok, but you can often get wonderfully exotic produce here. I found pea-sized bitter eggplants and water lily stems—the kind you find in hot and sour soup in authentic Thai restaurants.

Cathay isn't, strictly speaking, a Thai market. But like many Asian markets these days it serves a general Southeast Asian community. And it offers good prices on lemon grass, shallots, fresh coriander (cilantro), and other often-used Thai ingredients.

The best source for Thai ingredients in the South Bay is **Vinh Hao Super Market**, a multi-Asian store that concentrates on Southeast Asian products (see page 118).

L.A. Thai Market, 675 N. Spring Street, Chinatown, CENTRAL, 213-626-0844. In Chinatown, L.A. Thai Market can't hope to compete with the glitz of the Asian superchains. It has concrete floors, and the packaged goods are erratically arranged around its odd configuration. But when I telephone asking for frozen coconut milk, fresh kha (galangal), fresh *bai makrut* (kaffir lime), and fresh gwaytio, they have them all, unlike most of the tiny neighborhood Thai stores all over L.A. And in a nod to the recent trend in stylish markets, L.A. Thai now sports a high-style neon sign.

VIETNAM

It's hard to believe that just over 15 years ago the area we call Little Saigon was a forlorn patchwork of vacant lots, warehouses, and tiny stores. Now two gargantuan malls, Asian Gardens and Asian Plaza, on opposite sides of Bolsa Avenue near Magnolia Street, grab your attention with sweeping Asian architecture and hundreds of bright signs lettered in Vietnamese. The central core of Little Saigon spreads for several miles into Westminster, Garden Grove, and Santa Ana in Orange County, and without a doubt these are the best places to explore the delights and mysteries of Vietnamese food.

In the Asian Plaza, the enormous 99 Price supermarket is surrounded by a jumble of smaller shops and restaurants including Van's Bakery, which carries Western birthday cakes, Chinese sweets, and such Southeast Asian treats as young-coconut milkshakes and sticky rice with sweet plantain rolled in banana leaves. Across the street in the food court of the Asian Gardens mall you can munch on

Vietnamese-style egg rolls or green papaya salad garnished with beef jerky while shopping for gold jewelry or a stereo. Or you can sip a French café filtre at one of the Vietnamese coffee shops.

Other L.A. Vietnamese enclaves in the San Gabriel and San Fernando valleys and in Chinatown have their own restaurants and markets too, but nothing beats Little Saigon for unadulterated culture shock.

Vietnamese cooking is every bit as exotic as Thai and Indian. The country has long been a culinary crossroads: Trade with India introduced curry, while the French brought coffee, bread, and pâté. A thousand years of Chinese occupation contributed tofu, stir-frying, deep-frying, and the noodles that appear at almost every meal, sometimes to wrap in lettuce bundles with charcoal grilled meat, or to be eaten in the national soup dish called pho. As another legacy of its lengthy association with China, Vietnam is the only Southeast Asian country to use chopsticks.

— VIETNAMESE GLOSSARY —

Banh: The word means "cake" but indicates any item made from flour, whether it be rice, wheat, or tapioca flour. Thus banh canh is noodles made from rice and tapioca flours; banh chuoi is bread pudding made with bananas; banh cuon is a steamed rice-flour sheet; banh kong (or banh khot) is a deep-fried rice-flour cake; banh tom chien a deep-fried cake of shredded sweet potatoes; banh trang is rice paper; banh uot is an uncut rice-flour noodle sheet; and banh xeo is an omeletlike flour pancake folded over a filling of pork, shrimp, raw vegetables, and herbs.

Banh chung: Vietnamese New Year cake made of sticky rice filed with cured pork and mung beans. A sweet version with banana instead of meat and beans is banh tet chuoi.

Banh mi: The name for French bread and the Vietnamese submarine sandwiches of coldcuts on French-style rolls. When the ingredients are served as a cold-cut plate with bread on the side the dish is called banh mi dia.

Bo bay mon (bo 7 mon): Beef prepared seven different ways and served as seven courses.

Bo cha dum: Ground beef, clear noodles, and tree ears formed into a large ball and steamed.

Bo ko: Vietnamese-style pork or beef jerky.

Bo nhung dam: Thinly sliced beef

cooked at the table in a vinegar broth; often called "beef fondue."

Bun: Rice vermicelli, this is used hundreds of ways in Vietnamese meals, from soups to accompaniments for grilled meats.

Bun rieu: A light broth with bun, tomatoes, and small balls made with crab and pork.

Cha gio: Also known as "imperial roll," this is a Vietnamese-style egg roll of meat and clear noodles wrapped in rice paper and deep-fried.

Chao tom: Minced shrimp wrapped around a stalk of sugarcane, then grilled.

Che: The name for various sweet drinks and puddinglike desserts.

Dac biet: "Speciality of the house."

Du du: A salad of shredded green papaya topped with slivers of Vietnamese-style beef jerky.

Goi: The word for salads. Goi tom cang is a shrimp and cucumber salad.

Hu tieu: Clear potato starch noodles, and also the name of the southern regional soup noodle dish using them. Hu tieu dai tom cua xa xiu is a soup with seafood and Chinese-style barbecued pork.

La lot leaf: A broad leaf, rather like a grape leaf, grown in Hawaii and used to wrap around beef, which will then be grilled.

Mam nem: A potent dipping sauce

of anchovy paste and pineapple that accompanies grilled meats and the bo 7 mon dinners. Some prefer to substitute nuoc cham for this sauce.

Mien ga: A chicken broth with chicken and clear noodles.

Mi thit: Ham used in banh mi sandwiches.

Nem: A sausage of pork cured with garlic, wrapped in a banana leaf. It is usually consumed uncooked.

Nuoc cham: Vietnam's all-purpose dipping sauce, a clear light liquid made from nuoc mam, lime juice, vinegar, sugar, garlic, and hot chiles.

Nuoc mam: A clear liquid sauce made from fermented fish. Known as the soy sauce of Vietnam, it is the cuisine's major seasoning.

Nuong: Indicates charcoal-grilled foods on a menu. Nem nuong are barbecued meatballs, thit nuong is barbecued pork, and thit bo nuong is barbecued beef.

Pho: The northern regional beef soup noodle dish. Pho ga is made with chicken in place of beef.

Sinh to: A refreshing drink made of puréed fruit and ice.

Tau hu duong tau pho: Fresh tofu in a light caramel sauce.

Thit: Literally, meat, but often refers to ham when ordering Vietnamese sandwiches.

Thom (or tom): Shrimp.

ALL-PURPOSE RESTAURANTS

Most of the more than 200 Vietnamese restaurants scattered around Los Angeles and Orange County cater to a Vietnamese clientele. If you're just beginning to explore this cuisine, here are a few places with a comprehensive menu and a staff that will happily intro-duce you to the art of rolling rice-papers or the proper way to use the fresh herbs that accompany your soup.

Thiên Thanh No. I (Blue Sky), 5423 W. 1st Street, Santa Ana, OCOUNTY, 714-554-7260. **Thiên Thanh No. 2,** 10722 Westminster Avenue, Garden

---

Grove, OCOUNTY, 714-537-5563. Open breakfast through dinner daily and until 3:00 A.M. (No. 1) or 12:30 A.M. (No. 2) Friday and Saturday. The original, and more established Thiên Thanh No. 1, a fixture in Little Saigon, is always crowded with people eating in huge convivial groups. Over the years it has gained a following with occidental patrons, though they're still vastly in the minority. If your waiter's English is limited, he'll usually signal for the manager, who has plenty of experience explaining the dishes.

Start with the cha gio to get a good feel for the way Vietnamese eat. This crispy rice-paper-enclosed version of Chinese egg roll is served with a pile of lettuce and Vietnam's light, garlicky, all-purpose dipping sauce, nuoc cham (pronounced "nook chaam"). To eat cha gio, you wrap up the roll in a swatch of lettuce and dip the bundle into the nuoc cham. Another fine dish, eaten the same way, is the wonderful chopped shrimp on sugarcane, chao tom. One of Thiên Thanh's most popular items, pan-fried chicken with lemon grass, makes generous use of the aromatic lemony stalk that flavors almost every Vietnamese dish. Sour catfish soup, also perfumed with lemon grass, is a close cousin of Thai hot and sour shrimp soup.

Thiên Thanh No. 2, with a similar menu, excels at tabletop-grilled meats and seafood and the "fondue"-style dishes that you cook in a little pot of tart broth. You are brought a stack of sheer rice-paper crêpes and copious platters of fresh herbs, lettuce, and vegetables, pickled garlic cloves, and slices of starchy plantain among them. Enclose the herbs, vegetables, and meat or fish in rice-paper and roll up to eat. The eating style is usually a big hit with children. One of Thiên Thanh's best ver-

A waiter at Thiên Thanh No. 2 separates rice papers to wrap around grilled meats and fresh herbs.

sions of this extravaganza is the jumbo shrimp wrapped in thin beef slices.

For early risers, the restaurant serves an assortment of breakfast noodle dishes.

Favori, 3502 W. 1st Street, Santa Ana, OCOUNTY, 714-531-6838. Lunch and dinner daily. France's departure from Southeast Asia did little to diminish Vietnam's acquired fondness for bistro food, and several Vietnamese restaurants serve it. The menus at most of these places take a step back in culinary history to the times when the French held sway over Southeast Asia. Coq au vin and biftek with pommes frites are the mainstays, and Favori serves this cuisine with the utmost flair.

The restaurant glimmers with mirrors and candles, and the waiters wear proper satin cummerbunds. They bring on chateaubriand for two with the panache of seasoned Parisian garçons. And it's a very good chateaubriand too: a thick slice of tenderloin, perfectly cooked and topped with a crab leg and béarnaise sauce. Paella oriental, a bowl of tomatoey rice, is crammed with all sorts of seafood; and roasted quail comes on a bed of watercress.

But Favori also serves some of the best Vietnamese food I know—and it's what most non-Vietnamese patrons usually order. The cook-at-the-table beef and shrimp fondues are popular. And as at Thiên Thanh, they're served with a stack of rice-papers and assorted fresh herbs. These meals are abundant, but light enough to have room for Favori's dessert specialties, gooey ice cream sundaes or peach Melba.

Song Long, 9361 Bolsa Avenue, Suite 108, Westminster, OCOUNTY, 714-775-3724. Breakfast through dinner daily. **Bakery:** 9433 Bolsa Avenue, Suite C, Westminster, OCOUNTY, 714-531-0792. Many Vietnamese recommend Song Long, a stylish coffee shop serving French café fare and Vietnamese lunch plates (as opposed to full-fledged dinners with all the herbs, lettuce, rice-paper, and dips). This is where the local business people take their power breakfasts.

For breakfast there's pain français et beurre, or pâté chaud—meat-filled pastries—both baked at Song Long's French bakery nearby. Other dishes are omelettes au champignons, filet de sole gratin, and entrecote au poivre. On the Vietnamese side of the menu, barbecued pork chop with steamed pork cake over rice could stand in for an American blue-plate special, except for its distinctive Vietnamese seasonings. The café makes hu tieu in five varieties. This southern regional noodle soup comes with clear, chewy potato-starch noodles and a choice of toppings.

Anh Phuong, 633 S. San Gabriel Boulevard, No. 112, San Gabriel, SAN GABRIEL VALLEY, 818-309-1334. Lunch and dinner daily. Anh Phuong, a simple café, has a deli case full of strange and colorful beverages as its centerpiece. But the plain ambience belies its sophisticated and well-prepared food. Our warm salad with lean and meaty duck chunks had a tart, sassy dressing that epitomizes this cuisine: pungent, light, and completely satisfying. Remarkably, this masterpiece cost $3.95. In a chic East-West boite its price would be three times as much. A vast selection of noodle dishes includes the clear, chewy hu tieu noodles, and the thicker, fat (and also clear) banh canh noodles with all sorts of toppings. Perfect with any soup are the banh khot: crunchy light-as-air fried rice cakes topped with shrimp.

Nhà Hàng Sô 1, 14122 Brookhurst Street, Garden Grove, OCOUNTY, 714-537-5022. Lunch and dinner daily. Little Saigon's Nhà Hàng Sô 1 has a long and fascinating menu. In addition to the familiar noodle soups and grilled sates, you can get a beautifully roasted quail with crisp skin, or eel in various guises. Ours came in a hotpot fueled with live coals, and in its broth were tomatoes, pineapple, and banana flower buds. But the best dish was goi tom cang: grilled crayfish with their coral on a bed of tart-sweet cucumber salad.

Pho Lê Loi, 640 N. Spring Street, Chinatown, CENTRAL, 213-680-4644. Open 9:00 A.M. to 9:00 P.M. daily. Pho Lê Loi in Chinatown is probably the most centrally located restaurant to serve the seven-course beef meal, bo 7 mon. And it does a serviceable version, although the herbs and garnishes aren't as exotic as you'll find in Little Saigon. Even so, Pho Lê Loi has withstood the test of time while other Vietnamese restaurants around it have come and gone.

Pho Lê Loi does a fine job with imperial rolls. And one of the best items to follow these is the grilled beef dinner: A small brass stove comes to the table with a platter of thin meat slices sprinkled with scallions and peanuts. You can eat the sizzling meat with rice straight from the grill or roll it in rice paper with fresh herbs. Usually the waiter demonstrates the rolling procedure to newcomers. This food is so straightforward, and the flavors so beguiling, that you forgive them for omitting the pickled garlic that you'd find with these meals in Little Saigon.

Au Pagolac Cholon, 816 N. Spring Street, No. 103, Chinatown, CENTRAL, 213-680-8838. Lunch through dinner daily. Relatively new in Chinatown, and competition for Pho Lê Loi's seven-course beef meal, Au Pagolac concentrates on grilled dishes and combination rice plates rather than on noodle dishes or sandwiches as most Chinatown Vietnamese eateries do. Good things to try here: *com tam bi su on* (shredded pork and a marinated pork chop over rice) and the combination imperial roll and charbroiled beef plate.

Dông-Quê, 18601 Sherman Way, No. D, Reseda, S.F. VALLEY, 818-609-1039. Lunch through dinner daily. Dông-Quê, one of the San Fernando Valley's better Vietnamese places, started its life as a fast-food and noodle shop. Recently, a long list of more serious dishes was added to the menu, turning Dông-Quê into a fullfledged restaurant and a boon to the neighborhood. The shrimp fondue and the sliced beef marinated with lemon grass, *bo nuong vi,* are two of the kitchen's best efforts. (You might, however, want to request nuoc cham as a dipping sauce, since the accompanying special sauce for the fondue

is strong and fishy-tasting.) The familiar rice plates, noodle dishes, salads, and sandwiches are all here, too.

My Hanh, 9611 E. Garvey Avenue, No. 109, El Monte, SAN GABRIEL VALLEY, 818-579-5112. Lunch and dinner; closed Wednesday. At My Hanh in El Monte, any dish listed under "tiny rice stick" is a good bet. You'll be served a flavorful grilled meat on a bed of delicate rich vermicelli with the customary fresh herb, lettuce, and sauce trio for wrapping and dipping the meat and noodles. One of My Hanh's best plates is the combination grilled shrimp and cha gio on tiny rice sticks. (The kitchen turns out beef and pork versions of this dish, too.) On my last visit, the stuffed pancakelike banh xeo was enormously successful with my companions.

VIETNAMESE SPECIALTIES

In the world of everyday Asian eating, it's the specialists—the dumpling maker in his tiny shop, the humble sate griller, or the old woman dishing out sweet black sticky rice—who inspire midnight cravings. These artisans have perfected and serve only one item. And now that the Los Angeles area's Vietnamese population is firmly entrenched, traditional food specialists are beginning to flourish here. While the dishes they prepare may also be had in many all-purpose restaurants, they never seem quite as good as the versions made by the specialists.

♦ CHARCUTERIE AND SANDWICH DELIS

The French colonists, looking for a bit of their own cuisine, trained a legion of charcutiers who went on to develop their own cross-cultural pâtés, hams, and sausages. They piled these into crispy French baguettes slathered with mayonnaise and garnished with Vietnamese-style marinated vegetables to make Vietnamese-style submarine sandwiches known as banh mi. You can see banh mi signs all over little Saigon and China-town.

The Reseda branch of **Ba Le** excels in banh mi. The "combo sandwich" is the best introduction to this delicacy. Along with a wide variety of meats, the sheer quantity of filling makes it the most opulent banh mi anywhere. And Ba Le's rolls are always fresh and crunchy.

My Vi, an odd little restaurant with a Chinese-style barbecue offering glazed ducks and barbecued pork at one end of the room, makes banh mi dia. The meats that usually go into banh mi are arranged on a plate alongside two sunny-side-up eggs, a mound of homemade French-style mayonnaise, and the French roll. Occasionally I prefer this plate to the submarine sandwich that has everything piled into the bread.

At **Banh Mi Sô I,** a deli and restaurant in San Gabriel, you order banh mi from a lighted board behind the counter (there's no mention of banh mi on the written menu). You can choose many meat fillings: cha lua is a coldcut with a texture reminiscent bologna, and mi thit is lean ham, but the dac biet (house speciality) has all the meats. You might want to consume your sandwich with an "iced jelly drink" or "three-color porridge" (see **Banh Cuon Tây Hô,** page 109), and Banh Mi Sô I has a fascinating selection of snacks and sweets for sale in the deli area too.

- **Ba Le,** 18625 Sherman Way, Reseda, S.F. VALLEY, 818-342-9380. Open 8:00 A.M. to 9:00 P.M. daily.
- **My Vi,** 15709 Crenshaw Boulevard, Gardena, SOUTH, 310-644-0700. Open 10:00 A.M. to 10:00 P.M. daily.
- **Banh Mi Sô I,** 9000 E. Garvey Avenue, Rosemead, SAN GABRIEL VALLEY, 818-573-8333. Also in Little Saigon (Westminster). Lunch through dinner daily.

REGIONAL SOUP NOODLE RESTAURANTS

♦ **PHO**

Pho Hòa, 640 N. Broadway, No. 6, Chinatown, CENTRAL, 213-626-5530. Daily 7:00 A.M. to 9:00 P.M. Also **Hòa's House of Noodles,** 7255 Reseda Boulevard, Reseda, S.F. VALLEY, 818-705-6662; daily 8:00 A.M. to 9:00 P.M. Also in Monterey Park, SAN GABRIEL VALLEY, 818-281-6123, and Hawthorne, SOUTH, 310-644-4106. One of California's first pho shops and a chain with branches as far afield as Toronto and Falls Church, Virginia, is still among the best.

Pho Hòa sticks strictly to the business of making pho and as in all pho shops the soup is accompanied by two plates: a mountain of bean sprouts topped with fresh basil and cilantro sprigs on one, and another of lime wedges and fresh chile slices. On the table are bottles of chili-garlic sauce, fish sauce, and sugar.

With chopsticks in one hand and a soup spoon in the other, you alternately slurp noodles and soup, stopping occasionally to toss in some herbs or bean sprouts or a chile sliver. It's clear why there is little conversation at lunchtime and why it is hard to tire of the dish: Each bite has a different taste.

Pho 79, 727 N. Broadway, Suite 120, Chinatown, CENTRAL, 213-625-7026. Lunch through dinner; closed Tuesday. Also 881 E. Anaheim Street, Long Beach, SOUTH, 310-599-5305; open daily. Several locations in Monterey Park, SAN GABRIEL VALLEY, and Westminster, OCOUNTY. The chain of Pho 79 shops is complete with a logo and designer guest receipts. "In Saigon, Pho 79 was as famous as McDonald's," a friend explained. But there's no relation to the Sai-

Regional Soup Noodles: The Vietnamese Staff of Life

———

P ho, a beef-noodle soup and salad in a bowl, is Vietnam's national dish. All over Little Saigon and in other Vietnamese neighborhoods you see shops called Pho 99, Pho No. 1, Pho 54, Pho 86, Pho Anh, to name just a few. In Vietnam, pho is available around the clock as a quick breakfast or lunch in noisy, crowded cafes and at workaday stands. In the evenings, vendors pedal portable kitchens through residential streets; their cry—*"fuuhaaa?"*—is familiar.

A product of the north, pho became popular in Saigon when thousands of refugees fled there in 1954. In L.A., even at $3 a bowl, Vietnamese consumers seek out pho and debate whose broth is best. The mere suspicion of an institutional-sized can of premade broth in the pho kitchen would ruin a place's reputation. And it's considered gauche to use dry noodles now that fresh are available.

Each of Vietnam's distinct regions has its own cooking style and its own speciality noodle soup. In Hue, the ancient capital of the central region, the soup, like the cuisine in general, is spicy and elaborate. You find the best version of *bun bo Hue* at **Ngu Binh**.

In southern Vietnam, the traditional stronghold of seafood, the pho equivalent is hu tieu, a soup that replaces beef with seafood and pork and the rice noodles with clear chewy potato-starch noodles. **Ngan Dinh,** in San Gabriel, offers hu tieu in enormous variety.

PHO MENU GUIDE

Pho menus list many varieties; a close look, though, reveals these to be various combinations of the same six traditional beef topping ingredients: *tai* (thin slices of rare beef), *nam* (well-cooked flank), *gau* (well-cooked plate or brisket with alternating ribbons of fat and lean), *sach* (tripe), *gan* (beef tendons), and *bo vien* (meatballs) in any combination may be selected to top your noodles.

gon restaurant; they have merely borrowed the name to make everyone feel at home.

Like Pho Hòa, the restaurant's main concern is pho, and while the servings are not so artistically presented and Vietnamese friends say the broth may not be quite first-rate, it tasted great to me. Pho 79 also has a short list of other noodle and rice dishes and serves excellent crispy Vietnamese egg rolls. It's a little more mainstream than many shops, offering Cokes and fresh orange juice on the beverage list and flan au caramel for dessert.

Pho Bolsa, 9567 Bolsa Avenue, Westminster, OCOUNTY, 714-839-3380. Open daily. Morning is a busy time for Pho Bolsa, as many local merchants from the Bolsa Mini Mall breakfast there. Pho Bolsa isn't a chain, and my Vietnamese friends are of the opinion that its broth is the best. When the place first opened years ago, the menu was only in Vietnamese. But recently the restaurant expanded, and it now offers a translated menu with greater variety.

♦ **BUN BO HUE AND HU TIEU**

Ngu Binh Fast Food, 9361 Bolsa Avenue, No. 101 (Le Loi Center), Westminster, OCOUNTY, 714-839-2700. Open 8:00 A.M. to 8:00 P.M. daily. Also 4505 W. 1st Street, Santa Ana, OCOUNTY, 714-775-0134. Ngu Binh Fast Food is a tiny deli that specializes in bun bo Hue, the central region's speciality soup: it's a tomato-and-chile-laced broth simmered with pork hocks and beef. The shop orders its bun freshly made at a local factory. (Other restaurants use dried noodles.) Each huge, steaming bowl of noodles comes topped with the customary "salad" of fresh herbs and bean sprouts. Connoisseurs of the dish come to Ngu Binh because they can get the soup with little cubes of exceptionally fresh blood pudding and chewy beef ten-

don. If these traditional additions are to your liking, ask for *bun bo gan huyt.*

These hearty meals-in-a-bowl go well with one of the blended fruit drinks called sinh to. The flavors change; one day it may be jack-fruit, soursop, or sambutier—all tropical fruits. Don't be intimidated by the all-Vietnamese menu. Just consult with the servers for advice.

Ngan Dinh, 539 W. Valley Boulevard, San Gabriel, SAN GABRIEL VALLEY, 818-282-9996. Open daily. A popular breakfast and lunch spot offers pho and bun noodles, but the thing to get here are the hu tieu dishes. These come both with and without soup in about 30 guises. The traditional southern morning meal hu tieu dai tom cua xa xiu features the clear noodles in a broth with shrimp, crab, and barbecue pork. Like pho, the soup is accompanied by fresh herbs, lime, and chiles with which you do your own garnishing.

Also see **Song Long** (page 103).

♦ **BO BAY MON:**
"SEVEN-COURSE BEEF"

In Vietnam, good beef is so prized that it has always been entrusted to speciality chefs. Vietnam's favorite beef speciality, bo bay mon is an entire meal made of beef and served in seven differently prepared courses.

Seven courses of beef may sound like an unwieldy repast, but *these* courses are samplers of Vietnamese culinary artistry; they do not in any way resemble a lumberjack's dinner. Their well-bred lightness embodies the Vietnamese preference for the leanest meats cooked with barely any oil.

Bo bay mon is showing up on all sorts of Vietnamese menus these days, whether or not it's the restaurant's speciality. All over L.A. and Little Saigon, you find restaurants with a picture of a smiling cow and the words "bo 7 mon" on their signs. But you'll find the best versions in the speciality restaurants.

- **Pagode Saigon,** 710 W. Las Tunas Drive, No. 7, San Gabriel, SAN GABRIEL VALLEY, 818-282-6327. Lunch and dinner; closed Monday.
- **Pagolac,** 14564 Brookhurst Street, Westminster, OCOUNTY, 714-531-4740. Lunch and dinner; closed Monday.

Nine years ago Thomas Le and his wife Ly opened Pagolac, the first bo 7 mon restaurant in Little Saigon. The couple sold it to relatives when they moved to San Gabriel, where they established the popular Pagode Saigon. Both restaurants have similar menus.

Soon after you order, the table becomes a landscape of exotic vegetables, greens, and the inevitable stack of translucent rice papers. First comes bo nhung dam, beef fondue, which you cook in a little pot of seasoned vinegar and wrap to eat. Resist the temptation to pile too many aromatic goodies in the rice-papers, which tear easily when overfilled.

Before the last of the fondue has been cooked, the waiter brings bo cha dum, a steamed dumpling of seasoned chopped beef mixed with Chinese tree ear mushrooms and clear noodles; it resembles a savory minimeatloaf. Everyone uses the airy shrimp chips that accompany cha dum as edible spoons to eat pieces of dumpling along with a few herbs.

Courses three, four, and five are also eaten burrito style—although some people simply munch them down straight. Three grilled items are generally included: juicy little patties of seasoned minced beef; beef rolled in an elusively flavored Hawaiian la lot leaf; and sate: beef wrapped around ginger and pickled leeks, skewered, and cooked over an open flame.

A wonderful salad of hot grilled beef over lettuce with a vinaigrette owes a debt to France. The final course, a clear gingery broth scattered with rice and beef, is the traditional finish.

There's a menu offering each course separately, and a meal of marinated beef or shrimp grilled at the table.

Anh Hong, 10195 Westminster Avenue, Garden Grove, OCOUNTY, 714-537-5230. Lunch through dinner daily. For almost everyone who lived in Saigon in the last half century, Anh Hong was synonymous with bo 7 mon. The restaurant brought this dinner into fashion shortly after World War II. In suburban Saigon, Anh Hong had white-napped outdoor tables shaded by trees strung with little lights, and it served about 500 customers a day. After giving up his venerated Saigon establishment, owner Le Van Kah ran two restaurants in Belgium, and now different generations of the family own three Anh Hong restaurants in California.

Anh Hong's reputation was built on its mam nem dipping sauce, it's sweet-tart pickled lemon grass, and bo cha dum, translated on the menu as steamed "pâté" of beef. The meatball is so light it has an almost soufflé-like texture. Its complex flavor kept me eating and trying to figure out the enigmatic tastes. Instead of the usual commercially produced shrimp chips to accompany its cha dum, Anh Hong serves the authentic banh trang nuoc dua, a crisp, golden triangle made from rice flour and coconut milk. For anyone not up to all seven courses, the short menu offers each course separately. In addition, such dishes as shrimp fondue, or a beef and shrimp combination grilled at the table, ensure there's something for every taste.

Pho Sô 1, 7231 Reseda Boulevard, Reseda, S.F. VALLEY, 818-996-6515. Open 7:30 A.M. to

10:00 P.M. daily. As the name indicates, Pho Sô 1, ("Pho number one") serves pho. But the menu cover reads dac biet bo 7 mon ("house specialty, beef seven courses"), and it offers a chatty informative text carefully describing the conventions of the bo 7 mon dining ritual.

"For the beef salad," it reads, "you need only dip portions into the accompanying fish sauce." But mam nem, a potent blend of fermented anchovy paste and crushed pineapple, is an acquired taste. And though the Vietnamese consider this sauce an essential part of bo 7 mon, you must request it. Otherwise gringos automatically get the more familiar nuoc cham.

Another good thing about Pho Sô 1: it has three branches in various parts of town. Also at 120 E. Valley Boulevard, No. I-J, San Gabriel, SAN GABRIEL VALLEY, 818-571-7432. And 1015 S. Nogales Street, No. 127-A, Rowland Heights, EAST OF L.A., 818-964-5552.

VIETNAMESE MISCELLANY— REGIONAL DISHES TO DESSERTS

◆ NORTHERN VIETNAMESE CUISINE

Viên Dông, 9684 Westminster Avenue, Garden Grove, OCOUNTY, 714-539-4614, and 8966 E. Garvey Avenue, No. C & D, Rosemead, SAN GABRIEL VALLEY, 818-571-6807. Lunch through dinner daily. The cuisine from Vietnam's cooler northern region has a milder tone than the spicier foods of the south. And probably because of its proximity to China, more Chinese cooking techniques are in evidence. The specialties offered at Viên Dông illustrate the style. Mien ga, a mild chicken soup with bean thread noodles, stays close to similar Chinese recipes. Crispy fried sweet potatoes and deep-fried shrimp "banh tom co ngu" are not to be missed. Du du, a shredded green papaya salad with chewy strips of beef jerky; rice cakes with fried tofu; and

bun rieu, a soup with crab dumplings and tomato, all deliciously illustrate Viên Dông's northern cooking style.

◆ SEAFOOD

Grand Garden, 8894 Bolsa Avenue, Westminster, OCOUNTY, 714-893-1200. Lunch and dinner; closed Tuesday. Tiny Vietnam has 1,400 miles of shoreline, numerous rivers, and large deltas, so naturally fish and seafood of all sorts are staple foods. Most of the Vietnamese-owned seafood restaurants I've explored in the area, however, serve primarily Chinese-style dishes. An exception is Grand Garden, a fancy dinner house owned by the Pho 79 group. The restaurant offers more Vietnamese-style fish dishes than I've seen elsewhere. Most of these are listed on the menu under "house specialties and soups." Try fresh catfish hotpot, in which chunks of the mild fish float with tomatoes and pineapple in a fruity-tart tamarind broth; eel braised in coconut milk; crispy fried frogs' legs; or *thom kho to*: large spicy shrimp cooked in a clay pot.

◆ BANH CUON

Banh Cuon Tây Hô, 9242 Bolsa Avenue, No. C, Westminster, OCOUNTY, 714-895-4796, and 3520 W. 1st Street, Santa Ana, OCOUNTY, 714-839-7533. Lunch and dinner daily. If you've ever had fresh rice noodle sheets at a dim sum meal—the ones rolled around a filling and doused with black vinegar—you will recognize the origins of Vietnamese banh cuon. These steamed sheer rice sheets are thinner, more delicate, and less oily than their Chinese relatives. Tây Hô, a little café with two branches, specializes in banh cuon. Here the rice sheets are steamed without oil on a muslin drum rather than being cooked in a skillet as nonspecialty places are apt to do. The result is the sheerest, most elegant banh cuon of all, and Tây

Hô serves them myriad ways. When stuffed, they could be considered an Asian burrito.

For Americans, one of the most appealing versions is banh cuon *nhan thit* (No. 6), rolled around a filling of sautéed ground meat and tree ears. Other versions are stuffed with dried shrimp, or cut into strips and topped with *chua lua* (a Vietnamese cold sausage) or barbecued pork.

The house combination plate (No. 1) is, I think, the best banh cuon introduction. It includes both a meat-filled and a shrimp-filled rice sheet, a sample of crispy deep-fried banh kong, and a lacy tempuralike sweet potato patty called banh tom chien. For dipping, you ladle your own sweet-hot sauce into little soup bowls from gallon jugs on the table. This small banquet costs $3.45.

Tây Hô is also a wonderful source for che, most of which are coconut milk-based drinks with various ingredients like young coconut slivers or sweet red beans. My favorite, *suong xa hot luu,* is unappetizingly translated as "white jelly and cooked flour ball in coconut milk." It's a description that does a grave disservice to the sweet creamy drink with tiny chewy red nuggets and sparkling slivers of jelly. The sweet red bean in coconut milk with tapioca pearls (No. 11) is everyone's favorite.

♦ **DESSERT SHOP**
Hiên Khanh, 9784 Westminster Avenue, Garden Grove, OCOUNTY, 714-537-5105. Lunch through dinner; closed Wednesday. Also at 531 W. Valley Boulevard, San Gabriel, SAN GABRIEL VALLEY, 818-284-7931. Hiên Khanh, a shop resembling an old-fashioned ice cream parlor, specializes in che, Vietnamese desserts and sweet drinks. Customers at wrought-iron tables swirl their creamy iced drinks with long-handled spoons. Two serving counters with pots of pastel-colored dessert ingredients dominate the front part of the café. Although the pots look like drums of ice cream, you'll soon discover that their contents do not resemble ice cream in any way.

One of my favorite desserts is che *choi.* Like many offerings here, it is served warm and arranged in layers: first colorful green tapioca strands, then slices of cooked sweet plantain banana mixed with tiny tapioca pearls, and finally sweet creamy coconut milk poured over everything. Because the desserts are fashioned on the spot, served fresh at the perfect temperature, and never oversweetened, many Vietnamese go out of their way to come here, though the same items are widely available. Of the cold desserts, *tache che dau xanh,* whose menu description of "jello, mashed mung bean, and coconut" may sound entirely too weird for many Western palates, is, I'll admit, unique. But when you stir the sweet yellow bean paste into the thick creamy coconut milk along with the clear arrowroot strands, it becomes like an exotic sundae. Plenty of other choices, such as the tapioca balls stuffed with mung bean floating in sweet coconut milk, will keep you from dessert ennui.

SHOPS AND MARKETS
Thanh Son Tofu, 9688 Westminster Avenue, Garden Grove, OCOUNTY, 714-534-2100. Open 8:00 A.M. to 8:00 P.M. daily. Xuan Van Dang was a tofu maker in Vietnam, as was his father before him. Now he plies his craft in a delightful tofu "deli" on Westminster. In his large back kitchen, he runs through the small-scale tofu production process several times a day, so whenever you get there the tofu will still be warm. It isn't usually on display in the cooler with the soy milk; Dang or his wife goes back to the kitchen to get it. At a table squeezed into a corner

of the shop, you can have a bowl of tau hu duong tau pho: a chunk of tofu bathed in a pool of light caramel sauce flavored with slices of fresh ginger. It almost tastes like a rich crème caramel—without the cholesterol. The shop also makes fried tofu squares to use in stir-fries and vegetarian dishes.

Sau Voi Vietnamese Deli, 9066 Bolsa Avenue, Westminster, OCOUNTY, 714-895-4373. Open 7:00 A.M. to 9:00 P.M. daily. Sau Voi specializes in Vietnamese pâtés, coldcuts, and other deli items. In the deli cases there's *cha lua,* a smooth loaf of chicken with pork, and pâté *gan,* a long loaf of liver and pork sold in thick slices. Also look for *cha que nuong,* a baked pork pâté flavored with cinnamon, and Viet-namese-style head cheese, ham, and nem.

Delicious sticky rice balls are filled with pork and minced watercress. For the Vietnamese New Year, Sau Voi makes banh chung; a sticky rice roll with cured pork and mung beans, wrapped in a banana leaf.

Baron's, 14441 Brookhurst Street, No. 7 & 8, Garden Grove, OCOUNTY, 714-775-2074. Open daily. Over a cup of cappuccino with a classic éclair or Napoleon at Baron's bakery and café, the ambience is pure Parisian patisserie. But people also come here for the banh gan (a cross-cultural flan made with coconut milk, eggs, and sugar) and the banh cuon, and for the delicate open-faced pork dumplings (siu mai) topped with a slice of sausage.

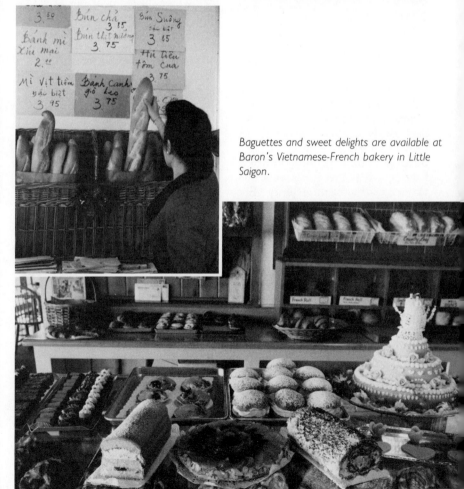

Baguettes and sweet delights are available at Baron's Vietnamese-French bakery in Little Saigon.

Van's Bakery, 121 E. Valley Boulevard, San Gabriel, SAN GABRIEL VALLEY, 818-571-5845. And 9211 Bolsa Avenue, No. 125, Westminster, OCOUNTY, 714-898-7065. Open 8:00 A.M. to 8:00 P.M. daily. At Van's, baroque Western-style birthday cakes and French-style desserts share display space with classic Chinese pastries and Vietnamese baked and steamed sweets. The banana leaf covering of banh tet chuoi holds sticky rice stuffed with a sweet banana. Bananas also figure in my favorite, banh chuoi, a rich bread pudding with layers of the cooked fruit. *Banh dau zanh* and *banh khoai mi* are both tortes (mung bean and cassava respectively); cut into wedges they look like the rich butter cakes of the West. Their chewy texture, however, is strictly Southeast Asian.

Bo Ko "Jerky Palace," 9651 Bolsa Avenue, Westminster, OCOUNTY, 714-531-7788. Open 9:00 A.M. to 8:00 P.M. daily. A familiar sight on many Vietnamese deli and snack shop counters is beef jerky. It tops shredded green papaya salads, seasons rice, or is just munched plain as a snack. Until I discovered Bo Ko "Jerky Palace," I thought that there was only one variety of Vietnamese jerky. But the deli case in this tiny shop holds seven varieties of dried yet moist and supple meats. Their rich earthy colors range from a deep dusty ocher to the blackest red. A row of plates filled with small samples lined up smartly on the countertop invites you to taste. These jerkys include extrahot spicy beef, sweet pork, sweet beef, fruit-flavored beef, and spicy beef cubes. Chinese-style hams and sausages are also manufactured here in a small factory at the rear of the shop. Jerky Palace is in the Today Plaza, beside Man Wha market.

Dong Loi Seafood Co., 13900–13902 Brookhurst Street, Garden Grove, OCOUNTY, 714-534-1410. Open 10:00 A.M. to 7:00 P.M. daily. Always one of the liveliest seafood shops in Little Saigon, Dong Loi has moved into large new aqua-blue-and-white-tile quarters with a nautical tone. At one end of the large room are tanks with several kinds of crabs: Dungeness, rock, spider, and yellow. Tilapia swim beside live carp and catfish; finicky cooks inspect the ice bins laden with green-lipped mussels, giant clams, oysters in several sizes, and baby shark. Dozens of fish in the round include milkfish, dace, mullet, and rabbit fish. In the freezer cases are crab claws, cuttlefish, chopped clam meat, and chopped shrimp to use in wontons or for other savory fillings. Huge, almost lobster-sized freshwater shrimp peer out at you from the fish case, and there are dressed shrimp of all colors and sizes.

Little Saigon Supermarket, 9822 Bolsa Avenue, Westminster, OCOUNTY, 714-531-7272. In Little Saigon Plaza across from a branch of Banh Mi Sô 1, Little Saigon Supermarket is the most polished food store in the neighborhood. "Material Girl" sung in Vietnamese wafts from speakers. Sparkling cases in the meat department hold well-trimmed meats—even tripe is completely cleaned and cut into delicate fettuccine-sized ribbons all read for making pho; some cuts come ready to stir-fry or grill.

In the produce area a well-kept shelf holds little pots of exotic herbs for the garden: lemon grass, the herb *rau ram,* and several kinds of basil. You'll find water spinach and other exotic leafy greens here. Also in the produce area is an array of fresh rice noodles; these come in sheets, wide ribbons, the skinny square-edged pho, and the clear, chewy spaghetti-shaped banh canh. Fresh rice noodles are never chilled but, like bread, are sold at room temperature the day they are made. Wheat-flour noodles and egg noodles, on the other hand, are stored in a cooler case. Frozen coconut comes in a variety of ways: grated, in young-coconut strips (for desserts and drinks), and as frozen milk, which I think is superior to the canned. Huge cloth sacks of rice are common in Asian markets, but also look for short-grained "sticky" rice or ebony-toned black sticky rice. And, naturally, all sorts of fish sauces and pastes, jars of chili sauces, and the ever essential rice-papers are located on the packaged-goods shelves. No matter what you need for Vietnamese cooking, it's here.

99 Price Market, 9221 Bolsa Avenue, Westminster, OCOUNTY, 714-894-3888. Open daily. Since Little Saigon Supermarket seems to have every Vietnamese foodstuff, you might suppose that the vast 99 Price Market would be redundant. Well, it is in many ways—with the same cans of lychee nuts and grass jelly, the same French champagne biscuits and durian-flavored cookies. But the warehouse-sized 99 has a different feel to it. Live fish swish in their tanks, and workers are at the ready with nets to pull them out for pointing customers. As you poke around the meat coolers you come across rarely seen items: pressed duck imported from Jimmy's in Canada, a "new"—the package says—Chinese sausage made from turkey meat. The produce section is large, with all the necessary herbs and vegetables for Chinese and Southeast Asian cooking. In the freezer are a wide selection of meatballs and fish balls and dozens of sizes and kinds of frozen shrimp. 99 Price has a full range of Chinese groceries plus Thai, Filipino, and Indonesian necessities, too.

In other parts of town, look for excellent Vietnamese provisions at the following stores:

- **Ai Hoa Supermarket,** 860 N. Hill Street, Chinatown, CENTRAL, 213-629-8121. Also in Reseda and Monterey Park.
- **Hawaii Supermarket,** 120 E. Valley Boulevard, San Gabriel, SAN GABRIEL VALLEY, 818-307-0062.
- **Vinh Hao Super Market** (see page 118).
- **Cathay Supermarket** (see page 97).

SOUTHEAST ASIAN CULINARY CROSSOVERS

Cambodia, Indonesia, Malaysia, and the Philippines

Thai restaurants may dominate the Southeast Asian dining scene, but L.A. has its share of other Southeast Asian restaurants, too.

CAMBODIA

You can easily spot Little Phnom Penh on Anaheim Street in Long Beach. Suddenly a plain American street sprouts dozens of signs in wiggly Khmer script—you're in the middle of the largest Cambodian expatriate community in the world.

More than 50,000 Cambodians live here, but until recently there were no Cambodian restaurants. Traditionally, Cambodians cooked their own food at home, and if they did go out to eat, it was usually to a Chinese restaurant. It's not surprising then that the first restaurants in the area were Chinese, serving only a few Cambodian dishes from a separate menu.

But after more than a decade of radical cultural adjustments, including the two-income family, Cambodian Americans have discovered the advantages of leaving the time-consuming preparation of their favorite dishes to restaurants.

If you ate Cambodian food not knowing its origin, you would recognize the familiar flavors of Thai and Vietnamese dishes. For centuries, Cambodia's borders with Thailand and Vietnam have been as fluid as Mekong Delta silt. Their kitchens borrowed copiously from one another—and from India and China. Still, each cuisine manages to have its own character, dictated by the supplies at hand. Cambodia's mainstays are the plentiful freshwater fish from the Mekong River and the country's great central lake, as well as the wild leafy herbs that grow along river banks. These—backed up with lemon grass, varieties of mints and basil, tamarind, and native limes—create a unique Cambodian flavor.

— CAMBODIAN GLOSSARY —

Amok: *Related to the Thai hormok, this is minced fish in spiced thick coconut cream wrapped in banana leaves and steamed.*

Nataing: *Related to northern Thailand's nam prik oong, nataing is one of Cambodia's many dips made with ground meat, fish paste, and coconut milk. These dips are eaten with raw vegetables, or, in* the case of nataing, bread.

Nhorm lahong: *A pork, shrimp, and shredded green papaya salad in a lime dressing.*

Samlaw kaw co: *All samlaws are thick, stewlike soups. This particular version is based on catfish with shredded green mango, green papaya, and Asian pumpkin.*

CAMBODIAN RESTAURANTS

New Paradise, 1350 E. Anaheim Street, Long Beach, SOUTH, 310-218-0066. Lunch through dinner daily. The flashiest establishment in Little Phnom Penh, the 400-seat New Paradise, with pink marble columns, brass wall accents, crystal chandeliers, and dim sum served from carts at lunch, is similar to the huge Hong Kong–style places in Monterey Park. Like many Cambodian restaurants, it has a full-fledged Cambodian-style Chinese menu, with a list of Cambodian dishes pasted to the back. These are written in Khmer script and described, if somewhat vaguely, in English. But the bilingual waitresses willingly add further information.

A dish from the Khmer menu seen on almost every table is the hot, tart pepper-spiked lobster soup. It resembles the Thai hot and sour shrimp soup, tam yam goong. Cambodian-style beef salad, another favorite here, is a fresh-tasting toss of thinly cut beef and cabbage, bathed in a sweet-tart lime dressing and festively garnished with red bell pepper strips and roasted peanuts. For some mysterious reason the extremely popular Cambodian-style sate isn't on the menu. I recommend amok—catfish steamed in well-seasoned coconut milk, wrapped in spinach and then banana leaves, it resembles a seafood pâté.

Monorom, 2150 E. Anaheim Street, Long Beach, SOUTH, 310-987-0130. Open 9:00 A.M. to 9:00 P.M. daily. With its plain, neat minimall storefront, Monorom is the least opulent of the area's Cambodian restaurants. But the frail-looking woman who works its stoves has a knack for creating spectacular flavors. The same items from other restaurants often pale by comparison. And Monorom has more Cambodian dishes than the restaurants serving both Chinese and Cambodian foods.

This is the place to try nataing, one of the most delicious Cambodian dishes I've ever eaten (ask for it; it's written on the wall in Khmer). It looks like a bowl of chili and comes with puffy rice cakes and French bread that you dip in the nataing. The secret of nataing's creaminess is the ground peanuts and coconut milk in the mild pepper-flavored sauce. *Tak kruen,* a dip made with grilled minced fish dressed with piquant lime sauce, lively with fresh Asian basil and fresh chiles, is accompanied with a plate of vegetables for dipping. Monorom's fish sour soup, with banana blossoms that taste like hearts of palm, comes in a clear, tangy broth with catfish slices, tomatoes, and pineapple generously sprinkled with fried garlic.

Other good dishes (needing a translation) are the beef salad (No. 10), Cambodian-style sates with shredded papaya and carrot salad (No. 12), samlaw kaw co (No. 15), and sautéed water spinach with pork (No. 16).

Banteay Srey Village Restaurant, 1020 E. Anaheim Street, Long Beach, SOUTH, 310-495-4140. Open 10:00 A.M. to 11:00 P.M. daily and until midnight on weekends. Banteay Srey Village, the local spot for weekend evening entertainment, has waitresses wearing long Cambodian-style dresses, and a thatched-roof decor combined inexplicably with a mirrored glass ball above its minute dance floor. It has an eerie somewhere-in-the-jungle nightclub feel to it, reminiscent of a Club Med. The entertainment, sung in Khmer to synthesized organ music, is equally novel.

Ordering here is relatively simple. Dishes are listed by categories such as soft noodles, appetizers, spicy soups, and so on. Banteay Srey's "hotpot" No. 47, one of the restaurant's cook-at-the-table communal meals, is, I think, the best dish in the house. You cook slices of beef, shrimp, and squid in a chafing dish filled with a slightly sweet curry and coconut milk broth, and eat them wrapped in lettuce with fresh herbs. Fresh rice noodles come with this, and at the end of the meal you cook them in the sensuously rich broth, which has absorbed the flavor of the meat and seafood.

Other good bets are the Cambodian sausage, any of the seafood hot and sour soups, the beef on skewers (sate), beef or squid salad, and the soft rice noodles Cambodian style.

Angkor, 16161 Ventura Boulevard, Suite B, Encino, S.F. VALLEY, 818-990-8491. Lunch and dinner Monday to Saturday; Sunday dinner only. Angkor is L.A.'s most assimilated Cambodian restaurant. I brought a Cambodian friend to lunch who thought the food tasted wonderful—but "not exactly Cambodian." That's probably OK, as authentic Cambodian food, with its emphatic use of pickled or fermented fish condiments, is a little unusual for many taste buds. But at Angkor, when you order the chicken, pineapple, and red curry soup, or the nhorm lahong salad of pork and prawns with shredded green papaya in a lime dressing, it won't be too spicy or fishy; it will be absolutely delicious. Furthermore, Ankgor has a much longer menu than the Long Beach restaurants, and every dish is both transliterated and clearly described. Angkor also serves beer and wine.

CAMBODIAN MARKETS
Shopping for Cambodian groceries is easy if you go to the right part of town. On nearly every block along Anaheim Street between Long Beach Boulevard and Redondo, small markets like **Kemara Market, Mekong Market** (2230 E. Anaheim), and **Siem Reip Market** serve the community. Also in the vicinity are two branches of the new **Vinh Hao Super Market** (1145 Long Beach Boulevard, Long Beach, SOUTH, 310-436-2332, and 1241 E. Anaheim Street, Long Beach, SOUTH, 310-599-3188), a multi-Asian market stocking foodstuffs for Cambodian, Thai, Indonesian, Filipino, and Chinese cooking.

MALAYSIA AND INDONESIA

Malaysia and Indonesia, for centuries the crossroads of international trade and political invasion, have inherited culinary influences from cultures as far-flung as Europe, the Americas, India, the Middle East, and several regions of China. Both cuisines show the Indian knack for blending spices in curries, the use of fresh hot chiles, and of pungent fish sauce as a flavoring. The Chinese, having owned most of the restaurants in these countries, evolved a cuisine that mixed their own cooking with the local ingredients and techniques. Interestingly, forks and fingers are the eating implements of choice except when dishes of Chinese origin—in particular noodle dishes—are eaten.

The Chinese and Indian influences that came separately to Malay and Indonesian cooking are now so integrated they show up together in the same dish: You find Chinese noodles dressed with curry and served with chutneylike sambals. The ever popular sates, initially Persian tandoor-cooked kebabs, now have thoroughly Southeast Asian flavorings. Such cross-cultural links make Indonesian-Malay cuisines some of the world's most intriguing.

— MALAY AND INDONESIAN GLOSSARY —

Ayam: Chicken. Ayam belado is chicken in an extremely hot red chili sauce; ayam kare is chicken curry, while soto ayam is chicken soup.

Bumbus: These spice pastes that are the bases for many Indonesian dishes can be bought premade in Indonesian markets. The bumbu is combined with coconut milk and cooked with other foods. Bumbu besengeh or bumbu sayur gudeg are but two varieties.

Dendeng belado: Highly seasoned dry-fried shredded meat eaten as part of a rice plate or rijsttafel.

Gado-gado: A vegetable salad topped with a peanut-tamarind dressing. When made with longtong, the dish is gadogado longtong.

Goreng: Fried.

Gulai otak: Beef brain curry.

Ketjap: A sweet thick soy sauce flavored with palm syrup, garlic, and other spices.

Kroket: A croquette, usually made of potato, adopted from the Dutch.

Krupek: Airy, deep-fried shrimp crackers eaten with meals.

Kwatiaw: Flat rice noodles that, when stir-fried, are called kwatiaw goreng.

Laksa: A rice noodle resembling spaghetti used in Malaysia. Every region in the country has its own laksa dish.

Lempur: Sticky rice rolled around a seasoned meat or chicken filling.

Longtong: A bland cake made from rice pressed into a smooth, compact log.

Minuman Indonesia: Tropical "shakes" with such intriguing ingredient combinations as coffee and avocado and fermented cassava with sugar.

Nasi goreng: Indonesian-style fried rice.

Nasi rames: A combination rice plate holding several curries or sauced dishes. Nasi rames is often called a minirijsttafel.

Opor ayam: A chicken stew cooked in coconut milk.

Pasteitjes: A Dutch-Indonesian half-moon-shaped beef-filled pastry.

Rambutan: A Ping-Pong-ball-sized Southeast Asian fruit related to the lichee nut, with a russet-colored bumpy exterior and delicate white interior.

Rendang: A dry beef curry cooked in coconut milk and seasoned liberally with hot chiles.

Rijsttafel: A multidish dinner—sometimes up to 50 dishes—is the ultimate combination plate. Rijsttafel is said to have been invented by Indonesian cooks to please their Dutch colonial rulers.

Risolles: A rectangular-shaped Dutch-Indonesian meat- and vegetable-filled pastry.

Rojak: A Malaysian fruit and vegetable salad dressed in a sweet-tart dressing.

Sambals: Intensely flavored condiments served alongside main dishes. Sambals are often, but not always, made from hot chiles.

Sambal goreng: This term indicates a food fried with lots of chiles; there is chicken sambal, dried fish sambal, and so on and they are always served with an assortment of other dishes.

Sate: Bite-sized pieces of marinated

meat or chicken, skewered, grilled over charcoal, and served with a peanut sauce.

Tape singkong: A milkshakelike drink made from sweetened, fermented cassava.

Tempeh: A soybean cake infused with a mouldlike culture, then pressed into a block. This versatile food, like tofu, is used as the protein in many dishes.

Trasi: A dry fermented fish paste used as a seasoning.

MALAY AND INDONESIAN RESTAURANTS

Agung, 3909 Beverly Boulevard, Koreatown, CENTRAL, 213-660-2113. Lunch through dinner; closed Tuesday. Down the street from a Korean pub and a cluster of Salvadoran pupuserias, Agung is one of those frozen-in-time ethnic places with posters and batik on the wall. It attracts a clientele who love to sniff out great food finds in this multiethnic patch of the city. This particular find happens to serve Pedang cuisine, the chile-hot cooking of West Sumatra, named after the Indonesian city in which rijsttafel was born. And rijsttafel, the café's specialty (it means rice table in Dutch), is a virtual banquet of many dishes and condiments to accompany rice. Unless you want to order the whole rijsttafel, select any combination of items from the list of side dishes. Try the dendeng belado to get a hint of the spicy Pedang style: beef slices cooked till they're as crisp as jerky and served in a dip that makes your ears glow. *Pedang agung* (the house barbecued chicken) along with gado-gado, and a couple of sate orders, also makes a well-rounded meal. Possibly the most exotic items served here are the "minuman Indonesia." These "shakes" range from a tame es *kelapa muda* (young coconut shreds in coconut milk), to the slightly more adventurous es *teler* (with avocado and jackfruit), to the outrageous es *alpukat*—sweet Indonesian-style iced coffee blended with avocado. All are weirdly delicious.

Cafe Krakatoa, 8206 Van Nuys Boulevard, Panorama City, S.F. VALLEY, 818-997-6171. Lunch through dinner; closed Tuesday. The owners of this delightful spot have taken a rather drab former Japanese restaurant and given it a quiet elegance simply by masking the entire ceiling with upended parasols hand-painted in pastel tones. What emerges from the kitchen reflects the tastes of a sophisticated Indonesian cook. Meats and chicken are generously served, well trimmed, and never over-sauced.

Early in the day, snacks are displayed near the cash register; the lempur, sticky rice rolls stuffed with minced chicken, are my favorites. Opor ayam, one of Indonesia's most popular chicken dishes and a staple of the rijsttafel table, comes as half a chicken, cut up and blanketed in a creamy well-spiced coconut milk sauce thickened with nuts. A fiery chicken dish, ayam belado, has a sauce of red chiles. Lone diners may want to try the longtong, a dish that's like a mini-rijsttafel in a bowl. Cafe Krakatoa's version is topped with three items: a piece of opor ayam, the currylike beef rendang, and a whole hard-cooked egg. But it's the rich coconut milk sauce together with all these items that make this dish so addictive.

Sri Ratu, 747 S. Vermont Avenue, Koreatown, CENTRAL, 213-480-0752. Lunch and dinner daily. Sri Ratu, something of a neighborhood institution, is extremely easy to miss in a crowded minimall with its nondescript storefront overshadowed by BIF Furniture. For nine years Budhi Brataatmadja has run the small recently remodeled dining room with its thoughtfully placed mementos. His wife, Hartini, does the cooking. The seating is pleasant, though many customers exit with puffy white bags filled with Hartini's wonderful boxed dinners. Each dinner holds rice and several accompaniments. My meal, the nasi rames, an astonishing feast for less than $5, includes a whole fried chicken leg basted with ketjap; a substantial chunk of beef rendang; a fried whole hard-cooked egg; and a cup of coconut soup brimming with vegetables. In the corner of the rice was a little patch of fried baby anchovies and peanuts.

The long menu at Sri Ratu includes both familiar items and the not so familiar: gulai otak, a curry made with beef brains, and tape singkong, a fermented cassava "milkshake."

Mawar Deli and Market, 534 E. Valley Boulevard, No. 8, San Gabriel, SAN GABRIEL VALLEY, 818-573-0506. Lunch through dinner; closed Sunday and Monday at 5:00 P.M. Mawar Deli is just few tables in one area of a mini Indonesian market. The owner's children often help with the serving, and grandma's home cooking is on the bill of fare. Her gado gado longtong makes an outstanding foil for its sumptuous peanut dressing, and her Indonesian-style fried chicken in a chili sauce has a sweet, irresistibly crackly skin. Each day there's a special dish and a changing array of little snacks including lempur and kroket. A small menu of Indonesian-style Chinese dishes includes *kwatiaw goreng* and an Indonesian-style wonton soup.

Like its population, Indonesia's beverages have a smidgen of Chinese heritage and a lot of Southeast Asian ancestry. Mawar's "ice Shanghai" clearly has Chinese roots: red beans, black Chinese jelly squares, soft young coconut shreds, and milk all top a mound of ice. Behind the counter Mawar has a heavy-duty iron ice shaver that scrapes the ice from a block. This is the only way to make these drinks—preshaved ice tastes stale. Other slushy ice drinks include ice lichee and ice rambutan, both made from tropical fruits.

Ramayani Westwood, 1777 Westwood Boulevard, Westwood, WEST, 310-477-3315. Lunch through dinner; closed Monday. Some complain that Ramayani, just down the road from U.C.L.A., is a college town version of an Indonesian restaurant. OK, so the dishes aren't as highly flavored with fish paste or as burning hot as they might be, and they do refer to their rijsttafel as "Indonesian combination tapas." But this is West L.A.'s only Indonesian restaurant. It also has a wonderfully long menu, and the kitchen uses good-quality ingredients. If you're not in the mood for a whole rijsttafel ceremony, entrées like ayam kare may be had à la carte or with rice, soup, and salad for under $10. Of course there are sates, rice dishes, and sambal goreng *tahu buncis*: green beans and tofu in a coconut milk sauce.

Kuala Lumpur, 133 Martin Alley (enter at 132 W. Colorado Boulevard), Pasadena, S.F. VALLEY, 818-577-5175. Lunch and dinner; closed Monday. The food at Kuala Lumpur, one of L.A.'s few Malaysian restaurants, shows off the Indian-Chinese mélange so deliciously that you wonder why more restaurants don't serve this exhilarating cooking. Curry laksa, a marvelous fusion of rich, slightly spicy coconut-milk curry sauce, could quickly turn rice noodles into an addiction. Kuala Lumpur's appetizers and noodles, all stellar examples of Malay market fare, include banana-leaf-wrapped sticky rice rolls stuffed with chicken, sausage, and vegetables. Rojak, a tropical fruit salad sold by Malay hawkers from ice carts, comes with mango, papaya, and crunchy chunks of cucumber and jicama dressed with a sharp "shrimp sauce." The taste is typical of the way Southeast Asian cooks unexpectedly blend salty and sweet elements.

But Kuala Lumpur does more than hawker dishes, as you might imagine glancing around this stylish dining room with its two-story ceilings and gorgeous flower bouquets. Rich curries come in elegant little chafing dishes; huge sambal shrimp are glazed in a tart-hot tamarind sauce, and *selangor*-style chicken has been marinated in lemon grass and cumin, then grilled.

INDONESIAN MARKETS

- **Ann's Dutch Imports,** 4357 Tujunga Avenue, Studio City, S.F. VALLEY, 818-985-5551; closed Monday.
- **Holland-American Market & Importing Corp.,** 10343 E. Artesia Boulevard, Bellflower, SOUTH, 310-867-7589; closed Sunday.

Run out of bumbu besengeh or bumbu sayur gudeg? The best places to stock up on these, along with ketjap, trasi, krupek and other Indonesian ingredients, are Ann's Dutch Imports and Holland-American Market. Both carry Dutch groceries—cheeses, herrings, and a selection of cakes and cookies—but Indonesian ingredients make up more than half their inventories.

Holland-American is near supermarket size, but carries no fresh meat or produce. A mainstay in the Indonesian department are bumbus. These spice bases for various curries come in soft blocks or small plastic containers. You mix their contents with coconut milk and meat or vegetables.

Even more convenient are the take-out foods at Ann's. In the cooler are take-away dishes and appetizers like filled croquettes, beef risolles resembling rectangular egg rolls, and pasteitjes. In freezer cartons you find nasi goreng, sambal goreng, and other ready-to-eat dishes.

At both stores look for jars of chile-based sambals to serve as table condiments, fermented shrimp, Indonesian laurel leaves, tempeh, and candle nuts (like macadamia nuts) to be ground and used to thicken curries.

THE PHILIPPINES

The Filipinos like to call their cooking a happy blend of East and West—it is certainly a hybrid. After almost 400 years of Spanish domination, the Filipino kitchen has made Spanish *guisado* (sautéing) and adobado (cooking in a marinade) the most common of their cooking methods. A little Chinese food is also factored in, so you get dishes like pancit guisado: Chinese noodles sautéed Spanish style with crisp chicharrones as a garnish.

But don't be misled by all this culture crossing. Filipino

food, except for a few instances, resembles neither Spanish nor Chinese cuisine. Native condiments of patis and bagoong, both fermented fish sauces, are major flavorings. Tart tamarind and native vinegars give dishes the sharp tang Filipinos love. Banana ketchup, another favorite condiment, even dresses French fries. And local foods like purple yam, immature coconut, coconut milk, and cassava root show up even when Spanish or Chinese cooking styles are used.

In spite of an enormous presence here—Filipinos are the largest Asian ethnic group in California—few outsiders actually know much about Filipino food. In the Filipino community, entertaining at home takes precedence over restaurant dining and the number of bona fide dinner houses is small. But there's plenty of authentic Filipino food to be had. Of Los Angeles' hundreds of Filipino eating establishments sprinkled widely across the county in minimalls, most are small take-out or specialty fast food places that do a substantial catering business on the side. And a number of Manila-based Filipino chains such as Goldilox, Mami King, and Max's Chicken have Filipinos lining up for the same food they'd be eating in Manila.

— FILIPINO GLOSSARY —

Adobo: Meat or fowl marinated in a palm vinegar-garlic-soy sauce mixture, and braised in the marinade. The meat is then fried and the marinade reduced by boiling before being recombined with the meat. Adobado is any dish cooked using this method.
Almondigas: Meatballs.
Ampalaya: Bitter melon.
Bagoong: There are dozens of varieties of this semiliquid fish paste made from fermented fish or shrimp. Bagoongs are often used as a condiment or dip and occasionally in cooking.
Balut: A duck egg containing a partially developed embryo. Balut are usually dyed a bright fuchsia color.
Bibingka: A flat rice pancake cooked in a special earthenware dish and topped with an egg, crumbled white cheese, and sugar.
Bulalo: Beef marrow bone soup.
Cocido: A beef, chicken, and vegetable stew with much garlic. Like puchero, some versions are

served with the cooking broth on the side.

Dinuguan: A pork and organ meat stew thickened with blood.

Ensaimada: A slightly sweet breakfast yeast bread topped with crumbled white cheese and sugar.

Goto: A thick rice purée soup often made with tripe—a close cousin of Chinese congee.

Guisado: Sautéed or to sauté.

Halo-halo: The Filipino version of a milkshake, which contains a large assortment of ingredients, including strips of young coconut, squares of egg custard, jackfruit, and sweet red beans.

Kare-kare: Oxtail stew with a peanut butter gravy.

Kalderetta: A stew usually made with goat or beef.

Leche flan: Egg custard.

Longaniza: Sausage.

Lumpia: There are two versions of lumpia: The deep-fried lumpia resemble egg rolls, although the fillings may be such things as banana or crab. Fresh lumpia is a crêpe rolled around lettuce and vegetables and served with a sweet, soy-based sauce.

Macapuno: Immature coconut.

Mami: Filipino-style Chinese wheat noodles in soup.

Mechado: A beef roast, sometimes with pork fat or bacon inserted into it, then braised. Sometimes termed Filipino-style pot roast.

Pan de sal: "Salt bread" in Spanish, pan de sal are plain yeast rolls eaten for breakfast.

Pancit: The Filipino term for noodle that includes pancit sotanghon (bean thread noodles) and pancit bihoon (rice noodles). Pancit guisado is pan-fried noodles and pancit lug lug, spaghettilike rice noodles topped with a wide assortment of ingredients including smoked fish.

Pastel: A large savory pie. Chicken and sausage, stewed tongue or fish are popular fillings.

Patis: Filipino-style fish sauce similar to Thai nam pla (page 85) but milder. As in Thailand, patis is used as a seasoning in cooking.

Pinakbet: A braised mixed vegetable dish that always includes eggplant.

Polvoron: Shortbreadlike cookies made with a large proportion of powdered milk.

Puchero or pucherong (also called cocido): This Filipino Sunday dinner staple is a hearty assortment of meats and vegetables cooked in a soup or broth. For some versions, the soup is served first, followed by the other ingredients. Pucherong manok is the chicken version.

Puto bumbong: A sweet made from purple sticky rice that is steamed and topped with butter and sugar.

Sinigang: A tart soup of meat or fish cooked with sour vegetables and flavored with tamarind, sinigang's variations are nearly endless.

Siomai: The Filipino version of siu mai—Chinese open-faced dumplings.

Siopao: The Filipino version of Chinese bao (filled, steamed breadlike buns).

Sitaw: Chinese long beans.

Taisan: A light chiffon cake.

Talong: Eggplant.

Tinapa: Flaked, smoked fish.

Turo-turo: A small restaurant selling rice plates with various toppings from a steam table.

Ube: A purple-colored yam used for desserts.

AN INTRODUCTION TO FILIPINO FOOD

Barrio Fiesta, 3821 W. 6th Street, Los Angeles, CENTRAL, 213-383-9762. Lunch and dinner; closed Tuesday. Barrio Fiesta (which means "neighborhood party," in Spanish) captures the Filipino outlook when it comes to socializing and food. A party atmosphere prevails here—large tables are nearly always filled with celebrants. The flagship restaurant of the Barrio Fiesta chain in Manila is a traditional venue for social gatherings. The custom has carried over to the Los Angeles branch.

Much of the decor, from its capiz shell lights to the mahogany floor, and even the waiters' native *barong tagalog* garb, was shipped from the Philippines.

Begin with the traditional pork or chicken adobo—both are long simmered in a soy-vinegar mixture, then crisped on a grill. Almost every restaurant will have adobo dishes, but Barrio Fiesta's are exceptional. Try crispy *pusit* (fried squid with a garlic-laced vinegar dipping sauce) and the peanut-sauced kare-kare.

Rey's Pinausukan, 1828–30 W. Rosecrans Avenue, Gardena, SOUTH, 310-323-7354. Lunch through dinner daily and until 1:00 A.M. Thursday to Saturday. Rey's Pinausukan, owned by videotape shop magnate Reynaldo Santos, is housed in an impressive Spanish hacienda-style building. Its multi-roomed dining area is elegantly appointed with imported hand-bent Filipino bamboo. Thursday to Sunday evenings a Filipina chanteuse who sings in one of the rooms always draws a little crowd.

Sinigang, the Philippines' famous tart tamarind soup, comes in nine versions including the additions of catfish, pompano, and beef. Dinner portions are huge and all à la carte; they seem designed for sharing. Though many menu terms are in Tagalog, the national language of the Philippines, the manager has a knack for explaining Pinausukan's dishes. He got me to try the *ginataang manok,* a dish of chicken and pork stewed in coconut milk sauce. As weird as crispy *pata* sounds (it's a deep-fried pork hock), the succulent meat is outrageously delicious, and the *guisadong* talong (sautéed eggplant) is a wonderful accompaniment. Fridays at lunch Pinausukan offers an all-you-can-eat buffet. Otherwise, be prepared to ask questions about Pinausukan's very long menu.

FILIPINO SPECIALTIES

♦ TURO-TURO

Turo-turo means "point, point" in Tagalog, and that's how you order at one of the many turo-turo restaurants scattered around L.A. The rules are the same at all of these places: Point to two choices from the steam table, and you get them served with rice and broth or a light soup. Or you can order à la carte. The prices are always streetside low, and in the good shops the food will be well cooked from scratch and won't suffer from standing on the steam table. Most places rotate their offerings, so you won't find all of the same dishes every day.

Little Quiapo, 4255 W. 3rd Street, Los Angeles, CENTRAL, 213-382-6308, and 1016 N. Vermont Avenue, Los Angeles, CENTRAL, 213-663-9450. Lunch and dinner; Sunday until 5:00 P.M. Little Quiapo is a minimall-bright turo-turo with tile walls and seating of a majestic, intense purple. Desserts at Little Quiapo seem color-coordinated to their surroundings: there's an astonishing purple-filled tart made from a purple yam called ube, and a purple yam pudding. The Third Street branch of Little Quiapo is just a basic, clean storefront that has been around much longer than the purple Vermont branch. At both branches, cocido brims with beef chunks and vegetables still firmly holding their shape, and the Chinese long beans with bacon are crisp and green. Good things to try: almondigas stew made with meatballs and vegetables, and adobo anything. If you're lucky, the day you visit they'll have pucherong manok (a chicken stew made with vegetables and garbanzo beans, flavored with Spanish sausage) and *la blanca maiz* (a yellow vanilla pudding flecked with specks of creamed corn).

D. J. Bibingkahan Restaurant, 13760 Roscoe Boulevard, Panorama City, S.F. VALLEY, 818-894-5688. Lunch and dinner daily. D. J.'s specialty, adobo rolls, always sell out fast. These resemble baked bao, the Chinese buns. But in place of the usual Chinese barbecue filling are chunks of pork adobo steeped in a heady vinegar and soy marinade.

D. J. makes fabulous mechado, a Filipino-style pot roast, and kare-kare. D. J.'s jovial proprietor says he doesn't put any bones or organ meats in this stew so it will appeal to "foreigners." Other specialties include kalderetta, a stew made of beef here rather than the traditional goat meat. Service is cafeteria-style, and the commodious seating area has etched-glass room dividers topped with brass railings.

Emmanuel's, 217 S. Vermont Avenue, Los Angeles, CENTRAL, 213-480-0898. Open 10:30 A.M. to 8:30 P.M.; closed Tuesday. At Emmanuel's such things as grilled oysters on the half shell served with a lime-garlic dip are cooked to order. Emmanuel feels these won't be satisfactory if they sit on the turo-turo steam table, nor will Emmanuel's voluptuous pancit lug lug, made from a special thick rice noodle and best cooked to order by dipping it in and out of hot water several times to keep the noodles firm. The pancit is garnished

splendidly with layers of stir-fried vegetables, pork, and shrimp, as well as crispy chicharrones, deep-fried garlic, flakes of a smoked fish called tinapa, and rounds of hard-cooked egg. The hot-table specials often depend on what Emmanuel's steady customers have requested. Most days you'll find Filipino-style pot roast and laing (taro leaves cooked in coconut milk), adobo pusit, or chicken pastel. To order at Emmanuel's you can turo-turo at the cooked-to-order items on the menu board or the steam table.

♦ **MAMI**

Chinese food has a long tradition in the Philipines. Manila has hundreds of Chinese restaurants, many of them specializing in mami, the Filipino version of Chinese-style soup noodles. These differ from pancit, which are noodles cooked in the Filipino-Spanish style.

Mami King, 4321 Sunset Boulevard, Los Angeles, CENTRAL, 213-669-1078, and 21209 Hawthorne Boulevard, Torrance, SOUTH, 310-540-3326; also Rowland Heights, EAST OF L.A. Open for lunch through dinner daily. The mami are made at Mami King's main Torrance branch and sent to other branches daily. You can buy bags of them to take home.

In the restaurant, mami come in soups with various toppings: chicken, barbecued pork, or wontons. Mami King also specializes in Chinese filled and steamed buns, called siopao in the Philippines. One version, the *bola-bola,* is filled with ground pork, chicken, sausage, salted egg, and mushroom. The siomai—pork-filled boiled dumplings open at the top—are large and hefty here.

Cathay Noodle House, 17806 Pioneer Boulevard, Suite 105 (World Plaza), Artesia, SOUTH, 310-402-8030. Open 11:00 A.M. to 8:30 P.M. daily. Mami King may have branches, but Cathay House is the only shop I know that makes its mami every day by hand. The noodles are slightly thicker and more al dente than the commercial kind. And an extrathick version called "lomi" in a soup that's almost a stew is a noodle-lover's dream come true. Cathay also makes wonderful fat wontons. Noodles and wontons may be had in a number of variations: topped with Chinese-style barbecued pork or beef or chicken, or as chow mien. Cathay House also makes chicken siopao and juicy siomai.

♦ **STREET FOODS IN A POSH GRILL**
Jeepney Grill, 3470 W. 6th Street, Koreatown, CENTRAL, 213-739-2971. Lunch through dinner daily. Jeepney Grill offers Manila-style street foods and Chinatown specialties in a sleek minimall café fitted out with Filipino lampposts and an authentic Jeepney: the popular mode of public transportation around Manila. Jeepneys, converted World War II Jeeps, are baroquely decorated over every surface with artwork that ranges from a mosaic portrait of Cory Aquino made from bottle caps to plastic flowers.

The streetside barbecue, Jeepney Grill's specialty, includes pork chunks, chicken, pork chops, and squid in a soy-based marinade. For Filipinos, these have unrelenting *sarap,* (a Filipino term for addictive flavor). Bulalo is available around the clock in Manila; you can get this hearty beef-shank soup for lunch at the Jeepney Grill along with goto, a Chinese-style soupy rice porridge made with simmered pork, tripe, lots of ginger, and topped with deep-fried garlic.

♦ **BIBINGKA AND PANCIT MALBON**
Manila Sunset, 2815 W. Sunset Boulevard, Los Angeles, CENTRAL, 213-484-5161. Open 11:00 A.M. to 8:00 P.M. daily. Also in Carson, Sepulveda, and West Covina. Bibingka—a traditional flat cake made from pulverized rice and steamed in an earthenware container with charcoal at the top—wasn't easy to find in L.A. before Manila Sunset opened. This American branch of a Manila chain called Mommy's Best specializes in bibingka, which once were sold—and probably still are—from December 16 until Christmas by vendors who offered their wares in front of churches after each Midnight Mass. The cakes are topped with a salted duck egg and a sprinkling of white cheese, sugar, and fresh coconut; it makes a pretty substantial meal. Another specialty of the house, puto bumbong (a delicious sweet made from naturally colored purple rice and steamed in a bamboo tube), is also brushed with butter and sprinkled with sugar and fresh coconut. Manila Sunset has a small menu of other specialties including their famous pancit *malabon:* rice noodles mixed with a shrimp sauce, then sprinkled with crispy chicharrones, fresh shrimp, deep-fried garlic, and egg slices, with a lime slice on the side.

SHOPS
Goldilocks, 209 S. Vermont Avenue, Los Angeles, CENTRAL, 213-382-2351. Also in Carson, Artesia, SOUTH, 310-860-7786, and West Covina, EAST OF L.A., 818-964-1811. Open daily. Tall ornate cakes with lush, gooey frosting are the pride of Goldilocks' pastry display. But this Filipino bakery and deli, a successful Philippines-based chain with several branches around Los Angeles, sells many more interesting items and everything is rendered exactly as it would be in Manila. The fresh lumpia, often called a Filipino egg roll, is a thin lettuce-lined crêpe rolled around pork and vegetables. It comes with a sweet-tart sauce. This is also where Filipinos come for their pan de sal and fragrant yeasty ensaimada. Farther out on the edge of the Pacific Rim are the purple ube tarts and pudding made from an amethyst-colored yam, and the

Tropical treats, gooey cakes, and deli to go from Goldilocks Filipino bakeshop.

macapuno tart with a jellylike young-coconut filling. You might want to sit at one of Goldilocks' tables and try a small snack of siopao and the outrageous milkshake drink called halo-halo, which means "mix mix." For this extravaganza Goldilocks combines approximately ten ingredients, including coconut jam, garbanzo beans cooked in sugar, squares of red gelatin, and leche flan in a tall ice cream glass. This may sound more like a stew than a shake, but it's really mostly milk and ice. The deluxe halo-halo comes with a scoop of ice cream.

Red Ribbon Bake Shop, 6091 Sunset Boulevard, Hollywood, CENTRAL, 213-465-5999. Open daily. Also in Cerritos, SOUTH, and West Covina, EAST OF L.A. This Manila-style pastry shop has drawn raves for its mango cake, which is tall, multilayered, and filled with mango purée mixed with whipped cream. The owner has a contract with Philippine mango growers to get the fruit at peak season; these are imported frozen; the Mexi-

can mangoes we get in our markets simply don't have the proper flavor.

The baked goods here reflect centuries of Spanish influence. The flaky chicken empanadas are big sellers, as are the empanaditas, little caramel-filled pastries wrapped in festive colored cellophane. Pan de sal and yeasted ensaimada are standard in all Filipino bakeries, but Red Ribbon does them elegantly. More popular sweets are taisan (a lighter-than-air chiffon loaf cake brushed with butter and sprinkled with sugar) and polvoron (shortbreadlike shaped cookies, gaily wrapped in tissue).

Asian Ranch Supermarket, Inc., 13722 Sherman Way, Van Nuys, S.F. VALLEY, 818-781-0385 or 781-0386. Asian Ranch, the newest and largest Filipino market in the Valley, has a large meat and seafood department with butchers on hand to answer your questions. The produce department is also impressively stocked with Chinese greens plus fresh cassava, ube, and, in season, mangoes imported from the islands. The freezer cases contain many whole fish imported from the Philippines. Unfortunately, the bangus, or milkfish, that Filipinos love isn't fresh; it only comes into this country frozen. In the meat department you'll also find Filipino longaniza of various brands and chorizo de bilbao sausage for making paella and other Spanish-influenced Filipino dishes.

Masagana, 4253 W. 3rd Street, Los Angeles, CENTRAL, 213-384-1160. A medium-size market, Masagana is one of the oldest and best stocked Filipino stores in central Los Angeles. On the packaged goods shelves you find such unique convenience foods as Mama Sita's singing soup mix, tamarind concentrate in jars, and annatto water—to eliminate using those messy seeds. You'll also see dried mango slices, the banana catsup used for sweet and sour sauces, and the palm vinegar essential for adobo dishes. Of course there's lots of patis and bagoong. The freezer area holds whole guava, palm nuts, coconut milk, and grated cassava convenient for making cassava pudding and other desserts.

Lorenzana Market, 627 N. Vermont Avenue, Los Angeles, CENTRAL, 213-665-5155, and 800 W. Carson Street, Torrance, SOUTH, 310-320-6103. Lorenzana, the granddaddy of Filipino supermarkets in Los Angeles, has a new branch in Torrance. Lorenzana still imports much of its own stock and finds local Chinese and Filipino vegetables for its good produce department. Look for green mangoes and papayas for salads, sitaw, and the tiny thumb-length bananas called *saba*. There's bitter melon *(ampalya)*; Asian eggplants to make pinakbet; and whole tamarind pods for flavoring sinigang.

The meat department carries every imaginable part of the pig including blood for dinuguan, plus pork snouts, maw, jowl, and pork butt for all sorts of stews. Beef offal are always plentiful here too. Lorenzana marinates its own milkfish ready to grill, as well as *tocino* (marinated pork belly). Baluts, brilliant magenta-colored salted eggs, are kept in the cooler. And you will find freezers filled with assorted sizes of shrimp, the sweetened young coconut called *buco* for desserts, fish and shrimp balls for soups, and lumpia wrappers.

INDIA

Not far from Malibu Beach, where surfers wait to catch the ultimate curl, is Sree Venkateswara Hindu Temple. It appears unexpectedly, its gold towers sparkling in the distance, as you navigate Malibu Canyon's winding roads.

The temple, built by Tamil craftsmen, is not the only surprising bit of Indian culture in L.A.: There's a shop on Pico Boulevard, next to a Jewish bakery, where you can have a sari made to order from the yards of sumptuously decorated fabrics on display—and this is only one of many such shops from Cerritos to Sherman Oaks. The Shakti School offers classes in Bharata Natyam classical dance at its five locations. And Sunderjeree Graphics will typeset copy in five Indian languages.

In Los Angeles you will find Punjabi, Gujarati, Bengali and other regional Indian cuisines. In fact, we can sample a larger variety of Indian dishes than most Indians would ever encounter in their homeland.

In India, cooks rely on what grows close at hand; there's

no transportation and usually no refrigeration. Indian cooks must also follow the dictates of their religion, and the rules of their sect or caste: Millions of Hindus are vegetarians; Jains never cook with garlic or onions. There is an old saying that you cannot be a good Muslim unless you eat plenty of meat—except, of course, pork, which is forbidden.

As any traveler who's eaten the local fare in India will tell you, restaurants, except in large tourist hotels, aren't likely to mix disparate cuisines. But here in L.A. they do so happily.

Once guided by unshakable dogma, some Indian cooks are adapting Western culinary notions. At Tikka, a small fast-food Indian take-out chain, dishes cooked with very little salt or fat bear the symbol of the American Heart Association. A lighter, California style is emerging in the Clay Pit and Nawab restaurants. And eyebrows would surely be raised back in India if they got wind of the tandoori-grilled pork baby back ribs at the East India Grill.

— INDIAN GLOSSARY —

See also Chat and Methai glossary (pages 141–142).

Alu gobi (or aloo gobi): *Potatoes and cauliflower dry-cooked with curry seasonings.*

Baegan bartha: *Charcoal-roasted eggplant simmered with seasonings and mashed.*

Basmati: *A strain of long-grained rice with a highly aromatic flavor grown and eaten in northern and western India but not in southern India (see chelo, page 212, for more on basmati rice).*

Batata bonda: *A deep-fried mashed potato ball.*

Bhajias: *Deep-fried vegetable fritters.*

Bhuna: *The technique of sautéing and stirring meats as they cook*

until spices cling to the meat and any liquid evaporates.

Biriyani: *Rice mixed with other ingredients, which might include meat, chicken, fish, or vegetables; often eaten as a main dish. A rice pilau, on the other hand, may be intricately spiced and even include meats, but is usually eaten as a side dish.*

Chat: *The general term for India's many and varied snack foods.*

Dahi: *Yogurt.*

Dal: *Beans or lentils, and also the name for many dishes using dals as the primary ingredient.*

Dhokla: *Cornbreadlike squares made from seasoned chick-pea* flour. Dhokla originated in western India.

Dudhi: A large pale green squash.

Ghee: Clarified butter used as a cooking medium.

Idli: Southern Indian steamed rice and lentil cakes.

Jelebi: A sweet deep-fried flour fritter made from a swirl of dough and flavored with syrup and rose water.

Katoris: Metal cups that hold dals and currys on a thali.

Kebab: Meats or chicken cooked on skewers, often in a tandoor oven or over an open grill. Several popular kebab styles are: bara kebab (skewered lamb chops); boti kebab (cubed marinated lamb); chicken tikka (boneless chicken marinated in yogurt and spices— there's also lamb tikka); and seekh kebab (seasoned ground meat formed into a sausage shape).

Kulcha: See roti.

Lassi: A beverage made from yogurt and ice either with salt or fruit.

Malai kofta: Balls made from fresh cheese with vegetables and nuts and cooked in a rich Moghlai-style sauce.

Masala: A mixture of spices.

Masala dosa (Punjabi) or dosai (southern): A thin rice and lentil flour crêpe stuffed with potato curry.

Moghlai: Refers to the rich cooking style of the northern Moghl rulers.

Murgh musallam: This traditional dish of whole chicken cooked in a rich spiced yogurt is often made here with chicken pieces.

Nan: See roti.

Oothappam or uthapam: A crêpe made of lentil flour and usually cooked with fresh onion and tomato.

Pakoras: Vegetables or other foods dipped in chick-pea flour and deep-fried.

Paneer: A fresh white cheese often made by Indians at home.

Pappadam (south Indian): A thin crisp-toasted wafer made of urad dal (a bean). In the north these are called papar.

Paratha: See roti.

Parval: A melonlike vegetable.

Pessret: A southern-style lentil crêpe made with minced chiles.

Petti: Mashed potato ball stuffed with seasoned fresh coconut and deep-fried.

Pilau: Rice cooked with other ingredients mixed into it.

Puri: See roti.

Raita: A cooling side dish made of cucumbers in yogurt.

Rava dosai: A southern Indian semolina pancake.

Roghan josh: Lamb cooked in a rich, complex northern-style yogurt sauce.

Roti: The general term for bread. Rotis include chapati, an unleavened whole wheat griddle-baked bread; nan, a yeast-leavened flat bread cooked against the walls of the tandoor; paratha, a flaky, unleavened whole wheat flat bread; and puri (or poori), a deep-fried whole wheat flat bread; kulcha, an oval yeast-leavened tandoor-baked or deep-fried white bread often containing onions (called onion kulcha).

Sag: The general term for leafy greens that includes methi ka sag (fenugreek leaves), palak ka sag (spinach), and sarson ka sag (mustard greens).

Sag paneer: Spinach cooked with white fresh cheese cubes.

Sambal: *Spicy condiments.*

Sambar: *A spicy southern-style dal dish made with whole and puréed lentils.*

Shrikhand: *A condensed yogurt dessert flavored with saffron.*

Tandoor: *Correctly spelled* tandur. *A barrel-shaped clay oven fueled by hot coals whose temperatures reach up to 800° F. The tandoor sears meats in seconds and bakes flat breads in minutes. On menus, foods cooked in the oven may be prefaced by the word* tandoori *(e.g.,* tandoori nan *or* tandoori chicken).

Tava: *A cast-iron convex griddle.*

Thali: *A complete meal on a tray arranged in a prescribed order and also the name of the tray itself (see page 138).*

Tikka: *Pieces. Chicken cut into chunks, marinated in spiced yogurt, and cooked in a tandoor is chicken tikka.*

Uthapam: *See oothappam.*

Vadai (southern) or vada (Punjabi): *A fritter made of lentil flour.*

Vindaloo: *An especially hot Goan-style curry for which the meat is marinated in vinegar.*

THE LIGHTER CAL-INDIAN STYLE

With an innovative bent and an inclination to lighten up on the oil, the ghee, and the heavy spicing of traditional Indian cooking, these restaurants are rethinking traditional Indian fare. Their food, in the current mode of California-style cuisine, emphasizes good fresh ingredients with spicing that complements rather than over-powers.

The Clay Pit, 3465 W. 6th Street, No. 110, Los Angeles, CENTRAL, 213-382-6300. Lunch and dinner daily. The Clay Pit, a room that's all angular natural surfaces and burnished metals, overlooks the patio at Chapman Market. Tandoor chefs work behind a glass partition thrusting long iron skewers of kebabs down into the center of the oven and shaping bread dough before deftly slapping it to the tandoor's clay walls to bake. The Clay Pit does traditional Punjabi-style cooking with a bright California twist to it. Some items are pure invention: The Clay Pit salad, strips of tandoori-baked chicken tikka scattered over a bed of greens, is drizzled with a vinaigrette or yogurt dressing. There's

also a marinated mesquite tandoori sirloin steak and a rack of baby lamb, both beautifully rare.

The Clay Pit hasn't ignored traditional dishes, and they do these equally well. Roghan josh, a rich Kashmiri-style lamb dish simmered in several types of masala—the ultimate test of a skilled Indian cook—is but one example.

Bombay Cafe, 12113 Santa Monica Boulevard, West Los Angeles, WEST, 310-820-2070. Lunch and dinner; closed Monday. The bright and multimirrored Bombay Cafe turns rough-and-ready Indian street foods into dainty West Side–style grazing fare. Where most sev puri comes in a free-form heap, the version at Bombay Cafe is as carefully planned as a composed salad: half a dozen crispy little wafers topped with potato and onion, and with sev—crunchy noodlelike strands of chick-pea flour—arranged on the top. Frankies, the owner's rendition of a popular snack sold at Candy Beach near Bombay, is a curry-filled flatbread rolled up like a burrito. The café isn't the best place for classic dishes: Chicken tikka, for example, is frankly dull. But the tandoori shrimp salad with pickled green mango on red leaf lettuce is a knockout.

Kenny's Kitchen, 14126 Sherman Way, No. 10, Van Nuys, S.F. VALLEY, 818-786-4868. Lunch and dinner; closed Monday. Kenny's is everything you always hoped a mom-and-pop restaurant would be. Kenny Sharma, an Oxford-educated gentleman who owns the tailoring business next to the restaurant, and his wife, Kiran, took up cooking for the love of it, and it shows. The menu is not the standard tandoori tome. Its mixed regional offerings include uthapam with a lightly cooked fresh-tomato-and-onion topping and coconut chutney. The meat and seafood curries are all low in sodium and prepared with corn oil. And Kenny's squeezes juices to order.

Kenny's dishes, full of sparkly fresh flavors, lift classical dishes like sag paneer—usually a murky rich spinach sauce with cubes of dense cheese—into the fresh-and-light school of cooking.

East India Grill, 345 N. La Brea Avenue, Los Angeles, CENTRAL, 213-936-8844 or 936-8845, and **East India Grill Santa Monica,** 318 Santa Monica Boulevard, Santa Monica, WEST, 310-917-6644. Lunch Monday to Saturday; dinner nightly. While Kenny's merely freshens up Indian classics, East India Grill has clearly been led—sometimes astray—by the trendy world of its surrounding neighborhood and the nearby ultrahip Melrose district. The appetizers are called "The First Experiment," and include curried mussels and "hot chicken wings from Hell." Nan, the chewy tandoori-baked bread, is topped pizza-style with garlic and basil or onion and cilantro; the baby back ribs are tandoor-cooked. Sometimes the experiments work wonderfully. Occasionally they don't.

But it's all very interesting.

East India Grill has opened a newer sibling, East India Grill Santa Monica, with a similarly innovative menu.

Tikka, 16101 Vanowen Street, Van Nuys, S.F. VALLEY, 818-781-5744; also 18966 Ventura Boulevard, Tarzana, S.F. VALLEY, 818-708-1448; 18110 Nordhoff Street, Northridge, S.F. VALLEY, 818-993-8529; 21915 Devonshire Street, Chatsworth, S.F. VALLEY, 818-998-6322. Lunch through dinner daily. About six years ago, Tikka's proprietor, a former burger-stand owner, decided to throw caution to the winds and turn his back on the staid burger and pastrami business in favor of a bold new idea: low-fat, low-sodium Indian-style grilled chicken. He painted the burger stand powder blue and installed a self-serve "salsa" bar stocked with various chutneys. And his dynamite, grilled yogurt-marinated skinless chicken was granted the American Heart Association's approval. Even the accompanying curried vegetables are healthy; they're steamed and seasoned with good masala. Now Tikka offers grilled Indian spiced fish and chicken tikka pita sandwiches at all four branches.

REGIONAL INDIAN CUISINES

Until recently, regional Indian foods were scarce in Los Angeles. The average Indian menu—practically interchangeable from one restaurant to the next—had a touristy, panregional mix of the subcontinent's most popular dishes. But a recent wave of Indian immigration has brought with it a demand for more authentic regional foods and eating places. Here are the best places to discover the regional differences of India's cooking.

♦ **THE NORTHERN CUISINES**
More than any other part of India, the northwest has borrowed cooking styles from a succession of

invaders and immigrants. The Near Eastern clay oven was first adopted by northern cooks, and thus Punjabi tandoori cooking was born. But Moghlai, the north's most opulent cuisine, was purloined from Persian royalty by India's Moghl rulers. Many dishes are sautés rich with cream, butter, nuts, and raisins, and the sweets are lavishly decorated with thin edible sheets of silver.

Akbar, 590 Washington Street, Marina del Rey, WEST, 310-822-4116, and 17049 Ventura Boulevard, Encino, S.F. VALLEY, 818-905-5129. Lunch and dinner daily. The elegant Akbar in Marina del Rey has a fine array of Punjabi grills with enough Moghlai specialties to allow a comparison of both cuisines. Chicken *akbari*, chicken chunks in an absolutely voluptuous nut-and-raisin-laced cream sauce, is the epitome of Moghlai richness; its spicing is complex but not too hot. And malai kofta, savory cheese balls stuffed with nuts in a creamy sauce flecked with minced vegetables, is another. Rice dishes such as biriyanis and pilaus can also exhibit the Moghlai richness, especially Akbar's Moghlai biriyani: your choice of seasoned lamb, chicken, or beef cooked with nuts and saffron. It's not likely the Moghuls ate much lobster, but in keeping with the theme of opulence Akbar offers tandoori lobster and lobster bhuna sautéed with fresh tomato, garlic, cilantro, and vegetables.

The plush Moghlesque decor is a contrast to the simple bilevel dining rooms of Akbar's Encino branch. And the menus follow suit. The Encino branch leans more toward the straight Punjabi style, and for diet-conscious Moghls its kitchen has initiated "Tandoori lite" dishes served in whole or half portions.

Mumtaz, 7166 Melrose Avenue, Los Angeles, CENTRAL, 213-933-2945. Lunch and dinner daily. Mumtaz, named after the woman for whom the Moghl emperor Sha Jehan built the Taj Mahal, serves whole Kashmiri tandoori chicken stuffed with minced seasoned lamb; the dish sums up the baroque thinking of Moghlai cooks. Game was favored at the Moghlai court, and Mumtaz serves a brace of marinated tandoori-cooked quail. If you order in advance you can get the Muglai *khurzi* lamb dinner, featuring a whole marinated lamb leg, six different vegetable dishes, basmati rice, and a selection of desserts including mango- or saffron-flavored ice cream with pistachios. All the standard tandoori à la carte items are also available. And though Mumtaz's prices are moderate, its upholstered chairs and linen-draped tables are plush enough for the Taj Mahal.

Bombay Palace, 8690 Wilshire Boulevard, Beverly Hills, WEST, 310-659-9944. Open for lunch and dinner daily. Although renowned for tandoori meat dishes, the north also has a complex vegetarian cuisine; in fact, most northerners are vegetarians. Bombay Palace is not a vegetarian restaurant, but it offers more than a dozen vegetable preparations, many as stunning in their execution as the glimmering Bombay Palace dining room filled with backlit recessed windows and antiques.

Two dishes that flaunt the subtle yet complex spicing of northern vegetarian cooking are this restaurant's malai kofta, vegetable fritters in a buttery sauce, and baegan bartha, tandoori-roasted eggplant simmered in tomatoes, onions, and masala. Another wonderful vegetable option, *bindi* masala, is okra sauteed with onion and tomato sparked with lots of cilantro. Add to these the tandoori onion kulcha bread stuffed with spiced onion and dry mango or the whole-wheat paratha stuffed with curried potatoes, and you have the makings of an unparalleled northern vegetarian meal.

Nawab of India, 1621 Wilshire Boulevard, Santa Monica, WEST, 310-829-1106. Lunch and dinner daily. Perhaps the most carefully executed traditional Punjabi food in the city comes from Nawab. The restaurant's dossier is a comment on the state of business in Los Angeles. It's owned by the Yugen Kaisha Himalaya partnership, a firm associated with the Indian-owned Japanese restaurant group that holds the Gaylord franchise in Japan. Appropriately, it's situated in a former sushi bar, which has been turned into a comfortable, understated dining room with soft gray linens and fresh flowers.

Huge prawns come from the tandoor au point, never dry; a fish curry holds moist-fleshed fish chunks. My favorite appetizer is the tandoori chicken chat, an Indian version of a Chinese chicken salad. Most of this food is light and clean-tasting, with occasional forays into Moghlai territory, such as murgh musallam: chunks of chicken on a bed of seasoned minced chicken in a cream-laced sauce topped with sliced egg.

♦ **THE SOUTH**
Madhu's Dasaprakash, 11312 E. 183rd Street, Cerritos, SOUTH, 310-924-0879. Lunch and dinner daily. The mainstay in the subtropical, rice-growing, primarily vegetarian south is dal with rice and rice with dal (beans and lentils). If the combination sounds monotonous, a meal at Madhu's Dasaprakash in Cerritos will dispel that notion. Centuries of ingenious Indian cooks have turned these lowly staples into a wildly diverse assortment of dumplings, cakes, crêpes, fritters, and porridge—each with its own textures and tastes. Madhu's, in its serene modern dining room, serves the widest

(and best) selection of all.

Seven types of crêpes and pancakes are made here, with varied batters and fillings. Rava dosai, a semolina pancake, plain or flecked with onions, has a completely different character from oothappam, a lentil pancake that comes with either tomato or onion. Pessret, a wafer-thin, light green lentil-and-fresh-chile crêpe, is the best example of south India's love affair with hot spicy food (which reputedly stimulates the liver).

With the pancakes and most every other dish, you are served Madhu's sambar, enhanced with the sharp tastes of tamarind, tomato, and fresh chiles. Three dazzling chutneys—coconut, refreshing mint, and sweet-hot tamarind—give each bite of the dal and rice combination even more variety.

But pancakes are only one category of Madhu's offerings. *Bondas,* a kind of fried dumpling, come in half a dozen varieties. Madhu's black lentil Mysore bondas are puffy and almost like sponge cake (in the wrong hands these can turn into paperweights). Six kinds of pakoras and bhajias include addicting cashew pakoras, dipped in a spiced chick-pea flour and fried tempura style. And of the vadai, or lentil-flour fritters, the house specialty, *medhu* vadai, is dappled with onion and green chiles. With all these, refreshing, salty yogurt lassi is the best drink. Like wine, it cleanses the palate.

Paru's, 5140 Sunset Boulevard, Hollywood, CENTRAL, 213-661-7600. Lunch through dinner; closed Tuesday. Also 9340 W. Pico Boulevard, West Los Angeles, WEST, 310-273-8088. Lunch through dinner; closed Monday. And 9545 Reseda Boulevard, Northridge, S.F. VALLEY, 818-349-3546. Lunch through dinner; closed Tuesday. Paru's in Hollywood introduced L.A. to southern Indian food in the late seventies.

Their masala dosai, a crisp sour-dough rice-and-lentil crêpe stuffed with potato curry and rolled into a cylinder the size of a small baseball bat, gained such a wide following that Paru's opened two more branches in West Los Angeles and Northridge. (I still think the original Hollywood branch is best). Other vegetarian specialties here include idli—steamed round rice cakes that Indians love for breakfast—and (if you can imagine this) a tomato oothappam with mozzarella cheese that resembles Indian pizza. As at Madhu's, you eat these (except for the pizza) with sambar and coconut chutney.

Paru's vegetable curries, whether cauliflower, mushroom, or eggplant, are made with the typical southern "wet" masalas as their flavoring base. For these, spices are pounded with fresh garlic, ginger, and cilantro leaves. Northern cooks, on the other hand, usually roast spices for their "dry" masalas.

♦ **THE WEST**
Sabra's, 18189 S. Pioneer Boulevard, Artesia, SOUTH, 310-924-4948. Lunch through dinner; closed Monday. Kathiawari and Surati vegetarian-style cooking belong to the western state of Gujarat, home of Mahatma Gandhi and the Jain religious sect. The best Surati kitchen, Sabra's, on Pioneer Boulevard in Little India, is a wonderful source for Gujarati dhokla, a steamed savory chick-pea flour cake sprinkled with mustard seeds and fresh coriander. Sabra's turns the humble potato into ethereally fluffy pettis deep-fried so there's just the thinnest crispy crust surrounding the soft interior. An unstuffed version, batata bonda, is great for dipping into a selection of chutneys.

You can see the north's influence on Gujarati food in Sabra's thali. The northern basmati rice at its center comes with a little cup of ghee to pour over it. Use the puris to scoop up the robust vegetable curry and dal. Alongside these main items comes pappadams, coconut chutney, and sweet lemon rind pickle—a fine orchestration of flavors.

Another spot in the neighborhood for Gujarati cooking is **Jay Bharat** (18701 Pioneer Boulevard, Artesia, SOUTH, 310-924-3310; lunch through dinner; closed Monday).

Diwana Restaurant, 1381 E. Las Tunas Drive, San Gabriel, SAN GABRIEL VALLEY, 818-287-8743. Lunch through dinner; closed Tuesday. Diwana, another Gujarati restaurant in San Gabriel, is the only place I know to serve Kathiawari or Jain-style cooking. Jains are such strict vegetarians that they avoid eating garlic, onions, and other vegetables that grow underground for fear of harming insects when the foods are harvested. But Kathiawari cooks supplant those flavors by blending sharp, fruity tamarind or lime with palm sugar. The food has a slight sweet tartness with the underlying notes of gentle chile heat and spices.

The restaurant's Gujarati thali is the best way to get acquainted with Jain-style food. The katoris hold two vegetable curries and a dal that change daily. These might be curries of green beans, eggplant, black-eyed peas, or mustard greens—dishes rarely seen in northern- or southern-style restaurants. Also on the thali are vegetable fritters and chapati.

The left side of the thali always holds the pickles, chutneys, and raitas—on which discerning Indians base their opinion of such a meal. Diwana's cook, Premila Khetani, creates her own selection, including an extraordinary lemon rind chutney with long red peppers in a sweet base.

Diwana cooks for non-Jain customers too, so you'll find onions and garlic in other dishes. And don't leave without trying shrikhand, a saffron-infused condensed yogurt dessert, so rich it almost seems like a sweet mayonnaise. (For Gujarati snacks, see **Surati Farsan Mart,** page 143.)

NEIGHBORHOOD RESTAURANTS

Shalimar Cuisine of India, 23011 Ventura Boulevard, Woodland Hills, S.F. VALLEY, 818-703-7794. Lunch and dinner daily. All those breads and meats brought smoking from the tandoor kept us returning to India Garden in Canoga Park. But now owner Sahik Miah has decided to move out to the bright lights of Ventura Boulevard. He opened Shalimar and broadened the menu slightly. His garlic nan, slapped on the side of the tandoor to cook, is as exquisite and chewy as always. His other breads (there are 9) include the deluxe Moghlai lamb-stuffed paratha, nearly a meal in itself. Plain paratha is wonderful for sopping up saucy curries. And onion-stuffed kulcha makes Miah's gently seasoned grilled meats taste all the better.

India's Cuisine, 19006 Ventura Boulevard, Tarzana, S.F. VALLEY, 818-342-9100. Lunch and dinner daily. Every time I stop by India's Cuisine on weekends, its elegantly dark dining room is jammed with Indian parties. The lure? According to my Indian friends it's the moderate prices, plus very good food. And India's Cuisine doesn't simply stick with the same humdrum menu you often see around town. Besides all the familiar tandoori meats and breads, they do a tandoori game hen, a wonderful rare rack of lamb, and, as an appetizer, fish pakoras, a sort of deep-fried fish fritter.

Anarkali, 7013 Melrose Avenue, Los Angeles, CENTRAL, 213-932-9913 or 934-6488, and 22721 Ventura Boulevard, Woodland Hills, S.F. VALLEY, 818-704-0533. Lunch and dinner daily. After you've eaten in about 50 Indian restaurants within a month's time you begin to notice subtle and not so subtle differences even when the menus seem alike. At both of Anarkali's restaurants—where there are few surprises—the seasonings are bold, full of depth, and very traditional. The vegetable curries, which in some places are cooked to death, here still resemble the fresh vegetables they were made from.

The Woodland Hills branch has dramatic undulating booths and is done in hues of reds and deep maroons—the look isn't nearly as traditional as Anarkali's superb food.

Gaylord, 50 N. La Cienega Boulevard, Beverly Hills, WEST, 310-652-3838. Lunch and dinner daily. There's something to be said for knowing that your chicken tikka and roghan josh will taste the same as it did on your last visit to Gaylord. As you sit in the comfortable room with its widely spaced cloth-draped tables, you know the service will be efficient and the food, if limited in choice, will be good. As one of a chain of restaurants with branches from Bombay to Hong Kong to Chicago, Gaylord's chefs have impeccable credentials. But with all that talent in the kitchen and prices that are higher than most, you'd think they would introduce us to something more exotic.

Raja, 8875 W. Pico Boulevard, West Los Angeles, WEST, 213-550-9176. Lunch and dinner daily. Recently the 9-year-old Raja, one of the first tandoori places to open in L.A., underwent a major facelift. The heavy Asian decor became stark and modern, with sculpted pale ocher walls and Indian antiques as accents. The familiar appetizer menu—pakoras, samosas, and such—has been extended to include a cucumber and tomato salad with chunks of lightly seasoned tandoori chicken drizzled with tamarind dressing that Raja calls "chicken chat," and also shrimp puri, a rich shrimp curry you eat with the accompanying fried puffy bread. Now the restaurant has added daily specials: tandoori-roasted leg of lamb and a Bombay specialty, salmon *koliwada*, (salmon rubbed in a lively spice mixture and expertly seared on a blazing hot tava).

FAST FOOD RESTAURANTS

Ten-year-old **India's Oven** (5897 W. Pico Boulevard, West Los Angeles, WEST, 213-936-1000) pioneered the open tandoori kitchen in restaurants. Back then, it surprised all those whose idea of inexpensive Indian food was curries with boiled rice and lots of soggy veggie dishes. Even though India's Oven serves everything on segmented Styrofoam plates with plastic cutlery, its boti kebab and chicken tikka are at least as good—and sometimes better—than those in tonier Indian dining rooms. Everything comes with the fragrant (and more expensive) basmati rice, and the chutneys and vegetables ring with freshness.

Chutneys Indian Fast Food (2406 S. Barrington [at Pico], West Los Angeles, WEST, 310-477-6263) is probably most famous for its yogurt-marinated grilled dahi chicken offered with freshly made chutneys at a self-serve bar—a sort of Indian version of El Pollo Loco. Not to be overlooked, however, are the excellent southern-style mini masala dosai and plain dosai served with sambar and coconut chutney; the various tandoori kebabs all served with nan, rice, and an excellent corn salad sprinkled with mustard seeds; and, of course, the chutney bar.

Also see **Tikka** (page 135).

India's Oven: The tandoor chef at work.

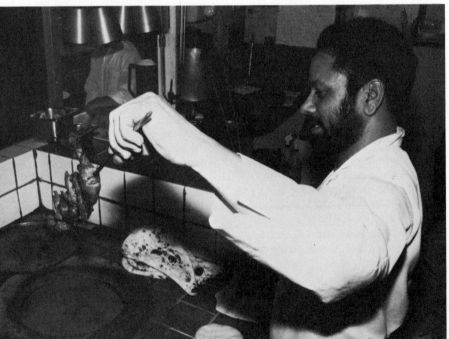

Chat and Methai:
Indian Snacks and Sweets

S ome of the best Indian eating is the *chat* (snacks) often sold wrapped in paper cones in market stalls and tiny specialty shops in India. *Methai* are a whole range of Indian sweets. For homesick Indians, nothing in the Western dessert repertoire can replace them—they're the Indian equivalent of cookies and ice cream.

DESCRIPTIONS AND GLOSSARY

MUNCHIES: Indians make a huge variety of crunchy snacks from besan, lentil flour, or rice flour. They're sold plain or in mixtures (called chevdas) with spices, nuts, roasted chick-peas, and other ingredients.

SMALL DISHES: The crunchy items above, when combined with potatoes, beans, chutneys, and sometimes yogurt, produce a large variety of saladlike chat. These may sound like health foods, but they're every bit as habit-forming as tortilla chips with salsa. Chat may vary from region to region.

Alu bonda or alu tikki (often written aloo): A small, spicy potato pancake or ball eaten with chutney.

Besan: Chick-pea flour.

Bhel: Puffed rice.

Bhel puri and sev puri: Bhel or sev mixed into a spicy potato, chick-pea, and yogurt combination sprinkled with green and tamarind chutneys.

Chakri: A Gujarati specialty—pretzel-shaped fried dough with a flavor reminiscent of onion rings.

Chevda: Assorted mixtures of crunchy snacks.

Dahi vadai (southern) or vada (Punjabi): Savory lentil patties or dumplings swimming in yogurt and topped with fresh coriander, hot pepper, and tamarind chutney.

Namkin: A general term for all salty-savory snacks.

Pakoras: Fritters of either vegetables, meat, fish or nuts held together with besan and deep-fried.

Pani puri (Gujarati): Thin semolina puffs that resemble Ping-Pong balls. You fill these from a dish of diced potato and beans, and add a dash of tamarind chutney and a dark, mysterious, minty water that come alongside.

Puchkas: The Bengali version of pani puri. In the north (Punjab), pani puri are called *golguppers*.

Samosas: Spicy pastry turnovers usually filled with potato.

Sev: A deep-fried noodlelike shape made of besan. A thicker, spicier ribbon of besan is called *gathia* (Gujarati).

The sweetmaster deep-fries jelebis at India Sweet House.

SWEETS (Methai—also spelled mathai or mithai).

Barfi (or burfi): An unfortunately named but delicious fudgy milk candy in many flavors and a rainbow of colors.

Cham cham: A confection made from thickened milk in various shapes, and often filled with custard cream.

Gulab jamun: A rich condensed-milk cheeselike ball fried and brushed with syrup.

Magaj (Gujarati): A sweet fried besan cake flavored with vanilla and cardamom.

Mohanthal (Gujarati): A sweet besan cake sprinkled with almonds.

Penda: Besan cookies in fanciful shapes.

Rasgolla: A white spongy cheese ball in sweet syrup.

Rasmalai: A ricotta cheese–like ball or patty in a sweet milk sauce with nuts.

SHOPS FEATURING CHAT AND METHAI

Surati Farsan Mart, 11814 E. 186th Street, Artesia, SOUTH, 310-860-2310. Lunch through dinner; closed Monday. *Farsan* means "snacks" in Gujarati. The best Gujarati farsan and chat come from Surati Farsan Mart, a rather spartan snack shop in Little India that constantly plays Indian rock music cassettes. Snacks include Gujarati-style pani puri with mung beans and minty water, and loads of crunchy snacks and small dishes. The barfi is special here—it has more texture and isn't as sweet as the smoother Bengali style sold elsewhere. Surati Farsan Mart makes three kinds, including my favorite with roasted coconut. Other Gujarati sweets include: mohanthal, magaj (crunchy as praline), and penda that look for all the world like spritz cookies.

India Sweet House, 5893 W. Pico Boulevard, West Los Angeles, WEST, 213-934-5193. Open daily. Crunchy savory sev and pani puri puffs are made hourly, so they are exquisitely fresh. The bhel puri, dahi vada and spicy samosas are equally wonderful here. Some like to buy components separately so the family can put their snacks together at home.

India Sweet House makes voluptuous rasmalai, cheese balls in a silky milk sauce loaded with pistachios and almonds. Other sweets include *rabri,* a milky pudding flavored with cardamom and pistachio nuts.

Standard Sweets & Snacks, 18600 Pioneer Boulevard, Artesia, SOUTH, 310-860-6364. Long an institution in the Indian community, this shop has imported its own *halwais,* or sweets chefs, who have years of experience in India making fine Indian sweets. Their paneer confections include the familiar rasmalai, rasagolla, and both the light and "black" versions of *gulab jamun.* The black is fried to a deep chocolate brown as opposed to the usual golden color, giving it a unique taste. Cham cham here is shaped like an éclair, filled with cream, and topped with a candied cherry. Standard Sweets makes Bengali-style barfis and all kinds of savory chat, too.

MARKETS WITH CHAT

Increasingly we are seeing combination chat and grocery stores—a kind of mini Indian-street-market street-food scene under one roof. Some of the best chat in this kind of setting is at **Mirch Masala** (8516 Reseda Boulevard, Northridge, S.F. VALLEY, 818-772-7691). Next to an Indian woman's boutique selling saris and *churidar* sets (the Punjabi gathered pants and flowing top sets), Mirch Masala displays its sweets and snacks in a well-kept array. The owners will guide you through the baffling realm of sev, namkin, pani puri, bhel puri, and *papri* chat. There are assorted paneer desserts of sweetened cheese, such as *dil bahar:* rounds of fried paneer topped with an elusively flavored thickened milk and sprinkled liberally with nuts.

The store is small but impressive, in that it carries seven varieties of basmati rice, good-looking fresh vegetables, and well-organized dals and spices.

Sweets and snacks are made hourly at India Sweet House.

India Sweets and Spices, 9409 Venice Boulevard, Culver City, WEST, 310-837-5286. And 22009–11 Sherman Way, Canoga Park, S.F. VALLEY, 818-887-0868. Also in Artesia, SOUTH, and Duarte, SAN GABRIEL VALLEY. The largest of the chat store-market enterprises, India Sweets and Spices, has four branches, with the newest in Canoga Park. Both the Culver City and Valley store have gleaming stainless steel kitchens where the chat, chevdas, and sweets are made. Look for aloo tikki studded with whole chunks of serrano chile that no amount of cooling raita or mint chutney can temper. All the markets are well stocked with Indian groceries, too.

INDIAN MARKETS

With so many Indian markets spread around L.A., you won't have any trouble locating Indian groceries near you. The following stores, however, are exceptional.

Bharat Bazaar, 11510 W. Washington Boulevard, Culver City, WEST, 310-398-6766. "A-safe-tida," a woman says, pointing to the word in her recipe book. By now, Phulan Chander, Bharat Bazaar's owner, is used to customers coming in to hunt down exotic Indian ingredients. Fortunately, most food products are labeled in English at Bharat Bazaar, one of the city's best-stocked Indian grocery stores. Chander's husband, Ramesh, who also runs a food wholesaling business, is as savvy as anyone when it comes to what's available in the Indian food marketplace.

Although the Chanders are Punjabis from the north, they stock ingredients needed for any Indian cooking: the rarely seen fresh curry leaves, essential to south Indian dishes, and of course *hing* (also known as asafetida). Like any of the L.A. area's more than 70 Indian markets, Bharat Bazaar's shelves are stocked with basmati rice, dozens of varieties of dals, and besan flour for making pakoras, chevdas, or sweets. They also stock a huge array of "convenience" foods: tandoori paste to spread on chicken or lamb before broiling, or vindaloo and other curry pastes for tossing together an almost instant curry.

Farm Fresh Produce (12621 Pioneer Boulevard, Norwalk, SOUTH, 310-929-8373), opposite the Gujarati Society Hall in Little India, specializes in fresh Asian fruit and vegetables. Owner Anita Keray procures such items as parval and dudhi from a friend who is a farmer. In season you'll find tender young *chori*: black-eyed peas that when mature are dried for dal. Indian cooks roast green chick-peas, still on the plant, over a coal fire; the fragrant leaves flavor the young beans, which are then picked off to eat. They stock sugar cane, lichees, green dates in season, fresh mango turmeric (which has a tart flavor), and little plants ready for your garden: guava, mango, *ramfal,* sugar apple, and more.

Nearby, **India Food and Gifts** (17820 Pioneer Boulevard, Artesia, SOUTH, 310-865-3678) has a good selection of groceries and much more. Piled in semidisarray are colorful glass bangles and little statues, comic book versions of classical literature, a full range of Indian cookbooks in paperback, stick-on *bindi* (the middle-of-the-forehead spot denoting marital status), plus a selection of frozen foods that includes samosas and many other treats. The store fills mail orders, too.

And at **Bombay Spices** (18628 Pioneer Boulevard, Artesia, SOUTH, 310-860-9949) are both Indian and Pakistani groceries, tons of movies in Hindi and Punjabi on videocassette, fancy gold and silver shoes, embroidered *dupattas* (scarves), hair ornaments called *prandas,* kohl, and sweaters from England.

Serious food shoppers in the southern part of the city will want to know about **Patel Brothers** (18636 Pioneer Boulevard, Artesia, SOUTH, 310-402-2953), with branches across the country including Houston, Chicago, and Cincinnati. It is one of the best-stocked markets in the Little India area.

A standout among the San Fernando Valley's many markets is **Bombay Spiceland** (8650 Reseda Boulevard, Northridge, S.F. VALLEY, 818-701-9383). Across the aisle from the store's huge selec-tion of rental films in various Indian languages is a small produce section. You'll find more fresh items in the cooler case at the back. Bombay Spiceland has a nice assortment of crunchy chevda snacks in a case near the cash register, as well as plenty of cooking implements including a brass sev maker, a chapati board and rolling pin sets, and heavy mortars for crushing spices.

The venerable **Bezjian's Grocery** in Hollywood (see page 227) also has a complete selection of Indian ingredients.

MEXICO

The very earliest Mexican eating places in L.A. were inexpensive stands and cafés that catered to immigrant laborers. The fare was strictly antojitos—tacos, burritos, gorditas, and other ground corn-based items—that is, the portable snack foods of the Mexican marketplace. As Southern Californians discovered this Mexican food and Mexican restaurateurs began catering to them, antojitos evolved into those ever popular combination plates loaded with a blanket of melted, gluey cheese that welded rice and beans to the dish. Local foods were liberally substituted for Mexican ingredients. But most of us who grew up eating in these restaurants loved the food, completely unaware of its lack of authenticity.

In the last two decades, new infusions of Mexican immigrants (almost half the population of Southern California is Latin American) created a demand for more authentic Mexican food. Today, any Mexican-food aficionado worth his salsa knows where to find the most authentic fare, and he also knows that there's much more to it than the tacos and enchiladas of the combination plate. Licuados, cocteles de mariscos, paletas, tortas, and a roast goat specialty called birria—all commonplace throughout Mexico—are also readily available on streets and in Mexican eating places throughout Los Angeles.

But very few of these places serve *comida casera,* or home cooking, and since Mexicans don't often entertain in restaurants—as for, example, Asians do—the better part of Mexican restaurant food is still based on antojitos.

Some restaurateurs, however, have rediscovered their culinary roots and are beginning to offer home cooking and regional dishes. We're starting to see Veracruz-style seafood, Yucatecan tamales wrapped in banana leaves, and Oaxacan moles. Both gringos and Mexicans are finding this food a welcome addition.

Another kind of Mexican cuisine has started to surface in the last few years. Adventurous non-Mexican chefs traveling back and forth across the border have devised a lighter, more sophisticated cooking combining the best California ingredients with the Mexican larder. This upscale fare based on authentic regional cooking has created a new food awareness among non-Latinos. Whereas once not so very long ago queso meant Cheddar or Jack, diners have also learned to appreciate panela and cotija. And epazote and chipotle have entered our culinary vocabulary.

— MEXICAN AND — — LATIN AMERICAN GLOSSARY —

Aceitunas: Olives.

Achiote: These bright orange mild-flavored seeds, called annatto in English, are used crushed as flavorings for marinades and stewed dishes. Achiote is especially popular in Oaxaca and the Yucatan.

Ackee: A bland white tree fruit popular in Jamaica, which is said to resemble scrambled eggs. Ackee often accompanies salt cod.

Adobado: A chile, garlic, and herb marinade used to season meat.

Aguas frescas: Fruit drinks made by steeping dried fruit or by blending fresh fruit with water.

Aji (Latin American): Pepper. Also the spicy, fresh green pepper condiment served at most Peruvian meals, as well as the general Peruvian term for peppers. Aji rocoto, a large red pepper, and aji marisol, a yellow moderately hot pepper, are both Peruvian.

Aji de gallina (Peruvian): Chicken stewed in a nut and chile cream sauce.

Al carbon: Cooked over coals or over an open grill.

Al pastor: Marinated pork slices stacked on a vertical spit and cooked on a rotisserie.

Albóndigas: Meatballs.

Antojitos: Snacks or light meals, usually consisting of something made with cornmeal. Tacos, burritos, and gorditas are examples.

Arepas: Colombian-style corn cakes. Arepas de queso are the same cakes made with the addition of cheese.

Arroz: Rice. Arroz con leche is rice pudding.

Arroz frito: Peruvian-Chinese-style fried rice.

Bacalao: Dried cod.

Barbacoa: Chile-marinated braised meat. Originally cooked wrapped in maguey leaves, now usually wrapped in banana leaves and steamed or simply braised. Popular as a taco filling.

Batidos (Cuban): Fruit and milk drinks—the Cuban version of licuados.

Birria: A specialty goat preparation in which the goat is braised, roasted, and served with its braising liquid.

Boliche: Cuban-style pot roast.

Bolillos (Mexican): French-style rolls.

Bolinhos de bacalhau: Brazilian codfish croquettes.

Botana: Appetizers or foods to accompany alcoholic beverages.

Brasero: A table-top grill.

Bun: A Jamaican/Belezian yeast-leavened sweet bread flavored with ginger.

Burrito: A flour tortilla wrapped around beans and any kind of meat or chile or cheese mixture or sundry other ingredients. Synonymous with the burro (donkey) that carries just about anything anywhere, burritos are an American invention and rarely found in Mexico.

Cabrito al horno: Roast baby goat.

Caldo: A souplike stew with a light broth. Caldo siete mares ("7 seas"), one well-known Mexican caldo, contains many kinds of seafood and fish.

Caldo de salchicha: An Ecuadoran blood soup with sausage.

Camarones: Shrimp.

Campechanas: A Guatemalan sweet roll eaten for breakfast.

Capirotada: Mexican-style bread pudding.

Carapulcra: A Peruvian stew made with pork and Andean-style freeze-dried potatoes that resemble meat.

Carne: Meat. Carne adobada (Central American) is a pork cutlet smeared with an achiote-vinegar paste. Carne asada: grilled steak. Carne desmenuzada: shredded meat Nicaraguan-style braised in spiced orange juice. Carne guisada (Central American): a stew of well-browned beef, usually with achiote and vinegar in the sauce. Carne seca: dried meat.

Carniceria: A butcher shop or small meat market.

Carnitas: Deep-fried pork chunks.

Cazuela: A heavy clay cooking pot.

Ceviche, cebiche (Mexican), or seviche: Raw fish or shellfish marinated in citrus juice with other spices. The acid in the citrus "cooks" the fish.

Cheeses: Mexican-style cheese now available in our markets include queso fresco (or ranchero), a fresh mild white cheese; cotija, a well-aged crumbly sharp cheese similar to Parmesan; manchego, a rich, well-ripened cheese excellent for melting; panela, a mozzarellalike mild cheese of compressed curds that holds its shape when heated.

Chicha morada: A sweet Peruvian drink made from purple corn and fruit juice.

Chicharrones: In Mexico deep-fried pork skin. In Central America chicharon is deep-fried chunks of pork (which are called carnitas in Mexico).

Chifles (Ecuadoran): Deep-fried sweet plantain slices.

Chile colorado: Braised meat or chicken in a red chile sauce; chile verde denotes a green chile sauce.

Chimichurri: Argentina's all-purpose dipping sauce made from raw chopped garlic, oregano, and fresh herbs.

Chipotle: A roasted dried jalapeño pepper with a smoky flavor.

Choclo (Peruvian): Giant white corn used in soups.

Chorizo: A variety of sausage.

Choros: Mussels.

Chupe de camarones: A Peruvian milk-based shrimp chowder.

Cilantro: Fresh coriander.

Cochinita pibil: Yucatecan-style pit-roasted young pig—now replaced by pork meat.

Cocido: Chunks of meat or chicken cooked in a mild broth with vegetables.

Coco bread: A dense, white Caribbean-style yeast-leavened bread made with coconut milk.

Cocteles de mariscos: Seafood cocktails.

Consume: Broth.

Criollo (criolla): Native or country-style.

Curtido (Salvadoran): From the Spanish encurtir, ''to pickle,'' this shredded, pickled, and usually spicy cabbage always accompanies pupusas.

Dende oil: Brazilian cooking wouldn't be Brazilian cooking without this highly saturated, bright orange palm kernel oil.

Empanadas: Mexican and South American half-moon-shaped pastry usually filled with meat or a sweet filling. In El Salvador, a small deep-fried pouch of mashed banana with a cream filling.

Epazote: A pungent weed/herb with jagged leaves used as seasoning in southern and western Mexican cooking—especially good in black beans or quesadillas. Available dried and occasionally fresh.

Escovich or escabeche: To cook or marinate with a mixture of vinegar and onions.

Farofa (Brazilian): Ground, dried cassava meal.

Feijoada: Brazil's national party dish of black beans stewed with a variety of meats and sausages.

Festival bread: Unsweetened Jamaican fried bread.

Flauta: Literally flute, this is a flour tortilla wrapped around various fillings and deep-fried. Flautas are often mistakenly called taquitos.

Frijol blanco (Guatemalan): White beans stewed with pork pieces.

Gallo pinto: A Nicaraguan rice and red bean dish whose name means ''spotted rooster.''

Gorditas: Flat grilled corn cakes split and stuffed.

Guanabana: Also known as soursop, this is a largely fleshy tropical fruit with a flavor similar to pears.

Guayaba: Guava. Mermelada de guayaba is the jellied fruit shaped into a log and served in slices for dessert.

Habañero chile: A small rumpled-looking chile pepper said to be the hottest on earth.

Harina de camote: Sweet potato flour.

Hilachas: Guatemalan-style braised, shredded beef.

Huacatay: Peruvian black mint.

Huachinango veracruzana: Red snapper deep-fried and served in a light tomato sauce with olives and capers.

Huancaina (Peruvian): Any dish served with the same sauce used for papas huancainas.

Huevos rancheros: "Ranch-style eggs"—sunny side up with a sauce of tomato and fresh chile or bell pepper.

Humitas: Unfilled South American corn tamales.

Jamaica: A juice made by steeping dried hibiscus flowers in water.

Jerk: A Jamaican seasoning mixture used on barbecued meats and chicken.

Jugo: Juice.

Lapping: Bolivian-style marinated, grilled steak.

Lengua: Tongue, usually braised.

Lentejas: Lentils; also, a thick Colombian pork and lentil stew accompanied with deep-fried pork rinds.

Licuados: A frothy Mexican drink made by blending fruit and milk.

Llapingachos: Ecuadoran potato and cheese pancakes.

Locos (Chilean): An abalonelike shellfish.

Lomo enchilado: Pork loin marinated in chile, garlic, and vinegar.

Longaniza: Sausage.

Loroco (Salvadoran): A flower used as an herb, especially popular in cheese pupusas.

Machaca: Shredded meat. Machaca also refers to the meat scrambled with eggs.

Mamey: A member of the sapote family, this large brown custard-textured fruit with a salmon interior is used to make desserts and frothy drinks known as licuados (Mexican) or batidos (Cuban).

Mariscos: Shellfish.

Marquesote (Guatemalan): A light cupcake made with whipped eggs. Salvadoran-style marquesote is a plain sponge cake.

Masa: A dough made from steeped, ground corn treated with lime. Masa preparada, used for making tamales, is masa whipped with seasonings and lard.

Matambre: This Argentinean-style rolled flank steak stuffed with ham, eggs, olives, and herbs, is sliced and eaten as a coldcut.

Mazamorra morada: A Peruvian gelatinlike dessert made from purple corn and cooked, dried fruits.

Membrillo: Jellied quince paste served in slices for dessert.

Menudo: A tripe soup, said to cure hangovers.

Milanesa: A thin steak with a bread-crumb coating.

Mole: A thick, rich, multispiced sauce often containing crushed nuts or seeds. Mole poblano, made with unsweetened chocolate, chiles, and nuts, is the most well known mole here.

Mollejas: Sweetbreads.

Morcilla: Blood sausage.
Moros: Cuban black beans. When mixed with rice they become Moros y Christianos.
Nacatamal: A Nicaraguan tamale.
Nixtamal: Dried soaked corn treated with slaked lime, used to make masa.
Nopalitos: Diminutive of nopales, cactus paddles, used in a salad.
Ocopa: A Peruvian dish of boiled sliced potatoes with a creamy chile-walnut sauce.
Olluquito con carne: A Peruvian stew made from a small potatolike vegetable grown in the Andes.
Orchata (or horchata): A cool drink made from rice with a flavor rather like rice pudding.
Paletas: Frozen fruit bars with or without milk.
Pan con gallina (Central American): A stewed chicken sandwich on a French roll, often garnished with curtido.
Pan dulces: Mexican sweet breads eaten for breakfast.
Panaderia: A bakery.
Panucho: A Yucatecan-style antojito; a fried tortilla with black beans, meat (usually turkey), and crumbled hard cheese.
Pão de queijo: Brazilian-style cheese rolls.
Papas chorreadas: Colombian-style potatoes in a cheese and egg cream sauce.
Papas huancainas (Peruvian): Potato slices topped with cheese sauce and served cold.
Papas rellenas (Peruvian): A ball of cheese-coated mashed potato stuffed with seasoned ground beef, olives, and raisins.
Parihuela: A Peruvian seafood soup.
Parillada: A mixed grill of meats served on a brazier at the table.
Parillas: An Argentine steakhouse.
Pastel de choclo: A Chilean casserole dish of chicken, olives, and tomato sauce with a slightly sweet cornmeal and egg topping.
Pastelitos: Small Salvadoran ground corn pastries filled with seasoned minced meat.
Patacones (Colombian and Ecuadoran): Deep-fried green plantain slices.
Pebre: The all-purpose Chilean fresh dipping sauce made of habañero chiles, garlic, herbs, olive oil, and vinegar.
Pepian (Guatemalan): A spicy stew, usually thickened with nuts (as in Mexican pipian), but occasionally thickened with toasted rice, bread, or tortillas.
Perujo: Guatemalan French-style rolls.
Pescado: Fish.
Pibil: The word originally meant "pit-cooked," a method replaced today by wrapping food in a banana leaf and steaming it.
Picadillo: A stew of ground meat in tomato sauce with raisins.
Picante de mariscos: A Peruvian shellfish and potato stew.
Picarones: Peruvian-style pumpkin doughnuts.
Piloncillo: Mexican-style raw sugar.
Pipian (Mexican): A spicy stew with nut- or seed-thickened sauce.
Pollo: Chicken.
Pollo en mani: Peruvian chicken dish in a ground peanut sauce.
Pozole: A hearty Mexican soup made with hominy.
Puchero yucateco: A soup-stew— the Yucatecan version of cocido.
Pukas: A Bolivian-style cheese- and olive-filled pastry.
Pulpo: Octopus.

Pupusas: Corn dough hand-patted around a filling and grilled to make a stuffed pancake.

Quesadilla: Here in California, a quesadilla is a flour tortilla folded around melting cheese. True Mexican quesadillas are corn-dough turnovers stuffed with stewed meat filling and eaten topped with cheese. Salvadoran quesadilla is a pound cake made with fresh cheese and topped with sesame seeds.

Queso fundido: A dish of baked melting cheese often served as an appetizer. Fresh chiles or chorizo may be added.

Rajas (Mexican): Fresh chile cut into strips.

Recado: Central American and Southern Mexican seasoning pastes made of ground chiles and/or other spices.

Refritos: Cooked and fried beans (refried beans).

Revolcado: Guatemalan pork-head and organ-meat stew.

Rodajas: An orange- or vanilla-flavored Guatemalan pound cake.

Ropa vieja: Literally "old clothes," ropa vieja is seasoned meat, braised until it can be separated into shreds.

Rundown (Jamaican): Salt cod simmered with coconut milk.

Salbutes: A Yucatecan-fried cornmeal cake filled with meat and served with red onions on top.

Salsa chimichurri: See chimichurri.

Seco de cordero (Peruvian): Lamb stewed in cilantro sauce.

Seviche: See ceviche.

Sopa marinera: Latin American seafood soup.

Sopes: Shallow rimmed corn cakes, deep-fried then topped with a filling of stewed or braised meats or carnitas.

Sorrel (Jamaican): A juice made from dried hibiscus flowers. (See jamaica).

Suchiles: A Guatemalan banana drink.

Taco: Corn tortillas wrapped around various meats or stews and served with onions, cilantro, and salsa. Tacos al carbon refers to tacos made with charcoal-grilled meats.

Tallarines (Latin American): Noodles.

Taqueria: A shop or stand where tacos are sold.

Tasajo: Cured dried beef imported from Brazil but often seen on Cuban menus.

Tinga: Central Mexican–style seasoned braised meat flavored with chipotle, poblano, or other chiles.

Tomatillo: A green tomatolike fruit used extensively in Mexican sauces.

Tortas: Mexican sandwiches on French rolls, often spread with beans and topped with mashed avocado.

Vigoron: A Nicaraguan yuca salad with diced tomato and crispy fried pork rind.

Yerba mate (Argentine): An herb tea.

Yuca: The Spanish name for cassava root or tapioca, yuca is a staple all over South and Central America and the Caribbean. Eaten boiled, or cut into strips and deep-fried, yuca often accompanies Central American–style chicharrones.

Yuca con mojo (Cuban): Boiled yuca with a sauce of minced fried garlic.

HOME COOKING

Though still rare in restaurants, Mexican home cooking is beginning to gain popularity.

Guadalajara Restaurant, 205 Broadway, Santa Monica, WEST, 310-395-5171. Lunch and dinner daily. Real Mexican home cooking turns up where you least expect it—just a few feet, for example, from Santa Monica's fashionable Broadway Deli. In a restaurant that looks as if it might serve fifties time-warp Mexican combination plates and slightly watery margaritas, Guadalajara offers pollo *à la jardinera:* chicken simmered in a sauce composed mostly of fresh vegetables with a hint of raisins. When you order carne asada *con chilaquiles*—a lasagna-style dish made with dry tortillas instead of noodles—the waitress actually asks you how you want your carne cooked. The kitchen garnishes many dishes with real *crema Mexicana*—a cultured cream rather than ordinary sour cream. And dinners come with a fresh vegetable soup that brims with lightly cooked chunks of chayote squash and carrot. And, yes, you can get a combination plate—the enchiladas verdes is the best.

Maria's Ramada, 1064 N. Kingsley Drive (corner of Santa Monica), Los Angeles, CENTRAL, 213-660-4436 or 669-9654. Lunch and dinner; closed Monday. It's more than just the corny romantic charm of Maria's cozy thatch-roofed booths, or the bargain prices, that makes this place worth knowing about. When you want to feel coddled and nourished, Maria's cocido of short ribs—or any of the made-from-scratch dishes from her native Ramada—will fix you right up. Gallina en mole is typical of the area's rich style. But the splendid cabrito al horno (a plate of lean, mild-tasting baby goat) is her forte. There are oysters on the half shell, and a terrific caldo siete mares overflowing with half a dozen kinds of seafood and vegetables, and Maria's cheese-rich enchiladas made with sautéed mushrooms are pure comfort food.

Mi Ranchito, 8694 Washington Boulevard, Culver City, WEST, 310-837-1461. Breakfast, lunch and dinner daily. Mi Ranchito, the kind of family place you expect to find in Whittier or Boyle Heights, has been a well-kept secret on a sleepy Washington Boulevard corner in Culver City. Though it's gone through several owners in the past 20 years, people working on the M-G-M or Zanuck movie lots always seem to know about the restaurant's cheap beer and great quesadillas. Meanwhile, local Latino merchants come in to scarf the cocido from enormous bowls. This is more than just a massive bowl of soup; it holds enough tender beef to feed the family for a week. You spoon the meat into warm tortillas and douse it with a little salsa. Then you squeeze juice from the accompanying lemon into the broth and sprinkle in chopped onions and cilantro. The combination is unbeatable.

While the M-G-M types stick to the combinaciones or try the slightly more daring Veracruz-style burrito *jacocho,* filled with shrimp, octopus, and abalone, locals and the more adventurous go with the birria or the huachinango relleno: stuffed red snapper. Or they order spicy-hot huevos *endiablados* for breakfast.

Zumaya's, 5722 Melrose Avenue, Hollywood, CENTRAL, 213-464-0624. Lunch and dinner; closed Sunday. Co-owner Emily Diaz describes Zumaya's food "just mom's home cooking." Diaz's mother has trained the restaurant's chef to follow her recipes that her children grew up on (and which, according to Emily, all the kids in the neighborhood loved).

The food you find at Zumaya's, in a hip, Spartan setting appropriate for this only slightly trendy part of Melrose, is Mexican cooking with an unaccustomed freshness: The potato-cheese soup has fresh chile strips in it. Side dishes of perfectly cooked zucchini with cheese, corn, and tomato, or a dish of soupy pinto beans, replaces the often heavy-handed refritos. Halibut comes sauced with a "pesto" of serrano chile, cilantro, and avocado, and a boneless chicken breast gets sauced with the scorchy taste of roasted chipotle chiles that add a good smoky flavor. As with much home cooking, though, some days the kitchen works wonders, while other days you get the feeling mom wasn't in the mood to cook.

Mi India Bonita, 4731 E. Olympic Boulevard, East Los Angeles, EAST OF L.A., 213-267-8505. Open 7:00 A.M. to 5:30 P.M.; closed Sunday. Mi India Bonita really jumps at lunchtime. Two customers in green scrub suits swap jokes with the cook, then head toward the refrigerator at the back of the café and help themselves to Cokes. They order lunch by saying "the special." Businessmen, mothers and kids—everyone seems to belong in this converted house with its open white-tiled kitchen trimmed in red and its small Naugahyde booths of a recent vintage. The beans are chunky and hand-mashed, the rice is flecked with bits of fresh vegetable, and the salsa is freshly made. It's the kind of place where nothing on the menu surprises, but the carnitas are crisp and sweet, the barbacoa unctuous, the chile colorado earthy, and the milanesa crunchy and perfectly fried. Try the rich bread pudding (capirotada), or take some home.

♦ **FONDITAS**
These are small family-style restaurants where the cooking is usually a little fancier than home cooking.

The Gardens of Taxco, 1113 N. Harper Avenue, West Hollywood, WEST, 213-654-1746. Dinner nightly. My friend from Mexico wasn't too surprised that the Gardens of Taxco had no written menu. "At a fonda," she explained, "the proprietor describes the daily specialties, discussing the condition of the vegetable and fish supply and advising his customers what's best." This dialogue is firmly entrenched in Mexican restaurant tradition.

That tradition is carried out at Gardens of Taxco, a comfortable, multiroomed house turned into a restaurant. The patron, Sr. Romero, describes to every customer the 14 entrées and a number of botanas (appetizers) on his unwritten menu.

Each dinner is a multicourse affair. Once you make your selections, albóndigas soup arrives; it has fine little meatballs in an unexceptional broth. The botanas are more interesting: The specialty of the casa is a double-decker California-style quesadilla with cheese and avocado, and there are succulent crunchy flautas with chunky guacamole for dipping. For an entrée, anything in mole will be worth a try. (Romero uses a recipe from the winner of the yearly mole contest in Puebla, Mexico). Another excellent choice is the chicken in a delicately spiced and very rich salsa crema.

To round out the meal, you're offered a creamy banana dessert and an after-dinner sherry—it's all very civilized considering the modest price of the meal (under $15).

Most entrées at the Gardens of Taxco display the Spanish side of Mexican cooking, so if you're looking for the strong, earthy flavors of Indian-influenced food, this isn't the place to dine.

La Serenata de Garibaldi, 1842 E. 1st Street, Boyle Heights, CENTRAL, 213-265-2887. Lunch through dinner; closed Monday. The best way to order at La Serenata de Garibaldi—named after the famous Mexico City square—is to consult Sr. Rodriguez, the owner. He always has a long list of unwritten daily specials to recommend.

Charming handwoven plaid tablecloths in near-neon colors, native art, and candles warm the room. At the back of the dining room a woman presses out tortillas and grills them minutes before they are rushed to the tables.

The quality and inventiveness of the seafood served here is amazing considering the sorry state of fish in many Mexican restaurants. The jumbo shrimp in piquant cilantro sauce and a seared chunk of perfectly cooked mahi mahi with meaty grilled mushroom slices in a rich pool of cream sauce are outstanding examples. Everything is beautifully presented, and some dishes are extraordinary: a quesadilla de pescado, one evening's special, was a piece of fish encased in corn dough, then poached in a sauce of fresh tomatillos flavored with dill. Five sauces, each made from a different variety of chile, show the kitchen's extraordinary range; many restaurants simply use the same one or two sauces for everything. And Serenata makes its own aguas frescas from fresh fruit—sometimes raspberries, melon, or papaya. Unlike at most East L.A. dining rooms, you can pay for your meal here with a credit card.

El Comal, 735 S. Atlantic Boulevard, East Los Angeles, EAST OF L.A., 213-266-0735. Lunch and dinner daily. El Comal, the first establishment in L.A. serving Jalisco-style braised dishes and stews, introduces a whole new kind of authentic cooking. Each meal is a mini King Henry VIII–style feast. *Chamoro* adobado, for example, is a long piece of lean pork hock stewed in a slightly vinegary roasted chile paste. It merely coats the meat. And though it looks hot enough to scorch the sidewalk, it emits only a faint chile heat.

The presentations, somewhat nouvelle in style, include a little patch of nopalito salad and another of diced tomatoes. Accompanying all the meals is a bowl of soupy, lightly pork-flavored *charro* beans and rice garnished with a nice fresh shrimp. Another standout, *cordoniz* adobada, is a whole baby game hen cut to lie flat and stewed in the same adobada marinade. There's a young-lamb stew (birria de *ternera),* marinated pork ribs, and more. The only other items El Comal serves are a few appetizers and side dishes: queso fundido, seafood cocktails.

Mexica, 7313 Beverly Boulevard, West Hollywood, CENTRAL, 213-933-7385. Lunch and dinner Monday to Saturday; dinner Sunday. Mexica's owner, Albert Solis, wanted to serve the kind of food people eat in cafés in Mexico. He painted up a thirties-era Chinese restaurant and added vibrantly colored postmodern Mexican murals, a little folk art, and a handmade tile frieze. A savvy clientele poured in and found traditional dishes that aren't too familiar here yet, prepared with up-to-date style: quesadillas filled with a shredded beef tinga flavored with chipotle and olives; carne asada topped with strips of lightly grilled fresh poblano chiles; and chicken enchiladas with a snappy tomatillo sauce that didn't obliterate the tortillas. From Mexico's repertoire of regional foods, the café serves a good Veracruz-style red snapper; Yucatan-style cochinita pibil; and marvelous green corn tamales.

MEXICAN SPECIALTIES

◆ TAQUERIAS

For me, the ultimate taquerias are **El Taurino** (1104 S. Hoover Street, Los Angeles, CENTRAL, 213-738-9197, open 24 hours) and **Rincon Taurino** (14551 Nordhoff Street, Panorama City, S.F. VALLEY, 818-893-5927, open daily). Their kitchens blend high tech—these places are practically wraparound stainless steel—with the authenticity of streetside taco vendors. The interiors, decorated with old photographs of matadors, are cheery and pleasant. Taurino caters to a varied clientele, from the lowered-Chevy drivers that congregate late at night to the middle-aged Korean couple I saw carefully studying the English menu.

Vertical spits of marinated pork rotate in front of a grill. The meat gets sliced off and folded into a warm tortilla when you order a taco al pastor. Taurino's burritos are long on shredded or grilled meat, short on rice, and have stewed whole beans instead of the mashed variety. The torta rolls are crisp: the torta milanesa with a breaded and deep-fried thin steak is wondrously crunchy.

Carne al Pastor sliced from the rotisserie at El Taurino taqueria.

King Taco No. 2, 4504 E. 3rd Street (junction of the 60 and 710 freeways), East Los Angeles, EAST OF L.A., 213-264-4067, open 24

Authentic taquerias serve all the traditional meats that are cooked and sold in Mexican marketplaces—marinated pork known as al pastor turns on a vertical rotisserie. There is grilled carne asada, *sesos* (stewed pork brains), lengua, *cabeza* (braised head meat), carnitas, and usually chile colorado, chile verde, and barbacoa, a deep shade of ruddy brown from its braising in roasted chile paste.

The taco cook wields a cleaver with a lightning-swift hand, hacking the meat into small bits before filling your order and splashing on some onion and cilantro or chile salsa. You choose any filling to go into the antojito you want, be it lightly warmed tortillas for tacos or burritos, gorditas, sopes or tortas.

Of L.A.'s mind boggling number of taco and burrito dispensaries, a distressingly large proportion serve soggy warmed-up meat on limp tortillas and refritos scooped from a No. 10 can. But those listed here, some true Mexican and others Cal-Mex style, represent the city's best taqueria cooking.

hours. Also 2020 W. Pico Boulevard, Los Angeles, CENTRAL, 213-384-8115, and 2400 Brooklyn Avenue, Boyle Heights, CENTRAL, 213-264-3940; open 24 hours. And citywide. Three cashier windows and four pickup stations at King Taco No. 2 aren't enough to accommodate the crowds on weekends. Around 11:00 P.M., when the place really starts to jump, they park a couple of taco trucks in their lot to take up some slack. Look in the kitchen window as you order; you'll see several rotating spits of marinated pork and a six-foot-long grill smothered in carne asada. The fry cook starts flipping steaks at one end and works his way down the grill. Unless you like your food *hot,* order the green sauce, *not* the red for any of the antojitos.

After you pick up your food, head for the huge garishly lit indoor eating area with its hand-painted wall murals of Aztec scenes. On weekends the hall is filled with the aroma of spit-roasted chickens as they turn to crisp, burnished perfection. Not all 18 of King Taco's branches are open 24 hours, though most are open until midnight.

Taco Sinaloa, 738 W. Anaheim Street, Wilmington, SOUTH, 310-518-7955. Open 7:00 A.M. to midnight daily. If you drive along Anaheim Street south of Pacific Coast Highway in Wilmington, Taco Sinaloa, an intense sky-blue-colored drive-through burger stand, will undoubtedly grab your attention. This busy but modest place does all the classic taqueria foods with a sure hand: marvelous tacos de lengua and carnitas, and all the various masa preparations, including the usual taco-burrito-torta trilogy and also gorditas and sopes. Awesome breakfast egg dishes tempt customers all day long. A functional dining area—also nicely painted intense blue—attracts a neighborhood crowd, and around 11:30 P.M., midnight munchers begin to trickle in.

El Gordito Taqueria, 11830 Valley Boulevard, El Monte, SAN GABRIEL VALLEY, 818-444-4912. Open daily. A popular El Monte taqueria, El Gordito has a drive-through window and orderly inside seating of molded orange plastic benches, as well as a couple of video games to amuse kids while their mothers pick up a quick family dinner. The translated menu on a backlit board offers pictures to help you remember your antojito vocabulary. Fat, juicy burritos come in an all-meat version—try the succulent chile verde—or any filling with beans. Or try the torta de lomo, a roast pork sandwich slathered with beans and guacamole. Serve yourself from the fresh salsa bar.

Yuca's, 2056 N. Hillhurst Avenue, Silverlake, CENTRAL, 213-662-1214. Lunch and dinner daily. By now most taqueria buffs know about Yuca's, a converted burger-stand hut, with blue sheeting stretched out to shade a few battered chairs and marbleized Formica tables in the middle of a parking lot. Yuca's serves Yucatecan-style foods, although they're toned down in heat for the gringo clientele. Still, nothing compares to Yuca's pibil pork steamed with red chiles and achiote in banana leaves. This is heaven itself spooned into a tortilla. Yuca's southern-style tamales wrapped in a banana leaf draw a crowd when they're sold on Saturdays. If you want a little extra chile heat to spice up your torta or taco made with Yuca's outstanding carnitas, ask for the pickled jalapeños.

El Tapatio, 22806 Victory Boulevard, Woodland Hills, S.F. VALLEY, 818-883-6142. Open 8:00 A.M. to 10:00 P.M. daily. Sitting in El Tapatio's comfortable seating area—a stylized ranchito with whitewashed walls and whitewashed artifacts—beats standing outdoors eating tacos with salsa dripping down your arm, and the food is just as good as at the stands. The especialidad de la casa is camarones a la diabla: shrimp sautéed in a brick-red chile sauce. But at lunchtime, most people order soft tacos and burritos. The cook grills marinated pork for al pastor items, quickly slipping the meat into a tortilla; it's still sizzling when you take your first bite.

There's an astonishingly good "Swiss quesadilla" of soft flour tortillas with beef and molten cheese. El Tapatio has a huge juicer pumping out jugos naturales: the carrot juice is sweet and refreshing. Menudo and birria are featured on weekends.

Las Fuentes (18415 Vanowen Street, Reseda, S.F. VALLEY, 818-708-3344; open 8:00 A.M. to 11:00 P.M. daily) has lots of lovely tile, a small gurgling courtyard-type fountain, and a large welcoming salsa bar that gives the place the feel of a well-run chain restaurant. A professor at Northridge tells me Las Fuentes is popular with the teaching staff. And though it's also frequented by Mexican merchants, it isn't hard-core authentic. While the flavors are right on target, dishes that gringos might find offensive—like cabeza, tacos made from offal, or even menudo—are absent. But the pollo con rajas burrito is terrific and the taco al pastor—my yardstick for judging taquerias—is juicy and fine. Huevos con chorizo makes the best breakfast imaginable, unless you're about to run a marathon.

Poquito Mas (3701 Cahuenga Boulevard W., Studio City, S.F. VALLEY, 818-760-8226; open daily until midnight) has captured the fancy of nearby entertainment studio employees. You see everyone from special-effects personnel to animal trainers and wannabe stars munching the tostadas in a bowl made from a tortilla and knocking back Penafiel Mexican sodas or New York seltzer under fringe-topped umbrellas on the little patio. They always rhapsodize about the fresh quality of the carne asada, the lean and barely spicy pollo in the soft tacos and burritos. And even people who like their food a little closer to its origins appreciate that Poquito Mas serves wonderful coffee (with Altadena half-and-half if you like),

definitely an exception in taquerias. Although Mexican grandmothers would probably have used lard to fry their carnitas and to make their red chile sauce, the restaurant uses vegetable oil. Most meat is grilled or broiled, and the food is full of good fresh flavors. (There is a branch at 10651 Magnolia Boulevard, North Hollywood, S.F. VALLEY, 818-994-8226.)

♦ **YUCATECAN COOKING**
Mayan-influenced Yucatecan food is so different from the rest of Mexican cooking that people who've only known the central or northern styles find it completely surprising. It's a more tropical cuisine: Tamales and pit-cooked meats are wrapped in banana leaves from the peninsula's humid rain forests; juice from Seville oranges combined with garlic is used to marinate foods. Black (not red) beans are the staple, and fish from the glorious Yucatecan coastline is used abundantly.

El Emperador Maya, 1823 S. San Gabriel Boulevard, San Gabriel, SAN GABRIEL VALLEY, 818-288-7265. Lunch and dinner; closed Monday. Yucatecan restaurants are in the minority in Los Angeles, but most serve considerably better than average Mexican food. El Emperador Maya, hands down the best, unfortunately abandons Yucatecan food halfway down its menu to offer "regular" Mexican items too. But even the non-Mayan dishes—say, the chicken and shrimps Azteca in chipotle sauce, topped with diced avocado—are something to write home about.

Outside, the place looks like a simple neighborhood cantina with neon beer signs in the window. But in the attractive little dining room with tablecloths and flowers, your leftovers come wrapped in foil shaped like a bird as if you were at L'Orangerie.

Start with panuchos yucatecos,

the Yucatan's favorite botana. It's a fried tortilla layered with black beans and shredded turkey, sprinkled with cotija cheese. You could just close your eyes and point at the menu and everything would be stupendous. But I'll recommend the "*poc chuc* Don Belos," three thin cutlets of pork coated with a mild orangy achiote sauce; it comes with spicy pickled cabbage and black beans on the side.

Balo's Place, 5672 York Boulevard, Eagle Rock, CENTRAL, 213-255-2878. Lunch and dinner daily. Balo's Place is even more down home, with its statuette of a saint and deep-blue painted tables gracing the dining room. But aficionados travel for miles to taste the roasted habañero salsa, one of those lip- and tonsil-numbing concoctions that is so dangerous it's never left sitting on the tables—you must ask for it. Balo's has a long menu of Yucatecan specialties, but, like El Emperador, it supplements the list with standard items. Look for huevos *motuleños,* a Yucatecan version of huevos rancheros; pollo pibil baked in a banana leaf that you get to unwrap at the table and eat with the soupy black beans and fried plantains; and *pavo en relleno negro,* a murky-looking dish of meatball-and-egg-stuffed turkey in a sauce made with a toasted black chile recado. This last dish may look uninviting, but the taste is unforgettable. Whet your whistle with a guanabana tropical fruit shake.

Merida, 20 E. Colorado Boulevard, Pasadena, SAN GABRIEL VALLEY, 818-792-7371. Lunch and dinner daily. The service is usually slow at Merida, but that gives diners more time to settle back in their chairs on the delightful shaded brick courtyard and pretend they're on a Mexican vacation. If you want a strictly Yucatecan meal, overlook such dishes as Guadalajara-style birria and Puebla-

style chicken in mole. Go for the Yucatan combination, an excellent sampling of cochinita pibil, pollo pibil, pork poc chuc, and a panucho served with black beans and rice; or order the puchero yucateco, a richly seasoned soupy stew of beef, chicken, and pork. Salbutes are puffy masa cakes filled with black beans or turkey. The food is sometimes a little rough around the edges here, but those Yucatecan flavors go a long way to make up for it.

La Paz, 21040 Victory Boulevard, Woodland Hills, S.F. VALLEY, 818-883-4761. Lunch through dinner daily. In its first location, a bandbox-tiny place at the back of a minimall, La Paz blew everyone away with its astonishingly different Yucatecan seafood dishes—in particular the huge rock cod marinated in achiote and garlic, served whole. But owner Oscar Iturralde spread himself too thin when he opened a larger restaurant and then a second in Calabasas. La Paz still draws the crowds, and its food appears to be some of the most interesting in L.A. But the cooking, at best, is uneven.

♦ **SEAFOOD**
It wasn't so long ago that you'd have to tour Mexico to find a good huachinango veracruzana or caldo de siete mares. But in the past four or five years it seems as though a seafood craze has hit the Mexican community. Everywhere you drive the word mariscos is replacing, or at least being added to, tacos and burritos on signs—even on taco-vending trucks. Unfortunately most of these places have jumped on the marisco and pescado bandwagon before they've learned the tricky art of handling fish. But the following restaurants do a creditable job.

Casa Carnitas, 4067 Beverly Boulevard, Koreatown, CENTRAL, 213-667-9953. Lunch and dinner daily. An old standby, Casa Carnitas is known for exceptional seafood in spite of its name ("house of meat pieces"). The dining room is an ultralow-lit red-tablecloth-and-velvet-painting sort of place that makes you expect mariachis will show up. Instead, the mostly Latino clientele makes do with an occasional tune on the loud jukebox. Seafood cocktails (there are 9 varieties) arrive in tall ice cream sundae dishes accompanied—as Mexican cocktails always are—with a heap of saltines. Hot seafood entrées range from the simplest lobster in butter to the more complex pulpo a la veracruzana, with olives and a touch of cinnamon in the sauce. Another reason to go to Casa Carnitas is for the well-made Yucatecan specialties such as cochinita pibil, and steak à la Yucateca, the latter rolled around chorizo and served with black beans.

Mariscos La Paz, 1227 N. Avalon Boulevard, Wilmington, SOUTH, 310-834-6567. Open 8:00 A.M. to 8:00 P.M. daily. When the Briseño family, the owners of one of my favorite marisquerias, moved into a redecorated fast-food outlet, they already had an enormous following. The family started in business with one of those huge catering trucks, and their tacos carnitas and rusty-colored, succulent barbacoa didn't take long to catch on. Their mariscos done Michoacan-style (the Briseños' home state) are as good as you'll find anywhere in the city. The seafood cocktails, traditionally served in tall ice cream sundae glasses, here come in paper cups. The sauce for these cocteles—be they shrimp, oysters, or other seafood—is made of seafood cooking liquid mixed with fresh cilantro, onion, and lime juice; the taste just sparkles. But to those used to the usual red sauce, this one may seem a little pale. Order your coctel "with everything," and they'll sprinkle in a little hot sauce and

catsup to brighten things up. Seafood tostadas seem to dot every table; be sure to order one topped with extra shrimp (it isn't listed on the menu, but all the customers know to ask). Go on the weekend if you like live mariachi music.

Casablanca, 220 Lincoln Boulevard, Venice, WEST, 310-392-5751. Lunch and dinner daily. In the center of the dining room a woman rolls out and grills fresh flour tortillas. Her handiwork is one good reason to eat at Casablanca. Another is the popular squid steaks that taste remarkably like abalone. Casablanca prepares these at least half a dozen ways—among them sautéed with garlic, in a Veracruz sauce, or spiked with tequila. The rest of Casablanca's seafood menu is interesting too, even if the dish names make corny references to the cast of the film *Casablanca*. Salmoncito Ingrid, for example, is whole baby butterflied salmon with chopped shrimp and crab meat. Pescado à la Warner—red snapper fillet with vegetables—comes in a caper-chili sauce. Most dinners are under $15, and the stagy *Casablanca* movie ambience is a kick.

Pescado Mojado, 1701 Sunset Boulevard, Los Angeles, CENTRAL, 213-413-8712, and 15233 Roscoe Boulevard, Panorama City, S.F. VALLEY, 818-893-4977. Also 6th and Rampart, Los Angeles, CENTRAL; Huntington Park, EAST OF L.A.; Lynwood, SOUTH; and Highland Park, CENTRAL. Lunch through dinner daily. Burt Galvez, the man who developed the El Pollo Loco chain and then sold it to Denny's, has created a fast-food seafood concept. The food at Pescado Mojado, always reliably fresh, is frequently of better quality than one finds at the plethora of more formal Mexican seafood places around town. Though still small, the chain has caught on, and branches are spreading rapidly. The thing to get here is *"levantate Lazarus,"* a mixed seafood cocktail rumored to cure hangovers, if not raise the dead, or caldo de pescado mojado, an oregano-laced tomato broth crowded with fish chunks. Oysters on the half shell are shucked to order, and the rich, molten queso fundido is the perfect way to begin your seafood meal.

Pepe's Ostioneria, 11740 Valley Boulevard, El Monte, SAN GABRIEL VALLEY, 818-401-1599. Lunch and dinner daily. Since the days of its modest beginnings, Pepe's has garnered a large San Gabriel following. Now that the restaurant has moved across the street into new and very fancy el rancho-style digs, with a splendid lofty ceiling and a leaded glass door, Pepe's parking lot is crowded with the Mercedeses and Lincoln Continentals of East L.A. politicians and business magnates. Pepe's still has the same cooks, however, as it did at the old location.

You'll need to go in a group to order the huge grilled-seafood appetizer, parillada aperitivo ($59.95 at this writing), or the smaller botana marina, a chilled mixed seafood platter. If you like whole fish Mexican style, deep-fried and crunchy, this is the best place to get it. But for the timid, Pepe's prepares a wide array of fillets. I'm sure Pepe's reason for using margarine was to gain the American Heart Association's symbol of approval; many menu items have the familiar heart next to them. For me, this is a shortcoming (maybe you could ask for butter).

Señor Fish, 5111 N. Figueroa Street, Highland Park, CENTRAL, 213-257-2498. Lunch and dinner; closed Monday evening. Most Mexican seafood houses stick to the traditional cocteles and variations of fish, rice, and beans on a plate. But at Señor Fish, situated in a former neighborhood burger stand (now painted with a saltwater aquarium scene), there are shrimp and scallop burritos, sea-

food quesadillas dripping with melted cheese, and tacos filled with fried fish garnished with fresh salsa. Señor Fish goes beyond the standard ceviche tostada to offer one with octopus salad and another with shrimp. The grilled fish is reasonably good, and a wonderful bouillabaisselike caldo siete mares is filled with all kinds of shellfish.

La Playita, 3306 Lincoln Boulevard, Santa Monica, WEST, 310-452-0090, open 9:30 A.M. to 8:00 P.M. daily. The most authentic marisquiera on the West Side, La Playita sells wonderful ceviches (especially the shrimp), cocteles, and seafood tostadas from a burger stand. Plan on take-out. The only seating is a few folding chairs under a dusty billboard. La Playita has much more than seafood: The burrito al pastor is a marvel of pork chunks in a bright chile- and achiote-laced sauce. And the tacos are almost as good as El Taurino's.

Other good seafood bets are **Guadalajara** (page 154) and **La Parrilla** (facing page).

♦ **BIRRIA**

Originally, birria de *chivo,* or roast goat, the west central relative of central Mexico's barbacoa, was cooked in a pit lined with maguey leaves. These days, specialty goat restaurants called birrierias season the meat with a light chile paste, steam or simmer it, and then roast it. You can order birria by part— leg, shoulder, spine (with marrow), or ribs. The meat comes in a bowl of consume made from the stock in which the goat was cooked. L.A. has at least 40 birrierias, from Pacoima to Long Beach. I haven't tried them all, but so far, these are my favorites.

Birrieria Jalisco, 1845 E. 1st Street, Boyle Heights, CENTRAL, 213-267-8821. Lunch through dinner daily. In business for 17 years, Birrieria Jalisco is an institution. Birria is all they sell, and it's made with rigorous attention to detail under the direction of proprietor Bonofacio Gonzales. Each day the kitchen grinds fresh peeled tomatoes for its consume in the same kind of stone mill used for grinding corn. The birria and chile-red, garlicky consume are only slightly spicy. But they come with a deep, dusky, spicy hot-chile sauce on the side. Lemon and freshly chopped onions, also on the side, are for sprinkling into the consume or adding to pieces of the meat, which you can wrap in a warm tortilla. The menu, on a light-up board in the ultraplain dining room, says only "birria, large and small." But if you ask the patron's extremely gracious son, he'll explain all the parts you can order.

At **Birrieria Tepechi** (1258 N. Avalon Boulevard, Wilmington, SOUTH, 310-513-8084; lunch through dinner daily), the rackety-rack of a computerized cash register lets you know that traditional birria has survived into the nineties. This light, modern café serves updated birria. It is well roasted, lean, and boneless, and my personal favorite. If you like, you can order birria with the consume on the side: some people like to eat the crispy roast pieces of meat without getting them soggy in the broth. Tepechi also has a well-rounded menu of other dinners and antojitos.

El Parian, 1528 W. Pico Boulevard, Los Angeles, CENTRAL, 213-386-7361. Breakfast and lunch daily. Near downtown, on the fringe of Koreatown, El Parian is named after the famous El Parian Plaza of Telaquepaque in suburban Guadalajara, where birria vendors roam near the tables selling their wares. There are no vendors at this funky spot, but the goat, crisp and oily, is absolutely authentic.

♦ **PARILLADA**
Mexicans love their parilladas. There's no better way to eat

meat, they feel, than sizzling hot from a charcoal brasier.

La Parrilla, 2126 Brooklyn Avenue, Boyle Heights, CENTRAL, 213-262-3434; 18716 Ventura Boulevard, Tarzana, S.F. VALLEY, 818-708-7422; and 19265 Roscoe Boulevard, Northridge, S.F. VALLEY, 818-993-7773. Lunch and dinner daily. La Parrilla's first restaurant (it now has three) opened in a simple storefront on Brooklyn Avenue. It was one of the first kitchens to show off the diversity of Mexico's cuisines by serving pollito en pipian, young chicken in a Oaxacan-style sauce of ground pumpkin seeds, and pork in chipotle sauce made with smoked jalapeño chiles.

The Northridge La Parrilla, the largest one, has a wonderful Mexico City ambience, and although no mariachis come in from the street to serenade as they used to on Brooklyn Avenue, a feeling of gaiety prevails. It's all those tiles, the native crafts, the cozy booths and little alcoves, and the expectant feeling you get watching sizzling minigrills, called *braseros,* being whisked still smoking to the tables. Each of the parilladas al brasero listed on the menu (it means a dish grilled over charcoal) is a different combination of items: No. 3, my favorite, is queso fundido, spare ribs, steak, and chorizo; No. 2 is carne asada, chicken and pork chops. These are served for two, but would probably satisfy three or four if you ordered a few of the very generous appetizers or an à la carte seafood dish.

El Chamizal, 7111 Pacific Boulevard, Huntington Park, EAST OF L.A., 213-583-3251. Lunch and dinner daily. At El Chamizal, the Cal-Spanish ambience is a little more understated, though still upscale. Here, although the menu isn't as interesting as La Parrilla's, the selection of parilladas (grilled dishes) is broader, and these, too, come to the table on a *brasero*. *Parillada jarocha* offers shrimp, scallops, squid, a fish fillet, and green plantains. The adobada has sausage, a pork chop, and a steak. Alongside the meats are roasted scallions and potatoes, and of course rice and beans. Apart from the parilladas, El Chamizal's selection runs the familiar gamut from fried whole red snapper to mole poblano and seafood cocktails.

♦ **TORTAS**
Almost every taco stand sells tortas, but what you often get is a soggy "French" roll slathered with beans and haphazardly filled with gooey stewed or grilled meats. Midway, you have to put the sandwich on a plate and finish eating it with a knife and fork. But **Super Tortas** (360 S. Alvarado Street, Los Angeles, CENTRAL, 213-413-7953; lunch and dinner daily) serves what must be the city's most refined tortas. And they're right at home in the shop's slick mauve interior. All start with ultrafresh and crispy bolillos, minus the customary bean spread; proprietor M. C. Guerrero thinks beans are too heavy for tortas. But perfect cooked-from-scratch beans can be had on the side. The machaca torta comes heaped with shredded beef and onion scrambled with eggs and topped with a fat slab of ripe tomato and vinegared chile slices. Ham tortas are amply filled and have a nice thick layer of avocado. And for the pork rib eye torta, the meat is always freshly grilled to order.

♦ **GORDITAS**
Gorditas, the Mexican equivalent of a stuffed pita, are thick corn pancakes that puff up as they grill. The center can be stuffed with anything: carne asada, chile verde, or *machaca* for example.

The best gorditas in town are at **Ana Maria's** in the Grand Central Public Market, next to **Roast to Go** (which has the reputation for L.A.'s best carnitas). Where many taquerias use premade gorditas (which toughen on standing), Ana Maria's makes them up fresh from the masa before your very eyes. For more detail, see description of **Grand Central Public Market,** page 171.

♦ **JUGOS, LICUADOS, AND PALETAS**
In recent years, frothy fruit and milk blender drinks (licuados), freshly squeezed juices (jugos), and frozen juice bars resembling popsicles (paletas) have become a Mexican national passion, and they are widely sold here. In many L.A. neighborhoods paleta vendors with mobile refrigerators ring bicycle bells to announce their arrival.

Cisco's Jugos Frescos, 696 S. Alvarado Street, Los Angeles, CENTRAL, 213-483-7225. Open all day; closed Monday. Cisco's juice bar, across the street from MacArthur Park, is an urbane version of the licuado trucks you see in most Mexican towns. Inside the tiny shop, you're surrounded by pyramids of fresh fruits and vegetables from which Cisco's extracts jugos frescos with the help of a heavy-duty juicer. But it's the creamy fruit-and-milk licuados that are most irresistible. Take your pick of fresh mango, papaya, strawberry, banana, melons, and more. And if you really want a substantial meal, Cisco's will whip an egg into your licuado.

Los Burritos, 4929 Sunset Boulevard, Los Angeles, CENTRAL, 213-669-9438. Open daily. Also at 8th and Alvarado, Los Angeles, CENTRAL, 213-386-5576; North Hollywood, S.F. VALLEY, 818-766-6546. Los Burritos makes some of the city's most voluptuous licuados. At some branches they've cordoned off a little area just for the drinks, which they call "Jugoslandia." Its menu features "fruit rainbow," a blend of watermelon, papaya, and blackberries. "Yogurt delight" includes papaya, strawberries, banana, and honey. The rest of their food though, is quite ordinary.

Paleteria El Oasis, 2758 E. Gage Avenue, Huntington Park, EAST OF L.A., 213-585-3561. The main Huntington Park shopping area, on a revitalized stretch of Pacific Boulevard, throbs on the weekends with street life and families out strolling, shopping, and eating. Tianguis and Viva Latin supermarkets both have branches there, and, just off Pacific on Gage, El Oasis offers icy snow cones made with mashed fruit instead of the usual insipid syrups. Leche paletas, made with milk, come in a dozen flavors including strawberry, rice, cocoa, guava, and the rich creamy coral-colored mamey. Paletas de agua, frozen fruit juice bars, are also made in a wide range of flavors including tamarind, melon, guanabana, and jamaica.

THE BEST CAL-MEX COMFORT FOOD

In most L.A. neighborhoods, including Mexican ones, the Californiaized combination plate holds sway. It's still as much a part of everyday eating as pizza or the deli sandwich. Though run-of-the-mill Cal-Mex can be pretty dreadful stuff, at the following restaurants is the best comfort food imaginable.

El Cholo (1121 S. Western Avenue, Koreatown, CENTRAL, 213-734-2773; lunch and dinner daily) is the grandaddy of Los Angeles Mexican restaurants. When it opened in 1927 in a Western Avenue storefront, it was on the outskirts of Los Angeles. In those days Mexican cooking was called "Spanish food"—even on El Cholo's sign. The restaurant, now run by the third generation of the Salisbury family, has kept pace with the times. Now a rambling multi-roomed hacienda-style place with a lushly planted patio and some say the best margaritas in town, its menu goes beyond the traditional

---

MARIACHIS

La Fonda, 2501 Wilshire Boulevard, Los Angeles, CENTRAL, 213-380-5055. You don't go to La Fonda for the food but for Los Camperos, a 12-piece mariachi orchestra (not band)—one of the finest anywhere, complete with a harpist and a full brass section.

These are Carnegie Hall–quality musicians in full formal dress, and in the elegant colonial-style surroundings, they sound little like the strolling mariachis that visit restaurants around town.

There's a full bar, and the limited menu is designed not to offend any palates: beef brochettes, large shrimp in a mild Veracruz sauce, arroz con pollo, and a daring mole poblano. The shows are three times nightly at 6:45, 9:00, and 11:00, and on weekends there's another performance at 12:45 A.M.

---

combinaciones. El Cholo's fresh corn tamales (June to September only) are famous, and the new soft tacos al carbon include one with lamb and a sauce of ancho chiles. Fajitas have been added, and there are daily specials—nothing too trendy but all very good.

More exciting than El Cholo's comfort foods are the stylized New Southwestern offerings at the Salisburys' other restaurant, **The Original Sonora Cafe** (445 S. Figueroa Street [in the Union Bank building], Los Angeles, CENTRAL, 213-624-1800). Sonora's comfortably stylish, adobe-style dining room is a welcome respite from the frenetic downtown traffic. And the hand-shaken Jose Cuervo 1800 tequila and Cointreau margaritas are as good as the ones that made El Cholo famous. With its duck confit tamales and lobster ravioli with ancho chile sauce, Sonora's menu might suggest that the food is designer Mexican concocted for L.A. foodies. But chef Felix Salcedo's cooking, though nothing you'd encounter in the Southwest or Mexico, has the taste and style of its Mexican origins.

Sierra's (6819 Canoga Avenue, Canoga Park, S.F. VALLEY, 818-884-0776; lunch and dinner daily), the San Fernando Valley equivalent of El Cholo and in business since 1937, is also family-run. Each room in the restaurant gives you the feeling you're in a Mexican colonial home, with artifacts, artwork, and books casually placed around. Taco, enchilada, and burrito plates are the best they can be, and home cooking–style dishes include daily specials of chicken adobada and marvelous carnitas sprinkled with just chopped onion and cilantro. The full bar is no slouch, with margaritas of all hues. (A second branch is at 500 Mission Boulevard, San Fernando, S.F. VALLEY, 818-365-9196.)

♦ **TREND-SETTERS**

El Porton, 1105 W. Whittier Boulevard, Montebello, EAST OF L.A., 213-888-8879. Open 7:00 A.M. to 11:00 P.M. daily. Across the parking lot from the huge Tianguis Mexican supermarket is El Porton, part of a large Mexico City chain. The coffee-shop-bright restaurant with a large open grill area at its center serves up comidas that Mexicans, until recent years, would eat almost exclusively at home: hearty regional stews and such grilled meats as lomo enchilado with its tangy vinegar-chile marinade. Many grilled meats—including the parillada—come with home-style papas con rajas (potatoes and strips of poblano chile cooked in cream) instead of the predictable beans. Fortunately, the menu is emblazoned with color photographs of many dishes, because likely as not your server won't be fluent in English. It's not that El Porton's food, which is somewhere between upscale taquiera and mom's cooking, is unique to Mexicans, but the restaurant itself is evidence of modern Mexico's changing restaurant-going habits.

The phenomenal success of the Montebello El Porton inspired its parent company to open a restaurant on the West Side, El Porton Grill. At this writing, this Westwood branch has closed. But it is expected to reopen in another West Side location in the summer of 1992.

Border Grill No. 1, 7407½ Melrose Avenue, Los Angeles, CENTRAL, 213-658-7495. Lunch and dinner daily. **Border Grill No. 2,** 1445 Fourth Street, Santa Monica, WEST, 310-451-1655. Lunch and dinner daily. At their first Border Grill on Melrose, chefs Mary Sue Milliken and Susan Feniger's tangential take on traditional Mexican cooking lured every foodie in town. Dishes like *huraches*—a masa turnover stuffed with black bean purée and plated on two pools of elegant and intensely flavored red and green sauces—exemplified the thinking of these two French-trained chefs. Their Border Grill No. 2 is even more daring, but differently so. It's a space of awesome proportions and sharp angles with bold semi-Mexican primitive caricatures painted over the walls. The food's flavors are amplified and rough-hewn, like the caldos and moles dished out from stoneware cazuelas in a Oaxacan marketplace.

A cook pats out handmade tortillas for exotic tacos near the front of the room. In spite of this, the tacos are the least successful items on the menu—but the Jaliscan pozole, the unctuous braised tongue, and the bright-tasting cocteles have altered L.A.'s perception of Mexican food.

Kaktus, 400 N. Canon Drive, Beverly Hills, WEST, 310-271-1856. Lunch Monday to Saturday; dinner nightly. Despite its upscale Beverly Hills location, chichi look, and trendy appellation, Kaktus turns out some wholly authentic dishes: fresh tomatillo salsa for just fried chips, enchiladas suisas with three Mexican cheeses (no Cheddar, thank you), and grilled nopalito salad with cotija cheese crumbled in. A certain refinement in preparing familiar dishes gives everything freshness. And the nouvelle Mexican dishes, like the slab of grilled swordfish with a bright cilantro sauce, stay close enough to tradition not to be branded as pure trendiness. Kaktus is a welcome addition to the Mexican food scene.

Rebecca's, 2025 Pacific Avenue, Venice, WEST, 310-306-6266. Dinner nightly. Every foodie knows this nuevo Mexican cantina owned by restaurant magnate Bruce Marder and his wife Rebecca. The restaurant's outrageous design by renowned architect Frank Gehry, with tree trunks dividing the polished cement block–floored dining room and huge alligators hanging from the ceiling, is perhaps as much a draw for the trendy bar crowd as the food. Rebecca's California-cuisine take on authentic Mexican cooking makes use of exceptional ingredients: just shucked baby oysters for cocktails and Norwegian salmon and Japanese yellowtail for the ceviche. The leanest lamb imaginable is spit-roasted for lamb adobada and served with the freshest salsa. Carnitas are never deep-fried but rotisserie-grilled. Rebecca's clean, lean food has an adoring following. But detractors find the kitchen uneven or complain it's too de-ethnicized. Rebecca's continues to pack 'em in, however; it

must be more than those alligators.

Lula, 2720 Main Street, Santa Monica, WEST, 310-392-5711. Lunch and dinner; closed Monday. Less stylized, and less expensive, then Rebecca's is Lula. Local chef, former cooking teacher and propriator of Gilliland's Cafe Gerri Gilliland (who's from Ireland) has been enamored with Mexican food since she arrived on our shores. She converted a tired beach-city seafood house into a contemporary cantina. Gilliland credits her teacher and mentor in Mexico, chef Lula Bertran (after whom the restaurant is named), for introducing her to a light, simple cuisine of the sort found in Mexico City's tonier modern fondas (and nothing like the lard-rich dishes of old-time authentic Mexican cooking). Lula's kitchen does succeed at lightening up Mexican cooking and it introduces dishes with a regional slant: *tiken xic pescado* (grilled fresh fish marinated in citrus and annatto-laced marinade typical of the Yucatan), and Guadalajara-style sopes (masa shells holding black beans, chorizo, and potato) and even Salvadoran tamales. The food is quite good, but as interesting as all this sounds, there's nothing particularly earth-shaking about the cooking.

La Salsa, 11075 W. Pico Boulevard, West Los Angeles, WEST, 310-479-0919. Many branches citywide. While some consider La Salsa's food "haute" Mexican, owner Howdy Kabrins, who introduced tacos al carbon to the mainstream and pioneered the salsa bar, says La Salsa's food is closer to what he ate while growing up in Mexico. His inspiration came from the Mexican kitchens of his travels and not the Californiaized food of East L.A. It's true he does mix the cooking of several regions in a sort of L.A. fantasy style—Yucatecan black beans and Sonoran carne asada, for example.

Cooks at La Salsa carve marinated beef from a spit and fold sizzling carne asada into soft tortillas that you squeeze with fresh lime, then sprinkle with just chopped cilantro and onion. The La Salsas serve huevos rancheros all day long and a slightly creamy orchata to drink—just as though they were in urban Mexico. These successful stylized taquerias, which gave us a fresh outlook on Mexican cooking, have inspired many clones. Also see **The Original Sonora Cafe,** page 165.

SHOPS AND MARKETS

The color and bustle of Mexican marketplaces is found in neighborhoods all over Los Angeles. But Boyle Heights and East Los Angeles are still the best places to seek out the finest Mexican specialties. **El Mercado** (3425 E. 1st Street, Boyle Heights, CENTRAL, 213-268-3451) isn't as lively as it once was. At the center is a modest food market with a good deli to the left, but most of the old-time food vendors have been replaced by swap-meet-style clothes-and-leather-goods hawkers. It's still fun to go to the top floor on a Sunday, take in the milling crowds, have a beer in one of the restaurants, and listen to the battle of the mariachi bands—usually there are at least three of them.

La Azteca Tortilleria (4538 Brooklyn Avenue, Boyle Heights, CENTRAL, 213-262-5977) is the ne plus ultra for handsome corn tortillas. Here they are patted out into thin rounds by a corps of aproned ladies starting at 6:00 A.M. Nothing compares to La Azteca's hand-rolled flour tortillas—they still use lard to get that fabulously authentic flavor—and the tortillas freeze beautifully. La Azteca makes some of the plumpest tacos with their just-off-the-grill tortillas. From the small menu on the wall, choose the awesome quesadillas with chorizo and a fresh

rough-hewn salsa, both made in the shop. Take home some of the finest tamales in town, filled with chunky meat.

You'll find the city's best pan dulce a few doors down at **El Gallo** (4546 Brooklyn Avenue, Boyle Heights, CENTRAL, 213-263-5528), a bakery with bulging cases, filled shelves, and fresh baked goods continually coming out of its ovens. El Gallo envelops you in temptations. The sweet breads (pan dulces) here bear no resemblance to most others around town. *Novios* are an eggy yeast bread encased in a swirl of short pastry; *cuernos* are the same barely sweet egg dough in a crescent shape; and *elotes,* corn-ear-shaped pan dulce, are another variation on the doughs. On weekends lines form for El Gallo's pan de agua (French rolls), pan dulces, and sweet fruit filled empanadas. Holidays bring traditional specialty breads: *pan de muerte* and *rasca de reyes.*

On a quiet residential street paralleling Brooklyn Avenue is **Juanito's Tamale Factory** (4214 Floral Drive, Boyle Heights, CENTRAL, 213-268-2365). Since 1957 Juanito's has been known in the community for its long, slender, refined tamales, both sweet and savory, wrapped in corn husks. Watch the women wrapping them in the stainless steel work area; smell the simmering aromas of the fillings wafting from the back kitchen. And go away with an armload of tamales.

Traveling up Whittier Boulevard, you can't miss **Al Salam Rancho** (3980 E. Whittier Boulevard, East Los Angeles, EAST OF L.A., 213-267-1857), with its huge chicken on the roof. Al Salam sells *aves vivas.* Pick out your live chicken, stewing hen, quail, or dove (or order ducks and squab), and the poultry will be dressed while you wait. With this supremely fresh bird, your caldo de pollo will be better than you can imagine. Back toward downtown on Whittier, you find **La Mascota** (2715 Whittier Boulevard, Boyle Heights, CENTRAL, 213-263-5513), one of the area's best-known bakeries. Their sumptuous capirotada, a bread pudding made with dark piloncillo sugar, cheese, and raisins, has no equal. La Mascota is also known for pan dulce—especially the large round white or whole wheat lightly sweetened morning breads called *semitas*—and for *rajas de queso,* a flat cheese-and-cherry-filled coffee cake sold in slices. La Mascota's tamales are made four ways: the traditional pork in red chile; with cheese; with chicken and green chile; and with pineapple.

El Gallo Giro (7136 Pacific, Huntington Park, EAST OF L.A., 213-585-4433) is the city's most complete prepared-food deli. The huge tiled store has various stations, each with a specialty. While your gordita is grilling, walk up to the "buffet" to select from various fillings: tinga flavored with chipotle or chicharron in green salsa. The bakery turns out hefty torta rolls to take home or to eat with a selected filling, perhaps roast pork with chile. A tortilla machine rolls off a constant supply. One counter sells various stews, including *picadillo;* another, roasted or braised meats. A little juice area offers jugos, licuados, and aguas frescas: cactus pear, mango, or banana. And in the next room El Gallo Giro has a small carniceria. (There's a second El Gallo Giro at 260 S. Broadway [across from Grand Central Public Market], Los Angeles, CENTRAL, 213-626-6926.)

Shoppers in the San Fernando Valley will want to know about **Lenchita's** (13612½ Van Nuys Boulevard, Pacoima, S.F. VALLEY, 818-899-2623), a fixture in Pacoima for more than 17 years.

People bring in their tubs to buy fresh masa, and they stock up on handmade corn tortillas and birria. Now that Lenchita's has taken over the Hub Market, you can eat in the front take-out area. But I prefer the tables in the back deli, with its smell of freshly ground corn. Take-out plates include chile verde, carne asada, and many caldos. Each comes with four handmade tortillas.

Gallegos Brothers, 1424 Broadway, Santa Monica, WEST, 310-395-0162. On the West Side since the 1930s, Gallegos Brothers, a small, family-run tortilleria, is where you can get warm tortillas sold with the steam still in the bag. The kitchen is in full view, with its bubbling vats of nixtamal waiting to be ground into masa. But Gallegos sells much more than tortillas and masa preparada for tamales. In the deli cases are lean little thumb-sized chorizos, crema fresca, and a selection of cheeses: cotija, asadero, Oaxaca, and queso quesadilla. For parties, Gallegos fries big batches of chips—either

Baking tortillas by the yard at Gallegos Brothers tortilleria and deli in Santa Monica.

thick or thin—and there are nine varieties of homemade salsas if you count the pickled chiles. There are big trays of enchiladas supremas filled with grilled chicken and crema, and take-out orders of very good soft tacos, burritos, and tortas too.

Mexico Supermarket (Carneceria Mexico), 21001 Sherman Way, Canoga Park, S.F. VALLEY, 818-992-3239. The East San Fernando Valley has plenty of Mexican markets, including Tresierras, La Placita, and a branch of Tianguis (see below). But in the West Valley the place to shop for Mexican goods, fresh meats, wonderful hand-tied chorizos, and piles of chiles or a packet of recado is Mexico Supermarket.

Foodies know by now that **Tianguis** (pronounced Tee-on-gees) (3610 N. Peck Road, El Monte, SAN GABRIEL VALLEY, 818-443-0499), a city-wide chain of huge Mexican supermercados owned by Vons, is the best for one-stop shopping. Go on a weekend—especially to the humongous 80,000-square-foot El Monte store. Mariachis play under piñatas shaped like rainbows and mutant ninja turtles that hang over the vast produce department with its cassavas, chipotles, poblanos, and guavas in massive piles on packing crates. The fruit and tomatoes always seem to be a little riper here. Go by the juice department and get a coconut with a straw in its center: You can drink the juice while you browse the cheese department and sample cotija, panela, or queso fresco, or taste one of five different crema Mexicanas. Look over Tianguis's enormous array of chorizos—brand names hang in ropes behind the deli, or you can buy one of the regional-style chorizos Tianguis makes in house. In the center of the store the bakers bake, the tortillas roll off a belt or are patted out, and the butchers will cut your order of oxtails or pigs' knuckles any way you like. Tianguis aims to create the same sort of social institution as the marketplace in Mexico, where people go in groups to shop and socialize. So far they are succeeding.

Numero Uno, 710 E. Jefferson Boulevard, Los Angeles, CENTRAL. The largest independent Mexican market in Los Angeles, Numero Uno looks exactly like any conventional supermarket until you start examining the ingredients.

Tianguis: Dozens of chorizo varieties.

Staples are sold in bulk at Tianguis Mexican supermarkets.

The produce section offers more kinds of fresh and dry chiles (at astonishingly low prices) than any market I know—including the elusive habañeros. Other rock-bottom-priced produce includes fresh epazote, *verdolaga* (purslane), fresh mamey, and heaps of hairy brown yuca root. The vast tortilla section, nearly half a block long, carries dozens of tortilla varieties including whole wheat, and also premade sopes, to be filled with your favorite chile or grilled meat. The frozen food department holds a large collection of fruit used in Southern Mexican and Central American cooking. Unlike conventional supermarkets, Numero Uno's meat and seafood section has a corps of butchers who cut meats to order. And Numero Uno's minivans provide transportation for those living in the neighborhood.

Since its inception in 1917, **Grand Central Public Market** (317 S. Broadway, Los Angeles, CENTRAL, 213-624-2378), the huge food bazaar in downtown Los Angeles, has been a boon for such shoppers as caterers in search of 25 pounds of ripe mangos and local families seeking to lower their food costs. It was getting seedy until developer Ira Yellen acquired it from its original owners and sank about $2 million into a facelift, rebuilding stalls and adding spiffy neon signs and a parking facility that is free with $15 worth of purchases. One stall sells Salvadoran, Guatemalan, and Mexican cultured creams, another various prepared moles—green and chocolate among them. The best gorditas in all L.A. are found at **Ana Maria's** (page 164); just look for the "gordita" neon sign near the center of the store. **Maria's Fried Fish,** which is connected to Norm's Fresh Fish, sells L.A.'s freshest Mexican-style cocteles de mariscos.

You can get Thai eggplants, Seville oranges, and beef cheeks here. And you might get a good deal from the dry fruit vendor, or on bulk rice, bulk dried chiles, longaniza, or carne seca.

The Grand Central Public Market. Left to right: A vendor shows off his "new crop" dried beans—the best quality; Saturday crowds; a staple stall.

CENTRAL AMERICA, SOUTH AMERICA, AND THE CARIBBEAN

Angelenos tend to assume that foods with Spanish names will be Mexican. But each Latin American country has its own culinary personality, with dishes that differ from Mexico's even when their names are the same. The quesadilla at any Salvadoran restaurant, for example, won't resemble in any way a Mexican quesadilla—it will be pound cake. If, you order a tortilla at La Cubana, what you get is a Spanish style omelet. And at Mi Guatemala, when you ask for an enchilada you may be surprised at what comes to the table. Guatamalan enchiladas resemble a Mexican tostada: a crisp corn tortilla layered with lettuce, cheese, and beans.

Everyone has stirred a little something different into Latin America's well-seasoned melting pot. The cooking of South and Central America is, to say the least, eclectic. Immigrants introduced German cheeses to Venezuela and Italian pasta to Argentina. The Spanish conquistadores, of course, brought over all kinds of new foods that got mixed into various Indian cultures. Europeans imported slaves, who added their cooking to the mix, particularly in Brazil.

South and Central American restaurants, in comparison to say, Thai or Chinese, are scarce. One exception to this is El Salvadoran restaurants.

Note: The glossary on pages 148–153 includes Latin American terms.

CENTRAL AMERICA

EL SALVADOR
♦ PUPUSERIAS

La Adelita, 1287 S. Union Avenue (at Pico), Los Angeles, CENTRAL, 213-487-0176; 5812 Santa Monica Boulevard, Los Angeles, CENTRAL, 213-465-6526; 1000 E. Washington Boulevard, Los Angeles, CENTRAL, 213-746-9520. Open 7:00 A.M. to 9:00 P.M. daily. For years, La Adelita gathered attention as a good place to buy hand-patted tortillas. They still make them, but now the bakery offerings have been broadened to include a toothsome selection of goodies from all over Central America and Mexico.

In the take-out area, pupusas are patted from a fresh scoop of masa (you can watch its production over on the bakery side). Whole fried bananas come smothered in sour cream or thinly sliced lengthwise and fried crisp. A Central American–style roast turkey makes great tortas; these come on special rolls baked in La Adelita's bakery. And La Adelita's selection of hot dishes includes both Mexican and Central American–style tamales.

Papaturro, 4109 W. Beverly Boulevard, Los Angeles, CENTRAL, 213-660-4363, and 1133 N. Vermont Avenue, Los Angeles, CENTRAL, 213-666-7290. Lunch through dinner; closed Tuesday. One of L.A.'s first pupuserias—and still one of the best—Papaturro has recently spiffed up its storefront with a chic new awning. Inside you find red-tablecloth-covered tables, smiling service, and some of the best Salvadoran cooking in town. Papaturro has opened a second branch on Vermont. **La Plancha** (2818 W. 9th Street, Koreatown, CENTRAL, 213-383-2009), owned by the Molina family who formerly ran the excellent La Plancha Nicaraguan restaurant next door, keeps its pupusa quality high. Mr. Molina picks out the lean pork shoulders for the chicharron filling himself. The same good meat goes into yuca con chicharron—the best in town. La Plancha also offers its original Nicaraguan dishes, but you have to ask for the menu.

A cook prepares ingredients for pupusas at La Plancha pupuseria.

SALVADORAN ANTOJITOS: PUPUSAS, TAMAL, AND YUCA CON CHICHARRON

It's been 8 or 9 years since the trickle of Salvadorans immigrating here turned into a flood. L.A. has over half a million Salvadorans and an estimated 250 pupuserias.

These restaurants, which are beginning to spread from the San Fernando Valley to Long Beach, serve El Salvador's national specialty, pupusas, and other dishes at extremely reasonable prices.

Pupusas—ground corn pancakes stuffed with melting cheese or meat—can vary tremendously in quality, but all Salvadoran cooks insist on patting them out by hand and grilling them to order. A good pupusa's filling is ample yet doesn't seep through its exterior, which should be quite thin. A typical choice of fillings will be: queso, chicharron (fried pork meat), *revueltas* (mixed cheese and meat), and cheese flavored with loroco, a mild-tasting flower used as an herb. All pupusas come with curtido, a lip-stinging spicy cabbage relish. The restaurants I've listed in this section do them right.

Other Salvadoran antojitos include the voluptuous tamal salvadoreño. Unlike Mexican tamales, these are made with smooth masa flavored with meat stock and filled with large chunks of marinated meat. The whole thing is wrapped in banana leaves and steamed.

Try the pastelitos, too: little ground corn envelopes filled with savory minced meat. Central American empanadas are not the usual stuffed pastry but a small pouch of mashed

Pupusas demonstrated step by step at La Plancha pupuseria.

banana formed around a cream filling and fried; each creamy bite is a little taste of heaven. Quesadilla is a sort of pound cake made with cheese in its batter. Most menus will also have yuca con chicharron: yuca root strips fried in oil like tropical French fries, served with lean crispy chunks of fried pork.

At **Atlacatl** (301 N. Berendo Street [at Beverly], Los Angeles, CENTRAL, 213-663-1404), the owners have painted up a large house and added a picket fence to make a charming restaurant. In its bright dining room, Atlacatl serves a greater variety of pupusas than do many places: There's a bean version, one with black beans and cheese, and another with chicken. **El Izalqueño** (1830 W. Pico Boulevard, Suite C, Los Angeles, CENTRAL, 213-387-2467), a bright room decorated with overstuffed tropical birds, offers both regular and rice flour pupusas, the latter a specialty of Izalco. The cooking is as creative as the decor. Try their fresh corn tamales, slightly sweet and light as a soufflé, served smothered in a sea of delicious, thick Salvadoran cream.

Anayas (1101 S. Vermont Avenue, No. 102, Koreatown, CENTRAL, 213-381-7582), with its high-tech pastel dining room, has the most upbeat surroundings of the restaurants in this group. The owners emphasize that they use the leanest meats—although I must say their *plato el pobre,* with its plump sausages, thick Salvadoran cream, and tortillas, is outrageously rich and good. And another great dish—especially for the price—is the paellalike arroz à la valenciana, the house specialty.

In Long Beach, the kitchen at Abel and Maria Salazar's **Ilopango** (1436 E. 7th Street, Long Beach, SOUTH, 310-432-6807) does every dish with great style. Even a humble chicken submarine sandwich (pan con gallina) uses a remarkable marinade, and the beautifully arranged fresh watercress, mild curtido, and the ripe tomato garnish could have come off the plates of Chaya Grill or Citrus.

♦ **SALVADORAN PANADERIA**
Of the Valley's new crop of pupuserias, **Mi Ranchito Salvadoreño** (14523 Vanowen Street, Van Nuys, S.F. VALLEY, 818-994-4562) is one with its own panaderia next door. Specialties of the dining room are generously filled pupusas and seafood mariscada, the Salvadoran equivalent of bouillabaisse. You're likely, though, to find yourself eating these to the beat of Latin music, which on weekends is often live.

The panaderia sells a full range of typical cakes and pastries: quesadilla is the most well known. Maria Louisa, a dense cake with a cream filling, comes topped with an even layer of red sugar—but it is not too sweet. Three plain cakes that Salvadorans love with their coffee are marquesote, an airy eggy yellow sponge cake; *paroza de arroz,* a dense, lightly sweet cake made with rice flour; and the tall, very compact torta de yema. Among the bakery's many sweets are *borrachos* (rum-flavored syrup-soaked cakes), and *ralampagos* (lightning)—a cream puff filled with thick custard and topped with crackly caramel.

GUATEMALA

- **Guatelinda,** 2220 W. 7th Street, Los Angeles, CENTRAL, 213-385-7420. Lunch and dinner; closed Monday.
- **Mi Guatemala,** 695 S. Hoover, Los Angeles, CENTRAL, 213-387-4296. Lunch and dinner daily.

It's been more than 20 years since these two Guatemalan restaurants opened. Guatelinda, now the fancier of the two since its remodeling, has white napery and pink walls that freshen this once barnlike space. The restaurant still features its signature marimba band on weekends—very popular with Guatemalans—so if you go then, don't plan on a whole lot of conversation.

One of L.A.'s truly great immoderate meals, the Guatelinda plate, is a combination that includes carne adobada, a pork cutlet smeared with a slightly vinegary achiote-laced marinade; a hunk of carne asada; and two juicy, intensely seasoned Guatemalan-style longaniza. With these come the familiar trio of fried plantains, mashed black beans (much thicker than the soupy Cuban kind), and rice. Pollo con crema shows off the European side of Guatemalan food. With its tart, light sauce made from rich silky Guatemalan-style cultured cream, the dish is unabashedly luxurious and more European than you expect Guatemalan food to be.

Mi Guatemala, still decorated in stereotypical "ethnic" style with travel posters and woven plastic-covered tablecloths, has a loud jukebox that plays "Lambada" and "Material Girl" in Spanish. The menu, almost identical to Guatelinda's, includes carne guisada, a beef stew with a slight kick of vinegar, and hilachas (it translates as threads), a braised shredded meat that is absolutely delicious rolled up in warm tortillas or eaten with the smashed beans and plantains. Revolcado, a soupy pork-head stew—the waitress was shocked when I ordered it—it is an ultrarich spicy broth, the product of simmering a pork head until the meat falls away. But the rest of Mi Guatemala's food isn't quite as exotic. With these selections try the intensely banana-flavored suchiles to drink.

La Mazateca, 524 Manchester Boulevard, Inglewood, SOUTH, 310-671-3910. Lunch and dinner; closed Tuesday. While driving through Inglewood from LAX, I discovered La Mazateca, a tiny market and café that has wonderful hand-painted scenes of rural Guatemala decorating the walls. It serves frijol blanco with large chunks of lean pork, and a typical pork pepián thickened with toasted bread and bright with orangy achiote. The Guatemalan-style tamal is always accompanied with a warm roll and coffee. "That's the way it's always eaten in Guatemala," the proprietor told me. La Mazateca's breakfasts—especially the longaniza with eggs and smashed beans—is something I'd return for, whether or not I'm driving home from the airport.

Guatemalteca Bakery, 4032 W. Beverly Boulevard, Los Angeles, CENTRAL, 213-382-9451. At Guatemalteca Bakery, a place with warm yeasty aromas drifting into the street early in the day, Guatemalan-style breads and French-style perujo, rolls, are heaped behind the counter. There are slightly sweet buns with a crunchy sugar topping and spiraled campechanas glazed with sugar. Rodajas, a pound cake flavored with orange, makes a perfect coffee accompaniment. The bakery now has several tables so you can enjoy the baked goods still warm on the spot. Also try the eggy light sponge cupcakes called marquesotes and the crescent-shaped empanadas filled with creamy custard. A small grocery section carries sieved Guatemalan-style black beans in cans, Guatemalan-style chorizo, and other typical ingredients.

NICARAGUA

La Plancha Grill, 6207 York Boulevard, Highland Park, CENTRAL, 213-255-1416. Lunch through dinner daily. When the old La Plancha turned into a travel agency, if you wanted their great Nicaraguan food you had to eat in the utilitarian dining room of the family's pupuseria next door. But now owner Milton Molina has bought a former neighborhood coffee shop and turned it into the La Plancha Grill. The newly remodeled restaurant has windows all around with a view of the Monterey hills.

The Grill serves many of the wonderful dishes that made the original La Plancha so famous: a nacatamal with its smooth exterior enveloping marinated meats and a prune; citrus-marinated grilled rib steaks, pork, and chicken; and the pollo *desmenuzado:* richly flavored shredded marinated chicken breast.

Managua, 1007 N. Alvarado Street, Los Angeles, CENTRAL, 213-413-9622. Lunch and dinner daily. Managua, on the bottom floor of a rambling two-story classic 1920s L.A. house, has an airy side porch where you can lunch outside, homey dining rooms with cushioned booths, and a loud jukebox with Nicaraguan selections. Proprietors Bismarck and Maria Morales are gracious hosts who don't mind explaining every detail of their dishes. Under "Especialidades", the *fritanga* is a good sampler plate—it's supposed to be a combination of appetizers, but by the time you work your way through the chunks of juicy fried pork and fried cheese, plantains drizzled with Nicaraguan-style cultured cream, yuca, gallo pinto, and a chopped salad with cabbage and tomato, you may find an entrée unnecessary. Order the arroz con leche pudding or the sliced guava jelly and cream cheese for dessert and call it a night. Another time be sure to have *lomito de cerdo,* pork marinated in spiced citrus juice and grilled. It's been a mainstay here for at least a decade, and now Managua does a chicken version they call "bistec de pollo." Of the frothy *refrescos,* creamy blends of milk whipped up with fruit, the guanabana drink is, for a change, not made with canned fruit.

El Floridita, 1253 N. Vine Street, Hollywood, CENTRAL, 213-871-0936. Lunch through dinner daily. El Floridita gained notice in the Latin community for its excellent Cuban food and for staging interesting entertainment: One night a reading from the Pulitzer Prize–winning novel *The Mambo Kings Play Songs of Love* was accompanied by the same drum music that was being described in that portion of the novel. Sometimes they'll have Brazilian salsa or a harpist.

El Floridita has so often been identified as a Cuban restaurant that its wonderful Nicaraguan menu comes as a surprise to many diners. There's the traditional Nicaraguan tamale, nacatamal, and vigoron: a yuca salad topped with crunchy fried pork skin. Carne desmenuzada, beef braised with Seville orange juice and onion, and then shredded, is addictive. Many dishes come with gallo pinto ("spotted rooster"), a popular Nicaraguan rice and pinto bean dish.

THE CARIBBEAN

♦ **RESTAURANTS**
Versailles, 10319 Venice Boulevard, Culver City, WEST, 310-558-3168, and 1415 S. La Cienega Boulevard, West Los Angeles, WEST, 310-289-0392. Lunch through dinner daily. Black bean fever seized L.A. about 7 or 8 years ago, when everybody began to get wind of Versailles. Once simply a mom-and-pop place serving Culver City's Cuban enclave, the restaurant finally had to expand, but nothing was lost in the translation: It's still the same unpolished roadhouse, with Cuban music blaring over the conversation of a high-energy crowd. Its second branch on La Cienega is a clone.

Famous for its citrus-drenched, onion-topped crisp roast chicken and marinated roast pork, Versailles serves a menuful of exotica including tasajo (imported dried beef in a sauce), all of which sound wonderful if you can forgo the fabulous chicken.

Rincon Criollo, 4361 Sepulveda Boulevard, Culver City, WEST, 310-397-9295 or 391-4478. Lunch and dinner daily. Farther west in Culver City is Rincon Criollo, a place with chicken almost identical to that at Versailles, except that it's accompanied by much larger portions of those devastatingly good fried plantains. The beans are beautifully spiced here, too, and prices are usually a dollar or so lower than at Versailles. But Rincon is quiet and small, without the flashy ambience. You sometimes get the sense you're not in L.A. here: One gentleman came in wearing a native tropical shirt, white shoes, and a Panama hat, lit up a hand-rolled cigar, and ordered a Cuban espresso while he waited for his food to go.

El Colmao, 2328 W. Pico Boulevard, Los Angeles, CENTRAL, 213-386-6131. Lunch and dinner; closed Tuesday. El Colmao's ads in the Cuban newspaper emphasize the paella, the comidas españolas (Spanish dinners) and the mariscos. Although the seafood-filled paella is some of the best in town, most gringos come for the Moros y Christianos—black beans fried with rice—and the long stewed, shredded beef, ropa vieja. El Colmao is etched-in-time Cuban—white tablecloths, veined mirrors, leatherette chairs—and almost anything you order will be good. Some are partial to the fried pork leg topped with a mound of slow-cooked onions; I love the shrimp in achiote-colored yellow rice. Saturday and Sunday, when all the Cubans gather for lunch, are the best times to soak up local color.

El Chori, 5147 Gage Avenue, Bell, EAST OF L.A., 213-773-3011. Lunch and dinner daily. El Chori's genteel dining room came as a real surprise—especially when the Venezuelan harpist started playing Latin music. From what I'd heard about the restaurant, I expected a Versailles East. But El Chori serves tapas, and there's a real Spanish emphasis to its food. Grilled chunks of Spanish chorizo spurt juice when you bite into them, thin slices of tongue come in a pungent garlic vinaigrette, and chicharron de pollo—quickly fried chicken chunks—are garnished with a tart garlic-onion relish.

El Chori makes soups so good and so hearty you may want to eat them as dinner. On Fridays, I like to take home the daily special of lentil soup made with ham, chorizo chunks, cubes of potato, and squash. On Mondays, it's navy bean soup richly flavored with lean Spanish bacon. Entrées come with the traditional black beans and garlic-drenched yuca. Many offerings go beyond the standard Cuban menu fare. The standouts include braised lamb in wine sauce, grilled brains with a crispy breading, and bacalao à la espanola: Spanish-style salted cod made into a stew (served Friday and Saturday). El Chori has a nice selection of familiar California wines and Spanish wines as well as well-chosen beers.

El Criollo, 13245 Victory Boulevard, Van Nuys, S.F. VALLEY, 818-760-9883. Lunch and dinner; closed Monday. El Criollo serves the best Cuban food in the Valley. Located next to a barbecue joint with a parking lot full of half-ton pickup trucks, the restaurant, with its faded sign, is so nondescript outside we drove by twice before finding it. But inside—especially in the back dining room painted fresh blue and wittily stenciled with palm trees—it's delightful. And so are El Criollo's waiters, all from the old school of hospitality. Mine put down my shrimp in wine sauce, then carefully constructed a little ditch in the accompanying heap of white rice. He spooned some of the black beans into it like a small river and stood back to admire his handiwork. "Whatever you want, senorita—just let me know," he said.

Taste one dish and you will probably want to try almost everything. The Cuban combination plate with substantial chunks of fried pork, next to a moist ham-spiked tamal and a garlicky chunk of yuca and black beans, is a good introduction. Pollo al *ajillo*—blanketed with minced stewed garlic—is another good choice. El Criollo also prepares different special dishes each day.

La Cubana (720 E. Colorado Street, Glendale, S.F. VALLEY, 818-243-4398; lunch and dinner; closed Monday) is an inviting peach-colored room with matching table-cloths, stained glass, and well-spaced tables that are as comfortable as the food. The service is friendly and Cubans from the neighborhood keep the place pretty full. Boliche—a juicy braised eye of round with a sausage in the center—shows off the restaurant's careful cooking. And the succulent achiote-laced ropa vieja is as good a version as I've ever tasted. Unfortunately, La Cubana's weekday menu is quite limited. To get the juicy roast pork or the garlicky yuca con mojo, you have to come on weekends. La Cubana's desserts are worth mentioning—especially the mermelada de guayaba, a big slice of the jellied fruit served with cream cheese.

SHOPS

Habana Bakery, 2346 W. Pico Boulevard, Los Angeles, CENTRAL, 213-389-3359. Open daily. Another fixture in the Cuban community, and right up the block from El Colmao, is Habana Bakery, with its assorted sock-it-to-you sweet *panatella borracha* (rum-soaked cakes), pastelitos filled with guava or pineapple, and *orejas* (puff pastry dipped in sugar). The empanadas here are like a huge pie baked in big trays and cut into serving-sized slices; some are stuffed with chicken and peas or spicy chorizo, or ham with peas

and onions. The hefty Cuban bread pudding makes a good breakfast, and Cuban-style bread and rolls are piled on the counters.

Tropical Ice Cream and Cuban Bakery, 2900 W. Sunset Boulevard, Los Angeles, CENTRAL, 213-661-8391. Open daily. The tiny tables at Tropical Ice Cream and Cuban Bakery are always filled with customers knocking back the mercilessly strong espresso and eating Cuban pastries. All the intriguing goodies are baked on the premises. The chocolate meringue cookies are an excellent chocolate fix, and the layered Monte Carlo cheesecake tempts. But the health-conscious stick with the batidos de leche: Tropical's milk and fruit shakes in such flavors as guanabana, mamey, or papaya.

JAMAICA: A HISTORY OF CROSS-CULTURAL CUISINE

A couple of years ago Caribbean food was briefly the hot trend. Restaurants called Sugar Shack and La Rumba have now faded like blue jeans in the wash. But the standby places frequented by Jamaicans, which were here before the passing trend, are still around. They serve Jamaica's evocatively named dishes—"stamp and go," "rundown" and "matrimony"—all a sprightly amalgam of West African and British cooking with a little East Indian and Chinese tossed in.

Stone's Restaurant, 6437 Crenshaw Boulevard, Los Angeles, CENTRAL, 213-971-1462. **Stone Bakery Co.,** 6700 Crenshaw Boulevard, Los Angeles, CENTRAL, 213-753-3847. Lunch through dinner daily; Sunday brunch.

"When Jamaicans first come to town they go to Stone's to get the grapevine," one Jamaican told me. The funky bakery and take-out kitchen next door to the 18-year-old Stone Caribbean Market has become an institution for Jamaicans in Los Angeles. What's more, some of the best Jamaican bun in the city comes out of its tiny kitchen (this sweet bread is like yeasted ginger cake, made with molasses, ginger, nutmeg, and honey). Stone's also sells a dense white bread made with coconut milk called coco bread, Jamaican-style carrot cake, and meat turnovers. And there's almost always a line of people waiting to pick up or order Stone's take-out dinners. These are listed on a blackboard and might include Jewish-mother-sized servings of stewed chicken, short ribs, or curried goat. All come with "rice and peas" (rice and beans cooked in coconut milk), several strips of fried plantain, and vegetables or a leaden boiled dumpling (Jamaican dumplings are always like paperweights).

Stone has finally opened a bona fide restaurant. The room is light and airy, with a mirrored wall opening up the space, a huge saltwater fish tank at the entryway, cozy booths, and large tables. The chefs are cruise-ship trained, and there are many things on the menu not available at Stone's take-out. And even old standbys like jerked beef look much better out of their Styrofoam boxes.

Stone's makes some real nostalgia dishes: For Sunday breakfast there's salt cod and ackee, and salt cod "rundown" simmered in a slightly curried coconut milk sauce. The wonderful tart, brilliant red sorrel juice and the creamy Irish moss drink are delicious here, as are the homemade desserts.

Janet's Original Jerk Chicken Pit, 1541 Martin Luther King Boulevard, Los Angeles, CENTRAL, 213-296-4621. Lunch and dinner daily. The aroma of smoldering "jerk" that wafts from the huge open grill and hovers near the ordering counter at Janet's Jerk Chicken Pit will sharpen your appetite in no time flat. At Janet's, barbecue meats are dry-marinated in the traditional currylike jerk seasoning.

Although it's the chicken that put Janet's on the foodie map, I am partial to the jerked pork. Beneath it's spicy (but not really hot) layer of seasoning, the meat is rich and juicy.

These dinners come with fried doughnutlike festival bread, fried plantains, and two additional side dishes selected from a lengthy list—definitely avoid the frozen "vegetables du jour." But do try the homemade lemonade or ginger beer made with fresh ginger and pineapple juice.

Del Rose Act I (2921 S. La Cienega Boulevard, Culver City, WEST, 310-558-9314; lunch through 8:30 P.M. [or as late as 10:00, depending on the flow of customers]; closed Sunday and Monday) is a plain storefront given the feeling of the sun-drenched Caribbean with colorful tableware and reggae concert flyers. Each time I've eaten here everything's been expertly prepared. Large red snappers are sliced into thick steaks, lightly dusted with flour, and "escoviched" with vinegar and onions. Del Rose's other Jamaican favorites, such as oxtail stew and meaty curry goat, all come with trencherman-sized servings of rice and peas, fried plantains, fresh vegetables and two triangles of festival bread—a much lighter version than most.

BELIZE: A CARIBBEAN-CENTRAL AMERICAN MÉLANGE

Belize, as British Honduras is known today, is a paradox in Central America. The country has strong cultural ties to the Caribbean Islands but can ignore neither its colonial past nor its Spanish-speaking Central American neighbors. The taste of its eclectic temperament is evident in every bite of the food.

You can order conch fritters, braised oxtails, and Central American–style tamales at the same sitting, And usually there's home-baked coco bread and bun, a gingery bread similar to Jamaica's. Most Belezean restaurants on Western or Vermont near the Coliseum cater to the neighborhood and do the largest part of their trade in take-out. Their dining rooms are storefront minimalist. Each restaurant cooks up a few daily specials so you never know exactly what they'll be serving. Here are the best of the lot:

- **Pelican Belizean Restaurant,** 4254 S. Vermont Avenue, Los Angeles, CENTRAL, 213-232-5487. Breakfast through 7:00 P.M. Monday to Saturday; breakfast only Sunday.
- **Mika's,** 4307 S. Vermont Avenue, Los Angeles, CENTRAL, 213-231-1207. Breakfast through dinner; Wednesday, closes at 6:00 P.M.; Sunday, closes at 8:00 P.M.
- **Tracy's Place,** 3810 S. Western Avenue, Los Angeles, CENTRAL, 213-735-2166. Lunch through 7:30 P.M. daily.

PAN-LATIN RESTAURANT
Prado, 244 N. Larchmont Boulevard, Los Angeles, CENTRAL, 213-467-3871. Lunch and dinner; closed Sunday. Somewhere between southern Mexico, the Car-

ibbean, and Hollywood is Prado. For this charming restaurant, Chief Torribio Parado of the post-trendy Cha Cha Cha and his brother Javier have snatched elements both from their homeland and their imaginations. The blue room, with rotund cherubs floating by puffy clouds on the ceiling, mixes touches of faded colonialism with native wit: crystal chandeliers, Gobelin tapestries, and tropical fabrics blend festively. Don't let the menu names—"gumbo ya ya" and "Black Beauty pizza" (with black beans)—convince you that the food is pop cuisine. In truth, most of the cooking is closer to its roots than the menu descriptions allow. Prado's famous spicy corn soup, though original, could be a Caribbean mom's home cooking. The chicken in black chili sauce, transplanted straight from southern Mexico and Guatemala, uses a black recado of toasted chiles as the base. Some food carries out the mixed colonial-native theme: Sweet corn tamales with a tomatillo sauce and cultured cream sport a caviar garnish. The result is some of the most satisfying food in town.

SOUTH AMERICA

PERU: ANDEAN CUISINE WITH EUROPEAN ACCENTS
When the Peruvian Indians introduced the Spanish to potatoes and tomatoes, and the Spanish in turn taught the Indians to make cheese, the result was magical: papas huancainas (a dish of boiled potatoes blanketed in a creamy cheese sauce with a subtle kick of chili) and picante de mariscos (a peppery shellfish stew with cubed potatoes in tomato sauce). A Chinese element crept into the cooking after the turn of the century, when immigrant chefs styled their own

food to the tastes of urban Peruvians.

El Pollo Inka, 15400 Hawthorne Boulevard, No. D, Lawndale, SOUTH, 310-676-6665. Also at 1425 W. Artesia Boulevard, Gardena, SOUTH, 310-516-7378; and 1100 Pacific Coast Highway, Hermosa Beach, SOUTH, 310-372-1433. At El Pollo Inka, probably the most popular restaurant among Peruvians right now, marinated chickens turn slowly on a spit over a big flame in the restaurant's front window. These pollos a la brasa are the house specialty. The juicy, crisp-skinned birds have a tangy aftertaste that accentuates their succulent meat. On the side comes a treacherous green hot sauce: an Incan-inspired purée of chiles simply called aji ("hot pepper"). Pollo Inka's extensive menu includes the best version of ocopa I've tasted. The dish—boiled potato slices smothered in a creamy sauce of ground walnuts, olive oil, and chiles—is another example of the Peruvian wizardry with potatoes. Just about everything else, from *seviche mixto* to lamb seco de cordero is prepared with finesse. Even the home-baked rolls that come to the table warm are uncommonly good. El Pollo Inka recently opened in Gardena and in Hermosa Beach.

Cafe Latino, 6772 Coldwater Canyon, North Hollywood, S.F. VALLEY, 818-503-8877. Lunch through dinner daily. The best place to go for platillos criollos, or native dishes (as opposed to the urbane café food most Peruvian restaurants serve) is Cafe Latino. This kitchen can't be beat for down-home Peruvian food. You find aji de gallina, an unbelievably rich chicken dish in a sauce of ground nuts, chiles, and cream, and pollo en mani, chicken in a peanut sauce. Carapulcra—a traditional Andean stew made from meatlike freeze-dried potatoes (a tradition that predates Birdseye) and pork—is more delicious than it sounds. Olluquito, one of the hundreds of potatolike tubers grown in the Andes, are stewed with meat to make olluquito con carne. Cafe Latino's owner, a veritable encyclopedia of Peruvian food lore, explained that in the Andes olluquito con carne is made with dried llama meat. In Lima, however, some chefs make substitutions for this unusual ingredient; on the other hand, some don't. Dried llama meat is unavailable in California, but Cafe Latino's version is otherwise authentic.

Los Andes, 9040 Slauson Avenue, Pico Rivera, EAST OF L.A., 213-948-4115. Lunch and dinner; Saturday until 2:00 A.M. Los Andes turns into a supper club on weekends. Starting around nine on Saturday night, the whole Peruvian community seems to be there table-hopping around the large open room or visiting in the tiny bar area. The restaurant features renowned Inkakena musicians, with their haunting wind instruments and vocals, along with other South American performers touring the United States.

If you've come to eat, Los Andes turns out an elegant seviche, full of firm, fleshy strips of fish. After it, try grilled beef strips with huancaina sauce over noodles, aji de gallina, or Peruvian-style chicharrones served with fried sweet potato.

El Silencio, 14111 Burbank Boulevard, Van Nuys, S.F. VALLEY, 818-997-9412. Lunch and dinner; closed Tuesday. One of Peru's greatest treasures, aside from its rich Indian civilizations, is the country's long, spectacular coastline. It's not surprising then that most Peruvians love seafood, or that El Silencio, a South American seafood restaurant, would serve primarily Peruvian dishes. I am partial to their conchas en salsa criolla. These raw scallops, marinated seviche-style, come served in individual seashells, topped with a fine dice of tomato, marinated onion, and corn kernels. A perfect complement is papas rellenas, mashed potatoes molded around a filling of seasoned beef with olives and raisins, rolled in grated cheese, and deep-fried; in each bite you get layers of crispy, creamy, and meaty textures.

Both the printed menu and the changing blackboard menu offer seafood prepared in almost every conceivable way: with spaghetti, in rich soups and stews, steamed, sauced, deep-fried, or grilled. Besides the icky sweet Inca Cola, there's a nice selection of South American beers and wines. For dessert, try the Peruvian-style pumpkin doughnuts called picarones.

El Sol, 15651 Hawthorne Boulevard, Lawndale, SOUTH, 310-973-2486. Lunch and dinner daily. Peruvian food aficionados who remember the now closed El Sol in Hollywood will be glad to hear that El Sol is still going strong in Lawndale. It has moved into a plain spacious dining room softened with pastel tablecloths, with a tiny bar tucked into one corner.

Everyone's favorite dish is *jalea de pescado,* a generous fillet of sautéed fish topped with lightly battered and deep-fried mixed seafood and sprinkled with enormous roasted corn kernels (one of Peru's many strains, we were told). Scattered over the top are red onion slivers, raw tomato, and a little lime juice. Peruvians love noodles, and tallarines con salsa de huancaina is sauced with the same creamy cheese mixture that tops papas huancainas. I'd like to try arroz frito de mariscos—a Chinese-style fried rice dish that includes fried plantains—next time.

- **Mario's Peruvian Seafood,** 5786 Melrose Avenue, Los Angeles, CENTRAL, 213-466-4181. Lunch through dinner; closed Monday.
- **Don Felix,** 305 N. Virgil Avenue, Los Angeles, CENTRAL, 213-663-1088. Lunch through dinner; closed Monday.

Just when I thought all the good Peruvian restaurants had vanished from the city's center, **Mario's Peruvian Seafood** restaurant, a modest storefront owned by Mario Tamashiro and his partner-chef, Juan Goto, opened in a mall at Melrose and Vine. Seafood fanciers can't go wrong with the café's parihuela, the Peruvian equivalent of Manhattan clam chowder with fish and assorted seafood, or the cold squid salad with Peruvian olives and marinated onions. There are seviches, of course, and a combination plate of papas huancainas with choros à la criolla: steamed mussels in the shell with a pickled onion salsa on top. I like to drizzle on a little aji over these. Drink the violet-hued chicha morada, or have the mazamorra morada dessert—both are colored with purple Peruvian corn. On weekends Mario's serves Peruvian breakfasts.

Chef Goto's brother Tsuyoshi owns **Don Felix,** a kitchen that prepares Peruvianized Italian dishes such as chicken cacciatore and tallarin saltado de pollo (stir-fried chicken breast, tomatoes, and onions over noodles). Don Felix may seem like a cross-cultural fantasy, but Italian foods are apparently as common in Peru as they are here. Don Felix's offers traditional Peruvian criollo items too: a bounteous tamal with red onion salsa criolla and that wonderful Peruvian shrimp chowder, chupe de camarones, with a poached egg in it.

ARGENTINA:
A LEGACY FROM THE GAUCHOS AND AN ITALIAN HERITAGE

Gaucho Grill, 7980 Sunset Boulevard, Hollywood, CENTRAL, 213-656-4152. And 11754 San Vincente Boulevard, Brentwood, WEST, 310-447-7898. Also in Studio City, S.F. VALLEY, 818-508-1030. Lunch and dinner daily. Argentines consume their famous beef with an almost religious reverence in the city's hundreds of parillas. Some restaurants have extravagant displays of meat carcasses in their windows, or stuffed bulls to greet you at the door. Steaks are grilled by the *parillero* (grill cook) over beds of charcoal.

Gaucho Grill doesn't have any stuffed bulls, but its grills are what carnivorous Angelenos are looking for. The restaurants are usually packed, though service is quick. Grilled appetizers include grilled sweetbreads and morcilla. Entrées—grilled, of course, and done with uncommon skill—include a selection of steaks and chicken prepared several ways; there's even a grilled chicken salad. Everything comes with pungent, garlic-laden salsa chimichurri for dipping, curly fresh French fries, and tomato-onion relish. And there is Argentine wine.

Don Felipe, 1050 N. Western Avenue, Los Angeles, CENTRAL, 213-464-3474. Lunch and dinner daily. At Don Felipe, a rather grand old-line Argentine dining room near Koreatown and up the block from Catalina's Argentine market, parillada is the specialty. A small barbecue smothered with a mixed grill of meats comes to your white-cloth-draped table still sizzling. A portion for two would probably feed a family of six. Being an Argentine restaurant, Don Filipe serves many other beefy options and reasonably good Italian dishes including excellent cioppino loaded with seafood, homemade agnolotti, and an outstanding marinated eggplant appetizer called *berenjenas* en escabeche. The service here is exceedingly gracious, and the powerful espresso will keep you awake after all that food.

Empanada's Place, 3811 Sawtelle Boulevard, Culver City, WEST, 310-391-0888; 8566 W. Pico Boulevard, West Los Angeles, WEST, 310-854-3373; 6136 Venice Boulevard, West Los Angeles, WEST, 310-838-3061. Also 1649 N. Cahuenga, Hollywood, CENTRAL, 213-465-8295. Open daily. In Argentina, fabricas de empanadas are a fairly recent phenomenon; they have sprung up everywhere in the last 10 years, and Empanada's Place, patterned after these Argentine turnover shops, is L.A.'s version. The small chain started as a tiny deli on a remote side street and now has several branches. Empanada's elevates this country's na-

tional snack to new heights. Fat little pillows of the thinnest pastry are stuffed to the max with fillings that are far more adventurous than the usual ground beef. At least a dozen varieties are available on any day, including chunky chicken, mushroom, cheese, or broccoli. These are not quite traditional; the chef uses vegetable oil instead of lard for frying.

Marcela's Restaurant and Tango Club, 14533 Gilmore Street, Van Nuys, S.F. VALLEY, 818-989-2581. Dinner Wednesday to Sunday. The first thing you learn at Marcela's is that Argentines aren't the only ones who love the tango. The second thing you learn is that this charming Van Nuys restaurant in a converted Spanish-style house is where impassioned tango devotees flock on weekends to show off their mastery of the seductive dance. Marcela's Argentine-continental menu offers nothing too exotic. But there's matambre, a rolled steak stuffed with herbs and vegetables that is sliced and eaten cold; a few pastas; Argentine-style steaks; and various grilled chicken-breast dishes. Tango, however, is the main course here, and there are tango classes several nights a week. On weekends the music is live. The restaurant even has a hotline for class information; it's 818-506-0780.

Tango and dinner at Marcela's Restaurant and Tango Club.

Norah's Place, 5667 Lankershim Boulevard, North Hollywood, S.F. VALLEY, 818-980-6900. Lunch and dinner; closed Monday and Tuesday. Tango lessons and weekend dancing are no less serious at Norah's Place. And Norah's is probably the only restaurant in town where you can eat Bolivian food. In addition to Argentine dishes, owner Norah Lopez, who's from Bolivia, serves such Bolivian specialties as pukas (a cheese turnover with fresh chiles and olives) and lapping, a hefty barbecued steak marinated in a well-seasoned orange juice-vinegar mixture.

Tango fans say that Norah's is a little more relaxed than the glitzy Marcela's, where the crowd tends to show up in sequins and Italian suits. The live weekend entertainment might also include Bolivian folk musicians.

Gardel's, 7963 Melrose Avenue, West Hollywood, WEST, 213-655-0891. Lunch and dinner; closed Sunday. The dulcet-voiced Carlos Gardel made the tango famous outside Argentina, and at this Melrose dinner house named after him, his songs still live as background music. Gardel's built a reputation for its baked garlic, which turns sweet and creamy in the oven; you squeeze it over bread to eat. Good solid food comes from this kitchen, including matambre, with its mosaic filling of Spanish pimiento and hard-cooked egg (occasionally made with chicken instead of the traditional beef), and a sublime roast garlic chicken. Argentine-style pastas, though, are not nearly as satisfying as those up the block at Rondo or Chianti. Argentine-style continental cuisine and parillada are what this restaurant is really about. Gardel's is nicely appointed, with double-draped tablecloths and an elegant bar with Melrosian prices—not too expensive, but not Gaucho Grill either.

CHILE

La Gaviota de Viña, 5254 Van Nuys Boulevard, Sherman Oaks, S.F. VALLEY, 818-788-4560. Lunch and dinner; closed Monday. Chile ambles down South America's Pacific coast in a long rattlesnake shape, its tail breaking into thousands of islands in the south. The cold Humboldt current gives Chile the most exotic seafood on earth: giant abalones called locos, pink clams, lobsters, giant sea urchins, and dozens of crab varieties. But our Chilean restaurants don't emphasize seafood, because we can't get these specialties fresh.

La Gaviota, a simple, smartly put together dining room on a restaurant-rich area of Van Nuys Boulevard, has at least a few seafood dishes. The cauldron of sopa marinera is a satisfying choice. Equally interesting are the appetizers, the southern Chilean specialties, and, believe it or not, the sandwiches (Chileans often eat sandwiches in the evening, lunch being the primary meal of the day).

This kitchen makes its own mayonnaise, which goes beautifully with any of the rolled-meat cold cuts: *arrollado de malaya* is beef rolled around Swiss chard and other seasoned vegetables; *pichanga* and *arrollado de chancho,* two kinds of rolled pork, are served as appetizers in sandwiches. The seviche is good here, if very mild (but you can spice it up with the exquisitely hot house salsa called pebre). Southern specialties include the popular pastel de choclo and cazuela de *vacuno:* stewed short ribs with corn, pumpkin, and green beans. Humitas, also from the south, is a creamy unfilled tamale made from grated corn.

Rincon Chileno Deli, 4354–56 Melrose Avenue, Los Angeles, CENTRAL, 213-666-6077. Lunch through dinner; closed Monday. Rincon Chileno has long been a fixture on the eastern end of Melrose Avenue. But Rincon's deli, where you can get the restaurant's food throughout the day, often gets overlooked. At almost any hour the ovens produce delectable, yeasty aromas that drift out into the street in appetizing little whiffs. Now and then during the afternoon, a baker brings a fresh tray of pastries from the kitchen. Try the sconelike pan huevo with your afternoon tea or breakfast coffee. Gloriously heavy dinner rolls come warm from the oven, as do calzone-sized beef empanadas.

The deli's most popular item, pastel de choclo, is packaged and ready to go in foil pans. Each "pie" is filled with ground meat and onions surrounding a piece of chicken and then topped by custardy ground corn sprinkled with sugar. These sweet and savory notes work so well that each bite tastes better than the last. Owners Ricardo and Christina Florez give advice on how to prepare the more unfamiliar foods. The seviche mixto appetizer from the regular menu will introduce you to *lenguas de machas,* a tender and triangular coral-colored shellfish. And probably nowhere else in the city can you take out *eriso matico* (sea urchins) with pebre: a piquant green fresh chili and cilantro sauce. The deli carries a good selection of Chilean wines.

COLOMBIA

La Fonda Antioqueña, 4903 Melrose Avenue, Los Angeles, CENTRAL, 213-957-5164. Lunch through dinner daily. La Fonda Antioqueña has moved from its somewhat unkempt former location to a charming refurbished house on the eastern end of Melrose. It shares this space with an art gallery that displays gargantuan canvases of wild Colombian art. But apart from that, the ambience is rather homey. On the handwritten blackboard menus placed

La Sultana del Valle, 14909 Vanowen Street, Van Nuys, S.F. VALLEY, 818-781-9056. Open 9:00 A.M. to 9:00 P.M. daily. The best place for sampling some of Colombia's most intriguing foods is not a restaurant but a bakery.

Proprietor Armando Barrios at La Sultana del Valle stocks dozens of breads, rolls, pastries, and take-out foods you rarely see elsewhere. The bakery makes Colombian corn cakes, arepas in a cheese version (arepas de queso), and many other delicious pastries.

Rolls are also made with cheese: *pandebono* (a fine chewy roll of yuca flour, corn, and cheese), tennis-ball-sized *buñuelos* (rather like a doughnut), and *almojabana,* a corn bun made with two kinds of cheese. Sweets are not overlooked. The *milojas,* fragile layers of puff pastry filled with chocolate cream, rivals only the baroque tropical concoction called *aborrajado,* guava and cheese sandwiched between slices of ripe plantain enclosed in egg batter and fried. The deli items include a spectacular marinated and roasted leg of pork, fried yuca, banana-wrapped tamales filled with three meats (chicken, pork, and beef), and fried green or ripe plantains accompanied by several dipping sauces.

around the room (written in Spanish and English), many dishes listed typify the well-defined regional cuisine of the Cauca Valley in western Colombia. The food is straightforward, copiously served and always comes with a side dish of pungent, herby aji sauce reminiscent of Argentine chimichurri. A good way to start is with sopa de platano, a starchy green plantain soup with vegetables. A few menu stars: the blood sausage plate served with corn cakes; the creamy cheese- and egg-sauced papas chorreadas; and lentejas, a substantial pork and lentil stew served with thick Colombian-style chicharrones.

Los Arrieros, 2619 Sunset Boulevard, Los Angeles, CENTRAL, 213-483-0074. Lunch and dinner; closed Tuesday. In a pleasant, comfortable dining room, Los Arrieros emphasizes the European-influenced cooking of Bogota rather than Colombia's Creole cooking. But for my tastes, the criollo dishes (mostly listed under side orders) are more interesting than the entrées. I could happily make a meal of Colombian chorizos with patacon, the fried green plantains, and arepa. Most entrées—the perfectly sautéed shrimp with garlic accompanied with a whole roasted potato and a mound of plain white rice—for example, aren't the sort of foods I envision going to an "ethnic" restaurant to eat, although my meat-and-potatoes-loving cousin from Des Moines would surely relish them. (It must be said the plain baked potato is a special Colombian variety.)

MORE SOUTH AMERICAN RESTAURANTS AND SHOPS

◆ BRAZIL
Café Brazil, 10831 Venice Boulevard, West Los Angeles, WEST, 310-837-8957. Open 10:00 A.M. to 10:00 P.M. daily. Brazil, with all its hectic industrialization, is still a land of parrots and macaws in the garden, lush tropical fruit, and a spirit of carnival that seems enshrined in every Brazilian soul. You feel it at Café Brazil, a revamped burger stand painted bright yellow with festive green accents, sidewalk tables, and blaring samba music. The menu

isn't lengthy here, but since the nearby Zilda's Brazilian deli closed down, it's the only Brazilian food in the area.

The minuscule dining room is dominated by a deli case holding snacks: There are *risoli* (deep-fried buttermilk turnovers stuffed with chicken, cheese, or shrimp) and *empadinha* (a cupcake-shaped pie filled with hearts of palm, chicken, or cheese). Other snacky items include codfish croquettes and *coxinha*, a chicken-stuffed potato croquette shaped like a chicken leg. Fresh sugarcane juice with a squirt of lemon is the favorite refreshment; it isn't as sweet as it sounds. Café Brazil offers only one entrée a day, but whatever it is it will be accompanied by fabulous black beans and fried bananas. And the café serves a Brazilian breakfast with pao de queijo, eggs, and passion fruit juice to drink.

◆ ECUADOR
Ecuatoriano No. 2, 1512 S. Vermont Avenue, Los Angeles, CENTRAL, 213-380-7928. Lunch through dinner daily. Some would compare Ecuador's thoroughly unique cuisine to Peru's (lots of potatoes, corn, and chiles). In fact, with the exception of high Andes cooking, the cuisines are dissimilar. Even within Ecuador, the cooking varies among its three major regions: Oriente (the upper Amazon basin east of the Andes), the highlands, and the coastal lowland. Ecuatoriano No. 2 serves primarily coastal lowland cooking.

The restaurant's dining room, reminiscent of a coffee shop with booths along one wall, has been a home away from home for Ecuadorans for over a decade. (If ever there was a No. 1, it hasn't been around for years.) On weekends they come in for the caldo de salchicha: blood soup with sausage. Other dishes may have broader appeal: Llapingachos, potato pancakes stuffed with cheese, always delight, and you can get them on a combination plate with sliced pork, two eggs, and rice. Another combination plate offers llapingacho with sausage, sliced pork, hominy, and fried sweet plantains. Chifles are fun to eat: You dip these deep-fried sweet plantain chips into a hot salsa. Patacones—smashed and deep-fried starchy green plantain slices—get dipped into the same sauce. The seviches, especially the one made with chocolate brown conch scattered with pickled red onion rings that have bled into a bright, bubble gum pink, are not your usual pickled fish. And the goat stew with tripe in a peanut sauce is another dish for sophisticated palates.

LATIN AMERICAN MARKETS

There is always some degree of overlap in South and Central American markets, since like ingredients are used throughout the region. But of L.A.'s many Latin stores, I like these for either the completeness of their stock or an emphasis on one particular country.

At one time, **Liborio** (864 S. Vermont Avenue, Los Angeles, CENTRAL, 213-386-1458) catered to Cubans. But as the neighborhood became more Central American, its stock branched out to include things like Salvadoran cheese and frozen loroco for making pupusas, banana leaves for wrapping tamales, and palm flowers—everything you need for Central American cooking. The shelves dazzle with plantain flour, frozen tropical fruit purées: guanabana, guava, and passion fruit. From Brazil there's farofa, dende oil, and black beans. The small but excellent produce department holds cactus fruit, taro, cassava, various yams, young coconut, and much more. And now Liborio has installed a Salvadoran bakery that sells quesadilla, marquesote and many of the same baked goods

found at panaderia Mi Ranchito Salvadoreño (see page 176).

At **Continental Gourmet** (12921 S. Prairie Avenue, Hawthorne, SOUTH, 310-676-5444), Argentine ingredients are the major attraction. The butcher carries all the cuts for the parillada, and they make their own Argentine-style chorizo, blood sausage, and matambre. The butcher also stocks tasajo, the dried Brazilian beef used all over South America, and the strong salty Argentine cotija cheese similar to Parmesan.

Homemade ravioli may be found in the freezer, along with empanada wrappers (the deli sells empanadas to go). A selection of South American wines, cookies, sweets (such as membrillo and caramel flan), and yerba mate, the evergreen leaf tea, rounds out the stock.

Catalina's Market (1070 Western Avenue, Los Angeles, CENTRAL, 213-461-2535), a prime source for South American ingredients, stocks many Peruvian items that include purple corn either whole or in powdered form for the Peruvian dessert mazamorra morada. Peruvian peppers include yellow aji marisol and red *rocoto* peppers in cans or ground conveniently into a paste for Peruvian recipes. There are Peruvian aceitunas negras (black olives); huacatay (black mint); the giant white corn called choclo for soups; freeze-dried potatoes, known as *chuño;* and harina de camote (sweet potato flour).

The butchers here cut meats South American style—you can get excellent thin steak for thin breaded beefstesk known as milanesa. Even the roasting and stewing beef has more color here than some of the pale stuff many supermarkets carry. The market stocks other items from all over South America, with an emphasis on Argentina.

EUROPE

It takes some snooping to find the wonderful Old World shops and restaurants that L.A. has to offer. They seem to turn up in unexpected locations: perhaps on a side street in Van Nuys or a shopping mall in Hollywood. When I tell hard-core food shoppers that my favorite German sausage maker is in Burbank, they look at me in mild disbelief. But this man sells the world's most succulent weisswurst and his shop also stocks all sorts of Eastern European items: Czech jaternice, Polish hunter's sausage, and fresh calves' liverwurst. Other surprising finds are Schreiner's in La Canada, well known among Germans for the Black Forest hams they cure on the premises; and J&T European Gourmet, a superb Polish meat shop in Santa Monica where the owners smoke their hams and sausages in a brick oven.

The European immigrants who once shared a common neighborhood with these businesses have long since moved away. The city's shifting population has left such anomalies as Olson's Scandinavian Delicatessen surrounded by an East Indian neighborhood, and Eisbach's German Meats in Torrance in the midst of a newly burgeoning Asian area. But business booms for such stores on weekends when their longtime clientele comes in for specialty items.

These places are social and cultural exchange depots too. They sell newspapers from the homeland and put up bulletin boards announcing events and festivals. Patrons stick their business cards on the boards to attract fellow countrymen; their addresses often range from San Diego to Bakersfield and beyond.

While we have an abundance of thriving, if scattered, European shops with a broad and authentic assortment of foods, good European restaurants are scarce as hen's teeth. Europeans are likely to dine out in a Chinese or American restaurant. But when it comes to eating the food of their own country, they want it just so—tradition has a stronghold on our culinary memories. More often than not, the ingredients are taken home to be prepared there. But these delis can be a good source for noncooks too; they often sell sandwiches, soups, and many interesting prepared items.

Fortunately, a few restaurateurs with a passion for holding on to the culinary treasures of their countries have kept the Old World candles burning in L.A. Quite often their restaurants serve as a sort of social club: There is entertainment, and they book parties and weddings.

These establishments continue to enrich the city's dining prospects. But if you long for the incomparable taste of Hungarian lekvar, German smoked goose breast, or Polish poppy seed roll, explore the shops and delis, for there you'll find the widest range of Old World foods.

— EUROPEAN GLOSSARY —

Bierschinken: German smoked ham to eat with beer.
Blood pudding: British-style blood sausage.

Bourek: A Yugoslavian stuffed savory pastry.
Butifarra (Spanish) or botifarra (Catalan): A chubby white mild-

---

tasting Catalonian-style fresh sausage.

Cevapcici: A Yugoslavian kebab of finely ground beef and lamb, seasoned with garlic and paprika and grilled on skewers.

Chistorra: A long thin Basque cooking sausage heavily flavored with garlic.

Chorizo de Bilbao: A popular Spanish cooking sausage flavored with garlic, Spanish paprika, and pepper.

Clatite: A Romanian dessert of crêpes filled with sour cherries.

Debreceni kolbasz: A Hungarian cured pork and beef sausage well seasoned with garlic and paprika; often used in stews.

Eccles cake: A British tea sweet of flaky pastry filled with currants and glazed with brown sugar.

Fustolt karaj: Hungarian smoked filet mignon served in paper-thin slices.

Fustolt szalona: A Hungarian-style aged smoked bacon.

Ikre: A Romanian-style dip of caviar whipped with olive oil rather like the Greek taramasalata.

Jaternice: This small Czechoslovakian sausage fastened with a tiny wooden pick at each end is eaten boiled or fried.

Jelita: A Czechoslovakian sausage eaten either boiled or fried.

Kabanos: A long thin dry Polish pork sausage.

Kashkaval: A mild, faintly salty Balkan-style cheese made from cooked cheese curds.

Kielbasa: A strong garlic-flavored Polish pork sausage usually smoked but also sold fresh.

Kippers (British): Herrings that have been split, salt-cured, and cold smoked.

Kneip: A Scandinavian bread of whole wheat, cracked wheat, and rye.

Kolbasz: A smoked Hungarian sausage heavily flavored with garlic and paprika.

Kommissbrot: This German bread known as soldiers' bread is a sturdy compact loaf made with crushed rye.

Kuchen: A German fruit or cheese yeast-raised coffee cake.

Kulebiaka: A large Russian pastry filled with layers of fish, rice, and eggs and seasoned with dill.

Lakschinken (German): Two pork loins pressed together in a roll and hot-smoked.

Landjager: A flat smoked German beef sausage.

Langos: A deep-fried Hungarian bread that diners rub with fresh garlic before eating.

Lappi: A slicing cheese from Finland.

Leberkäs: A large German tubular sausage with a smooth texture eaten in thick slices as a coldcut, or served warm with eggs (leberkäs mit ei). Despite its translation as "liver cheese," leberkäs often contains no liver.

Leberwurst (liverwurst): A smooth spreadable pork liver sausage.

Lecsó: Basic to Hungarian cooking, this mixture of sautéed onion, sweet pepper, and garlic is the base for many stews and is often eaten topped with a fried egg.

Lekvar: A Hungarian fruit butter eaten with toast or used in desserts.

Limpa: A light Swedish rye flavored with anise, fennel, and orange rind.

Lomo embuchado: A Spanish coldcut made from lean cured pork loin.

Lutefisk: Scandinavian-style dried codfish.

Mamaliga: Romanian-style cornmeal mush similar to polenta.

Manchego cheese: A rich firm Spanish slicing cheese.

Mett: A German pork sausage made with onions.

Mititei: A Romanian grilled seasoned mixture of beef, pork, and lamb shaped like a sausage.

Morcilla con cebolla: A Spanish blood sausage made with onions.

Nusschinken: A German-style cold smoked pork tenderloin eaten sliced thin as a coldcut.

Paella: There are many regional differences in paellas but the base is always saffron-flavored rice cooked with a variety of ingredients such as shellfish, sausage, ham, chicken, peas, or artichoke hearts.

Palacsinta: A thin Hungarian pancake usually stacked or rolled around sweet or savory fillings. As a dessert, half a dozen of the pancakes are layered with filling and cut into wedges.

Pavlova: An Australian soft meringue dessert garnished with fresh fruit.

Pelmeni: Russian boiled dumplings made of noodle dough stuffed either with potato, meat, or cheese and eaten fried with sour cream or in soup.

Pierogi: The Polish term for filled dumplings that are the same as Russian pelmeni.

Pirozhki: Pastry turnovers, usually savory, filled with meat, cheese, or vegetables.

Raznjici: Yugoslavian veal or pork kebabs.

Schlachtplatte: A German combination sausage plate with sauerkraut and potatoes.

Schnitzel: German-style breaded meat cutlet, usually veal.

Scotch egg: This standard British pub food is a sausage-wrapped hard-cooked egg dusted with bread crumbs and fried.

Serrano ham: A dry-cured Spanish-style ham similar to prosciutto.

Sikte: A light Norwegian-style rye bread.

Spaetzle (German): Tiny boiled wheat flour and egg dumplings.

Spritz: Shaped butter cookies made by pushing dough through a cookie press.

Tabaka: A Georgian- and Armenian-style pressed and pan-grilled young chicken that is weighted down as it cooks. (A game hen is usually used in the United States.)

Tarhónya: Hungarian noodles known as egg barley, made by pushing dough through a sieve.

Thüringer: A German sausage that comes in numerous styles, the most popular of which is an all-beef smoked and dried sausage.

Vareniki (Ukranian or Hungarian): Noodle-dough dumplings with a variety of fillings, from potato to sour cherries, eaten boiled or fried with various toppings.

Västerbotten: A Swedish cheese similar to Swiss cheese with tiny holes.

Vollkornbrot: A traditional heavy German bread made from crushed whole rye grains.

Weinbrod (or weinerbrød): The Danish term for the pastries we know as "Danish."

Weisswürst: A delicate German sausage made with veal, eggs, and cream.

Wiejska: A very garlicky coarse smoked Polish pork sausage.

GERMANY

♦ SAUSAGE MAKERS

European Deluxe Sausage Kitchen, 9109 W. Olympic Boulevard, Beverly Hills, WEST, 310-276-1331. At the back of European Deluxe Sausage Kitchen, the shop's own very lean salamis, meats, and sausages are smoked over smoldering hickory chips in a brick pit. Especially wonderful is the cold smoked beef that's hung over the coals for three days. Proprietors Peter Kienzle and Willy Kossbiel were trained in Germany and have served the Beverly Hills area for about 20 years. The ultra-plain shop's cases hold perfectly spiced veal wieners, fat bratwurst, German veal liver pâté, and smoked beef tongue; the butcher counter stocks excellent veal that's cut to order. I've received free veal bones for soup and ordered sausage casings and caul fat that are almost impossible to find elsewhere.

Schreiner's Fine Sausages, 3417–19 Ocean View Boulevard, Glendale, S.F. VALLEY, 818-244-4735. Schreiner's, one of L.A.'s largest German stores, wholesales its house-made sausages and cured meats across the nation. Schreiner's smokehouse turns out wonderful Canadian bacon and Black Forest ham with a sweet hickory flavor. The best days to shop are Thursday to Saturday, when the butchers make fresh bangers, apple sausage, and Swedish sausage.

In the huge, long deli cases you'll find German mett, tea rings, landjager, and thüringer: all fine examples of the sausage maker's art. Schreiner's huge selection of German and Dutch cheeses are a good accompaniment to the many imported and locally made German breads the store sells. And you'll find all sorts of European groceries, including rollmop herring marinating in stocky glass jars,

Hungarian noodles, Swiss spaetzle, and a good selection of German wines and beers.

Alpine Village Market and Bakery, 833 W. Torrance Boulevard, Torrance, SOUTH, 310-327-2483 or 321-5660. Driving down the Harbor Freeway, you can't miss the kitschy Alpine Plaza with its Bavarianesque architecture. But don't pass off the Alpine Market within it as a tourist attraction. The sausages made here are among the city's best, and the butcher shop has introduced a small line of low-fat and low-sodium sausage products. Because Alpine makes sausages several times a week, heavy salting isn't needed as a preservative, even for its regular line. You'll find a huge selection of salamis of every size and description, cured pork and freshly smoked bierschinken, big rounds of country pâté, European-style hams, and all kinds of pork for Eastern European dishes.

Besides its smoking facilities, the market has its own bakery. Traditional German rye breads baked daily include vollkornbrot and German farmer's bread. The sturdy kommissbrot is known for its long keeping ability. For something sweet there's kuchen with a crumbly streusel topping, crisp apple strudel, and Sacher and other European-style tortes for teatime or intimate little dinners.

In the market area, look for a huge supply of cheese, pickles, German butter, and all sorts of imported jams and baking ingredients.

Alpena Sausage (no retail shop; see next entry), 818-505-9482. Fred Thaller grew up working in his father's Austrian sausage business. He did his apprenticeship in Germany and served as a journeyman in Switzerland. Perhaps that's why his sausage recipes come from all over the Austro-Hungarian Empire. Thaller's traditional links include smoky Hungarian kolbasz and debreceni kolbasz; the dry German landjager flavored with caraway; the pale Swiss bratwurst; and hearty blood sausages. Lately, Thaller's Alpena Sausage Company has added nitrate-free chicken franks sold at Trader Joe's markets and Mrs. Gooch's markets. For years Alpena produced and sold its sausages from a tiny store in Burbank but they've now moved into a factory. You can still get Alpena sausage, however, in German delis and specialty shops citywide.

Atlas Sausage Kitchen, 10626 Burbank Boulevard, North Hollywood, s.f. valley, 818-763-2692. Fred Thaller (see above) also formerly owned Atlas Sausage Company, just a short trip way from Alpena. Though Atlas has been sold to a longtime Alpena employee, it still specializes in a wide variety of fresh European sausages and coldcuts made on the premises, just as it always has. Its cases are amply stocked with Irish pork sausages, French head cheese, Austrian-style debreceni kolbasz, Czech jaternice, German blood-tongue sausage, Austrian leberwurst made with cream, and Austrian mountain-grown herbs among the shop's nearly 100 sausage styles.

Also, look for fresh meat specialties like triple-ground extralean beef for making steak tartare and cubed veal for goulash or stews. Atlas carries a good selection of German cheese and, to go with it, more kinds of rye than you ever knew existed. There's also imported German butter and many varieties of mustard.

Eschbach's Meat Products, 18045 S. Western Avenue, Gardena, south, 310-324-1376. Also in Alpine Village Market and Bakery (see above). Fritz Am-

beuhl, the owner of the German food landmark Hildesia Sausages in Orange, took over Eschbach's more than half a dozen years ago. He's kept up the high standards of this fine old-fashioned company: The workers still trim the meats by hand for over 65 types of European sausages, coldcuts, and hams. Ambeuhl keeps the cases at both the Gardena and Alpine Village locations well stocked with plump all-veal Bavarian bratwursts and landjager as well as Italian and Hungarian sausages, and Louisiana hot links. The coldcut selection boggles the mind with its many kinds of blood sausage, veal loaf, and various styles of head cheese. There's house-made pastrami and corned beef. And the store will custom-age meat for its customers.

♦ **DELICATESSENS**
Van Nuys German Deli, 16155 Roscoe Boulevard, Sepulveda, s.f. valley, 818-892-2212. The Van Nuys German Deli, one of the best-stocked stores of its kind in the Valley, has moved from its original Woodley address to a location across from the huge Anheuser-Busch brewery on Roscoe. I've always gone there for the fabulous smoked goose breast, which they usually stock only in the wintertime. Of course they sell sausages and coldcuts, and owner Wilma Rosner combs the marketplace to find the very best. I love the pepper loaf and the interesting hams like nusschinken and *zigeuner*. You'll find rich-tasting venison sausage, New Zealand smoked eel, and smoked fillet of pork. And there is a good selection of dessert making and baking supplies and, of course, breads and condiments.

Old Country Delicatessen, 2621 Lincoln Boulevard, Santa Monica, west, 310-452-1019. At Old Country Deli near Marina del Rey, owner Mrs. Sangler cooks up a huge pot of fresh, hearty soup every day to go with the shop's excellent sandwiches and wursts. Depending on the day, it might be lentil with smoked pork chop, pea, or cabbage soup. The small store has a few cloth-covered tables set behind the old-fashioned, lace-curtained windows. To decide on your sandwich, check the cold case for nusschinken, lakschinken, leberkäs, and lots of coldcuts and cheeses.

After lunch you can work off a few calories by browsing the large table that holds many kinds and brands of German breads. And on the shelves you'll find European ingredients: cheesecake stabilizer, rolls of Danish almond paste, imported flavorings for baking, and more.

Two other well-stocked German delis are:

- **Ernie's European Imports,** 8400 Eighth Avenue, Inglewood, SOUTH, 213-752-1002.
- **German Cold Cuts International,** 6019 Topanga Canyon Boulevard, Woodland Hills, S.F. VALLEY, 818-883-8051.

◆ **BAKERIES**

B&L Gourmet Pastries, 8556 W. 3rd Street, Los Angeles, WEST, 310-271-8333. B&L German bakery has been a fixture on Third Street since the days the red trolley cars ran in L.A. In recent times, its owners opened a shop and tearoom at 246 N. Larchmont, Los Angeles, CENTRAL, 213-464-4126, in Larchmont Village. It's reminiscent of the tearooms where Germans linger over their afternoon coffee with a good piece of strudel. Both shops carry B&L's renowned Black Forest cake and the Vienna torte with its sweet pastry crust and cheese filling. Other Viennoiserie include excellent European-style cookies: florentines, crunchy hazelnut cookies filled with chocolate, and petits fours.

Erika's Bake Shop, 1014–22 Westlake Boulevard, Westlake Village, S.F. VALLEY, 805-495-0266. Baker Dieterich Heinzelmann apprenticed in pastry making in Stuttgart, Germany, and achieved his master baker status there. His first shop was Cathy's in Encino; then eighteen years ago Heinzelmann moved to Westlake Village and opened Erika's. Customers flock in for the beehive pastry, a Danish dough topped with melted butter and toasted almonds and filled with Bavarian cream. Popular too is the streusel-topped yeasted kuchen, also filled with Bavarian cream, and the multilayered fruit-and-cream-filled Dutch cherry cake on a base of puff pastry. Erika's pure butter cookies include the ever popular Linzer tarts and classic spritz.

◆ **RESTAURANTS**

Red Lion Tavern, 2366 Glendale Boulevard, Silverlake, CENTRAL, 213-662-5337. German restaurants are few in Los Angeles; good German restaurants are fewer still. I've had frozen and reheated sauerbraten, and duck that tasted as if it had been around for a week or two.

But at the Red Lion Tavern, really more of a bierstube than a formal restaurant, everything is fresh and well put together. The restaurant has an understated, cozy beer-hall ambience; the seating is on two levels, with a bar on each. On tap is beer from the Alpine Village microbrewery, plus Beck's and Dortmunder Ritter Brau in dark or light. And there's a long list of bottled beers and many types of schnapps.

The schlachtplatte is a real farmer's meal, a combination of blood and liver sausages served with sauerkraut and boiled potatoes. A personal favorite is the leberkäs mit ei: veal loaf topped with a gently fried egg served with mashed potatoes and tart-sweet red cabbage. The extensive menu offers half a dozen sausage plates and hearty sandwiches in addition to more complete dinners.

Knoll's Black Forest Inn, 2454 Wilshire Boulevard, Santa Monica, WEST, 310-395-2212. Chef Norbert Knoll and his wife Hildegard started in a tiny one-room place in Santa Monica that attracted college students in the mood for the best wursts. Even then, Mrs. Knoll, a product of very formal Swabian upbringing, would call customers—even the ones in faded blue jeans—to the table saying, very properly, "Mr. So-and-So, your table is ready." Over the years, both the food and ambience became even more formal, especially when the Knolls moved into a large restaurant on Wilshire Boulevard with a stone fireplace, a lovely garden patio, and a rather corny indoor-gazebolike "winter garden."

The traditional well-prepared dishes lean to homemade sausages and roast duck (and goose on winter holidays). A "new" German menu offers items you don't expect to find in a German restaurant outside of urban Germany: mache and smoked trout salad, creamy smoked salmon soup with peppercorns, and Swabian dumplings (like ravioli) with various sauces.

But the real strength of the restaurant is in its wines. Ronald Knoll, son of the owners and the resident wine expert, took classes at the esteemed German Wine Academy in the Reingau and worked in Munich restaurants. His collection of modestly priced and rare wines is highly regarded by critics.

RUSSIA
♦ **RESTAURANTS**

The Russian population, and consequently its food, has always been extraordinarily varied in ethnic origins. In Los Angeles, you find Armenians and Georgians whose foods are linked to those of the Middle East, Russians with culinary ties to the Balkan countries, and Russians from whom we've inherited such familiar fare as gefilte fish, borscht, stuffed cabbage, and dill pickles.

Russians insist that dining out "should be like a party." L.A.'s Russian restaurants—even small cafés—accommodate this desire with evening entertainment. The splashiest and most successful Russian dining and entertainment spot is **Moscow Nights** (11345 Ventura Boulevard, Studio City, S.F. VALLEY, 818-980-8854; open for lunch and dinner; closed Monday). Moscow Nights moved from its minimall location on Sherman Way and has reappeared in a higher rent district on Ventura Boulevard. Its new palatial interior has a sweeping polished wood bar running the length of the huge room. Antique samovars enclosed in glass lend Czarist elegance, and the banquet room is lavished with the same hand-painted details as the old restaurant. This is a place to immerse yourself in Russian cabaret and sample a little pre-Bolshevik opulence with servings of caviar and vodka (or more modest choices of stroganoff and chicken Kiev, vareniki dumplings and pelmeni). There's a dance floor and on weekends the Moscow Nights band entertains along with Russian singers of international repute. During the week you can get the same classic Russian fare but without the cabaret.

Violet's, 1712 Colorado Boulevard, Eagle Rock, CENTRAL, 213-255-4562. Dinner Wednesday to Sunday; entertainment on weekends. Sink back into Violet's plush armchairs in the dimness of an Old World dining room graced by Czarist art and formal Florentine wallpaper. Order beluga or sevruga with traditional toast rounds and chopped egg. Select a French or Mendocino champagne and while away a few hours listening to the haunting strains of melodic gypsy music. An evening at Violet's will transport you to a vanished era.

The restaurant has a pedigree: Russian-Armenian owner Violet Pashinian, born in Shanghai into a family of restaurateurs, grew up in Brazil and later Los Angeles, where her parents opened Kavkaz, a spirited Russian cabaret and restaurant popular with Hollywood's old guard (the building now holds Spago, another Hollywood haunt). Violet's husband, Andy, the restaurant's chef, also from a family of restaurateurs, cooked at Kavkaz for 20 years with Violet's mother, Miriam, who learned her culinary art from one of the former chefs at Czar Nicholas II's court.

Violet's Russian-Armenian menu blends the best of both cultures: First-rate appetizers include meat-stuffed grape leaves and pelmeni, Siberia's answer to the wonton, in a dill-flavored broth or deep-fried and served with sour cream for dipping.

Violet's exceptional borscht, a deeply flavored beef broth swimming with crunchy vegetables, precedes the entrées. Tender, juicy rack of lamb marinated in pomegranate juice is the house specialty; the stroganoff is sliced filet mignon smothered in mushrooms; and of course Violet's serves shish kebabs. The Brazilian rasco steak and several Chinese-inspired dishes would seem odd in any Russian restaurant but Violet's. Raisa Dewar, a Russian pianist who sings gypsy music, and Harach Yacoubian, a violinist well known in the international Russian-Armenian community, entertain on weekends.

Little Russia, 1132 E. Broadway, Glendale, S.F. VALLEY, 818-243-4787. Lunch and dinner daily. Little Russia, a halfheartedly decorated café with deep red tablecloths and bare walls, attempts to be all things to all Russians. From 11:00 A.M. it offers good Arme-

nian sandwiches and cold plates at rock-bottom lunchroom prices. And at lunch you don't have to shout over the relentless gypsy music that plays in the evening.

Beyond the clichés of stroganoff and shish kebab, a host of Middle Eastern–style appetizers represent the best of Little Russia's Armenian-Russian kitchen. There's *basturma,* the thinly sliced, spicy, air-dried Armenian-style beef; hummus; eggplant caviar; and also mutabbal, the roasted eggplant dip. Georgian-style meat stuffed dumplings of a preposterous size will take more than the edge off your appetite; share them. *Kharcho,* a stewlike Armenian meat and vegetable soup, warms the soul. The restaurant's many kebabs include well-seasoned (and well-grilled) *lule* kebab (ground meat rolled into a sausage form) and chicken tabaka, a whole marinated game hen, oozing with delicious juice.

Little Russia's prices must have been translated from Russian rubles: The last time I looked, the fish of the day was $7.93 and the kebab sandwiches were $3.76.

♦ **DELICATESSENS AND MARKETS**
Most of "Little Russia" is in Hollywood along Santa Monica, east of Fairfax up to Gardner Street. Along that stretch, you find a collection of Russian markets—the Continental, Arcadia, and Berouzka among them. I prefer **Gastronom** for smoked fish. Though it's obscurely located at 7859 Fairfax Avenue, Hollywood, CENTRAL, 213-654-9456, down a few stairs in the back corner of a shopping mall that holds an Alpha Beta Market, Russians beat a path to its door. The smoked fish include meaty eel, baby whitefish, silky cold-smoked salmon and hot-smoked salmon, along with silvery mackerel and shad, to name a few. Gastronom's cheese selection seems wider than that of many Russian stores: There's smooth

pot cheese for baking cheese buns, or the Georgian cheese bread called *khachapuri*, or Ukrainian-style stuffed vareniki dumplings. In the same case look for creamy Russian yogurt; giant logs of sweet, farmhouse butter; and thick cultured cream. Don't miss the selection of Polish and Hungarian sausages and smoked meats.

Tatiana, 8205 Santa Monica Boulevard, Hollywood, CENTRAL, 213-656-7500. My Russian food information source, Sophia, tells me she's "crazy for the plates to go" at Tatiana, a jam-packed Russian deli and market. The prepared dishes include fat cabbage rolls stuffed with dill-flavored chopped chicken and rice. Plump chickens are baked with garlic and paprika. Everything is lovingly cooked by co-owners Rosalia Tisprin and her sister Bronya. The sisters excel at cold appetizers and such salads as fresh sliced beets in a zingy, tart marinade, and puréed roasted eggplant spiked with lemon and garlic.

Tatiana also has a huge deli case filled with smoked fish and meats, sausages, and cheeses. I like to buy the fresh anchovies for Caesar salad. Mid-store, several shelves hold boxes of cookies, jams, esoteric canned items, and sturdy Russian breads.

Tatiana caters parties and is known in Russian circles for its kulebiaka, an opulent layered pastry filled with dill-infused salmon, rice, and eggs. Kulebiaka must be ordered in advance.

At **International Food Center** (7754 Santa Monica Boulevard, West Hollywood, WEST, 213-656-1868), salmon caviar, luxuriously displayed in tubs, seems so decadent—such a large volume of it piled up in one container. The crushed-egg type is less expensive than the perfect whole eggs, and often just as delicious. The astoundingly varied deli cases hold at least half a dozen types of sweet butter, eight kinds of hams, and a host of international salamis, smoked meats, roast pork, sausages, and jellied tongue. In the salad section you can choose from several styles of eggplant salads or spreads to accompany the delicious sandwiches to go.

There are quarts of chopped garlic, and International makes several homemade desserts including pirozhki filled with sweet cheese or with cherries, and cream-filled Napoleons and cakes.

CENTRAL EUROPEAN SHOPS AND RESTAURANTS

People outside Central Europe usually perceive the region's food as a single entity: all that cabbage, yards of sausages, mountains of dumplings, and vats of sour cream. The Central European cuisines do have undeniable similarities, as they are related to the German and Austrian-Hungarian cultures and to Turkey. But each cuisine has a distinct personality.

♦ POLAND

L.A. has little Polish food—just one restaurant and a few stores. Although close to Russian cooking, especially in the sweet-sour taste of some of its soups or meats and its fondness for sour cream—Poland has its own way with sauces and game, inspired somewhat by the French.

Warszawa, 1414 Lincoln Boulevard, Santa Monica, WEST, 310-393-8831. Open for dinner daily. Fortunately the Polish restaurant, Warszawa (pronounced Var-schav-ah) has an accomplished kitchen. In a converted house, its dining rooms are small and intimate, with whitewashed walls that glow with candlelight. Don't expect this fare to be all goulash and dumplings. OK, so they do have pierogi, and *paprykarz cielecy:* a cousin of veal paprikash. But there's also fresh rainbow trout simmered with fresh dill, lemon, and leeks and *z czerwonej kapusty,* a salad of slivered

red cabbage with yellow, red, and green bell peppers mixed with leeks and walnuts. The crackly skinned roast duck with apple stuffing is a wonder, as are the crispy potato pancakes with dried plums, cinnamon, apples, and sour cream. Warszawa has a full bar and a good list of California wines.

J&T European Gourmet, 1128 Wilshire Boulevard, Santa Monica, WEST, 310-394-7227. Country dwellers in Eastern Europe have traditionally smoked sausages to preserve them through the long winter. J&T Gourmet, a handsome meat-and-sausage shop, continues the tradition by smoking dozens of sausages and hams, all cured on the premises. Sausage makers John Pikula and Ted Maslo, both from Poland and employees of the establishment when it was called Andrezj, now own the business. They butcher meat to their own specifications, so their sausages are often much leaner than traditional and commercially produced items.

Sausages smoked on the premises at J&T European Gourmet Polish deli in Santa Monica.

The cured sausages dangling behind the deli case include kabanos, or stick sausages; garlicky kielbasa; and a meaty farmer's sausage called wiejska. J&T's hams are lean, smoky, and, best of all, never too salty. You can really taste the mix of smoke and meat. Any one of J&T's three styles of bacon can add pungent smokiness to soups or vegetable dishes. And the smoked pork tenderloin goes wonderfully with saucy red cabbage and the potato dumplings from the store's freezer case. The selection of smoked and cured fish is worth investigating; eat any of these the European way with a slice of hearty rye that the shop procures from Baltic Bakery in San Pedro.

♦ **HUNGARY**

Hortobágy Hungarian Restaurant, 11138 Ventura Boulevard, Studio City, S.F. VALLEY, 818-980-2273. Open for lunch and dinner; closed Monday. Nearly 20 years ago, Hortobágy was a favorite haunt of USC students seeking a hearty dinner for small change. About a decade ago it followed its clientele over the hill to Ventura Boulevard, where it remains one of the city's favorite Hungarian restaurants. It's the place to pig out on the vast Hortobágy wooden platter of mixed meats: veal, pork sausages, and liver, along with red cabbage. The platter is supposed to serve two but it would satisfy four, especially if they wanted to leave room for the knockout palacsinta (sweet crêpes filled with cheese and poppy seeds) or for the unbelievably rich chestnut torte. This is satisfying food unless you're thinking about a spa diet.

Hungarian Budapest, 7986 Sunset Boulevard, Hollywood, CENTRAL, 310-654-3744 or 654-3745. Open for lunch and dinner daily. I should tell you right off that Hungarian Budapest is not related to the dreary old restaurant of the same name that used to be on Fairfax. This spiffy modern Hungarian café is wedged between the Gaucho Grill and Don Corleone in Hollywood. It's weird to see rapper-rocker groupie-type customers in studded leather downing traditional smoky Transylvanian goulash or consommé with liver dumplings at the café's pristine, cloth-covered tables.

The café's food is lighter than the lard-fried, onion-based stews of its ancestry. Besides the main dishes there are Hungarian salami sandwiches on good Hungarian bread, and a marvelous pastry case holding a multitiered palacsinta torte filled with sweet crushed walnuts and lightly drizzled with bittersweet chocolate sauce.

Monique's, 618 Shoppers Lane, Covina, EAST OF L.A., 818-332-4902. Open for lunch and dinner; closed Monday. Monique's bills itself as a French-Hungarian restaurant. "Les Hors d'oeuvres" offers escargots and moules mariniere, and under "Les Poissons" you find fillet of sole amandine and snapper grenobloise. "Les Specialities," however, are pure Hungarian. Monique's Hungarian chef, Sandor Fekete, prepares the expected beef goulash with spaetzle, and veal paprikash, but also sautéed calves' brains, roast duckling with braised red cabbage, and an addictive fried country bread called langos that you rub with garlic while it's still hot. The vast potpourri combination dinner reflects the "eat, eat" mentality of Eastern Europe. If you make it through half the sausage, pork chops, stuffed cabbage, weiner schnitzle, beef goulash, red cabbage, and spaetzle on the platter, you may have room to sample "les tentations du diable," one of Monique's desserts, but you'll probably want to bring lots of the food home.

Otto's Hungarian Market, 2320 W. Clark Avenue, Burbank, S.F. VALLEY, 818-845-0433. When you step into Otto's Hungarian Market, you're instantly in Budapest. Old-fashioned cookware lines the walls. Polka music plays on a stereo. There's a comfortable clutter of imported ingredients that an Eastern European grandmother would clasp to her apron with joy.

Otto's, with its huge selection of Hungarian and other European hams, sausages, and salamis, makes some of the best sandwiches in the city. Smoked Hungarian-style string ham or lean Polish ham on Otto's farmhouse rye are sandwiches worth a drive. Of Otto's smoked meats, I particularly like the fustolt karaj, a filet mignon smoked and air-cured, and the fustolt szalona, an aged smoked bacon that adds a wonderful rich flavor to all kinds of soups and potato dishes.

Irma, Otto's wife, will counsel you on using the store's lesser known ingredients; lecsó, for example, a mixture of braised onions, sweet peppers, and paprika, is the base for many Hungarian stews and soups. There's a wonderful collection of eggy Hungarian noodles: tarhónya, known as egg barley, are tiny noodle pellets made by pushing the dough through a sieve. These are unbelievably good with meat juices.

Dedicated cooks should be sure to explore the lekvar, an intense fruit butter used in pastries, or the sweetened chestnut purée. Otto's also stocks an old-fashioned selection of cooking equipment including torte pans, nut grinders, and potato ricers. And Otto's carries Hungarian wines.

♦ **YUGOSLAVIA**
Yugoslavian food, with its Turkish-style kebabs, its tradition of the *meze* table, and its countless ways with eggplant, reveals the influence of Turkish cooking. But each area of the country has taken something from its five indigenous nationalities and from countries that ruled before Yugoslavia's independence: Austria, Hungary, and Turkey. And from Yugoslavia's coast comes Mediterranean seafood.

Beograd, 10540 Magnolia Boulevard, North Hollywood, S.F. VALLEY, 818-766-8689. Open for dinner; closed Monday. You might think of the food at Beograd Restaurant as Yugoslavian heartland cooking—unfortunately the glorious seafood dishes are missing. Otherwise, Beograd currently serves the best Yugoslavian fare in town. The warm bread that comes to the table first is baked in the restaurant's kitchen. The well-wrought appetizers represent familiar Balkan fare and include *pohovani kackavalj*: barely breaded and fried kashkaval cheese, which flows from its crispy exterior into a delicious molten puddle. The untraditional boureks are light puffy crowns of crisp filo filled with meat or cheese. The entrées are simple but as carefully prepared as the appetizers. Cevapcici (seasoned ground meat formed into a sausage shape, grilled, and served on a bed of onions) and raznjici (skewered, marinated pork tenderloin chunks) both vie for the title of Yugoslavia's national dish. Potatoes sautéed in just a little chicken fat with onions are just the way Yugoslavian grandmothers make them. And for desserts there are sinful layered tortes. Ours, filled with chocolate "creme" and crushed walnuts, was not too sweet and perfect with coffee. It also came from Beograd's kitchen.

◆ ALBANIA

Ajetis Albanian, 425 Pier Avenue, Hermosa Beach, SOUTH, 310-379-9012. Open for dinner; closed Monday. In 1978 Dino Ajetis (pronounced Aye-en-tees) opened what was then—and probably still is—California's only Albanian restaurant. He specialized in cooking subtly spiced lamb, the customary meat in Muslim Albania. Present owner Thomas Thompson turned Ajetis into a romantic dining spot with flickering candles, beguiling homemade desserts, and a gypsy violinist who plays by the fireplace on Friday nights. Thompson still serves plenty of subtly spiced lamb, but he's broadened the menu to include Albanian-style vegetarian dishes. These are so richly flavored and interestingly spiced that you never miss the meat. Most entrées, including the traditional lamb dishes, bear the American Heart Association's little heart because they're made with such lean meat.

◆ ROMANIA

Mignon, 1253 N. Vine Street, No. 11, Hollywood, CENTRAL, 213-461-4192. Open for lunch and dinner Tuesday through Saturday; closed Monday. Romanians are Latins, but their Balkan cuisine blends the influences of Turkish, Russian, and Viennese cooking. Mignon's pork schnitzel will remind you of Vienna, its stuffed cabbage of Moscow, and its mititei of Istanbul. But listen closely, and you'll hear conversation in Romanian, and the soft lilt of Romanian folk songs on the Muzak. Mignon's food, like most Romanian cooking, is somewhat lighter than other Eastern European cuisines.

Most people start with the *vinete,* a garlicky eggplant pâté, and ikre, a caviar whipped up with olive oil rather like the Greek *taramasalata.* You'll probably want to try the Romanian national dish, mamaliga *cu brinza si smintina.* This cornmeal "polenta" is served with crumbled fetalike cheese and sour cream. Drink a toast with Romanian cabernet, try the *clatite* (dessert crêpes filled with sour cherries), and for a short while you're in Romania.

Ron's Market, 5270 W. Sunset Boulevard, Los Angeles, CENTRAL, 213-465-1164. Open 8:00 A.M. to 10:00 P.M. daily. Nowhere else in the city is there anything quite like Ron's Market, a multi-ethnic shopping experience at bargain prices. Inside the converted Von's supermarket, shoppers line up at the deli area for Polish, Hungarian, Russian, Romanian, and assorted Middle Eastern specialties. Dozens of smoked fish varieties from sturgeon to eel, as well as caviar, Romanian sausage, Russian farmhouse butter, and yogurt, are arranged in abundant piles. The produce section often features incredible deals on Hungarian yellow peppers, purple basil, or Asian eggplant. Bread varieties run the gamut from Lithuanian and Polish ryes to Arabic tanur lavash and Armenian madnakosh. And the aisles are crammed with low-priced Romanian wines, Polish jams, Italian chocolates, and German cookies.

SCANDINAVIA

Ever since Scandia, Carl Andersen's, and Ben's closed their doors, we have had little in the way of Scandinavian food—only a few smorgasbord places, the authenticity of whose meatballs is questionable.

We do, however, have the delightful **The Danish Pastry** (11726 W. Pico Boulevard, West Los Angeles, WEST, 310-477-9954). Whether you call it wiener-brød or Danish pastry, the real thing is very different from what most commercial bakers make. Each creation here is puffy, light, and meltingly flaky, with fillings that are not overly sweet. I love the apple custard pastry, the cardamom buns, and the fragrant orange-almond coffee cake.

Hokan Gath, the shop's Swedish-trained pastry chef, also makes splendid marzipan cakes, Budapest meringue cake, and petits fours. And now The Danish Pastry has a little café next door, where they serve lovely sandwiches on their own breads and rolls. The Norwegian shrimp with dill sprinkled with caviar is particularly nice, and there's a wonderful rich onion pie flecked with cheese and bacon. All the pastries are available here too.

For voluptuous sandwiches made with European-style meats and a broader selection of Scandinavian groceries, try **Olson's Deli** (5660–62 Pico Boulevard, Los Angeles, CENTRAL, 213-938-0742). Olson's does most of its grocery business in the wintertime when homesick Scandinavians flock there for Scandinavian-style *julskinka* hams made specifically for the shop just for the holidays. They also stock up on flash-frozen lingonberries to roll up in thin pancakes, and lutefisk (a dried fish) already soaked and ready to cook. There's an enormous selection of cured and pickled fish, Danish cheeses including Norwegian *lepse,* Finnish *lappi,* and Swedish västerbotten. The Olsons make their own liver

An array of pastries at The Danish Pastry in West Los Angeles.

pâté, Swedish pork and potato sausage, Danish pork sausage, and other Scandinavian sausages.

Early every morning, **Norwegian Imports & Bakery** (1231 S. Pacific Avenue, San Pedro, SOUTH, 310-832-0206) bakes Swedish limpa bread flavored with anise and orange peel; large ovals of light Norwegian rye; long loaves of sikte; and kneip made from a mix of whole wheat, cracked wheat, and rye. There are cardamom buns and almond coffee cake whose tempting spicy aromas linger in the shop through the afternoon. The bakery cases hold many sweets, but the showstopper is the marzipan-covered cake filled with fruit and whipped cream.

This stark, barnlike market and bakery hasn't changed in nearly 30 years. Scandinavians have long come here for their deli items: Gothenburg salami made from mutton, and mutton legs cured like prosciutto to be eaten in thin slices. There's a whole parade of pickled fish and Scandinavian cheeses, including Norwegian goat cheese. The ancient shelves bulge with imported Scandinavian groceries and an ample selection of rare preserves, including one of the pale yellow Arctic-grown raspberries called cloudberries.

BRITAIN, IRELAND, AND AUSTRALIA

British pubs and shops are stashed in almost every corner of Los Angeles County. This small selection represents the best, but it's by no means comprehensive.

I've always thought of **The John Bull Pub** (958 S. Fair Oaks Avenue, Pasadena, SAN GABRIEL VALLEY, 818-441-4353; open for lunch and dinner daily) as a fantasy of a classic English pub come true. It has all that wonderful dark paneling and leaded glass and many marvelous dark ales "on draught." These are drawn with authentic English hand

pumps that use no carbon dioxide gas to "inflate" the beer. But the fantasy part is the food: They serve pies made from *lean* meats with flaky fragile crusts. They also serve salads and fresh fruit—try to get those in a pub in England. For steak and kidney pie the meats are simmered with Harvey's dry sherry, and for steak and mushroom pie, in Guinness Stout. The shepherd's pie, topped with real mashed potatoes, has Cheddar cheese crumbled over it.

Santa Monica has long had a large British population. Now many of the shops and eating establishments that were scattered around town have moved to a concentrated area near the Third Street Mall. Right across the street from the King George V Pub, which recently moved from its old location at Sixth and Santa Monica Boulevard, is **Ye Olde King's Head** (116 Santa Monica Boulevard, Santa Monica, WEST, 310-451-1402). An institution for lovers of fish and chips, the pub serves possibly the best version in the Los Angeles area. The large rambling multiroomed pub draws a lively, sociable, and only partially British crowd. On draft are Harp lager, Fullers, Watney's, Bass, and Guinness, to name only a few. With these, Welsh rarebit or Scotch eggs—encased in a thin layer of cooked sausage and dusted with bread crumbs—are the perfect pub grub. More substantial fare includes the renowned fish, fried in a puffy, heavenly light beer batter; pub pies; and, for dessert, Midland English trifle. Next door to the pub, look for the more recently opened **Ye Olde King's Head Shoppe** (132 Santa Monica Boulevard, Santa Monica, WEST, 310-394-8765). This terribly British movie-set quaint shop stocks the prestigious Duchess of Devonshire line of fancy foods, including Seville orange marmalade with whis-

Jolly good fare and beer at Ye Olde King's Head British pub in Santa Monica.

key. Also look for the Fortnum and Mason line of teas, jellies, and jams in their dignified containers; Irish bacon; and bake-at-home sausage rolls. And for gifts, see the Aynsley and Portmeirion china pieces and the David Winter porcelain cottages.

For afternoon tea, walk up Santa Monica Boulevard to **Tudor House** (1403 Second Street, Santa Monica, WEST, 310-451-4107), a bakery shop and tearoom. You can get all the makings of a proper high tea in the bakery or have tea served to you in the old-fashioned tearoom. Tudor House bakes good hefty scones with plump golden raisins. The cases also hold rows of currant cakes, Eccles cakes, lemon curd tarts, and traditional meat pies and sausage rolls. This is where West Side Brits come for their Tips tea, Walker's buttery shortbread, and Scotch oats. The shop stocks Stilton, Cheshire, and Leicester cheeses; very good frozen bangers; Devonshire double cream; and assorted British groceries and newspapers.

With a large British following from the Long Beach area, **Gwen's Pantry** (443 E. Broadway, Long Beach, SOUTH, 310-437-7037) serves a true English cream tea: It begins with Stilton and cucumber sandwiches, followed by a scone or crumpet with Devon cream and English preserves, and tea cake. Gwen's carefully crafts homemade pasties (man-sized meat and vegetable turnovers) and flaky-crusted chicken and Scotch pies. Gwen's hearty weekend English breakfasts of eggs with your choice of bangers, British bacon, smoked kippers, or blood pudding along with a grilled tomato and potatoes are substantial enough to inspire you to walk home from Long Beach.

Closer to the center of town, **Paddington's Tea Room** (729 N. La Cienega Boulevard, West Los Angeles, WEST, 310-652-0624), with its tea-rose wallpaper and veddy British decor, gives you the feeling you're sitting in Kensington or Shepherd's Bush. It does a splendid tea from 9:00 A.M. to 5:30 P.M.: curried egg sandwiches, potted meats, scones with cream, and even Jamaican Blue Mountain coffee if you like.

In the San Fernando Valley, a goldmine for pub crawlers, you have Bucannan Arms, Bully Pub, and Kavanaugh's, among others. **Scotland Yard** (22041 Sherman Way, Canoga Park, S.F. VALLEY, 818-703-9523), its ceiling and walls virtually covered with police hats from all over Europe, is home to three soccer teams and several dart teams. The favorite pub food here is grilled cheese toasties, to go with the Fullers ESP and other lagers on tap.

The best and most complete range of Valley Britannia is at the **Robin Hood British Pub** with its adjoining **Friar Tuck Shoppe**

(13638 Burbank Boulevard, Burbank, S.F. VALLEY, 818-994-6045 [pub] or 785-4814 [shop]). Friar Tuck is an English bakery, grocery, and gift store. The shop bakes a full line of savory pies (including cheese with onion, chicken, and mushroom) and tea cakes (rock cake, scones, custard tarts, and vanilla slices), and it also stocks British groceries. Robin Hood draws a crowd for its Sunday roast dinners from 2:00 to 11:00 P.M. The roast changes weekly, alternating between beef, pork, and a "joint" of lamb. Robin Hood has nine beers on draught including Newcastle Brown, Watney's, and McEwan's. During the week the dining room offers its own steak and mushroom pie with wine sauce and a puff pastry lid, exceptionally good fish and chips, and other traditional fare. Earlier on Sunday, Robin Hood's hearty English breakfast offers up bangers with eggs, grilled fresh mushrooms, and tomato.

In an entirely different setting is the **Cat & Fiddle Pub and Restaurant** (6530 Sunset Boulevard, Hollywood, CENTRAL, 213-468-3800), a hangout for Brits in the music industry. A charming old California-style building with thick arches, a heavy tile roof, and a lovely central patio like a hacienda's makes for delightful—if somewhat incongruous—English dining. Inside, a cozy fireplace warms the comfortable room. And there's live jazz on Sundays.

The Bass, Guinness, and Harp lager on tap; a bountiful mixed grill of meats; homemade sherry trifle; and more nouvelle Anglo dishes, such as poached Norwegian salmon salad with new potatoes, appeal to a diverse clientele.

The same Long Beach Brits who go to Gwen's for tea shop at **British Imports** (2013 Pacific Avenue, Long Beach, SOUTH, 310-599-5119). This 30-year-old British-owned provision shop is the third oldest in the country. The mainstay here is the sausage. British Imports sells about 300 pounds a week of locally made sausage based on the recipes of Wall's and Sainsbury's, two well-known British firms. The shop also stocks such popular British standbys as Danish bacon, all kinds of meat pies (ploughman's pork pies are a favorite), Batchelor's mushy peas, and pharmaceuticals like Lemsip for colds and Radox bath salts for aches and pains.

The place to go for lean rashers of Limerick Irish bacon, Irish boiling bacon, and for sausagelike black pudding, and white pudding, is **Irish Imports** (738 N. Vine Street, Hollywood, CENTRAL, 213-467-6714). Among the many Irish foods are Bewely's all-butter shortbread, Erin marrowfat peas, and naturally smoked kipper fillets. There's also Duskie hand-cut glass and other chinaware.

Wallaby Darned, 617 S. Centre Street, San Pedro, SOUTH, 310-833-3629. The little glossary of Aussie slang on the back of Wallaby Darned's menu defines *razoo*: "Worth nothing [as in] 'not worth a brass razoo.'" This Dingo Lingo slang guide, along with the drunk kangaroo on the front of the hokey newsprint menu, and even the pub's corny name, could lead you to believe that the cooking at this Aussie pub might not be worth a brass razoo. That isn't the case. "Shrimp from the barbie" are huge tiger prawns grilled but still moist. There's roustabout's salad: a plate of thinly sliced cold lamb on lettuces and vegetables with tomato relish; it's a lot more genteel than something a ranch hand might eat. The pub has the largest selection of Australian wines and beers in California, and its homemade trifle and Pavlova, an airy meringue cake, couldn't be better. And this is "the drum" (straight, honest information).

SPAIN

The vivid earthy flavors and Mediterranean accents of Spanish cooking seem natural for California, but this cooking hasn't found much of a following here. Only tapas have caught our fancy. Tapas might be viewed as Spain's answer to dim sum or sushi—well, almost—because in Spain tapas aren't considered a meal. They are just little snacks to tide you over while drinking sherry until the traditional dinner hour at 10:00 P.M.

Tasca (6266½ Sunset Boulevard, Hollywood, CENTRAL, 213-465-7747), however, encourages you to make a meal of tapas. For single diners or couples, Tasca has wisely provided several tapas combination plates, allowing a good range of nibbles at a modest price. "El Probador" offers five cold tapas, and the Tasca combination is an arrangement of serrano ham (Spain's answer to prosciutto), rich manchego sheep's milk cheese, and chunks of Spanish sausage. Some of the single dishes include the Catalan-style *ensalada de berengena*: a garlicky stew of minced eggplant, red pepper, and tomato. Deep-fried squid and the tender clams sautéed with ham in a sherry sauce are among the hot tapas.

If you're not in the mood to nibble, Tasca's entrées are equally good. Paella comes loaded with plump shrimp and the sea bass is cooked to buttery tenderness in a smooth champagne sauce. Tasca has a full bar, a short list of Spanish wines and sangrias, and, of course, to go with the tapas, five varieties of Spanish sherries from the dry fino to sweet.

From Spain, 11510 W. Pico Boulevard, West Los Angeles, WEST, 310-479-6740. In a simple storefront with very blue tablecloths, chef Juan Rodriguez, who's from Barcelona, concentrates more on entrées, though he offers 17 tapas, too. A few of these and a bowl of his Catalan *suquet de peix*, a hearty fisherman's soup, and you've got a meal. From Spain serves all the familiar tapas: stuffed olives with anchovies, grilled shrimp with meltingly sweet garlic, chicken empanadas, and the Spanish-style "tortilla": a potato omelet cut into thick wedges.

Consider, too, Rodriguez's Catalan specialties: breast of chicken with shrimps in tomato sauce with almonds and grilled thin lamb chops with aïoli—a garlicky mayonnaise-like sauce—alongside.

El Cid Show, 4212 W. Sunset Boulevard, Los Angeles, CENTRAL, 213-668-0318. Open Wednesday through Sunday. Without leaving Hollywood, the ambience of a sixteenth-century Spanish taverna complete with passionate flamenco guitar riffs, castanets, clicking heels, and the swirl of ruffled skirts, can be yours for an evening at El Cid Show. The show is riveting and expertly performed. The menu, naturally, includes a paella and quasi-continental fare of almost cafeteria quality. They're edible—but remember, you came for the show.

La Española Deli, 2020 Lomita Boulevard, No. 7, Lomita, SOUTH, 310-539-0455. Open Monday to Friday 7:00 A.M. to 5:00 P.M.; Saturday, 9:00 A.M. to 5:00 P.M. La Española, Los Angeles's only Spanish market, is more than a place to buy real paella rice, Spanish manchego cheese, and serrano ham. La Española's minuscule store fronts its main enterprise as a manufacturer of serrano ham and Spanish sausages. Owner Juana Faraone has traveled all over Spain to study sausage-making techniques from various regions. In her USDA-approved kitchen she turns out about 20 sausage types, including plump white Catalan-style butifarras, long, skinny Basque chistorra; and Spain's most popular cooking sausage, chorizo de Bilbao. Her lomo embuchado is a lean cured pork loin. The sausages include salami style, which Faraone cures several months in her curing room; semicured sausages; and fresh sausages like morcilla con cebolla: a blood sausage with onions often served as tapas.

GREECE,
THE MIDDLE EAST,
AND AFRICA

Section Introductions by Charles Perry

In Los Angeles, we have a ringside seat on all the cuisines of the Middle Eastern regions as well as those countries that their cooking has influenced, namely Greece, North Africa, and the Balkan states. Each recent political disturbance in these areas has given our city a new style of Middle Eastern cooking, the newest being Iranian—or as most Iranian expatriates prefer to call anything pertaining to their culture, Persian. Los Angeles is home to more than a quarter million Iranians and has an abundance of restaurants to serve them.

IRAN

The most influential cuisine in history until modern times was that of the ancient Persian court. It became the haute cuisine of medieval Islam and followed the Muslim banner everywhere from Spain to India, even as far as the gates of China in Central Asia. The Persian influence remains throughout this whole area today: Many Indian dishes still have Persian names, including kofta, pilaf, paneer, and sa-mosas.

But Iran does not have a strong restaurant tradition. The great dishes are still made at home, and travelers complain that eating your way across Iran is a little like eating your way across Nevada. Thus it is not surprising that many of the Persian restaurants here are kebaberias, serving the simplest steak-and-fries version of the cuisine. —C.P.

In Iran the best kebabs, grilled over live coals, are sold by vendors in the bazaars. So the widespread popularity of fast-food kebab outlets here isn't surprising. These citified versions of bazaar stalls are variously named Kebab King-dom, Kebab Broiler, Kebab Palace, and Kebab King—practically every large shopping mall has one.

But a number of L.A. kebab restaurants have pleasant dining rooms, linen-covered tables, and even live music on weekends. They're great places to know about. The food is simple and usually good, and prices for a meal hover around $10, making them some of the most remarkable dining bargains in town.

— PERSIAN GLOSSARY —

Alabaloo: Dried sour cherries.
Ash-e mast: A traditional Iranian yogurt-based soup with leafy greens and mint.
Baghlava: See baklava (page 220).
Bamieh: Okra; also Persian sweet syrup-soaked cakes shaped like okra.
Barg: Thin meat strips about 1½ inches wide marinated, threaded onto skewers, and grilled.
Borani-e esfenaj: A side dish of yogurt mixed with steamed spinach, beets, or other cooked vegetables.
Chelo: Boiled basmati rice

topped with saffron-flavored rice grains. Chelo combined with egg yolk and oil, spread thin, and baked to form a crisp crust, becomes chelo tah deg, which often accompanies Persian stews. It is offered to the guest in Persian homes as a delicacy. (The ultra long-grained basmati rice strain grows only in limited areas of the Middle East and northern India. The grains are smoked for several days, giving it a unique fragrance.)
Doogh: A palate-cleansing yogurt and soda water drink flavored with dried mint.

Faludeh: Rose-water-flavored sherbet with vermicellilike strands of cornstarch.

Fesenjan: A meat or chicken stew (khoresh) flavored with crushed walnuts and concentrated sour pomegranate juice.

Kashk: Dried reconstituted yogurt whey.

Khoresh: Persia's rich array of stews, long cooked to achieve a slow fusing of flavors, are often made of vegetables or a mixture of meat and vegetables. Served atop chelo the meal becomes chelo khoresh. A few well-known khoresh are: khoresh bademjan (lamb shank braised with eggplant and flavored with dried lime and saffron), khoresh loobia (with green beans), khoresh bamieh (with okra), khoresh gheimeh (with yellow split peas).

Lavash: A large oval flat bread, often 2 1/2 feet long. When baked in a tanur oven (see below) it's called tanur lavash.

Madnakosh: This large oval semiflat bread, scored in two directions to create squares on its surface, is sold in Persian and Armenian markets.

Mokhalafat: Side dishes in a Persian meal, which may include pickles, relishes, condiments, plates of fresh herbs, vegetables, cheese, and yogurt.

Panir o sabzi: A tray of herbs, raw vegetables, and cheese that accompanies most Persian meals.

Polos: Iran's pilaf-style dishes differ from chelo in being cooked with another ingredient besides rice. They include alabaloo polo (cooked with dried morello cherries), and zereshk polo (cooked with tiny tart red barberries).

Sangak bread: A large (3 feet by 1 foot) chewy flat bread originally cooked on hot stones, giving the baked bread a Swiss-cheeselike texture.

Somagh (or sumac): A tart dry condiment made from grated, dried sumac berries to sprinkle on rice and kebabs.

Taftoon bread: A large flat wheat bread over a foot in diameter with a pocket like pita bread.

Tah deg: Rice and egg baked in a thin sheet until it is crisp (in a restaurant). Tah deg usually accompanies chelo khoresh.

Tanur: A cylindrical clay oven, the ancestor of the Indian tandoor oven. Breads and skewered meats, among other things, are cooked in it at high temperatures.

Tanur (or tanour) lavash: See lavash.

Zereshk: Tiny tart dried red berries that when mixed with rice become zereshk polo.

Zulubia: A fried cake soaked with rose-water-flavored syrup.

PERSIAN KEBAB RESTAURANTS

Of course you'll find beef shish ke-bab in all Persian restaurants but there's also a long list of other ke-babs: *jujeh* kebab (made with chicken or game hen), *barreh* ke-bab (small lamb chops), and kofta kebab (ground meat with parsley and onions). Barg, which may also be called chelo kebab on menus, is long strips of marinated meat or chicken threaded onto skewers. It is traditional to sprinkle kebabs and especially barg, with somagh, that sourish purple spice made of dried sumac berries that Persian restaurants keep on every table.

A grilled tomato and a huge mound of basmati rice drizzled with butter accompany these dishes. You mix the rice and tomato and sprinkle on somagh for additional zip. Traditionally chelo kebab is accompanied with a raw egg yolk to mix into the rice; at most restaurants, the yolks must be ordered separately.

The best appetizer is kashk o bademjan, a rich purée of eggplant seasoned with tart somagh and drizzled with white creamy kashk, a sauce made from dried and reconstituted yogurt whey. Scoop it up with warm pita bread. Most of the restaurants serve mastokhiar, a tangy garlic-laced yogurt and cucumber mixture similar to an Indian raita; it adds a lot of zing to kebabs. All the dishes are best washed down with doogh, a sprightly, palate-cleansing yogurt and soda water drink flavored with mint.—C.P.

Shekarchi, 1712 Westwood Boulevard, West Los Angeles, WEST, 310-474-6911. Lunch through dinner daily. The Shekarchi name is well known in the Iranian community. Its reputation as a high-quality restaurant was built in Tehran by the grandfather of the present owner, Habib Shekarchi. Now in its ninth year in California, it has recently expanded to a stunning ultra-modern dining room of blond wood beams and slate. The menu, fully translated into English, has excellent descriptions of the foods.

A chef working at an open grill behind a plate-glass partition sears kebabs threaded onto huge sword-like skewers. Shekarchi's traditional plates offer a choice of grills and a variety of rice preparations: Fragrant basmati rice comes with saffron butter, or with wild barberries (zereshk), or with tart cherries or sweet orange peel and almonds. A much longer than usual

list of grilled fish includes salmon and mahi-mahi.

Shahrezad, 17547 Ventura Boulevard, Encino, S.F. VALLEY, 818-906-1616, and 1422 Westwood Boulevard, Westwood, WEST, 310-470-3242. **Darband/ Shahrezad,** 138 S. Beverly Drive, Beverly Hills, WEST, 310-859-8585. Lunch and dinner daily. (See also Shahrezad Flame, facing page.) In the past several years, Shahrezad has bought out a few of its competitors and is now a chain. Each of its four branches has its own personality; the menus, though, are nearly identical. From the start, the original Westwood Shahrezad, with its casual café-style ambience, was popular with Iranian businessmen discussing real estate transactions and calling on their cellular phones.

The fancier Beverly Hills branch (formerly Darband) offers hard liquor, evening entertainment, and a few higher-end items like quail kebab. Shahrezad's barg is always succulent and juicy. For fish enthusiasts, the grilled marinated rainbow trout or whitefish arrives crisp-skinned and moist.

The perfect way to preface these grilled foods is with ash-e mast. The thick yogurt-based broth flavored with mint and generously filled with spinachlike greens comes strewn with grilled slivered onions. A changing selection of traditional Persian-style stews called khoresh is offered daily.

Shamshiri, 19249 Roscoe Boulevard, Canoga Park, S.F. VALLEY, 818-885-7846; 1916 Westwood Boulevard, West Los Angeles, WEST, 310-474-1410; Also in Hollywood and Glendale. Lunch and dinner daily. Now with four branches, Shamshiri offers a standard Persian menu and cooking that is always reliable. They serve wonderful baby lamb chop kebabs—something their closest competitor, Shahrezad, lacks. Each day three or four Persian-style stews rotate as daily specials. They'll always have chicken fesenjan khoresh, rich and tart in its potent pomegranate and ground walnut sauce.

Saam, 39 S. Raymond Avenue, Pasadena, SAN GABRIEL VALLEY, 818-793-8496. Lunch and dinner daily. Unlike the Westwood Boulevard restaurants whose clientele is almost exclusively Iranian, Saam attracts a mixed crowd. My guess is that's why it offers a handful of non-Persian Middle Eastern items: hummus, falafel, tabbouli, and a Greek salad (what most people expect Middle Eastern food to be). But in its sleek dining room overlooking a brick courtyard you'll find mostly Persian dishes. There's a monumental combination plate ($40 at this writing) with all the many kebabs, a veritable meat extravaganza: skewered meat in chunks, strips, and various ground forms, plus chops, a game hen, and a braised lamb shank served with a polo, or pilaf, of rice mixed with dill and tiny green fava beans.

BEYOND KEBABS

Today Persian cuisine retains its ancient taste for cooking fruit with meat, for complex spicing, and for the thick-sauced stews called khoresh. The national dish, khoresh-e-fesenjan, for example, is a rich, molelike concoction of meat, ground walnuts, and concentrated sour pomegranate juice. Khoresh—and just about everything else—is served on rice, the staple grain of Iran and one that Iranians prepare particularly well. Persian cooks have developed a varied catalogue of rice dishes. These fall into two categories—chelo, plain boiled rice with food served over it (usually kebabs or khoresh), or polo, a pilaf-style dish of rice mixed together with other ingredients.

At some Persian restaurants,

you'll notice distinctive Iranian breads, such as the flat tanur and sangak breads that are much larger than the Arab pita.—C.P.

A large variety of Persian-style breads is available all over the city in Middle Eastern markets and at **Shahrezad Flame** (1442 Westwood Boulevard, West Los Angeles, WEST, 310-470-9131; lunch and dinner daily). Flame prepares tanur lavash bread in a marvelous wood-burning clay oven at the front of the dining room; occasionally flames leap from its tiled opening. A worker slaps large thin ovals of tanuri bread dough onto the oven walls—this is the warm earthy bread that comes to your table after you're seated. Now that Flame—which used to be an independently owned restaurant called Tanouri—is part of the Shahrezad chain, it has the same menu as the other branches. But this is the only branch to bake its own tanuri bread.

Javan Restaurant, 11628 Santa Monica Boulevard, No. 9, West Los Angeles, WEST, 310-207-5555. Lunch through dinner daily. At Javan, one of the city's best Near Eastern restaurants, I learned the rituals of Persian dining: The minute you sit down you're brought a basket tanur lavash and a whole raw onion with a knife plunged into its center. These are for munching while you decide on dinner. My Iranian friend explained that one must order panir o sabzi, a tray of herbs and vegetables that includes watercress, radishes, and feta cheese; these are to be nibbled as a refreshing counterpoint to the main course. At most Persian meals, the entrées are surrounded by several such dishes, collectively called mokhalafat. For our mokhalafat we ordered whole heads of pickled garlic, bright pink pickled turnips colored with beet juice, and borani, a bowl of thick, creamy house-made yogurt mixed with steamed fresh spinach.

Javan's unusually long menu offers 23 main dishes, among them the familiar kebabs, including barreh kebab, a skewer full of tiny, tender sweet-fleshed lamb chops. There are several khoresh and one of Iran's favorite polo dishes, alabaloo polo: half a braised chicken served over basmati rice that has been mixed with sweetened tart cherries. One of the two changing daily specials might be the remarkable *tachin*—chopped roasted lamb mixed with rice, yogurt, saffron, and egg, and oven-baked until it forms a loaf with a slightly crisp bottom. It's served with tart barberries over the top.

Javan also does well with desserts. The cigar-shaped baghlava is familiar, but the delicious syrup-soaked zulubia, which resembles a doughnut or beignet, is more exotic. An unusual frozen dessert (for Western palates), faludeh, has what seems like sweet noodles in it.

Shiraz, 15472 Ventura Boulevard, Sherman Oaks, S.F. VALLEY, 818-789-7788. Lunch through dinner daily. Named after the Iranian city, Shiraz offers the familiar chelo kebab dishes and also five khoresh, each served over chelo rice, plus one or two different polo dishes each day.

Meat khoresh include fesenjan and khoresh bademjan: a lamb shank braised with eggplant, dried limes, saffron, and tomatoes. Shiraz also offers five vegetarian khoresh. One, khoresh loobia, is a mixed vegetable stew with French mange-tout beans and baby new potatoes simmered in a saffron-tomato sauce. Khoresh bamieh, with okra, is similar.

The changing selection of two or three polo dishes might include zereshk polo: a succulent chicken with saffron-infused rice flecked with tiny tart red barberries.

With these you might want to try tangy pomegranate juice or fresh carrot juice, and for dessert the sticky but delicious Persian-style rose-water ice cream.

Two other restaurants in the same chain with virtually the same menu are **Sallar's Restaurant,** (1240 S. Glendale Avenue, Glendale, S.F. VALLEY, 818-500-8661) and **Up All Night** (4505 Sepulveda Boulevard, Sherman Oaks, S.F. VALLEY, 818-501-8661).

Golestan, 1398 Westwood Boulevard, West Los Angeles, WEST, 310-470-3867. Lunch through dinner daily. There are two good reasons to eat at Golestan. One is to sit in its dreamy, fantasylike dining room, in which every inch of wall and ceiling are adorned with pastel mirror-mosaics, and listen to the slightly mournful taped Iranian music. The other is to sample several khoresh at once from the hot buffet. So far as I know, Golestan is the only place that offers this all-you-can-eat sort of arrangement.

While you can select kebab dinners cooked to order, for the inquisitive, the hot table holds khoresh bademjan and whole baby lamb shanks stewed with tart dried lemon and onion. Next to these, and several more vegetable and meat khoresh, is a golden pyramid of crispy tah deg. Once the rice that came from the bottom of the pan, this crisp rice is now made in large quantities by mixing rice with egg and baking it in sheets. To accompany the khoresh, the kitchen constantly replenishes the tah deg and a fragrant heap of basmati.

Golestan's owners, who are delightful happily cater to your every whim and will give detailed explanations of their khoresh assortment.

Your Place, 354 N. Beverly Drive, Beverly Hills, WEST, 310-858-1977. Lunch and dinner daily; until 5:00 A.M. Friday and Saturday.

This lively mirror-lined café, which opens out onto Beverly Drive, is crowded with shoppers and businessmen during the day and families in the evening. You get the feeling that it was transported from Tehran during happier times when "French" eating places flourished there. Along with the familiar kebabs, fesenjan, and zereshk polo, there is "continental" food in the form of omelets, ratatouille au gratin, chicken-stuffed crêpes, endive salad, and French pastries. Café au lait and espresso are available, along with Persian black tea.

Cabaret Tehran, 12229 Ventura Boulevard, Studio City, S.F. VALLEY, 818-985-5800. Dinner nightly. Without having to worry about travelers' warnings for the Near East, anyone can easily be transported to this faraway land with a brief visit to Cabaret Tehran. Enter the fairy-tale kingdom above a savings and loan and you see graceful arches and sculpted columns surrounding a dining room that seems the size of the Convention Center's hall. Soft, tiny lights illuminate every arch. The cabaret lives with the spirit of prerevolutionary days. You will also see a Farsi-speaking comedian, a crooner delivering melodic phrases in Farsi, belly dancers, and occasionally customers twirling on the dance floor.

How's the food? Limited to a few kebab dishes, sole meuniere, and a short list of appetizers. It is quite fine—but not the main event. Call for show and dinner prices; they vary on different days.

PERSIAN MARKETS

Super Jordan, 1449 Westwood Boulevard, West Los Angeles, WEST, 310-478-1706. Open daily. This minisupermarket, the largest in the Iranian enclave along Westwood Boulevard, is named after a well-known supermarket in Iran. A baroque window display of beautiful fruits—huge pomegranates, luscious juicy grapes, pineapples, and quinces—lures you in. At the back of the store in the produce department, where customers weigh out their Persian-style cucumbers and pick up bushy bunches of mint, tarragon, dill, and basil. Iranian breads—pillow-case-sized sangak, and white and wheat tanuri—are stacked like yardage in a bazaar.

The meat department cuts its beef and lamb for kebabs to order. You can get the long strips of meat for barg, or chunks of lamb, beef, and chicken for kebabs. Small lamb shanks and veal shanks are popular too. On the shelves you'll find bags of somagh, dried kaffir limes for adding a tart elusive flavor to braised meats, pomegranate syrup (not the

Yards and yards of Middle Eastern–style breads at Super Jordan market in West Los Angeles.

sticky-sweet variety, but a juice concentrate for cooking), and the tart juice from unripe grapes used to flavor khoresh. Pickles abound here: whole heads of garlic, beet-dyed turnips, chile peppers, and all kinds of other vegetables in brine.

Across from the cash register behind an art deco glass-block room divider, a pastry department holds a fairy-tale collection of fancy Persian-style pastries and cookies. There are the sticky syrup-soaked bamieh, and tiny flower-shaped cookies, smaller than a dime, macaroonlike almond cookies, and fancy pastry twists. Some cookies are made mostly of crushed nuts or chick-pea flour.

Miller's Market, 18248 Sherman Way, Reseda, S.F. VALLEY, 818-345-9222. Open daily. Miller's got its name from the old-fashioned Valley supermarket on Vanowen it took over about 10 years ago. It was the largest, if not the best kept, Middle Eastern store in the country. Miller's has now moved—adopted name and all—to a smaller but freshly appointed store on Sherman Way, updated with item-print-out cash registers, bar code scanners, and other modern market amenities.

Though Iranian-owned, Miller's carries both Persian and Arab ingredients, and the butcher offers only kosher meats. The bread department has a fascinating collection of breads: huge flat tanuri and chewy sangak breads to serve under grilled kebabs and to soak up their juices; taftoon breads that look like hubcap-sized pitas; flat yeasty Afghani bread strewn with sesame seeds; and inch-thick yeasted Armenian madnakosh the size of a banquet platter. The shelves hold about ten kinds of pita, including the small puffy Israeli variety. And there are round, slightly sweet breakfast breads for your morning coffee. In the produce department you'll see shahi, a Near Eastern–style watercress, jahiar (Persian cucumbers), and fresh quince for making jellies and for cooking up with meat in a khoresh. In season, there are green almonds with jellylike centers.

Delights for the Persian table from Miller's Market.

Pastries and caviar—a few of the delicacies from a Persian market.

MIDDLE EASTERN FOOD
FROM ARMENIA, LEBANON,
AND SYRIA

Greece, Armenia, Syria, and Lebanon have very similar cuisines. The reason is simple: All were under the rule of the Ottoman Empire from the fifteenth to the nineteenth centuries, and their most popular dishes are Turkish—kebabs, stuffed vegetables, such elaborate eggplant dishes as moussaka, simple meat and vegetable stews called *yakhni,* and baklavalike desserts based on filo.

Understandably, though, Greeks, Armenians, and Arabs may not particularly relish being reminded of their debt to the Ottoman oppressor, any more than Americans like being reminded that apple pie is English. In any case, the dishes are now thoroughly part of their own cuisines and are usually prepared in a distinctive national way.

Each of these cultures has kept its own traditions as well: the seafood repertoire of the Greeks, and the Syrian kibbeh made of lamb and bulgur wheat pounded together. The Arab appetizers hummus and tabbouli are also popular with everybody in the region, particularly the Armenians. Most Armenian families came to this country by way of Syria and Lebanon and know Arab food intimately. In fact, most of our Lebanese restaurants and delicatessens are run by Armenians.

The Ottoman style of cooking, which replaced the Persian medieval haute cuisine of the Islamic world, differed from it in two ways: It avoided cooking fruit with meat, and it went easy on the spices. —C.P.

— ARMENIAN, LEBANESE, AND —
— SYRIAN GLOSSARY —

Arayes (Syrian and Armenian): A grilled beef patty sprinkled with pine nuts and grilled inside a pita bread.
Babaghannouj: One of the Middle East's many meze. A dip made from puréed roasted eggplant, tahini, lemon juice, garlic and olive oil. (Also see mutabbal.)

Baklava or baghlava (Persian): A rich pastry composed of thin buttered filo layers and sweetened nuts.

Basturma: Lean dry-cured beef rubbed with hot pepper and spices, served in very thin slices.

Borek: Savory pastries of short dough or filo dough filled with either meat, cheese, or spinach.

Falafel: Small, round deep-fried fritters made of chick-peas or fava beans, blended with parsley and other seasonings.

Fool: Fava beans sold dried, canned, frozen, or, in season, fresh.

Gata (Armenian): A sweet, soft bun enclosed in a firmer dough.

Hummus: A dip made from puréed chick-peas, tahini, garlic, and lemon juice.

Kashkaval: A smooth eating cheese, the same as Italian caciocavallo, used all over the eastern Mediterranean and Balkan countries. Kashkavals vary from country to country and can be delicate and mozzarellalike or sharp and salty.

Kataif: A shredded-wheatlike pastry used in the same ways as filo dough.

Kibbeh: Lamb and cracked wheat pounded together in a stone mortar to form a smooth paste. Eaten baked, fried, or raw with lettuce and lemon juice.

Kofta (keufta, kefta, kafta, kufta): Near Eastern minced meat mixtures made into balls or cooked in other shapes. The most well known kofta preparation is kibbeh maqli: kibbeh stuffed with the kofta mixture and deep-fried.

Labneh: A fresh soft cheese made from drained yogurt.

Lahmajun: Thin bread rounds topped with minced meat and seasonings; often called Armenian pizza.

Lule kebab: Ground seasoned meat formed into a sausage shape around a skewer and grilled.

Mahleb: Cherry pits crushed to a powder and used to give breads and pastries an elusive fruity aroma.

Meze: A selection of small dishes, usually considered appetizers but may also constitute an entire meal.

Molukhia: A green vegetable used in soups and casseroles sold dried and, in season, fresh. Molukhia has a viscous quality similar to okra.

Moughrabiyeh: Couscous topped with chicken and chick-peas in a brown sauce.

Muhammara: A dip made of crushed walnuts and hot chiles often with the addition of sour pomegranate juice.

Mutabbal: Another word for babaghannouj.

Nazuk (Armenian and Persian): A layered sweet pastry composed of two different doughs.

Pirozhki (Russian/Armenian): Savory filled pastry turnovers; the Armenian name is the Turkish borek.

Ras nana (Armenian): A large, flat minced beef patty with a garlic vinegar sauce.

Sahlab: Dried orchid root used as a flavoring for desserts.

Sarma (Armenian): Grape leaves stuffed with rice or meat and rice.

Shanklish cheese: A small round medium-hard sour cheese made from yogurt and coated with zatar.

Shawarma: Marinated sliced meat threaded onto a large skewer to form a loaf shape and grilled on a rotisserie.

Shish kebab: Marinated lamb chunks skewered and grilled.

Sujuk (or soudjuk): The most popular Armenian sausage, almost as dry as salami; has a flavor and texture similar to spicy pepperoni.

Tabbouli: A salad made of bulgur wheat, parsley, mint, onion, and tomatoes, dressed with lemon juice and olive oil.

Tahini: A paste made from crushed sesame seeds resembling peanut butter.

Tahn (Armenian): A liquid yogurt drink equivalent to Persian doogh and Lebanese ayran.

Torshi: Pickles.

Zatar: Called Middle Eastern thyme, this has a taste somewhere between thyme and oregano. Blends of zatar and sumac are also labeled simply zatar.

MEZE SOURCES: RESTAURANTS AND DELIS

Tarzana Armenian Grocery (café and restaurant), 22776 Ventura Boulevard, Woodland Hills, S.F. VALLEY, 818-703-7836. And (market and deli), 18598 Ventura Boulevard, Tarzana, S.F. VALLEY, 818-881-6278. Closed Sunday. Tarzana may not carry 200 meze items, but the shops' cases hold one of the best meze selections around. When the deli was a tiny hole in the wall on Clark Street, owner Rose Chelebian's kids would stock shelves and marinate olives after school. Now they help run a business that includes a trilevel café and deli with full dinner service in Woodland Hills and a well-stocked grocery and deli in Tarzana. But what made the deli/grocery a citywide destination for lovers of Armenian food was more than just Mrs. Chelebian's kids' ambitions. Over the years, her exquisite Syrian-style stuffed grape leaves, her luxurious falafel, and her home recipes such as *mujaddara,* a wheat and lentil pilaf smothered in almost caramel-sweet onions, have spread the deli's reputation beyond its Tarzana location. The deli's selection includes stuffed meatball-like kofta, lahmajun (Armenian pizza), cheese borek, pickled baby eggplant, sujuk sausage, and basturma.

The Woodland Hills branch serves a selection of kebabs, sandwiches, and deli items for lunch and dinner, while the Tarzana store has a wide selection of groceries plus a full range of deli items and sandwiches. Both have beautiful homemade pastries baked by Esther, one of the Chelebian sisters.

Al Amir, 5750 Wilshire Boulevard, No. 195, Los Angeles, CENTRAL, 213-931-8740. Lunch Sunday to Friday; dinner nightly. It isn't just the intimacy of Al Amir's heavy linen-draped tables behind etched-glass room dividers, or the

MEZE

The appetizer table, or meze, is the heart and soul of Middle Eastern eating. Sharing food and hospitality with guests is a matter of honor and ritual in the Middle East, and a spread of meze—which can be a few olives and pickles with cheese, or a banquet table laden with such dishes as stuffed eggplant, kibbeh stuffed with lamb, and various kinds of salad—is a symbol of a host's generosity.

Meze might make up a whole meal or be just a snack of roasted melon seeds and nuts with drinks, but it is a daily ritual. The endless possibilities for meze are reflected in the yarn of a Lebanese café owner who bet he could set a table with 200 meze in an afternoon. Because his butcher ran out of lamb, the poor fellow could come up with only 178 items and lost his bet.

luxurious silverware, or even the tuxedoed waiters that have given Al Amir its reputation as Los Angeles's premier Near Eastern restaurant. Lebanese connoisseurs say it is the meze (the menu lists 53, both hot and cold) and the consummate skill that goes into their preparation: A butcher is on the premises to prepare meats. A baker bakes pita all day and evening long. There's a special cook devoted to making nothing but kibbeh maqli—these are little football-shaped stuffed meatballs with seasoned lamb and pine nuts inside a thin, crisp shell of toasted wheat pounded with lamb. Getting the kibbeh's exterior thin without allowing the filling to escape is an art.

Surprisingly, all this skill and luxury is modestly priced. A party of 8 could order 32 meze (4 plates apiece) for under $20 per person, and fewer dishes would probably be ample. The possibilities run from the clichéd (but truly wonderful) falafel and hummus (the latter comes plain or with various grilled meats) to lamb brains in a vinaigrette. If you still have room after the meze, the grilled meat or fowl entrées are equally well prepared, and the Lebanese dessert pastries are particularly authentic.

Caroussel, 5112 Hollywood Boulevard, No. 107, Hollywood, CENTRAL, 213-660-8060. Lunch through dinner daily. The neighborhood once flourished as "Little Armenia." Even now, though most Armenians have headed for suburbia, there's a cluster of Armenian businesses and eateries mixed in with the pupuserias, Russian markets, and body shops. When Armenians do come this way, it's usually to take home a few dozen of Caroussel's juicy stuffed grape leaves (sarma) or a tray full of the excellent kofta. Caroussel sells its barbecue-to-go by the pound: you can get lule kebab, chicken kebab, or liver kebab this way, or in a sandwich.

In Caroussel's homey dining room, appointed rather charmingly with mismatched decor, no one minds if you share one of the long banquet-style tables. The conservative order the chicken kebab plate that comes with a mountain of smoky eggplant dip, mutabbal, or hummus, and a fresh tabbouli with plenty of parsley and mint and very little wheat—the way it's supposed to be. The more inquisitive will want to order the spicy muhammara, a paste of crushed walnuts, tart pomegranate, and blazing hot pepper, or the spicy sujuk sausage.

Marouch, 4905 Santa Monica Boulevard, Hollywood, CENTRAL, 213-662-9325. Lunch through dinner; closed Monday. One of the pleasures of eating at Marouch—besides the great food and upbeat café atmosphere—is its menu. Owner Serge Braidi has gone to the trouble of explaining every dish—you'll know your labneh from your *makanek* in no time.

At the back of the room, three spits of shawarma—beef, lamb, or lemon-marinated chicken breasts—turn slowly in front of their grills beside the rotisserie of roasting juicy chickens. It's tempting just to order one of these and forget about the menu. But don't. The meze for 6 with 20 items served in devastatingly large quantities is worth getting a crowd together to try.

Daily specials are chalked on a board and might include bamieh (a beef-okra stew) or Serge's favorite, moughrabiyeh, chicken in a rich brown sauce with a few chick-peas, served over couscous—Lebanese home cooking at its best. With any meal, you munch on refreshing green olives, pickled turnip, or chiles and green onions from a complimentary relish tray.

The Middle East, 910 E. Main Street, Alhambra, SAN GABRIEL

VALLEY, 818-281-1006. Breakfast through dinner daily. Hand-painted signs listing daily specials that cover almost every inch of wall space and the loud, taped Arabic music add a modicum of character to this undistinguished storefront. Huge trays of baklava sit golden and puffy alongside the borek on the long bank of deli counters. Inside the cases are more meat pies and unbaked baklava awaiting a turn in the oven. Plain as it is—and out of the way as it seems—this place, not surprisingly, does a massive business. They've thought of everyone: Kebab dinners come in large and small sizes; more than a dozen vegetarian plates include rotund, tasty stuffed cabbage, fava bean stew, and stuffed zucchini. The olives are fresh, the eggplant-tahini dip (called *imtabbal* here, not mutabbal) is smoky, and the roast lamb drizzled with yogurt sauce is juicy and succulent. This place is worth a trip—but don't bother to put on a tie.

Cafe Mediterranean, 10151½ Riverside Drive, Toluca Lake, S.F. VALLEY, 818-769-0865. Lunch through dinner daily. Popular with people working at the studios nearby, Cafe Med—as it is affectionately called by its followers— had to expand its tiny storefront to accommodate the growing following it has acquired over the years. In its new pink incarnation— pink tablecloths, walls, and menu— the room and the food (though usually good) seem Valleyized. I can't quite put my finger on what it is—perhaps the fact that you can get kebabs rare if you like (most Middle Eastern restaurants tend to cook them well done), or that Cafe Med serves no tongue or brains but does offer unusual (for Middle Eastern restaurants) shrimp kebabs. Even so, everyone in its skylit dining room seems to relish dipping into the bowls of creamy hummus and babaghannouj and nib-

bling its extra crunchy filo-wrapped borek, which include uncommon shrimp and chicken versions.

Hagop, 14228 Ventura Boulevard, Sherman Oaks, S.F. VALLEY, 818-995-8254. Lunch through dinner; closed Monday. Less Valleyized—although still very nicely appointed, with glass-covered peach tablecloths and a full bar— Hagop is an Armenian restaurant with soul and a few dishes you don't see on every menu. Tongue-numbing spicy muhammara dip made from pomegranate juice, crushed walnuts, and pepper is on the long meze list, as are beef brains marinated in lemon and garlic. Paprika-dusted basturma comes in thin slices, and of course there are the ever popular stuffed grape leaves, tabbouli, mutabbal, hummus, and barbecued quail. With these you can sample the Near Eastern anise-flavored aperitif, *arak,* or Lebanese beer. One sensational entrée, ras nana, is a plate-sized patty of grilled minced beef doused with a powerful garlic vinaigrette. And arayes-maria, a sort of wonderfully seasoned Middle Eastern hamburger, is spread inside a pita bread, sprinkled with pine nuts, then grilled.

TAKE-OUT SPECIALTIES

Some of the best Middle Eastern food is sold to go. Here are the best places to eat when you're not concerned about tablecloths and silverware.

Zankou Chicken, 5065 Sunset Boulevard, Hollywood, CENTRAL, 213-665-7842 or 665-7845. Also at 1415 E. Colorado Street, Glendale, S.F. VALLEY, 818-244-2237. Open 10:00 A.M. to 10:00 P.M. daily. "One becomes a chef, but one is *born* knowing how to roast" is a proverb attributed to Brillat-Savarin. Someone at Zankou Chicken, who tends as many as 80 plump, juicy chickens rotating slowly in front of the bank of rotisseries, must have been born knowing how to roast. Whatever the secret, these crisp-skinned, golden birds bear no resemblance to supermarket barbecued chickens.

But the frosting on the cake—or in this case the chicken—is Zankou's incredibly fresh, slightly lemony garlic paste, which accompanies each order. You spread this over the hot chicken, then carve off slices of meat and crispy skin to eat between small pieces of pita bread. Since Zankou's opening in 1986, many have jumped on the Middle Eastern roast chicken bandwagon, but none can duplicate Zankou's famous sauce.

Zankou also serves juicy shawarma, shish kebab, and lule kebab on a plate or in a sandwich. Though commercially produced sujuk sausage is available, Zankou makes its own as part of a selection of meze.

Parking in Zankou's small Hollywood minimall lot is often impossible. But food this good is worth the hassle of finding a place on the street.

Falafel Arax, 5101 Santa Monica Boulevard, No. 2, Hollywood, CENTRAL, 213-663-9687. Open 10:00 A.M. to 9:00 P.M. daily. Lebanese friends say this bright, white fast-food shop in "Little Armenia" serves the best shawarma and falafel. But the shop also makes fine, Lebanese-style sandwiches using meze ingredients: juicy Armenian sujuk sausage, and thinly sliced basturma that, although often likened to pastrami, is much closer to the dry-cured Italian bresaola. Brains, so popular as meze, are arranged on a French roll, garnished only with a little fresh lemon juice and a drizzle of olive oil, then heated on a double grill—the kind used for grilled cheese sandwiches—until they're crispy and slightly flattened. Hot pickled peppers and torshi-left, a bright pink pickled turnip, come on the side. To go with these, order the tangy yogurt tahn to drink for a perfect combination.

Chicken Rotissary, 5658 Sepulveda Boulevard, Van Nuys, S.F. VALLEY, 818-781-0615. Open 10:00 A.M. to 10:00 P.M. daily. A number of Zankou chicken clones have surfaced in recent years. Most are poor substitutes for the real thing, but Chicken Rotissary, in the middle of the Valley, comes fairly close. The rotisserie-broiled chickens are crisp and juicy, and the garlic sauce—while not Zankou's—tops any other facsimiles I've tried. Rotissary has lots of other things going for it: excellent falafel and shawarma; a respectable lule kebab; the usual hummus, tabbouli, and mutabbal; and a large pleasant tiled dining area with plenty of parking close by.

Alwazir (6051 Hollywood Boulevard, No. 104, Hollywood, CENTRAL, 213-856-0660; open 10:00 A.M. to 10:00 P.M. daily) pays attention to little details. You won't always find babaghannouj so nice and smoky, or tabbouli packed with such fresh parsley and tasting of good olive oil, or borek stuffed with plenty of cheese or spinach. The real surprise is the stuffed kibbeh, which takes so much skill to prepare that Al Amir (see page 221) has a special kibbeh chef. Alwazir's kibbeh has a delicate, thin crust with a juicy, well-seasoned filling. All this great Lebanese-style food is dished up in a pristine, sparkling fast-food outlet.

♦ **LAHMAJUN**
Hagop Danaian (Uncle Jack's) 1108 N. Kenmore Street, Hollywood, CENTRAL, 213-664-8842. Open 7:00 A.M. to 6:00 P.M.; closed Sunday. Hagop Danaian, also known as "Uncle Jack," is the premier lahmajun baker in Los Angeles. You'll often see his product—which some call Armenian pizza—in the freezer cases of Middle Eastern markets and delis all

over the city. But you can get Uncle Jack's lahmajun hot and fresh right at the source: Hagop Danaian's No. I Lahmajun, a funky bakery that's an extension of a house. The thin-crusted bread rounds topped with tomatoey minced meat, lots of herbs, garlic, and minced bell peppers come in dozen and half-dozen stacks. Some people eat them on the spot rolled up like a burrito or folded into a half circle in the traditional way. Danaian also bakes the zatar bread that Armenians love for breakfast. This base like a pizza crust sprinkled with Middle Eastern thyme (zatar) and sumac, has a tart, earthy flavor. Typically zatar breads are eaten with chopped tomatoes and olives or with thin slices of onion strewn over the top—but you'll have to add these extras at home.

FALAFEL

Sometimes called the Israeli hot dog, falafel wrapped in pita with a smooth tahini sauce is sold from stands on almost every urban streetcorner in Israel. Falafel originated in Egypt in the days of the pharaohs and spread throughout neighboring Syria, Lebanon, and Israel. Each country has its own variation of these deep-fried fritters made from seasoned ground beans and herbs; Egyptian cooks use fava beans, while Israelis use chick-peas.

The best falafel places always make the fritters from dried beans that are not too old, rather than the packaged preseasoned mixes now on the market. Comparing falafel from a mix with freshly made falafel is like comparing dried instant soup with grandma's homemade version.

FALAFEL RESTAURANTS

Amer's Falafel, 17334 Ventura Boulevard, Encino, S.F. VALLEY, 818-995-6332. Lunch through dinner daily. There always seems to be a gaggle of young kids at Amer's, craning their necks over the counter to watch the cook flip the mashed chick-pea and parsley mixture from its mold into the sizzling oil. Pini and Shoshana, Amir's owners, make up batches of Middle Eastern salads every day: a Turkish salad of chopped tomato and parsley, a standout chopped eggplant salad with sweet red pepper, and the traditional hummus. The shawarma and kebabs are juicy here too, and so is a marinated grilled chicken breast in pita drizzled with creamy tahini sauce.

The Falafel Palace, 9255 Reseda Boulevard, Northridge, S.F. VALLEY, 818-993-0734. Open 10:00 A.M. to 10:00 P.M. daily. What California Pizza Kitchen does for the Italian pie, this place does for chick-pea fritters: It pushes the frontiers of the falafel sandwich. Falafel Palace serves the traditional falafel sandwich, but you can also satisfy any urge for novelty from a long list of specials—the avocado, mushroom, and cheese falafel; the artichoke and cheese falafel; or the tuna falafel. Shawarma sandwiches show the same Californiaesque bent; cheese shawarma might not be the choice of purists, but it's delicious. The Falafel Palace does the familiar array of Near Eastern salads and dips beautifully.

Falafel King, 10940 Weyburn Avenue, Westwood, WEST, 310-208-5782. Lunch through 1:00 A.M. daily. In the heart of Westwood Village, Falafel King bubbles over with a mixed bag of humanity: college students escaping the mystery meat in the dorm dining room, hordes of film enthusiasts fortifying themselves before standing in line at a dozen-odd movie houses, and window shoppers cruising Westwood. After 20 years in the same location, Falafel King has amassed a huge and loyal following. Especially popular is the plate of 6 kinds of Near Eastern salads with falafel or with still sizzling shawarma.

Noura Cafe, 8479 Melrose Avenue (at La Cienega), West Hollywood, WEST, 213-651-4581. Lunch through dinner; closed Sunday. Located among the chic designer home-decorating boutiques of West Hollywood, Noura is one of the better West L.A. places for freshly made falafel and for Middle Eastern salads, shawarma, and kebabs. The "taster's delight" for vegetarians is a well-filled plate of falafel, several salads (including marinated eggplant and mushroom), fried eggplant slices, and a stuffed grape leaf. Fresh-squeezed fruit juices, lemonade, and good cappuccino add to Noura's appeal. There's a pleasant plant-filled patio with a skylight, but parking in the area can be difficult. Most people call their order in ahead and make a quick escape.

Noura also owns the equally good **Eat a Pita** (465 N. Fairfax Avenue, Los Angeles, CENTRAL, 213-651-0188; lunch through dinner daily), a converted burger stand with a pleasant enclosed patio. For some reason the falafel seems even fresher and plumper here, even though Eat a Pita's menu is not as extensive as Noura's—there's only one kebab.

NEAR EASTERN SHOPS AND MARKETS

Panos Pastry, 5150 Hollywood Boulevard, Hollywood, CENTRAL, 213-661-0335, and 418 S. Central Avenue, Glendale, S.F. VALLEY, 818-502-0549. Open daily. Lebanese from Beirut know the Panos name and its Middle Eastern pastries; master baker Panos Zetlian owned a shop there for many years. His filo and kataif are unrivaled in Los Angeles and, I'd venture to say, al-

Top: Kataif bakes on the rotating copper grill at Panos Pastry. Above: Panos Zetlian, master Lebanese baker, displays his wares.

most anywhere else in the world.

Every morning under Zetlian's watchful eye, workers hand-stretch the filo that will soon be turned into light-as-air baklava in all its many forms (rolled, stacked, and "queen" style). Kataif, the most difficult pastry to make, starts with a smooth batter poured onto an udder-shaped container with a row of tiny holes at the bottom. It streams out onto a hot rotating circular griddle when the baker removes his finger; seconds later, the tiny strings of pastry are whisked, like tangled skeins of silk, from the grill. These will be tightly rolled around plump, meaty pista-

Top: Hand-rolling filo dough at Panos Pastry. Above: Handmade filo pastries emerge from the oven at Panos Pastry.

chios or layered with walnuts or rich pastry cream.

Panos's other passion is chocolate, and he makes exquisite French-style truffles and other bonbons. The exotic Middle Eastern ice cream in sahlab, pistachio, melon, and berry flavors is prepared on the premises.

Village Pastry, 1414 W. Kenneth Road, Glendale, S.F. VALLEY, 818-241-2521. Open 8:00 A.M. to 7:00 P.M.; closed Sunday. For more than 47 years, since baker Artavazd Mirzayan opened Village Pastry, the shop, now run by his son Jon, has been serving the Glendale Armenian enclave. Sweet

and savory baked goods from all over the Levant and Russia include bamieh and zulubia, those ultra sweet Persian syrup-soaked cakes shaped like fancy airy doughnuts. Persian-style crushed almond cookies made with egg white melt in your mouth. The Armenian cookies are studded with tiny black raisins, and a dense raisin loaf cake with walnuts is perfumed with a hint of orange.

For breakfast pick up gata, a slightly sweet, soft bun enclosed in a firmer dough, and nazuk, the same differently textured doughs in layers. Both are wonderful with a big cup of café au lait. Eastertime brings Russian-style *paskhas,* the tall, yeasted buttery sweet breads flavored with cardamom and orange peel. A favorite with regular customers are the large meat *pirozhki,* and *pirozhki* with chunks of potato and flecks of green onion. Village Pastry is known also for its rich whipped cream cakes layered with fresh berries or swirled into rolls.

The best new Armenian bakery, **Avo's Bakery** (6740 Reseda Boulevard, Reseda, S.F. VALLEY, 818-774-1032), has recently opened in the Valley. This place is a wonderland of Middle Eastern pastries and breads. Look for all sorts of handcrafted cookies, like the fat nut-filled *m'amool,* plus gata, nazuk and tahini bread.

Bezjian's Grocery Inc., 4725 Santa Monica Boulevard, Hollywood, CENTRAL, 213-663-1503. Open daily. For many years, Bezjian's has been the holy grail for any cook wanting to explore all the cuisines of the Near East and India. The shelves are a goldmine of hard-to-find ingredients, from Lebanese olive oil, hot *ajvar* peppers, and morello cherry preserves for Near Eastern dishes to Indian lime pickle, mango in oil, and asafetida for exotic Indian cooking. In the past, cooks with lists of ingredients and questions would consult Mrs. Bezjian, owner and cookbook author, who would dispense valuable advice.

The market is still in the family, though Alice, as Mrs. Bezjian was fondly known to all her followers, has retired. These days the market, which for many years baked fresh Armenian-style breads, lavash, pita, and Indian nan in its brick oven, has added a line of house-baked sourdough breads in an array of delectable flavors: round crisp-crusted loaves come studded with Kalamata olives or seasoned with rosemary or garlic. The sun-dried tomato with basil bread is a good seller. None of these contains any oil or shortening. And all the breads are stored on open shelves and never bagged until they are sold, to keep their texture perfect.

The lingering aroma of baking yeast dough will coax you toward the store's well-stocked deli case, where you'll find about 17 varieties of olives—the largest selection anywhere—from dark meaty Greeks and Peruvian alpozos to crunchy bitter Lebanese and wrinkly oil-cured Moroccans. For the meze table, the deli case holds Armenian sujuk sausage, basturma, and a wide range of cheeses: fetas, kashkavals, and the hard-to-find tennis-ball-size shanklish cheese, with a shaggy herb covering, to crumble into salads. More meze include eggplant salad and house-made borek.

Al Tayebat, 1217 S. Brookhurst Street, Anaheim, OCOUNTY, 714-520-4723. Open 9:00 A.M. to 7:00 P.M.; closed Sunday. Serious Middle Eastern cooks will want to know about Al Tayebat. The store's name means "wonderful things." It's fitting. For along with the usual array of Middle Eastern spices, grains, pickles, and exotic fruit syrups and preserves, Al Tayebat's meat and produce departments are particularly outstanding. Butchers make several kinds of Middle Eastern sausage, including *ma'ani* (a regional pronunciation of *naqaniq),* an allspice-seasoned lamb sausage studded with pine nuts. And their sujuk, a lightly cured Turkish- and Armenian-style beef sausage, is more moist than the commercially made kind. Kofta (minced meat) is seasoned to order for kebabs or to be baked.

The produce offerings change continually; in the proper season you'll find fresh (not dried) dates still in a bunch; white cherries and sour red cherries used for khoresh; yellow wax beans, tender baby fava beans that don't need peeling; and huge English butter gourds to stuff with meat and rice.

Cooks also single out the store for certain specialty items: Lebanese olive oil, Syrian olives, Middle Eastern fresh cheese for baking, and cheese marinated in oil with herbs Syrian style.

Hawthorne Market and International Grocery, 24202 Hawthorne Boulevard, Torrance, SOUTH, 310-373-4448. Open daily. This market has the most complete stock of Arab, Persian, and Afghani ingredients in the South Bay. Stocking the shelves are huge sacks of basmati rice, wheat kernels and various sizes of bulgur, cans of fool, packets of zatar, sumac, dried mint, and all kinds of Near Eastern breads.

For Persian dishes look for dried alabaloo (sour cherries), dried limes, and zereshk (tiny garnet barberries). For baking there's *mahleb,* and mastic, rose water, and orange flower water. And in the cooler you'll find various types of filo and kataif dough, and blocks of sweet butter for pastry making.

See also **Ron's Market** (page 203).

ISRAEL

I grew up in the neighborhood where Haifa now serves weekend cholent to transplanted Israelis. In those days the "Jewish" shops in the neighborhood were a kosher butcher, a good bakery that specialized in unseeded rye and challah, and a deli with an abbreviated Canter's deli-style menu—cheese blintzes, potato latkes, knishes and lox with cream cheese and bagels.

I always thought those Eastern European-style dishes were what all Jewish people ate until a boyfriend from Israel took me to a real Israeli restaurant: I tried my first falafel and hummus there, and ate the kind of dinners served at Habayit and Tempo—mainly all the Near Eastern basics from stuffed kibbeh and chopped eggplant salad with roasted peppers to grilled kebabs.

Our supply of true kosher restaurants (as opposed to kosher-style restaurants), those that observe kashrut—the Jewish dietary laws—is small. And most of these places don't serve "ethnic" Israeli food but rather international cooking—or even American food such as at the Kosher Colonel Chicken or Peking Tam's New York-style Chinese Kosher Restaurant. But Grill Express, Haifa, and Dizengoff are kosher and Israeli.

— ISRAELI GLOSSARY —

Challah: A traditional Jewish yeast bread rich with eggs.
Cholent: A hearty, long-cooking stew that includes meats, vegetables, and sometimes whole eggs and rice, typically served at midday on the Sabbath.
Knish: A savory pastry of Russian origin with fillings that might include potato, ground meat with buckwheat groats, or cheese.
Latkes: Savory pancakes usually made from grated potato and onion.
Saniyeh: Beef brisket baked with tahini sauce.
Shakshuka: A mixture of sautéed onions, peppers, and tomatoes topped with a fried egg, originally from Algeria and Morocco.

Habayit (11921 W. Pico Boulevard, West Los Angeles, WEST, 310-479-5444; open 10:00 A.M. to 10:00 P.M. daily) is the best place for superfresh Middle Eastern salads, excellent kibbeh, falafel, and satisfying homemade soups: white bean, lentil, and more. Homey entrées include stuffed Cornish game hen and chicken schnitzel.

Tempo, 16610 Ventura Boulevard, Encino, S.F. VALLEY, 818-905-5855. Lunch and dinner daily. A hangout for Valley Israelis, Tempo is part piano bar, part restaurant, and part sidewalk café. The most formal of the Israeli restaurants listed, it serves familiar Near Eastern fare. But besides the kebabs, shawarma, and stuffed grape leaves, the restaurant—with a nod to international cuisine—cooks orange roughy about half a dozen ways, including a peppery Cajun style and a dish called "orange roughy piccata."

KOSHER RESTAURANTS
Grill Express, 501 N. Fairfax Avenue, Los Angeles, CENTRAL, 213-665-0649. Lunch and dinner; closed Friday night and Saturday until sunset. Wonderful plates of cracked olives, pickled turnips, and cabbage arrive as soon as you're seated. At the Grill Express the main courses include huge platters of kebabs served with fresh vegetables; braised stuffed artichoke hearts; and shakshuka: fried eggs resting on a bed of slowly cooked onions, peppers, and tomatoes.

Haifa, 8717 W. Pico Boulevard, West Los Angeles, WEST, 310-550-2704. And 15464 Ventura Boulevard, Sherman Oaks, S.F. VALLEY, 818-995-7325. Open 9:00 A.M. to 10:00 P.M.; closed Friday night and Saturday. Haifa, a Glat kosher restaurant, has now sprouted a branch in the Valley and aficionados say its even better than the older Pico Boulevard restaurant. Besides the familiar Near Eastern salads and kebabs, an unusually good specialty is the saniyeh, brisket baked with tahini sauce. The traditional Sabbath meal cholent—a long simmered stew of meat, beans, vegetables, and hard-cooked egg—is served here on Sunday.

Dizengoff, 8103½ Beverly Boulevard, West Hollywood, WEST, 213-651-4465. Lunch Monday to Friday and Sunday; dinner nightly. Named after a famous boulevard in Tel Aviv, Dizengoff does the popular Near Eastern favorites, as well as smatterings of the sort of dishes brought by Europeans to Israel: chicken schnitzel, moussaka, goulash, and nondairy Bavarian cream. Lemony, garlic-laced baked chicken and other entrées come with rice topped with a small pile of garlicky stewed white beans and a refreshing chopped vegetable salad. Pickled turnips and a spicy Yemenite sauce made with hot peppers, fresh coriander, and lots of garlic are always on the tables.

GREECE

— GREEK GLOSSARY —

Bakaliaros: Dried codfish.
Dolmas: Grape leaves stuffed with seasoned rice, or with a meat and rice mixture.

Kasseri: A cheese similar to provolone or mozzarella.
Kefalotiri: A medium-hard ewe's milk cheese.

Keftedhes: *Meatballs.*
Kourabiedes: *S-shaped butter cookies coated in powdered sugar.*
Lakerdes: *Salt-cured bonito eaten as an appetizer.*
Loukanika: *A sausage flavored with orange peel and fennel.*
Loukoumi: *Jelled fruit candies coated in starch and powdered sugar.*
Mizithra: *A whey cheese similar to ricotta when soft and used for grating when aged.*
Moussaka: *A dish made by layering meat, eggplant, tomatoes, and topped with a custardlike cheese mixture.*
Pastitsio: *The lasagna of Greece—macaroni and meat with a cheese-custard topping.*

Retsina: *Greek wine treated with pine tree resin. Its turpentinelike flavor is an acquired taste.*
Saganaki: *Sliced kasseri cheese fried in butter and olive oil and set aflame at the table. Recently, other flamed foods such as shrimp have also taken the name.*
Souvlaki: *Marinated, grilled skewered meat cubes.*
Spanakopita: *A flaky pastry filled with spinach and feta cheese.*
Taramasalata: *Carp roe blended with bread, olive oil, and lemon juice to make a dip.*
Tzatziki: *A side dish of yogurt-dressed sliced or shredded cucumbers.*

RESTAURANTS

Sofi Estiatorion, 8030¾ W. 3rd Street, Los Angeles, WEST, 213-651-0346. Lunch Monday to Saturday; dinner nightly. The courtyard at Sofi, with its tree-and-vine-shaded trellises and filtered sunlight, resembles the one in which I ate my first home-cooked Greek meal. My companion and I had given up on the Corfu bus service, and we had the good fortune to be offered a lift to our pension by a doctor and his wife—with an unexpected stop-off for supper at her mother's. It's not just Sofi's courtyard that brings back those times, it's the taste of her kitchen's uncompromisingly Greek home-style food. It must remind Greeks of their homeland too; a good deal of the clientele is Greek.

Sofi's recipes are based on those she learned from her mother's family; her aunts and grandmother, she says, were all superb cooks. She studied pharmacology and medicine at UCLA, but her nostalgia for home inspired her to open the restaurant, which Konstantin Konstantinidis, her architect husband, has imbued with an understated European elegance. Light woods, a few well-placed museum-quality artifacts, and several levels of seating make diners feel as if they are in a home.

Many dishes will be familiar to lovers of Greek food. But others, such as the *kakavia* (a seafood soup with fresh herbs and vegetables) and *patzari* (diced fresh beets with walnuts in a garlic-laced yogurt), are straight off the family table.

Papadakis Taverna, 301 W. 6th Street, San Pedro, SOUTH, 310-548-1186. Dinner nightly; lunch Fridays. At one of L.A.'s first Athenian-style tavernas, there is still much enthusiastic hand-clapping, cheek-kissing, and a concern for customers having a good time. The hoopla and the opahs have been more subdued in recent years, the novelty of plate throwing and glass smashing having worn off. But the restaurant is still full of infectious gaiety and warmth.

And Papadakis's Greek dishes go beyond the generic souvlaki and dolmas menu. White veal fillet with kasseri cheese in pastry and a creamy basil sauce; a saddle of lamb, also pastry-wrapped; and huge meaty shrimp in a tomato wine sauce are a little fancier than your average taverna grub. There's retsina, but also an ample collection of California wines. And the waiters still break into song as they bring on Bacchanalian-sized servings of food.

Corfu, 1383 Westwood Boulevard, West Los Angeles, WEST, 310-479-8892. Lunch Monday through Friday; dinner nightly. The food at Corfu, a quintessential mom-and-pop taverna, tastes as though *mitera* and *patera* have plenty of cooking experience. The only problem I have with this place is their remodeling job. They painted over the wonderfully corny mural of Corfu and hung mediocre art in its place.

But Corfu's food is a result of caring, from-scratch cooking: The kitchen blends its own tarama, the carp roe, bread, and olive oil dip, and makes an egg-rich, lemony avgolemono soup based on a long simmered chicken broth. Vegetarian customers are catered to with a nonmeat moussaka. At dinner, a plate of tiny grilled lamb chops is cooked rare, if you request it, and comes with delicious roasted potatoes. *Kleftiko,* piquant marinated and roasted spring lamb—deemed "world famous" on the menu—is just as good. The fish, which varies from day to day, is always fresh.

Joseph's Cafe, 1775 N. Ivar Avenue, Hollywood, CENTRAL, 213-462-8697. Breakfast, lunch, and dinner; closed Sunday. This revamped 1940s coffee shop, whose prices hark back to another era, serves pancakes and bacon, saganaki, souvlaki, and Sparta beer. Except for the American breakfast items and standard coffee-shop

sandwiches, you'll recognize most of the dishes as Greek. The chicken shish kebab is marinated in homemade yogurt; ground veal patties come sprinkled with fresh-snipped parsley; and spanakopita, an unbelievably crispy filo wrapping is stuffed with plenty of spinach and feta cheese. The juices are freshly squeezed, and the French fries are freshly cut too. Regulars might dine at the counter but there's also a huge, very blue back room with one wall painted to resemble the Aegean Sea.

Cafe Athens, 1000 Wilshire Boulevard, Santa Monica, WEST, 310-395-1000. Dinner nightly; lunch Monday through Friday. An updated designer Greek taverna. The huge pictures of famous Greeks, with color-coordinated inscriptions of their names, show a graphic designer's hand in composing this large room. But Cafe Athens's singing and dancing waiters, for all their effervescence, don't seem to engage the jaded West Side crowd, who appear more interested in the baby octopus salad, the Cognac-flamed cheese, and the chopped peasant salad in a light Mediterranean vinaigrette. This is definitely not mom and pop's cuisine, although you can get keftedhes, hummus, and moussaka. Among the nouveau dishes are an herb-and-lemon-rubbed rack of baby lamb; deep-fried battered squid reminiscent of tempura; and grilled Greek lamb sausages with oven-roasted potatoes.

The Great Greek (13362 Ventura Boulevard, Sherman Oaks, S.F. VALLEY, 818-905-5250; lunch and dinner daily) is another, earlier Greek rendition from the owners of Cafe Athens. But here the dancing waiters are more successful at getting the clientele into the aisles. The mood and the decor—old Greek newspapers collaged onto the walls and photos of Greek luminaries—work in this

Waiters take to the dance floor at Cafe Athens.

Valley location. A party-time atmosphere prevails. Fans of the Great Greek love the joyous music and expertly performed and sometimes intricate Greek dancing, especially after a few ouzos. The menu is almost identical to that of Cafe Athens in Santa Monica, with a few of the fancier items (like the pasta sauced with lobster in cream) omitted.

Marathon, 1064 E. Broadway, Long Beach, SOUTH, 310-437-6346. Lunch and dinner; closed Monday. One of the handful of good old ethnic standbys in Long Beach, Marathon has been dishing up souvlaki for more than 25 years. This is a kitchen with plenty of soul, and even better, plenty of skill. Nothing is fancy, but the vegetables that come with your meal are fresh and chunky and not cooked to mush. The rice is perfectly firm, and the moussaka—rich layers of meat and eggplant—holds its form. Some have dubbed Marathon ''home of the combination plate,'' because there are a dozen dinners that combine two entrées—veal in wine sauce with pastitsio, for example. Each dinner is served with fresh soup, a Greek salad, taramasalata, tzatziki, and bread, and each costs under $10. Marathon's dining room, while not from the pages of *Architectural Digest,* is comfortably formal, and next door is a take-out area more like a coffee shop.

Alexis' (9034 Tampa Avenue, Northridge, S.F. VALLEY, 818-349-9689; lunch and dinner; closed Sunday) started out almost 20 years ago as a market and deli combined, serving the only respectable Greek food in this section of the Valley. In those days there were only a few tables. But chef Alexis Kavvadias's fans would come early for one of them, and if you got there late it meant a long wait or take-out. Roast shoulder of lamb in its own juices, stuffed grape leaves under a lemony sauce, and anything made with homemade yogurt are among the many dishes worth the wait.

In recent years Alexis abandoned its market to expand the restaurant substantially; some say the food isn't as good as it used to be. I still think there's much on this menu worth notice, especially the roasted and grilled meat dishes served with potatoes roasted in butter and good olive oil, and the shrimp saganaki with feta cheese and fresh tomatoes. In the grand style of Greek dining there's a 17-course dinner. You're served a meze of a dozen appetizers—including most of the usual Greek menu stalwarts—and an entrée platter with roast lamb, beef kebabs, pastitsio, moussaka, and rice or potatoes and vegetables.

Le Petit Greek, 127 N. Larchmont Boulevard, Los Angeles, CENTRAL, 213-464-5160. Lunch and dinner Tuesday through Saturday; Sunday dinner only; closed Monday. Opinions vary markedly regarding this upscale restaurant. Some rave about its refined Greek cooking. Others find it too "de-ethnicized." The stark white-washed stucco dining room with sophisticated black and white photographs on the walls and a back-lit designer floral arrangement in a small alcove set the tone. It's not the sort of place where people get up and dance. The food, too, is most untavernalike, although you will find excellent versions of moussaka and souvlaki (called simply "kebabs" on this menu). One specialty, chicken Olympia, combines gently melting feta, roasted peppers, and chicken seasoned with minced fresh coriander, all wrapped in crispy filo pastry. Served only at lunchtime, "Le Petit Greek Special" is another filo-wrapped extravaganza that layers turkey, ham, mortadella, and Greek cheeses with spinach.

All this is skillfully prepared, as are the several fresh fish dishes offered each day. What I miss is the rich, fishy flavor of *taramasalata* in the Petit Greek's fluffy pink version; you can barely taste the roe. And there's no wonderfully garlicky, greasy roast chicken like the ones most mom-and-pop places serve.

SHOPS

C&K Importing Co., 2771 W. Pico Boulevard, Los Angeles, CENTRAL, 213-737-2970 or 737-2880. Closed Monday. The tiny café next door to C&K sells L.A.'s best Greek take-out food. The souvlaki gets a light grilling before being folded into thick Greek-style pita (imported from Chicago) and dabbed with a garlicky yogurt sauce. Lean lamb and chicken kebabs marinated in lemon may be had this way too, or on a plate with a mound of rice and Greek salad. There's also a juicy Greek burger.

The market itself, started by present owner Chrys Chrys's father, has served the community since 1948. Many of C&K's long-time customers have been ordering their whole baby lamb or their *loukanika* (sausage made with wine, orange peel, and an hint of fennel seed) since the time that the store

Provisions from Greece, the Middle East, and Ethiopia at C&K Importing Co.

bordered a Greek community. The Greek Orthodox Church is just a stone's throw away. And on Sundays, even before the last bell has tolled at the end of services, a stream of regulars is stocking up on buttery kourabiedes cookies, the jewellike loukoumi fruit candies, and the shop's ready-to-cook homemade spinach-filled spanakopitas or cheese-filled *tiropites*.

In the freezer you'll find lean slices of lamb leg and other cuts for Greek dishes. Of course, there are olives, breads, and several varieties of filo dough. On hand are bakaliaros (dried codfish) for cooking and lakerdes (salt-cured fillet of bonito), to be served with lemon juice and a drizzle of olive oil. For meze, there's tarama and a wonderful selection of Greek cheeses: mountain kasseri, hard and soft mizithra (a kind of Greek ricotta), and sheep's milk kefalotiri for grating or for cutting into cubes and grilling, then serving with a squeeze of lemon.

C&K also has a full line of Ethiopian and Middle Eastern groceries and an excellent selection of international wines.

S&J Importing Co., 1770 Pacific Avenue, Long Beach, SOUTH, 310-599-1341 or 774-9525. Closed Monday. An importer and distributor of Greek, Arabic, and Balkan foods, S&J is particularly well known for its own filo dough, which it sells unfrozen. The white-labeled Long Beach brand is sturdier and better for making *borek*, chefs say, while the more delicate Omega brand is better for sweet pastries.

The company has long had a retail store, and its excellent prices on Greek olives, olive oils, and Greek and Balkan cheeses attracted a large ethnic population from the Long Beach area. The neighborhood has changed, but customers still travel from all over the city for S&J's impressive range of grains, beans, flours, and spices for all types of Near Eastern cooking. Look for zatar, Greek oregano on the stem, molukhia for soups and casseroles, mahleb for baking, mastic, kashk, and all kinds of nuts. There's also a deli case with sausages, cured meats, and fish, as well as Greek and Yugoslavian fruit preserves and estate-bottled Greek and Yugoslavian wines.

MOROCCO AND TUNISIA

Morocco and Tunisia keep up the medieval Persian culinary tradition of using spices liberally. Not as liberally as India, of course, but the cuisine is rich and perfumy, almost dreamlike, marked by stews in which meat is cooked until it falls off the bone, and a distinctive repertoire of filo pastries including the giant chicken pie, bestila.

Only a few ingredients are unique to North Africa: couscous, the steamed grain product; harisa, the spicy sauce; and the peppery spice mixture ras el hanut. As a result, shopping for North African cooking means going to Near Eastern markets for staples such as olives, and to Indian import stores for spices. —C.P.

— MOROCCAN AND TUNISIAN —
— GLOSSARY —

Baklava: See page 220.
Bestila: A large filo-dough-crusted pie of chicken or pigeon, eggs, and ground almonds sprinkled with powdered sugar and cinnamon.
Brik (Tunisian): A semolina crêpe with various stuffings and an egg folded inside.
Harira: A lentil soup made with lamb stock.
Harisa: This traditional accompaniment to couscous dishes in Morocco and Tunisia is a hot chile paste that includes garlic, cumin, and other spices. It can be purchased in Middle Eastern markets and some Italian grocery stores.
Ras el hanut: An all-purpose dry Moroccan seasoning mixture composed chiefly of hot red pepper, cinnamon, cloves, and black pepper. Available in tins in Middle Eastern stores.
Tajines: Moroccan stews, often mixtures of fruit and meat, slow-cooked in special earthenware pots with conical lids.

RESTAURANTS

In the late 1970s, Moroccan food swept into Los Angeles when Pierre Dupart built the enormously successful Dar Maghreb. A few other restaurants followed its successful format, which has barely changed since. What you got at these places, and still do, is the whole Moroccan enchilada—reclining on pillows while eating with your fingers or with anise bread from a low table, accompanied by the swish of a belly dancer's skirts.

Dar Maghreb, 7651 Sunset Boulevard, Hollywood, CENTRAL, 213-876-7651. Dinner nightly. In the Maghreb—as North Africa is called by its inhabitants—white-domed Islamic architecture is a familiar sight. And on Sunset Boulevard, the Islamic-style white-domed building housing Dar Maghreb, the city's most opulent Moroccan restaurant, has become a landmark that some have called "Hollywood ethnic." You enter a cool, ornately tiled courtyard with a central pool reminiscent of those late-1930s Foreign Legion movie sets. Inside the cool recesses of the imposing building, hand-painted tiles, pillowed benches, and fez-wearing costumed waiters complete the effect. Fortunately, there's more than illusion to the fantasy. Dar Maghreb's food, though fairly standard now that other restaurants have copied its menu format, is well prepared. Groups, however, must order one of the set menus for the whole table—a system that is likely to cause discontent among those who have their heart set on a favorite dish that isn't on the chosen dinner.

Koutoubia, 2116 Westwood Boulevard, West Los Angeles, WEST, 310-475-0729. Dinner only; closed Monday. As you would expect from a Moroccan restaurant, Koutoubia is ornately exotic, with a tented ceiling, and sofa-sized puffy pillows on which to recline. But belly dancing is only occasional, allowing you to concentrate on your *diffa* (Moroccan for meal).

Koutoubia goes beyond the familiar prix fixe meals. Chef-owner Michel Ohayon's varied daily specials and adventurous à la carte dishes delve more deeply into the mysteries of this flamboyant cuisine.

Ohayon is a chef who cures his own pink olives, after waiting to obtain them when they reach a stage between green and ripe; these are strewn generously into a lamb tajine. He preserves his own lemons, which are also used in tajines, and makes a delicate mint-laced duck-and-chicken sausage to serve on lettuce leaves with a spicy dipping sauce.

Other dishes offer more insights into Moroccan cooking: 5 different styles of couscous; sea bass seasoned with a garlic, coriander, and paprika mixture surrounded by roasted red chiles; brains gently poached and served in a lemony coriander sauce; and crisp-skinned roasted squab.

Babouch Moroccan, 810 S. Gaffey, San Pedro, SOUTH, 310-831-0246. Dinner Tuesday to Sunday. At Babouch, a family-owned place, Youssef Keroles is the chef while his brother Kamal runs the dining room. Babouch has the expected *Thousand and One Nights* ambience, including a belly dancer and a predining hand-washing ceremony, but it lacks the formula feeling sometimes present in Moroccan restaurants.

Part of this is because people dining together here aren't required to eat the same dishes. The regular dinner, for example, offers a choice from 9 entrées. Each dinner starts with gently spiced harira—the lamb-based lentil soup with which Muslims end their Ramadan fast—and a cumin-laced salad. The appetizer bestila is a "pie" of richly stewed chicken, egg, and almonds imbued with cinnamon and encased in crispy, paper-thin layers of pastry sprinkled with powdered sugar: all the elements that made Persia's royal cuisine so seductive. Your entrée might be chicken stewed with preserved lemons; vegetable or lamb couscous; lamb stewed with prunes; or rabbit simmered in paprika. And there are changing daily specials.

Marrakesh, 13003 Ventura Boulevard, Studio City, S.F. VALLEY, 818-788-6354. Dinner nightly. In a series of tented rooms to which a belly dancer will come at your request, Marrakesh offers 4 well-priced Moroccan feasts. What you can't guess by reading the menu is that dishes listed simply as salads turn out to be major extravaganzas—a tray full of vegetable dishes including marinated carrots flavored with ginger and cumin; a little mountain of diced, spiced tomato and cucumber; and a well-seasoned eggplant made with parsley and cilantro. Dinners include bestila and a choice of entrée: couscous, rabbit simmered in a peppery sauce, or quail. All end with a huge bowl of fresh fruit, nuts and baklava. Marrakesh has two other branches in La Mesa and Newport Beach; each has a different menu.

Moun of Tunis, 7445½ Sunset Boulevard, Hollywood, CENTRAL, 213-874-3333. Dinner nightly. Tunisian food is very close to what you find in Morocco. There are tajines in conical-topped ceramic dishes, couscous prepared many ways, and harisa, a searingly hot chile paste, which Tunisians use more liberally than Moroccans.

At Moun of Tunis the differences between Moroccan and Tunisian food are only slightly apparent. From a series of 7 set meals, your table may choose anything from the inexpensive 4-course couscous feast to a special feast of the day.

Each meal begins with a strictly Tunisian specialty, brik, a thin griddle-baked semolina pastry sheet into which various fillings (in this case potatoes and onions) topped with a raw egg are folded. The egg inside cooks when the brik is fried. The salads with each meal are similar to Moroccan ones but have their own flavorings. A carrot salad, for example, is grated and flavored with rose water. You'll also find the entrées very close to Moroccan dishes, with slightly different flavorings. Moun of Tunis is more modest in decor and price than other North African restaurants.

ETHIOPIA

In an attempt to give the Ethiopian community more visibility, the Ethiopian Restaurant Association—L.A. does have such a thing—urged its members to relocate to Fairfax Avenue near Olympic. The Fairfax Ethiopian district now boasts a variety of restaurants, a market, and several other businesses. It's similar to the Ethiopian enclave on 18th Street in Washington, D.C.

Ethiopia is a mostly Christian country and was not part of the medieval Islamic culinary world. Its cooking is similar to Morocco's though: rich and perfumy, but a little more earthy. Of the many spices it uses, the dominant note is cardamom—Ethiopia has several native varieties. Berberé, an intricate blend of ground chiles and a host of spices, is the major flavoring in many dishes. Most meals include spicy stews known as *wot's*, and are served in a strikingly exotic way, on chewy, millet crêpes called injera that serve as both plate and napkin: You tear off a swatch of injera and use it to pick up your food and to mop up the delicious Ethiopian sauces. Injera must be eaten very fresh, and it is tricky to make. Anybody who enjoys this cuisine and wants to cook it at home can breathe a sigh of relief now that this unusual bread is available ready-made. —C.P.

— *ETHIOPIAN GLOSSARY* —

Awazé: One of Ethiopia's trilogy of hot pepper mixtures, awazé is a blend of chiles, garlic, red onion, and numerous spices in a paste or powder.

Berberé: The most complex of Ethiopia's seasoning mixes used in many wot's and t'ibs, berberé is based on hot red pepper and includes rue seed, sacred basil, and bishop's weed.

Doro wot': A spicy chicken stew made with berberé and nit'r k'ibé.

Dulet: A honeycomb tripe stew.

Firfir (also fitfit): A dish made with pieces of injera mixed with a spicy wot'.

Injera: This huge washclothlike pancake-bread, Ethiopia's staff of life, is usually made from a native millet called teff in Ethiopia. Here it is often made with wheat and buckwheat flours.

Jabana: A special ceramic coffeepot used for making Ethiopian-style coffee.

Kitfo: This steak tartare of Ethiopia is lean minced beef flavored with nit'r k'ibé and hot pepper.

Mit'mit'a: The hottest among the spice mixes, mit'mit'a is also the least complex, relying primarily on red pepper, cardamon, and salt for its flavor.

Nit'r k'ibé: Seasoned clarified butter.

Quanta: Spicy dried beef.

Sambusa: A pastry turnover filled with meat or lentils and hot chiles.

T'ej: Ethiopian mead wine made from honey.

Tere sega: Cubes of raw beef served with awazé.

T'ibs: Complexly seasoned dry cooked meat.

Wot': Stew, the backbone of most Ethiopian meals. Wot's may be made with meats or with vegetables and legumes.

RESTAURANTS

Keste Demena, 5779 W. Venice Boulevard, Los Angeles, CENTRAL, 213-937-5144. Lunch and dinner daily. Outside the Fairfax enclave, Keste Demena, with its modest travel-poster decor, comes highly recommended by Ethiopians. Its food makes liberal use of berberé, mit'mit'a, and awazé. These three spice blends, all with loads of hot dry pepper, and a long list of other exotic spices—including bishop's weed and plenty of cardamom—are basic to Ethiopian cooking. Doro wot', the national chicken stew simmered with berberé and a seasoned butter called nit'r k'ibé, is not for the timid of tongue. Keste Demena cooks up other wot's of all kinds: yesega wot' with beef and yemiser wot' with lentils to eat with the washclothlike injera.

Because Ethiopians fast, and because they avoid eating meat almost 200 days a year, Ethiopian cooks have developed many vegetarian preparations. Keste Demena excels in these, calling them "scrumptious vegetarian entrées." One particularly good dish is a red lentil salad, crunchy with minced fresh chiles and shallots. Most of the vegetable dishes may be had without butter or oil on request.

But Ethiopians love meat, and raw is one of their favorite ways to eat it. For true carnivores there is tere sega, cubes of raw beef served with a scorching hot awazé dipping sauce—a carpaccio of sorts. On weekends Keste Demena offers Ethiopian-style breakfast dishes.

Rosalind's, 1044 S. Fairfax Avenue, Los Angeles, CENTRAL, 213-936-2486. Lunch through dinner daily. Of the restaurants in the Ethiopian townlet along Fairfax, Rosalind's has the most varied menu, in that it serves both Ethiopian and West African dishes.

All sorts of Ethiopian wot's include yeduba wot', with chunks of pumpkin, and yemiser wot', a spicy lentil stew. Several dishes called t'ibs, unlike the stews, are dry-cooked with seasonings. The most popular of these, *adulis tib's*, is made with beef and is served in a special charcoal-fired pot.

But the unique dishes here are from the West African states and Central Africa. *Ojojo,* or meat and vegetable meatballs, arrives with *pili pili,* a chile-laced dipping sauce that's sure to call your taste buds to attention. Garnishing the plate are plantains and patties of ground deep-fried black-eyed peas. The fascinating menu works its way through the African states offering groundnut (peanut) stew, a rich peanut sauce simmered with beef and chicken; Niger-style goat; Sierra Leone–style beef in a complex peppery sauce; and Senegalese lemon-marinated broiled chicken served with additional lemon sauce as a garnish. These dishes come with rice and a rather Californiaized "jungle salad," something I don't think they do back in West Africa. On weekends Rosalind's offers live African music.

Blue Nile, 1066–70 S. Fairfax Avenue, Los Angeles, CENTRAL, 213-933-0960 or 933-0588. Open 10:00 A.M. to 11:00 P.M. daily. The Blue Nile, which used to be on Washington Boulevard, is just up the street from Rosalind's. Ethiopians say the seasonings are toned down to cater to American tastes. But the sambusa appetizer—a beef turnover laced with minced green chiles that made my mascara run—wasn't all that mild. Blue Nile's wot's, however, are definitely mellowed out a bit. Although forks are offered on request, eating with cutlery would be a shame, because half the fun of Ethiopian food is being allowed to lick your fingers in public.

Ethiopian coffee comes with great ceremony in a ceramic carafe called a jabana, served on a tray with burning incense; you drink the thick, dark spiced liquid in tiny cups. Blue Nile also, as do many Ethiopian places, offers t'ej—or mead—a wine fermented from Ethiopia's famous honey.

There are even a few pasta dishes here, including lasagna with garlic bread—a reminder of the years when Ethiopia was occupied by Italy.

Messob, 1041 S. Fairfax Avenue, Los Angeles, CENTRAL, 213-938-8827. Open 9:00 A.M. to 10:00 P.M. daily. Across the street from Rosalind's and the Blue Nile, Messob, an Ethiopian café and hangout, isn't as splashy as those larger restaurants. In its homey booths you can try out Ethiopian-style breakfasts until 11:30 A.M.

It's also a good place to sample kitfo, the steak tartare of Ethiopia, which blends mit'mit'a and nit'r k'ibé. Several firfir dishes, based on injera torn into pieces then mixed with chicken or beef wot', are unique here. And on weekends Messob makes dulet: honeycomb tripe minced with beef and liver, and cooked with onions and the spiced butter mit'mit'a.

Walia, 5881 W. Pico Boulevard, Los Angeles, CENTRAL, 213-933-1215. Dinner nightly. Not on Fairfax but close enough to Ethiopian Town, Walia is one of the city's oldest Ethiopian restaurants. Its thatched hut decor is divided into intimate booths. Combination dinners called *beyaynetu* are an excellent way to experiment. The "B" beyaynetu gives you a beef wot', a boneless sautéed chicken t'ibs, a variety of cooked vegetable dishes, and salad, along with injera that comes rolled up like those washcloths in a sushi bar. There's also a vegetarian combination meal, Ethiopian coffee, and beers.

SHOPS

Merkato, 1036½ S. Fairfax Avenue, Los Angeles, CENTRAL, 213-935-1775. Open daily and evenings. No trip to Ethiopian Fairfax would be complete without a visit to Merkato, a small market with all the ingredients you'll need for Ethiopian cooking. Stacks of injera flank the deli case, and other Ethiopian breads include flat, round chewy loaves made from wheat and semolina. Merkato has on hand three "convenience" foods used for Ethiopian cooking. In the past, if you wanted to cook an Ethiopian meal you'd have to begin by tracking down a bevy of unfamiliar spices and grind them all together in a stone mortar with plenty of hot peppers. Now you can use the spice blends sold here: *berberé, mit'mit'a,* and awazé, as well as prepared nit'r k'ibé. Merkato also has quanta—a

spicy beef jerky eaten in Ethiopia as a snack—and Ethiopian beer and wine. The colorful shop is full of artwork and artifacts, and has a rack of beautiful American women's clothing for sale. And perhaps most important for Ethiopian food buffs, there is an Ethiopian cookbook in English.

C&K Importing Co. (see page 234) on Pico Boulevard also sells a complete line of Ethiopian spices and ingredients, plus Ethiopian *harrar* coffee, the special coffeepots called jabana, and Ethiopian handwoven basket tables in various sizes. In the freezer, look for uncooked sambusa, the very spicy meat or lentil appetizer turnovers, to bake at home. C&K also sells fresh injera.

Ethiopian injera and a typical Ethiopian basket-weave table for sale at C&K Importing Co.

City Index

Alhambra, SAN GABRIEL VALLEY
Anaheim, OCOUNTY
Artesia, SOUTH
Bell, EAST OF L.A.
Bellflower, SOUTH
Beverly Hills, WEST
Boyle Heights, CENTRAL
Brentwood, WEST
Buena Park, OCOUNTY
Burbank, S.F. VALLEY
Canoga Park, S.F. VALLEY
Carson, SOUTH
Cerritos, SOUTH
Chatsworth, S.F. VALLEY
Chinatown, CENTRAL
Costa Mesa, OCOUNTY
Covina, EAST OF L.A.
Culver City, WEST
Duarte, SAN GABRIEL VALLEY
Eagle Rock, CENTRAL
East Los Angeles, EAST OF L.A.
El Monte, SAN GABRIEL VALLEY
Encino, S.F. VALLEY
Garden Grove, OCOUNTY
Gardena, SOUTH
Glendale, S.F. VALLEY
Harbor City, SOUTH
Hawthorne, SOUTH
Hermosa Beach, SOUTH
Highland Park, CENTRAL
Hollywood, CENTRAL
Huntington Park, EAST OF L.A.
Inglewood, SOUTH
Koreatown, CENTRAL
Lakewood, SOUTH
Lawndale, SOUTH
Little Tokyo, CENTRAL
Lomita, SOUTH
Long Beach, SOUTH
Los Angeles, part CENTRAL,
   part WEST

Lynwood, SOUTH
Marina Del Rey, WEST
Montebello, EAST OF L.A.
Monterey Park, SAN GABRIEL
   VALLEY
North Hollywood, S.F. VALLEY
Northridge, S.F. VALLEY
Norwalk, SOUTH
Pacific Palisades, WEST
Pacoima, S.F. VALLEY
Panorama City, S.F. VALLEY
Pasadena, SAN GABRIEL VALLEY
Pico Rivera, EAST OF L.A.
Pomona, EAST OF L.A.
Rancho Palos Verdes, SOUTH
Reseda, S.F. VALLEY
Rosemead, SAN GABRIEL VALLEY
Rowland Heights, EAST OF L.A.
San Gabriel, SAN GABRIEL VALLEY
San Marino, SAN GABRIEL VALLEY
San Pedro, SOUTH
Santa Ana, OCOUNTY
Santa Monica, WEST
Sepulveda, S.F. VALLEY
Sherman Oaks, S.F. VALLEY
Silverlake, CENTRAL
Studio City, S.F. VALLEY
Tarzana, S.F. VALLEY
Temple City, SAN GABRIEL VALLEY
Toluca Lake, S.F. VALLEY
Torrance, SOUTH
Van Nuys, S.F. VALLEY
Venice, WEST
West Covina, EAST OF L.A.
West Hollywood, WEST
West Los Angeles, WEST
Westlake Village, S.F. VALLEY
Westminster, OCOUNTY
Westwood, WEST
Wilmington, SOUTH
Woodland Hills, S.F. VALLEY

Geographical Index

CENTRAL

Belizean
Mika's (Los Angeles), 182
Pelican Belizean Restaurant (Los Angeles), 182
Prado (Los Angeles), 182
Tracy's Place (Los Angeles), 182

British
Cat & Fiddle Pub and Restaurant (Hollywood), 206

Chinese/Asian Shops and Markets
Ai Hoa Supermarket (Chinatown), 34
Canton Poultry (Chinatown), 35
Cathay Supermarket (Los Angeles), 97, 113
Family Pastry (Chinatown), 31–32
Hong Kong Supermarket (Chinatown), 33–34
Man Wah Market (Chinatown), 33
99 Ranch Market (Chinatown), 32–33
Shang Lee Poultry (Chinatown), 35
Sun Long Tea (Chinatown), 33, 34
Superior Poultry (Chinatown), 35
United Foods Company (Chinatown), 35

Chinese Restaurants
A B C Seafood (Chinatown), 21
Empress Pavilion (Chinatown), 19–20
Fortune (Chinatown), 20
Full House Seafood (Chinatown), 20–21
Green Jade (Chinatown), 13
Hop Li (Chinatown), 20
Hunan Taste (Los Angeles), 31
Kim Chuy (Chinatown), 25

Luk Yue (Chinatown), 25–26
Mandarin Deli (Chinatown and Little Tokyo), 24–25
Mandarin Shanghai (Chinatown), 7
May Flower (Chinatown), 26–27
Mon Kee (Chinatown), 21
Ocean Seafood (Chinatown), 20
V B C Seafood (Chinatown), 21

Ethiopian/African
Blue Nile (Los Angeles), 240
Keste Demena (Los Angeles), 239
Merkato (Los Angeles), 240–41
Messob (Los Angeles), 240
Rosalind's (Los Angeles), 239–40
Walia (Los Angeles), 240

Filipino Shops and Markets
Goldilocks (Los Angeles), 127–28
Lorenzana Market (Los Angeles), 129
Masagana (Los Angeles), 129
Red Ribbon Bake Shop (Hollywood), 128

Filipino Restaurants
Barrio Fiesta (Los Angeles), 125
Emmanuel's (Los Angeles), 126
Jeepney Grill (Koreatown), 127
Little Quiapo (Los Angeles), 125–26
Mami King (Los Angeles), 126
Manila Sunset (Los Angeles), 127

German
Red Lion Tavern (Silverlake), 197

Greek
C&K Importing Co. (Los Angeles), 234–35, 241
Joseph's Cafe (Hollywood), 232
Petit Greek Restaurant, Le (Los Angeles), 233–34

Hungarian
Hungarian Budapest (Los
	Angeles), 201–2

Indian and Pakistani
Anarkali (Los Angeles), 139
Clay Pit, The (Los Angeles), 134
East India Grill (Los Angeles), 135
Mumtaz (Los Angeles), 136
Paru's (Hollywood), 137–38

Indonesian
Agung (Koreatown), 120
Sri Ratu (Los Angeles), 120–21

Irish
Irish Imports (Hollywood), 207

Jamaican
Janet's Original Jerk Chicken Pit
	(Los Angeles), 180
Stone's Bakery & Grocery Co.
	(Los Angeles), 180
Stone's Restaurant (Los Angeles),
	180

Japanese Shops and Markets
Enbun Market (Little Tokyo), 65
Frances (Little Tokyo), 59
Fugetsu-Do (Little Tokyo), 63
Ginza Ya (Little Tokyo), 59
Ikeda Bakery (Little Tokyo), 65
Mikawaya (Little Tokyo), 65
Modern Food Market (Little
	Tokyo), 65
Ryoku Shu En (Little Tokyo), 64–65
Yaohan Market (Little Tokyo), 62–
	63

Japanese Restaurants
Apple (Little Tokyo), 50–51
Atch-Kotch (Hollywood), 49–50
Curry Club (Hollywood), 57–58
Focus Salon de Café (Little Tokyo),
	51–52
Ginza Sushi-Ko (Los Angeles), 54
Horikawa (Little Tokyo), 61
Inagiku (Los Angeles), 53
Issenjoki (Little Tokyo), 42
Ita-Cho (Hollywood), 41
Kappo Kyara (Little Tokyo), 45
Katsu (Silverlake), 54
Kokekokko (Little Tokyo), 47
Kushinobo (Little Tokyo), 51

Mikoshi (Los Angeles), 50
Mitsuki (Los Angeles), 44
Nanban-Tei of Tokyo (Little
	Tokyo), 47
Okonomiyaki Koma (Little
	Tokyo), 51
Sai Sai (Los Angeles), 59–60
Sarashina (Little Tokyo), 48
Senbazuru (A Thousand Cranes)
	(Little Tokyo), 61
Shibucho (Silverlake and Little
	Tokyo), 54
Suehiro (Little Tokyo), 61–62
Takaya (Little Tokyo), 52
Tatsuki (Little Tokyo), 53
Tokyo Kaikan (Little Tokyo), 61
Umemura (Little Tokyo), 50
Yoro No Taki (Los Angeles and
	Little Tokyo), 44

Korean Markets
Hannam Chain Super Market
	(Koreatown), 80–81
Koreatown Plaza Market and
	International Food Court
	(Koreatown), 81–82

Korean Restaurants
Beverly Soon Tofu Restaurant
	(Koreatown), 78
Boh Tong Zip (Koreatown), 82
Corner Place, The (Koreatown), 71
Ddo Wa Dumpling (Koreatown), 79
Ham Hung (Koreatown), 71–72
In Cheon Restaurant (Koreatown),
	76
Jangtoh Soontofu (Koreatown), 78
Kobawoo House (Koreatown), 77
Kong-Joo (Koreatown), 80
Korean Express (Koreatown), 82
Korean Gardens (Koreatown), 74–
	75
Lotte Buffet (Koreatown), 72
Mandarin Garden (Koreatown), 78
Mandarin House (Koreatown), 78
Myung Dong Noodle House
	(Koreatown), 77–78
Nakwon Jip (Koreatown), 79–80
Nam Kang (Koreatown), 73–74
Panda Dumpling (Koreatown), 79
Peking Yuen (Koreatown), 78
Siyeon (Koreatown), 75
Song Do Sea Food (Koreatown),
	75–76

Soot Bull Jeep (Koreatown), 70–71

Toad (Koreatown), 77

V.I.P. Buffet Palace (Koreatown), 72

Woo Lae Oak of Seoul (Koreatown), 75

Yeejoh (Koreatown), 76–77

Latin American Shops and Markets

Catalina's Market (Los Angeles), 189

Guatemalteca (Los Angeles), 177

Habana Bakery (Los Angeles), 180

Liborio (Los Angeles), 189

Tropical Ice Cream and Cuban Bakery (Los Angeles), 180

Latin American Restaurants

Adelita, La (Los Angeles), 174

Anayas (Los Angeles), 176

Arrieros, Los (Los Angeles), 188

Atlacatl (Los Angeles), 176

Colmao, El (Los Angeles), 179

Don Felipe (Los Angeles), 185

Don Felix (Los Angeles), 184

Ecuatoriano No 2. (Los Angeles), 188–89

Empanada's Place (Hollywood), 185

Floradita, El (Hollywood), 178

Fonda Antioqueña, La (Los Angeles), 187–88

Gaucho Grill (Hollywood), 184–85

Guatelinda (Los Angeles), 176–77

Izalqueño, El (Los Angeles), 176

Managua (Los Angeles), 178

Mario's Peruvian Seafood (Los Angeles), 184

Mexica (Los Angeles), 156

Mi Guatemala (Los Angeles), 176–77

Papaturro (Los Angeles), 174

Plancha, La (Koreatown), 174

Plancha Grill, La (Highland Park), 177–78

Prado (Los Angeles), 182

Rincon Chileno Deli (Los Angeles), 186–87

Mexican Shops and Markets

Azteca Tortilleria, La (Boyle Heights), 168

Gallo, El (Boyle Heights), 168

Gallo Giro, El (Los Angeles), 169

Grand Central Public Market (Los Angeles), 164, 171

Juanito's Tamale Factory (Boyle Heights), 168

Mascota, La (Boyle Heights), 168–69

Mercado, El (Boyle Heights), 168

Numero Uno (Los Angeles), 170–71

Tianguis (Los Angeles), 170

Mexican Restaurants

Balo's Place (Highland Park), 160

Birriera Jalisco (Boyle Heights), 162–63

Border Grill No. 1 (Los Angeles), 166

Burritos, Los (Los Angeles), 164–65

Casa Carnitas (Los Angeles), 160–61

Cholo, El (Koreatown), 165

Cisco's Jugos Frescos (Los Angeles), 164

Fonda, La (Los Angeles), 165

Gallo Giro, El (Los Angeles), 169

King Taco No. 2 (Los Angeles and Boyle Heights), 157–58

Maria's Ramada (Los Angeles), 154

Mexica (Los Angeles), 156

Original Sonora Cafe, The (Los Angeles), 165–66

Parian, El (Los Angeles), 163

Parrilla, La (Boyle Heights), 163

Pescado Mojado (Los Angeles and Highland Park), 161–62

Salsa, La (Los Angeles), 167–68

Señor Fish (Highland Park), 162

Serenata de Garibaldi, La (Boyle Heights), 156

Super Tortas (Los Angeles), 164

Taurino, El (Los Angeles), 157

Yuca's (Silverlake), 158

Zumaya's (Los Angeles), 154–55

Middle Eastern Shops and Markets
Bezjian's Grocery Inc.
(Hollywood), 227–28
Hagop Danian (Hollywood), 224–25
Panos Pastry (Hollywood), 226–27
Ron's Market (Los Angeles), 203–4

Middle Eastern Restaurants
Al Amir (Los Angeles), 221–22
Alwazir (Hollywood), 224
Caroussel (Hollywood), 222
Eat a Pita (Los Angeles), 226
Falafel Arax (Hollywood), 224
Grill Express (Los Angeles), 230
Marouch (Hollywood), 222
Moun of Tunis (Hollywood), 237–38
Shamshiri (Hollywood), 214–15
Zankou Chicken (Hollywood), 223–24

Moroccan
Dar Maghreb Restaurant (Hollywood), 236

Romanian
Mignon (Hollywood), 203
Ron's Market (Los Angeles), 203–4

Russian
Gastronom (Los Angeles), 199–200
Tatiana (Hollywood), 200
Violet's Restaurant (Eagle Rock), 198

Scandinavian
Olson's Deli (Los Angeles), 204–5

Spanish
El Cid Show (Los Angeles), 208
Tasca (Hollywood), 208

Thai Markets
Bangkok Market (Los Angeles), 96–97
Bangluck Market Inc. (Hollywood), 97
Cathay Supermarket (Hollywood), 97
L.A. Thai Market (Chinatown), 97

Thai Restaurants
Alisa (Chao Nue) (Los Angeles), 87–88
Chan Dara (Hollywood and Los Angeles), 92
Jitlada Restaurant (Hollywood), 91
Palm Restaurant (Hollywood), 94
Pi Yai Restaurant (Hollywood), 90
Renoo's Kitchen (Hollywood), 94
Sanamluang Cafe (Hollywood), 93
Sompun (Los Angeles), 92
Sunshine Thai (Koreatown), 93
Tepparod Thai Restaurant (Hollywood), 94–95
Tommy Tang's (Los Angeles), 91–92
Torung (Hollywood), 95
V.P. Cafe (Hollywood), 88

Vietnamese
Au Pagolac Cholon (Chinatown), 104
Pho 79 (Chinatown), 105–107
Pho Lê Loi (Chinatown), 103
Pho Hòa (Chinatown), 105

EAST OF L.A.

Chinese
China Muslim (Rowland Heights), 15
99 Ranch Market (Montebello and Rowland Heights), 32–33

Filipino
Goldilocks (West Covina), 127
Mami King (Rowland Heights), 126
Red Ribbon Bake Shop (West Covina), 128

Hungarian
Monique's (Covina), 202

Latin American
Andes, Los (Pico Rivera),
202
183
Chori, El (Bell), 179

Mexican
Al Salam Rancho (East Los
Angeles), 168
Chamizal, El (Huntington Park),
163–64
Comal, El (East Los Angeles),
156
Gallo Giro, El (Huntington Park),
169

King Taco No. 2 (East Los
Angeles), 157–58
Mi India Bonita (East Los
Angeles), 155
Paleteria El Oasis (Huntington
Park), 165
Pescado Mojado (Huntington
Park), 161–62
Tianguis (Montebello), 170

Thai
Sanamluang Cafe (Pomona),
93

Vietnamese
Pho Sô 1 (Rowland Heights),
108–109

OCOUNTY

Japanese
Horikawa (Santa Ana),
61
Yaohan Market (Costa Mesa),
62–63

Mexican
Gallo Giro, El (Santa Ana),
169

Middle Eastern
Al Tayebat (Anaheim), 228

Thai
Thai Nakorn (Buena Park), 90

Vietnamese Shops and Markets
Baron's (Garden Grove), 111
Bo Ko "Jerky Palace"
(Westminster), 112
Dong Loi Seafood Co. (Garden
Grove), 112
Little Saigon Supermarket
(Westminster), 112–13
Man Wah Supermarket
(Westminster), 33
99 Price Market (Westminster
and Anaheim), 113
Sau Voi Vietnamese Deli
(Westminster), 111
Thanh Son Tofu (Garden Grove),
110–11

Van's Bakery (Westminster),
112

Vietnamese Restaurants
Anh Hong (Garden Grove),
108
Banh Cuon Tây Hô (Westminster
and Santa Ana), 109–110
Banh Mi Sô 1 (Westminster),
105
Favori (Santa Ana), 102–103
Grand Garden (Westminster),
109
Hiên Khanh (Garden Grove),
110
Ngu Binh Fast Food (Westminster
and Santa Ana), 107
Nhà Hàng Sô 1 (Garden Grove),
103
Pagolac (Westminster),
108
Pho Bolsa (Westminster),
107
Pho 79 (Westminster), 105–
107
Song Long (Westminster),
103
Thiên Thanh (No. 1 and 2)
(Garden Grove and Santa Ana),
101–102
Viên Dông (Garden Grove),
109

SAN FERNANDO (S.F.) VALLEY

British
Friar Tuck Shoppe (Burbank), 206–7
Robin Hood British Pub (Burbank), 206–7
Scotland Yard (Canoga Park), 206

Cambodian
Angkor Restaurant (Encino), 117–18

Chinese
Ai Hoa Supermarket (Reseda), 34
Fortune West (Studio City), 30
Hong Kong Restaurant (Northridge), 27
Mandarin Deli (Reseda), 24–25
Oriental Seafood Inn (Encino), 21
Szechuan Garden (Reseda), 31

Filipino
Asian Ranch Supermarket, Inc. (Van Nuys), 128–29
D.J. Bibingkahan Restaurant (Panorama City), 126

German
Atlas Sausage Kitchen (North Hollywood), 196
Erika's Bake Shop (Westlake Village), 197
German Cold Cuts International (Woodland Hills), 197
Schreiner's Fine Sausages (Glendale), 195
Van Nuys German Deli (Sepulveda), 196

Greek
Alexis' (Northridge), 233
Great Greek, The (Sherman Oaks), 232–33

Hungarian
Hortóbagy Hungarian Restaurant (Studio City), 201
Otto's Hungarian Market (Burbank), 202

Indian Shops and Markets
Bombay Spiceland (Northridge), 145
India Sweets and Spices (Canoga Park), 144
Mirch Masala (Northridge), 143

Indian Restaurants
Akbar (Encino), 136
Anarkali (Woodland Hills), 139
India's Cuisine (Tarzana), 139
Kenny's Kitchen (Van Nuys), 134
Paru's (Northridge), 137–38
Shalimar Cuisine of India (Woodland Hills), 139
Tikka (Van Nuys, Tarzana, Northridge, and Chatsworth), 135

Indonesian
Ann's Dutch Imports (North Hollywood), 122
Cafe Krakatoa (Panorama City), 120

Japanese
Cho Cho San (Tarzana), 55–56
Edo Sushi (Woodland Hills), 60–61
Iroha (Studio City), 55
Kazu Sushi (Studio City), 56–57
Kushiyu (Tarzana), 56
Kyushu Ramen (Van Nuys), 50
Mako Sushi (Sherman Oaks), 57
Megu's Japanese Food Mart (Canoga Park), 55
Pasta House (Sherman Oaks), 58
Ramen Nippon (Reseda), 50
Shihoya (Sherman Oaks), 55
Sushi Nozawa (Studio City), 55
Teru Sushi (Studio City), 61
Ueru-Ka-Mu (Tarzana), 56

Korean
Green Oaks (Van Nuys), 74
Pine Tree Korean BBQ (Northridge), 75

Latin American
Cafe Latino (North Hollywood), 183

Criollo, El (Van Nuys), 179–80
Cubana, La (Glendale), 180
Gaucho Grill (Studio City), 184–85
Gaviota de Viña, La (Sherman Oaks), 186
Marcela's Restaurant and Tango Club (Van Nuys), 185
Mi Ranchito Salvadoreño (Van Nuys), 176
Norah's Place (North Hollywood), 185
Silencio, El (Van Nuys), 183–84
Sultana del Valle, La (Van Nuys), 187

Mexican Shops and Markets
Lenchita's (Pacoima), 169
Mexico Supermarket (Canoga Park), 169–70
Tianguis (Pacoima), 170

Mexican Restaurants
Burritos, Los (North Hollywood), 164–65
Fuentes, Las (Reseda), 159
Parrilla, La (Northridge and Tarzana), 163
Paz, La (Woodland Hills), 160
Pescado Mojado (Panorama City), 161–62
Poquito Mas (Studio City and North Hollywood), 159
Rincon Taurino, El (Panorama City), 157
Sierra's (Canoga Park and San Fernando), 166
Tapatio, El (Woodland Hills), 158–59

Middle Eastern Shops and Markets
Avo's Bakery (Reseda), 227
Miller's Market (Reseda), 218
Panos Pastry (Glendale), 226–27
Village Pastry Shop (Glendale), 227

Middle Eastern Restaurants
Amer's Falafel (Encino), 225
Cabaret Tehran (Studio City), 217
Cafe Mediterranean (Toluca Lake), 223
Chicken Rotissary (Van Nuys), 224

Falafel Palace, The (Northridge), 225
Hagop (Sherman Oaks), 223
Haifa (Sherman Oaks), 230
Sallar's Restaurant (Glendale), 216
Shahrezad (Encino), 214
Shamshiri (Canoga Park), 214–15
Shiraz (Sherman Oaks), 216
Tarzana Armenian Grocery (Woodland Hills and Tarzana), 221
Tempo (Encino), 230
Up All Night (Sherman Oaks), 216
Zankou Chicken (Glendale), 223–24

Moroccan
Marrakesh (Studio City), 237

Russian
Little Russia (Glendale), 199
Moscow Nights (Studio City), 198

Thai
Anajak Thai Cuisine (Sherman Oaks), 92
Bangluck Market (North Hollywood), 97
Gulf of Siam (Woodland Hills), 95
Indra (Glendale), 93–94
Jitlada West (Studio City), 91
Khun Khao (Panorama City), 93–94
Sanamluang Cafe (North Hollywood), 93
Satang Thai (Panorama City), 90–91
Talesai (Studio City), 86
Thai 'n I (Encino), 92

Vietnamese
Ba Le (Reseda), 105
Dông Quê (Reseda), 104
Hoa's House of Noodles (Reseda), 105
Pho Sô I (Reseda), 108–109

Yugoslavian
Beograd (North Hollywood), 203

Asian Shops and Markets
Ai Hoa Supermarket (Monterey Park), 34
Daiyu Discount Warehouse (Rosemead), 65
DiHo (Monterey Park), 34
Hawaii Supermarket (San Gabriel), 113
Hong Kong Supermarket (Monterey Park and San Gabriel), 33–34
Kuo's Bakery (Alhambra), 32
Monterey Fish Market (Monterey Park), 34
99 Ranch Market (San Gabriel), 32–33
Sun Long Tea (Monterey Park), 34
Yi Mei Bakery (Monterey Park), 31

British
John Bull Pub (Pasadena), 205

Chinese Restaurants
A A A Seafood (Monterey Park), 8
China Islamic (Rosemead), 14–15
Chiu Chow Garden (Monterey Park), 7–8
Cocary (Monterey Park), 15
Coriya (Alhambra), 15
Deli World Café (Monterey Park), 10
Dow Shaw Noodle House (San Gabriel), 24
Dragon Regency (Monterey Park), 18–19
Dragon Villages (San Gabriel), 5
Dumpling House (Temple City), 23–24
Dumpling Master (Monterey Park), 24
Fragrant Vegetable (Monterey Park), 27
Fu Shing (San Gabriel), 12–13
Good Shine Kitchen (Monterey Park), 10–11
Harbor Seafood (San Gabriel), 16–17

Harbor Village (Monterey Park), 17–18
Helena Restaurant (San Gabriel), 28–29
Lake Spring Cuisine (Monterey Park), 5
Litz (Monterey Park), 28
Live Fish (Monterey Park), 12
Luk Yue (Monterey Park), 25–26
Lu's Garden Taiwanese Congee Shop (San Gabriel), 28
MaMa's Kitchen (San Gabriel), 11
Mandarin Deli (Monterey Park), 24–25
Meitze (Monterey Park), 11
Merit Grove (Monterey Park), 27–28
N B C Seafood (Monterey Park), 18
Ocean Seafood (Alhambra), 18
Ocean Star Seafood (Monterey Park), 19
Pearl's Oriental Restaurant and Dumpling House (Monterey Park), 27
Peony (San Gabriel), 16
Plaza Deli (San Gabriel), 28
Royal House (Alhambra), 14
Seafood City (Rosemead), 17
Shanghai Palace (San Marino), 5
Shau May (Alhambra and San Gabriel), 28
Silver Wing (Alhambra), 26
Sun Shine (San Gabriel), 10
3 6 9 (San Gabriel), 6
3 6 9 Shanghai (Alhambra), 6–7
Wei Fun (San Gabriel), 13–14
Yung Ho (San Gabriel), 9–10

Indian
Diwana Restaurant (San Gabriel), 138–39
India Sweets and Spices (Duarte), 144

Indonesian
Mawar Deli and Market (San Gabriel), 120

Japanese
Genghiskhan Bar-B-Q Buffet
  House (Alhambra), 59
Kayo (Monterey Park), 46

Korean
Pete Wood B-B-Q (Monterey
  Park), 71

Malaysian
Kuala Lumpur (Pasadena),
  121–22

Mexican
Emperador Maya, El (San
  Gabriel), 159–60
Gordito Taqueria, El (El Monte),
  158
Merida (Pasadena), 160
Pepe's Ostioneria (El Monte), 162
Tianguis (El Monte), 170

Middle Eastern
Middle East, The (Alhambra),
  222–23
Saam (Pasadena), 215

Thai
Pataya Cafe (Pasadena),
  95–96
Suvanee Siam (Monterey Park),
  86–87
Thai Dynasty (Alhambra), 96

Vietnamese
Anh Phuong (San Gabriel),
  103
Bánh Mi Sô 1 (Rosemead),
  105
Hiên Khanh (San Gabriel),
  110
My Hanh (El Monte), 104
Ngan Dinh (San Gabriel),
  107
Pagode Saigon (San Gabriel),
  108
Pho Hòa (Monterey Park), 105
Pho 79 (Monterey Park), 105–
  107
Pho Sô 1 (San Gabriel), 108–9
Van's Bakery (San Gabriel),
  112
Viên Dông (Rosemead), 109

SOUTH

Albanian
Ajetis Albanian (Hermosa Beach),
  203

Australian
Wallaby Darned (San Pedro),
  207

British
British Imports (Long Beach),
  207
Gwen's Pantry (Long Beach),
  206

Cambodian
Banteay Srey Village Restaurant
  (Long Beach), 117
Monorom (Long Beach),
  117
New Paradise (Long Beach),
  116–17
Vinh Hao Super Market (Long
  Beach), 118

Chinese
Big Wok (Torrance), 15–16
DiHo Market (Artesia), 34
Formosan (Artesia), 11–12
Golden Lotus (Rancho Palos
  Verdes), 30
Hunan Garden (Lomita), 30
99 Ranch Market (Gardena), 32–
  33
Sea Food House #3, The
  (Artesia), 21
Sir Charles Dumpling House
  (Artesia), 26

Dutch
Holland-American Market &
  Importing Corp. (Bellflower),
  122

Filipino
Cathay Noodle House (Artesia),
  126–27
Goldilocks (Artesia), 127

Lorenzana Market (Torrance), 129
Mami King (Torrance), 126
Red Ribbon Bake Shop (Cerritos), 128
Rey's Pinausukan (Gardena), 125

German
Alpine Village Market and Bakery (Torrance), 195
Ernie's European Imports (Inglewood), 197
Eschbach's Meat Products (Gardena), 196

Greek
Marathon (Long Beach), 233
Papadakis Taverna (San Pedro), 231–32
S&J Importing Co. (Long Beach), 235

Indian
Bombay Spices (Artesia), 144–45
Farm Fresh Produce (Norwalk), 144
India Food and Gifts (Artesia), 144
India Sweets and Spices (Artesia), 144
Jay Bharat (Artesia), 138
Madhu's Dasaprakash (Cerritos), 137
Patel Brothers (Artesia), 145
Sabra's (Artesia), 138
Standard Sweets & Snacks (Artesia), 143
Surati Farsan Mart (Artesia), 143

Indonesian
Holland-American Market & Importing Corp. (Bellflower), 122

Japanese Shops and Markets
Bonjour French Pastry (Gardena), 59
Chikara Mochi (Gardena), 63–64
Ikeda Bakery (Torrance), 65
Meiji Tofu (Gardena), 65
Mikawaya (Gardena), 63

Pacific Supermarket (Gardena and Torrance), 65
Pasco (Gardena), 58
Sakura Ya (Gardena), 63
Yaohan Market (Torrance), 62–63

Japanese Restaurants
Chin-Chin Tei (Gardena), 57
Curry House (Torrance), 58
Daruma (Gardena), 42–44
Fukuhime (Gardena), 42
Furaibo (Gardena), 51
Genghiskhan Bar-B-Q Buffet House (Harbor City), 59
Hakone Sushi (Torrance), 57
Kanpachi Sushi (Gardena), 53–54
Masukawa (Gardena), 60
Moc-Moc (Gardena), 52–53
Oishii (Long Beach), 60
Ran-zan (Torrance), 54–55
Rokumeikan Cutlet Parlor (Gardena), 51
Sanuki no Sato (Gardena), 48–49
Sarashina (Gardena), 48
Seafood Club (Torrance), 53
SeiKo-En (Torrance), 58–59
Spoon House (Gardena), 58
Sushi Boy (Torrance), 56
Tampopo (Gardena), 50
Tokyo Sushi (Gardena), 56
Tomo (Torrance), 51
Tori-zen (Gardena), 47–48
Torimatsu (Gardena), 47
Tsukiji (Gardena), 54
Tsukuba (Torrance), 60
Umemura (Gardena), 50
Yoro No Taki (Gardena), 44

Korean
Corner Place, The (Cerritos), 71
Shilla (Gardena), 72
Yet Gol (Gardena), 74

Latin American
Continental Gourmet (Hawthorne), 189
Ilopango (Long Beach), 176
Mazateca, La (Inglewood), 177
Pollo Inka, El (Hermosa Beach, Lawndale, and Gardena), 182–83
Sol, El (Lawndale), 184

Mexican
Birrieria Tepechi (Wilmington),
163
Mariscos La Paz (Wilmington), 161
Pescado Mojado (Lynwood), 161–
62
Taco Sinaloa (Wilmington), 158

Middle Eastern
Hawthorne Market and
International Grocery
(Torrance), 228

Moroccan
Babouch Moroccan (San Pedro),
237

Norwegian
Norwegian Imports & Bakery (San
Pedro), 205

Spanish
Española Deli, La (Lomita),
208–9

Thai
Renu Nakorn (Norwalk),
88–89
Siamese Restaurant (Long Beach),
92
Thai Villa (Lakewood),
89–90
Thai Tiffany (Lomita), 96

Vietnamese
My Vi (Gardena), 105
Pho Hòa (Hawthorne), 105
Pho 79 (Long Beach),
105–106
Vinh Hao Super Market (Long
Beach), 113

WEST

British
Paddington's Tea Room (West
Los Angeles), 206
Tudor House (Santa Monica), 206
Ye Olde King's Head (Santa
Monica), 205
Ye Olde King's Head Shoppe
(Santa Monica), 205–6

Chinese
Fragrant Vegetable (West Los
Angeles), 27
Jasmine Tree (West Los Angeles),
30–31
Joss (Beverly Hills), 29
Mandarette Cafe (West
Hollywood), 27
Mandarin, The (Beverly Hills), 29
Oriental Seafood Inn (Marina del
Rey), 21
Plum West (Westwood), 29
Twin Dragon (West Los Angeles),
29–30

German
B&L Gourmet Pastries (Los
Angeles), 197
European Deluxe Sausage Kitchen
(Beverly Hills), 195
Knoll's Black Forest Inn (Santa
Monica), 198

Old Country Delicatessen (Santa
Monica), 196–97

Greek
Cafe Athens (Santa Monica),
232
Corfu (West Los Angeles), 232
Sofi Estiatorion (Los Angeles),
231

Indian Shops and Markets
Bharat Bazaar (Culver City), 144
India Sweet House (West Los
Angeles), 143
India Sweets and Spices (Culver
City), 144

Indian Restaurants
Akbar (Marina del Rey), 136
Bombay Cafe (West Los
Angeles), 134–135
Bombay Palace (Beverly Hills),
136–37
Chutneys Indian Fast Food (West
Los Angeles), 140
East India Grill Santa Monica
(Santa Monica), 135
Gaylord (Beverly Hills), 139–40
India's Oven (West Los Angeles),
140

Nawab of India (Santa Monica),
137
Paru's (West Los Angeles), 137–
38
Raja (West Los Angeles), 140

Indonesian
Ramayani Westwood (West Los
Angeles), 121

Jamaican
Del Rose Act I (Culver City), 181

Japanese Shops and Markets
Aloha Grocery (West Los
Angeles), 62
Ginza Ya Bakery (West Los
Angeles), 59
Mousse Fantasy (West Los
Angeles), 59
Safe and Save (West Los
Angeles), 65

Japanese Restaurants
Asahi Ramen (West Los Angeles),
49
Asuka (West Los Angeles), 56
Hirozen (West Hollywood), 41–
42
Hurry Curry of Tokyo (West Los
Angeles), 58
Ike-Ichi. *See* U-Zen *below*
Matsuhisa (Beverly Hills), 45
Mikoshi (Los Angeles), 50
Mishima (West Los Angeles), 49
Nanbankan (West Los Angeles),
47
Robata Beverly Hills (Beverly
Hills), 45–46
Sakura House (Marina Del Rey),
47
Sushi Boy (West Los Angeles),
56
Terried Sake House (West Los
Angeles), 44
Totoraku (West Los Angeles),
58–59
Umemura (West Los Angeles), 50
U-Zen (Ike-Ichi) (West Los
Angeles), 55
Yokohama Ramen (West Los
Angeles), 49
Yoro No Taki (West Los
Angeles), 44

Yuu (West Los Angeles),
44

Latin American
Café Brazil (West Los Angeles),
188
Empanada's Place (Culver City
and West Los Angeles), 185
Gardel's (West Hollywood), 186
Gaucho Grill (Brentwood), 184–85
Rincon Criollo (Culver City),
178–79
Versailles (Culver City and West
Los Angeles), 178

Mexican
Border Grill No. 2 (Santa
Monica), 166
Casablanca (Venice), 161
Gallegos Brothers (Santa Monica),
169
Gardens of Taxco, The (West
Hollywood), 155–56
Guadalajara Restaurant (Santa
Monica), 154
Kaktus (Beverly Hills), 166–67
Lula (Santa Monica), 167
Mi Ranchito (Culver City), 154
Playita, La (Santa Monica), 162
Rebecca's (Venice), 167
Salsa, La (West Los Angeles),
167–68

Middle Eastern
Darband/Shahrezad (Beverly
Hills), 214
Dizengoff (West Hollywood),
230
Falafel King (Westwood), 225–26
Golestan (West Los Angeles),
216
Habayit (West Los Angeles), 230
Haifa (West Los Angeles), 230
Javan Restaurant (West Los
Angeles), 215–16
Noura Cafe (West Hollywood),
226
Shahrezad (Westwood), 214
Shahrezad Flame (West Los
Angeles), 215
Shamshiri (West Los Angeles),
214–15
Shekarchi (West Los Angeles),
214

Super Jordan (West Los Angeles),
217–18
Your Place (Beverly Hills), 216

Moroccan
Koutoubia (West Los Angeles),
236–37

Polish
J&T European Gourmet (Santa
Monica), 200–201
Warszawa (Santa Monica),
201

Russian
International Food Center (West
Hollywood), 200

Scandinavian
Danish Pastry, The (West Los
Angeles), 204

Spanish
From Spain (West Los Angeles),
208

Thai
Chan Dara (West Los Angeles), 92
D. J. Thai (Pacific Palisades), 96
Natalee Thai Cuisine (Los
Angeles), 96
Talesai (West Hollywood), 86
Talking Thai (Santa Monica), 87
Tusk Thai Cuisine (West Los
Angeles), 87

General Index

A A A Seafood, 8
A B C Seafood, 21
Adelita, La, 174
Agung, 120
Ai Hoa Supermarket, 34, 113
Akbar, 136
Al Amir, 221–22
Albanian food, 203
Alexis', 233
Alisa, 87–88
Aloha Grocery, 62
Alpena Sausage, 195–96
Alpine Village Market and Bakery, 195
Al Salam Rancho, 168
Al Tayebat, 228
Alwazir, 224
Amer's Falafel, 225
Anajak Thai, 92
Ana Maria's, 164, 171
Anarkali, 139
Anayas, 176
Andes, Los, 183
Angkor, 117–18
Anh Hong, 108
Anh Phuong, 103
Anju (Korean pubs), 76–77
Ann's Dutch Imports, 122
Antojitos (Salvadoran snacks), 175
Argentinian food, 185–86
Armenian food, 219–28
Arrieros, Los, 188
Asahi Ramen, 49
Asian Ranch Supermarket, Inc., 128–29
Asuka, 56
Atch–Kotch, 49–50
Atlacatl, 176
Atlas Sausage Kitchen, 196
Au Pagolac Cholon, 104
Australian food, 207
Avo's Bakery, 227
Azteca Tortilleria, La, 168

B&L Gourmet Pastries, 197
Babouch Moroccan, 237
Bakeries
  British, 206–7
  Central American, 176, 177
  Chinese, 31–32

Colombian, 187
Cuban, 180
Filipino, 128
German, 195, 197
Jamaican, 180–81
Japanese, 58–59
Near Eastern, 226–27
Scandinavian, 204, 205
Vietnamese, 111–12
Ba Le, 105
Balo's Place, 160
Bangkok Market, 96–97
Bangluck Market, 97
Banh cuon (Vietnamese rice sheets), 109–10
Banh Cuon Tây Hô, 105, 109–10
Banh Mi Sô, 105
Banteay Srey Village Restaurant, 117
Barbecue
  Filipino, 127
  Japanese, 46–48
  Japanese–style Korean, 58–59
  Korean, 70–72
Baron's, 111
Barrio Fiesta, 125
Belizean food, 181–82
Bento (Japanese portable boxed meals), 52–53
Beograd, 203
Beverly Soon Tofu Restaurant, 78–79
Bezjian's Grocery Inc., 145, 227–28
Bharat Bazaar, 144
Bibingka (Filipino flat cakes), 127
Big Wok, 15–16
Birrieria Jalisco, 162–63
Birrierias (Mexican goat restaurants), 162–63
Birrieria Tepechi, 163
Blue Nile, 240
Bo Bay Mon (Vietnamese beef meal), 107–9
Boh Tong Zip, 82
Bo Ko "Jerky Palace," 112
Bombay Cafe, 134–35
Bombay Palace, 136–37
Bombay Spiceland, 145
Bombay Spices, 144–45
Bonjour French Pastry, 59
Border Grill No. 1, 166

Border Grill No. 2, 166
Brazilian food, 188
British food, 205–7
British Imports, 207
Buffet restaurants (Korean), 72
Burritos, Los, 164–65

C&K Importing Co., 234–35, 241
Cabaret Tehran, 217
Cafe Athens, 232
Cafe Brazil, 188
Cafe Krakatoa, 120
Cafe Latino, 183
Cafe Mediterranean, 223
Cal–Mex comfort food, 165–66
Cambodian food, 115–18
Cantonese restaurants, 16–21
Canton Poultry, 35
Caribbean food, 173–74, 178–81
Caroussel, 222
Casablanca, 161
Casa Carnitas, 160–61
Catalina's Market, 189
Cat & Fiddle Pub and Restaurant, 207
Cathay Noodle House, 126–27
Cathay Supermarket, 97, 113
Central American food, 173–77, 181–82
Central European food, 200–204
Chamizal, El, 163–64
Chan Dara, 92
Charcuterie, Vietnamese, 104–5
Chat (Indian snacks), 141–44
Chicken Rotissary, 224
Chikara Mochi, 63–64
Chilean food, 186–87
China Islamic, 14–15
China Muslim, 15
Chinatown, Cantonese restaurants in, 19–21
Chin–Chin Tei, 57
Chinese food, 1–35
  bakeries, 31–32
  Chiu Chow, 7
  dim sum, 23–24
  dumplings, 26–27
  Hunan, 13–14
  markets, 32–35
  noodles, 23–26
  northern–style, 14–16
  regional restaurants, 4–21
  Sichuan, 12
  specialties, 27–29
  Taiwanese, 8–12
  vegetarian, 27–28
  wontons, 26–27
Chiu Chow Garden, 7–8
Chiu Chow restaurants, 7–8
Cho Cho San, 55–56
Cholo, El, 165
Chori, El, 179
Chutneys Indian Fast Food, 140
Cisco's Jugos Frescos, 164
Clay Pit, The, 134
Cocary, 15
Coffee shops, Japanese, 58–59
Colmao, El, 179

Colombian food, 187–88
Comal, El, 156
Confectioneries, Japanese, 63–64
Continental Gourmet, 189
Corfu, 232
Coriya, 15
Corner Place, The, 71
Criollo, El, 179–80
Cubana, La, 180
Cuban food, 178–80
Curry, Japanese–style, 57–58
Curry Club, 57–58
Curry House, 58

Daiyu Discount Warehouse, 65
Danish food, 204
Danish Pastry, The, 204
Darband/Shahrezad, 124
Dar Maghreb, 236
Daruma, 42–44
Ddo Wa Dumpling, 79
Delicatessens. See also specific
    establishments
  German, 196–97
  Russian, 200
  Scandinavian, 204–5
  Spanish, 208–9
  Taiwanese, 8–11
  Vietnamese, 104–5, 111
Deli World Café, 10
Del Rose Act I, 181
Dessert shops
  Cuban, 180
  Thai, 93–94
  Vietnamese, 110
DiHo, 34
Dim sum, 23–24
Diwana Restaurant, 138–39
Dizengoff, 230
D. J. Bibingkahan Restaurant, 126
D. J. Thai, 96
Don Felipe, 185
Don Felix, 184
Dong Loi Seafood Co., 112
Dông–Quê, 104
Dow Shaw Noodle House, 22, 24
Dragon Regency, 18–19
Dragon Villages, 5–6
Dumpling House, 22
Dumpling Master, 24
Dumplings
  Chinese, 26–27
  Korean, 79

East India Grill, 135
East India Grill Santa Monica, 135
Eat a Pita, 226
Ecuadoran food, 188–89
Ecuatoriano No. 2, 188–89
Edo Sushi, 53, 60–61
Edun Market, 65
El Cid Show, 208
Emmanuel's, 126
Empanada's Place, 185
Emperador Maya, El, 159–60
Empress Pavilion, 19–20

Erika's Bake Shop, 197
Ernie's European Imports, 197
Eschbach's Meat Products, 196
Española Deli, El, 208–9
Ethiopian food, 238–41
European Deluxe Sausage Kitchen, 195
European food, 191–209
  Albanian, 203
  British, 205–7
  German, 195–200
  Hungarian, 201–2
  Irish, 205–7
  Polish, 200–201
  Romanian, 203–4
  Scandinavian, 204–5
  Yugoslavian, 202–3

Falafel (Middle Eastern deep–fried bean
    fritters), 225–26
Falafel Arax, 224
Falafel King, 225–26
Falafel Palace, The, 225
Family Pastry, 31–32
Farm Fresh Produce, 144
Fast food, Indian, 140
Favori, 102–3
Filipino food, 122–29
Floridita, El, 178
Focus Salon de Café, 51–52
Fonda, La, 165
Fonda Antioqueña, La, 187–88
Fonditas (family–style Mexican restaurants),
    155–56
Formosan Restaurant, 11–12
Fortune, 20
Fortune West, 30
Fragrant Vegetable, 27
Frances, 59
Friar Tuck Shoppe, 206–7
From Spain, 208
Fuentes, Las, 159
Fugetsu-Do, 63
Fukuhime, 42
Full House Seafood, 20–21
Furaibo, 51
Fu Shing, 12–13

Gallegos Brothers, 169
Gallo, El, 168
Gallo Giro, El, 169
Gardels, 186
Gardens of Taxco, The, 155–56
Gaucho Grill, 184–85
Gaviota de Viña, 186
Gaylord, 139
Genghiskhan Bar-B-Q Buffet
    House, 59
German Cold Cuts International, 197
German food, 195–98
Ginza Sushi-Ko, 54
Ginza Ya Bakery, 59
Goat specialty restaurants
  Korean, 80
  Mexican, 162–63
Golden Lotus, 30
Goldilocks, 127–28

Golestan, 216
Good Shine Kitchen, 10–11
Gorditas (Mexican stuffed corn cakes), 164
Gordito Taqueria, El, 158
Grand Central Public Market, 170
Great Greek, The, 232–33
Greek food, 230–35
Green Jade, 13
Green Oaks, 72, 74
Grill Express, 230
Guadalajara Restaurant, 154
Guatelinda, 176–77
Guatemalan food, 176–77
Guatemalteca Bakery, 177
Gujarati (Indian) food, 138–39
Gulf of Siam, 95
Gwen's Pantry, 206

Habana Bakery, 180
Habayit, 231
Hagop, 223
Hagop Danian (Uncle Jack's), 224–25
Haifa, 230
Hakone Sushi, 57
Ham Hung, 71–72
Hannam Chain Super Market, 80–81
Harbor Seafood, 16–17
Harbor Village, 17–18
Hawaii Supermarket, 113
Hawthorne Market and International
    Grocery, 228
Helena Restaurant, 28–29
Hiên Khanh, 110
Hirozen, 41–42
Hoa's House of Noodles, 105
Holland-American Market & Importing
    Corp., 122
Hong Kong Restaurant, 27
Hong Kong Supermarket, 33
Hop Li Seafood, 20
Horikawa, 61
Hortobágy Hungarian Restaurant, 201
Hunan Garden, 30
Hunan restaurants, 12–14
Hunan Taste, 31
Hungarian Budapest, 201–2
Hungarian food, 201–2
Hurry Curry of Tokyo, 58

Ikeda Bakery, 65
Ike-Ichi. See U-Zen
Ilopango, 176
Inagiku, 53
In Cheon Restaurant, 76
Indian food, 131–45
  California-style, 134–35
  chat (snacks), 141–44
  markets, 143–45
  methai (sweets), 141–44
  northern, 135–37
  Pakistani, 139
  southern, 137–38
  western, 138–39
Indian Food and Gifts, 144
India's Cuisine, 139
India's Oven, 140

India Sweet House, 143
India Sweets and Spices, 144
Indonesian food, 118–22
Indra, 93–94
International Food Center, 200
Iranian food. *See* Persian food
Irish food, 207
Irish Imports, 207
Iroha, 55
Israeli food, 229–30
Issenjoki, 42
Ita-Cho, 41
Izaka-ya (Japanese pubs), 42–44
Izalqueño, El, 176

J&T European Gourmet, 201
Jamaican food, 180–81
Janet's Original Jerk Chicken Pit, 181
Jangtoh Soontofu, 79
Japanese food, 37–65
    a shokudo (borrowed foods), 57
    bakeries, 58–59, 65
    coffee shops, 58–59
    confectioneries, 63–64
    ippin-ryori, 43
    kappo restaurants, 45–46
    kari-raisu (curry), 57–58
    Korean barbecue, 58–59
    koryori-ya, 41–42, 43
    kushi-yaki, 47–48
    noodles, 48–50
    patisserie, 59
    pubs, 42–44
    ramen shops, 49–50
    raw fish, 56–57
    robata restaurants, 45–46
    spaghetti, 58
    specialties, 50–53
    sushi, 53–57
    tea, 64–65
    tofu, 62, 65
    yakitori, 46–47
Jasmine Tree, 30–31
Javan Restaurant, 215–16
Jay Bharat, 138
Jeepney Grill, 127
Jitlada Restaurant, 91
Jitlada West, 91
John Bull Pub, The, 205
Joseph's Cafe, 232
Joss, 29
Juanito's Tamale Factory, 168
Jugos (Mexican blender drinks), 164–65

Kaktus, 166–67
Kamameshi-ya (Japanese rice–dish
    restaurant), 52
Kanom (Thai desserts), 93–94
Kanpachi Sushi, 53–54
Kappo Kyara, 45, 53
Kappo (Japanese) restaurants, 45–46
Kari-raisu (Japanese curry), 57–58
Katsu, 53, 54
Kayo, 46
Kazu Sushi, 56–57
Kebabs, 213–15

Kemara Market, 118
Kenny's Kitchen, 135
Keste Demena, 239
Khun Khao, 93–94
Kim Chuy, 25
King Taco No. 2, 157–58
Kissaten (Japanese coffee lounge), 51–52
Kitayama, 61
Knoll's Black Forest Inn, 198
Kobawoo House, 77
Kokekokko, 46–47
Kong-Joo, 80
Korean Express, 82
Korean food, 67–82
    barbecue, 70–72
    buffets, 72
    dumplings, 79
    goat, 80
    pubs, 76–77
    seafood, 75–76
    soups, 79–80
    tofu, 78–79
Korean Gardens, 74–75
Koreatown Plaza Market and International
    Food Court, 81–82
Koryori-ya (Japanese restaurants), 41–42,
    43
Kosher restaurants, 230
Koutoubia, 236–37
Kuala Lumpur, 121–22
Kuo's Bakery, 32
Kushi-age (Japanese skewered fried foods),
    50–51
Kushinobo, 51
Kushi-yaki (Japanese) restaurants, 47–48
Kushiyu, 56
Kyushu Ramen, 50

Lake Spring Cuisine, 5
Lao Dah Fung, 33
L.A. Thai Market, 97
Latin American markets, 189
Lebanese food, 219–28
Lenchita's, 169
Liborio, 189
Licuados (Mexican fruit juices), 164–65
Little Quiapo, 125–26
Little Russia, 199–200
Little Saigon Supermarket, 112
Litz, 28
Live Fish, 12
Lorenzana Market, 129
Lotte Buffet, 72
Luk Yue, 25–26
Lula, 167
Lu's Garden Taiwanese Congee Shop, 28

Madhu's Dasaprakash, 137
Makkolli (Korean pubs), 76–77
Mako Sushi, 57
Malaysian food, 118–22
    introduction to, 118–20
MaMa's Kitchen, 11
Mami (Chinese-style Filipino soup noodles),
    126–27
Mami King, 126

Managua, 178
Mandarette Chinese Cafe, 27
Mandarin, The, 27, 29
Mandarin Deli, 24–25
Mandarin Garden, 78
Mandarin House, 78
Mandarin Noodle House, 25
Mandarin Shanghai, 7
Manila Sunset, 127
Man Wah Supermarket, 33
Marathon, 233
Marcela's Restaurant and Tango Club, 185
Mariachis, 165
Maria's Ramada, 154
Mario's Peruvian Seafood, 184
Mariscos La Paz, 161
Markets
  British, 205–7
  Cambodian, 118
  Central European, 203
  Chinese, 32–35
  Ethiopian, 240–41
  Filipino, 127–29
  Greek, 234–35
  Hungarian, 202
  Indian, 143–45
  Indonesian, 122
  Japanese, 62–65
  Korean, 80–82
  Latin American, 189
  Mexican, 168–71
  Middle Eastern, 218, 221
  Near Eastern, 226–28
  Persian, 217–18
  Polish, 201
  Russian, 200
  Spanish, 208–9
  Thai, 96–97
  Vietnamese, 110–13
Marouch, 222
Marrakesh, 237
Masagana, 129
Mascota, La, 168–69
Masukawa, 52, 60
Matsuhisa, 45
Mawar Deli and Market, 121
May Flower, 26–27
Mazateca, La, 177
Megu's Japanese Food Mart, 55
Meitze, 11
Mejii Tofu, 65
Mekong Market, 118
Mercado, El, 168
Merida, 160
Merit Grove, 27–28
Merkato, 240–41
Messob, 240
Mexica, 156
Mexican food, 147–71
  birria (goat), 162–63
  Cal-Mex comfort food, 165–66
  fonditas (family-style restaurants), 155–56
  gorditas (stuffed corn cakes), 164
  home cooking, 154–55
  jugos (blender drinks), 164–65
  licuados (fruit juices), 164–65

markets, 168–71
  paletas (Popsicles), 164–65
  parillada (grilled meat), 163–64
  seafood, 160–62
  tortas (sandwiches), 164
  trend-setting restaurants, 166–68
  Yucatecan, 159–60
Mexico Supermarket (Carneceria Mexico), 169–70
Meze (Middle Eastern appetizer table), 221–25
Middle East, The, 222–23
Middle Eastern food, 211–30
  falafel (deep-fried bean fritters), 225–26
  Israeli, 229–30
  meze (appetizer table), 221–25
  Persian, 211–18
  take-out, 223–25
Mignon, 203
Mi Guatemala, 176–77
Mi India Bonita, 155
Mika's, 182
Mikawaya, 63
Mikoshi, 50
Miller's Market, 218
Mi Ranchito, 154
Mi Ranchito Salvadoreño, 176
Mirch Masala, 143
Mishima, 49
Mitsuki, 44
Moc-Moc, 52–53
Modern Food Market, 65
Monique's, 201
Mon Kee, 21
Monorom, 117
Monterey Fish Market, 34
Morrocan food, 235–38
Moscow nights, 198
Moun of Tunis, 237–38
Mousse Fantasy, 59
Mumtaz, 136
My Hanh, 104
Myung Dong Noodle House, 77–78
My Vi, 105

Nakwon Jip, 79–80
Nam Kang, 73–74
Nanbanken, 47
Nanban–Tei of Tokyo, 47
Natalee Thai Cuisine, 96
Nawab of India, 137
N B C Seafood, 18
New Paradise, 116
Ngan Dinh, 107
Ngu Binh Fast Food, 107
Nhà Hàng Sô 1, 103
Nicaraguan food, 177–78
99 Frice Market, 113
99 Ranch Market, 32–33
Nomi-ya (Japanese pubs), 42–44
Noodles
  Chinese, 22, 24–26
  Filipino, 126–27
  Japanese, 48–50
  Korean, 77–78
  Thai, 93

Noodles (cont.)
   Vietnamese, 105–7
Norah's Place, 186
North African food, 235–38
Northern-style Chinese cooking, 14–16
Norwegian food, 205
Norwegian Imports & Bakery, 205
Noura Cafe, 226
Numero Uno, 170–71

Ocean Seafood, 18, 20
Ocean Star Seafood, 19
Oishii, 60
Okonomiyaki (Japanese pizza), 51
Okonomiyaki Komo, 51
Old Country Delicatessen, 196–97
Olson's Deli, 204–5
Oriental Seafood Inn, 21
Original Sonora Cafe, The, 165–66
Otto's Hungarian Market, 202

Pacific Supermarket, 65
Paddington's Tea Room, 206
Pagode Saigon, 108
Pagolac, 108
Pakistani food, 139
Paletas (Mexican Popsicles), 164–65
Paleteria El Oasis, 165
Palm Restaurant, 94
Pancit (Filipino noodles), 127
Panda Dumpling, 79, 82
Panderia (bakery), 176
Panos Pastry, 226–27
Papadakis Taverna, 231–32
Papaturro, 174
Papusas (Salvadoran stuffed corn cakes), 175
Parian, El, 163
Parillada (Mexican grilled meat), 163–64
Parrilla, 163
Paru's 137–38
Pasco, 58
Pasta House, 58
Pataya Cafe, 95–96
Patel Brothers, 145
Patisserie (Japanese), 59
Paz, La, 160
Pearl's Oriental Restaurant and Dumpling
   House, 26
Peking Yuen, 78
Pelican Belizean Restaurant, 182
Peony, 16
Pepe's Ostioneria, 162
Persian food, 211–14, 217–18
Peruvian food, 182–84
Pescado Mojado, 161–62
Pete Wood B-B-Q, 71
Petit Greek, Le, 233–34
Pho (Vietnamese beef-noodle soup), 106
Pho Bolsa, 107
Pho Hòa, 105
Pho Lê Loi, 103–4
Pho 79, 105–7
Pho Sô 1, 108–9
Pine Tree Korean BBQ, 75
Pi Yai Restaurant (Yai), 90
Plancha, La, 174

Plancha Grill, La, 177–78
Playita, La, 162
Plaza Deli, 28
Plum West, 29
Polish food, 200–201
Pollo Inka, El, 182–83
Poquito Mas, 159
Porton, El, 166
Poultry markets (Chinese), 35
Prado, 182
Pubs
   British, 205–7
   Japanese, 42–44
   Korean, 76–77

Raja, 139–40
Ramayani Westwood, 121
Ramen Nippon, 50
Ramen shops, 49–50
Ran-zan, 53, 54–55
Rebecca's, 167
Red Lion Tavern, 197
Red Ribbon Bake Shop, 128
Renoo's Kitchen, 94
Renu Nakorn, 88–89
Rey's Pinausukan, 125
Rincon Chileno Deli, 186
Rincon Criollo, 178–79
Rincon Taurino, El, 157
Robata Beverly Hills, 45–46
Robata (Japanese) restaurants, 45–46
Robin Hood British Pub, 206–7
Rokumeikan Cutlet Parlor, 51
Romanian food, 203–4
Ron's Market, 203–4
Rosalind's, 239–40
Royal House, 14
Russian food, 198–200
Ryoku Shu En, 64–65

S&J Importing Co., 235
Saam, 215
Sabra's, 138
Safe and Save, 65
Sai Sai, 59–60
Sakura House, 47
Sakura-Ya, 63
Sallar's Restaurant, 216
Salsa, La, 167–68
Salvadoran food, 174–76
Sanamluang Cafe, 93
San Gabriel Valley, Cantonese restaurants
   in, 16–19
Sanuki no Sato, 48–49
Sarashina, 48
Sashimi, 56–57
   Korean-style, 75–76
Satang Thai, 90–91
Sausage, German, 195–96
Sau Voi Vietnamese Deli, 111
Scandinavian food, 204–5
Schreiner's Fine Sausages, 195
Scotland Yard, 206
Seafood
   Korean, 75–76
   Mexican, 160–62

Vietnamese, 109
Seafood City, 17
Seafood Club, 53
Sea Food House, The, 21
SeiKo-En, 58–59
Senbarzuru (A Thousand Cranes),
    53, 61
Señor Fish, 162
Serenata de Garibaldi, La, 156
Shahrezad, 214
Shahrezad Flame, 215
Shalimar Cuisine of India, 139
Shamshiri, 214–15
Shanghainese restaurants, 5–7
Shanghai Palace, 5
Shang Lee Poultry, 35
Shau May, 28
Shekarchi, 214
Shibucho, 54
Shilla, 72
Shioya, 55
Shiraz, 216
Siamese Restaurant, 92
Sichuan restaurants, 12–14
Sierra's, 166
Silencio, El, 183–84
Silver Wing, 26
Sir Charles Dumpling
    House, 26
Siyeon, 75
Sofi Estiatorion, 231
Sol, El, 184
Sompun, 92
Song Do Sea Food, 75–76
Song Long, 103
Song Long Bakery, 103
Soot Bull Jeep, 70–71
Soups
    Korean, 79–80
    Vietnamese, 105–7
South American food, 182–89
Southeast Asian food, 115–29
Spaghetti, Japanese–style, 58
Spanish food, 208–9
Spoon House, 58
Sri Ratu, 120–21
Stone Bakery Co., 180–81
Stone's Restaurant, 180–81
Street foods, Filipino, 127
Suehiro, 61–62
Sultana del Valle, La, 187
Sun Long Tea, 34
Sun Shine, 10
Sunshine Thai Restaurant, 93
Superior Poultry, 35
Super Jordan, 217–18
Super Tortas, 164
Supper clubs, Thai, 94–95
Surati Farsan Mart, 143
Sushi, 53–57
    Korean-style, 75–76
Sushi Boy, 56
Sushi Nozawa, 55
Suvanee Siam, 86–87
Syrian food, 219–28
Szechuan Garden, 31

Taco Sinaloa, 158
Taiwanese food, 8–12
Takaya, 52
Talesai, 86
Talking Thai, 87
Tampopo, 50
Tapatio, El, 158–59
Taquerias, 157–59
Tarzana Armenian Grocery, 221
Tasca, 208
Tatiana, 200
Tatsuki, 53
Taurino, El, 157
Tea
    British, 206
    Japanese, 64–65
Tempo, 230
Tempura, 53
Tepparod Thai Restaurant, 94–95
Terried Sake House, 44
Teru Sushi, 61
Thai Dynasty, 96
Thai food, 83–97
    classic L.A., 91–92
    curry, 93–94
    Isaan (northeast provinces), 88–90
    kanom (desserts), 93–94
    markets, 96–97
    new California–style, 86–87
    noodles, 93
    northern, 87–88
    southern, 90–91
Thai 'n I, 92
Thai Nokorn Restaurant, 90
Thai supper clubs, 94–95
Thai Tiffany, 96
Thai Villa, 89–90
Thanh Son Tofu, 110–11
Thiên Thanh No. 1, 101–2
Thiên Thanh No. 2, 101–2
3 6 9, 6
3 6 9 Shanghai, 6–7
Tianguis, 170
Tikka, 135
Toad, 77
Tofu
    Japanese, 62, 65
    Korean, 78–79
    Vietnamese, 110–11
Tokatsu (Japanese pork cutlet), 50–51
Tokyo Kaikan, 61
Tokyo Sushi, 56
Tommy Tang's, 91–92
Tomo, 51
Torimatsu, 46–47
Tori no karaage (Japanese fried chicken), 51
Tori-zen, 47–48
Tortas (Mexican sandwiches), 164
Torung, 95
Totoraku, 58–59
Tracy's Place, 182
Tropical Ice Cream and Cuban Bakery, 180
Tsukiji, 54
Tsukuba, 60
Tudor House, 206
Tunisian food, 235–38

Turo–turo (Filipino restaurants), 125–27
Tusk Thai Cuisine, 87
Twin Dragon, 29–30

Ueru-Ka-Mu, 56
Umemura, 50
Unagi-ya (Japanese eel restaurant), 52
United Foods Company, 35
Up All Night, 216
U-Zen, 55

Van Nuys German Deli, 196
Van's Bakery, 112
V B C Seafood, 21
Versailles, 178
Viên Dông, 109
Vietnamese food, 99–113
  bakeries, 111–12
  banh cuon (rice sheets), 109–10
  bo bay mon (seven–course beef), 107–9
  charcuterie, 104–5, 111
  delis, 104–5, 111
  desserts, 110
  markets, 110–13
  northern, 109
  seafood, 109
  soup noodle restaurants, 105–7
Village Pastry, 227
Vinh Hao Super Market, 34, 97, 113, 118

Violet's 198–99
V.I.P. Buffet Palace, 72
V.P. Cafe, 88

Walia, 240
Wallaby Darned, 207
Warszawa, 200–201
Wei Fun, 13–14
Woo Lae Oak of Seoul, 75

Yakitori (Japanese) restaurants, 46–47
Yaohan Market, 62–63
Yeejoh, 76–77
Ye Olde King's Head, 205
Ye Olde King's Head Shoppe, 205–6
Yet Gol, 74
Yi Mei Bakery, 31
Yokohama Ramen, 49
Yoro No Taki, 44
Your Place, 216–17
Yuca con chicharron (Salvadoran fried yuca
    with pork), 175
Yucatecan food, 159–60
Yugoslavian food, 202–3
Yung Ho, 9–10
Yuu, 44

Zankou Chicken, 223–24
Zumaya's, 154–55